Lecture Notes in Computer Scie

Commenced Publication in 1973
Founding and Former Series Editors:
Gerhard Goos, Juris Hartmanis, and Jan van Leeuwen

T.C. Nicholas Graham   Philippe Palanque (Eds.)

Interactive Systems

Design, Specification, and Verification

15th International Workshop, DSV-IS 2008
Kingston, Canada, July 16-18, 2008
Proceedings

 Springer

Volume Editors

T.C. Nicholas Graham
School of Computing
Queen's University
Kingston, Ontario, Canada
E-mail: graham@cs.queensu.ca

Philippe Palanque
IRIT
University Paul Sabatier (Toulouse 3)
Toulouse, France
E-mail: palanque@irit.fr

Library of Congress Control Number: 2008930133

CR Subject Classification (1998): H.5.2, H.5, I.3, D.2, F.3

LNCS Sublibrary: SL 2 – Programming and Software Engineering

ISSN 0302-9743

ISBN 978-3-540-70568-0 Springer Berlin Heidelberg New York

Springer is a part of Springer Science+Business Media

springer.com

© Springer-Verlag Berlin Heidelberg 2008

Typesetting: Camera-ready by author, data conversion by Scientific Publishing Services, Chennai, India
Printed on acid-free paper   SPIN: 12436422   06/3180   5 4 3 2 1 0

Preface

The modern world has made available a wealth of new possibilities for interacting with computers, through advanced Web applications, while on the go with handheld smart telephones or using electronic tabletops or wall-sized displays. Developers of modern interactive systems face great problems: how to design applications which will work well with newly available technologies, and how to efficiently and correctly implement such designs. Design, Specification and Verification of Interactive Systems 2008 was the 15th of a series of annual workshops devoted to helping designers and implementers of interactive systems unleash the power of modern interaction devices and techniques.

DSV-IS 2008 was held at Queen's University in Kingston, Canada, during July 16–18, 2008. This book collects the best papers submitted to the workshop. There were 17 full papers, 10 late-breaking and experience report papers, and two demonstrations. Keynote presentations were provided by Judy Brown of Carleton University and Randy Ellis of Queen's University.

The first day of the workshop addressed the problems of user interface evaluation and specification, with particular emphasis on the use of task models to provide high-level approaches for capturing the intended functionality of a user interface. Day two continued this theme, examining techniques for modeling user interfaces, particularly for mobile and ubiquitous applications. Presenters also discussed advanced implementation techniques for interactive systems. Finally, day three considered how to architect interactive systems, and returned to the themes of evaluation and specification.

The workshop was hosted by IFIP Working Group 2.7/13.4 on User Interface Engineering. We thank the 30 members of our international Program Committee for their hard work in the paper selection process. We also gratefully acknowledge Precision Conference for their generous donation of the PCS reviewing system.

We hope that you enjoy this record of the DSV-IS 2008 workshop, and find it fruitful for your work and research.

July 2008   T.C. Nicholas Graham
                                                             Philippe Palanque

Organization

Conference Chairs

T.C. Nicholas Graham, Queen's University, Canada
Philippe Palanque, IHCS-IRIT, Université Paul Sabatier, France

Program Committee

Simone Diniz Junqueira Barbosa, PUC-Rio, Brazil
Rémi Bastide, IRIT - C.U. Jean-François Champollion, France
Regina Bernhaupt, ICT&S, University of Salzburg, Austria
Ann Blandford, UCL, UK
Judith Brown, Carleton University, Canada
Gaelle Calvary, University of Grenoble, France
José Creissac Campos, University of Minho, Portugal
Stéphane Chatty, ENAC, France
Prasun Dewan, University of North Carolina, USA
Anke Dittmar, University of Rostock, Germany
Alan Dix, Lancaster University, UK
Gavin Doherty, Trinity College Dublin, Ireland
Peter Forbrig, University of Rostock, Germany
Philip Gray, University of Glasgow, UK
Morten Borup Harning, Priway, Denmark
Michael Harrison, University of Newcastle, UK
Chris Johnson, University of Glasgow, UK
Joaquim A Jorge, Technical University of Lisbon, Portugal
Kris Luyten, Expertise Centre for Digital Media, Hasselt University, Belgium
Mieke Massink, CNR, Pisa, Italy
Francisco Montero, UCLM, Spain
Laurence Nigay, University of Grenoble, France
Nuno Nunes, University of Madeira, Portugal
Fabio Paterno, ISTI-CNR, Pisa, Italy
Greg Phillips, Royal Military College, Canada
Kevin Scheider, University of Saskatchewan, Canada
Harold Thimbleby, University of Swansea, Wales
Claus Unger, University of Hagen, Germany
Jean Vanderdonckt, Université Catholique de Louvain, Belgium
Marco Winckler, IHCS-IRIT, Université Paul Sabatier, France

Table of Contents

EMU in the Car: Evaluating Multimodal Usability of a Satellite Navigation System

Ann Blandford[1], Paul Curzon[2], Joanne Hyde[3], and George Papatzanis[2]

[1] UCL Interaction Centre, University College London, Remax House, 31-32 Alfred Place
London WC1E 7DP, U.K
A.Blandford@ucl.ac.uk
http://www.uclic.ucl.ac.uk/annb/
[2] Queen Mary, University of London, U.K
[3] formerly at Middlesex University U.K

Abstract. The design and evaluation of multimodal systems has traditionally been a craft skill. There are some well established heuristics, guidelines and frameworks for assessing multimodal interactions, but no established methodologies that focus on the design of the interaction between user and system in context. In this paper, we present EMU, a systematic evaluation methodology for reasoning about the usability of an interactive system in terms of the modalities of interaction. We illustrate its application using an example of in-car navigation. EMU fills a niche in the repertoire of analytical evaluation approaches by focusing on the quality of interaction in terms of the modalities of interaction, how modalities are integrated, and where there may be interaction breakdowns due to modality clashes, synchronisation difficulties or distractions.

Keywords: usability evaluation, multimodal systems, in-car navigation systems, satellite navigation systems.

1 Introduction

There is a substantial literature on the design and use of multimodal systems, most of which takes either a system or a user perspective. Taking a system perspective, issues of concern include how to select output modalities to communicate most effectively (e.g. [9]) and how to integrate user input expressed through multiple modalities to correctly interpret the user's meaning (e.g. [15]). Conversely, much work from a user perspective is concerned with how users perceive and work with system output in different modalities (e.g. [8]) or how users select modalities of communication (e.g. [14]). Little work has taken an integrative approach, considering both user and system perspectives in parallel. The work reported here takes such an approach, developing a prototype methodology for reasoning about the design of multimodal interactive systems to accommodate both input and output within the interaction. As an integrative approach, it does not consider the fine-grained details of either system implementation or user cognition, but focuses more broadly on how the two interact.

T.C.N. Graham and P. Palanque (Eds.): DSVIS 2008, LNCS 5136, pp. 1–14, 2008.

The method, Evaluating Multimodal Usability (EMU) was initially developed and tested using as the main case study a robotic arm interface [10]. The approach presented and illustrated here is a refinement of the method, as described below.

2 Background: Multimodal Interaction

Multimodal systems are widely considered to be ones that integrate multiple modes of input or output, typically using non-standard interaction devices. The standard configuration of keyboard and mouse for input and graphics, text and audio for output is rarely described as "multimodal", though for our purposes it would class as such. Many definitions of a "modality" effectively consider a data stream from a particular source. For example Lin and Imamiya [13] discuss assessing user experience by measuring various user attributes – eye gaze, pupil size, hand movements, verbal reports – and refer to each of these inputs as a modality. Similarly, Sun et al [15] discuss data fusion across speech and gesture modalities, and Oviatt et al [14] focus on how people select alternative modalities (i.e. input devices) for interacting with a computer system. Considering both user input and computer system output, Coutaz et al [5] consider the combinations of modalities in terms of Complementarity, Assignment, Redundancy and Equivalence. Here, 'assignment' means that information has to be communicated through a particular modality and 'equivalence' means that the same information can be communicated equally effectively through alternative modalities. Complementarity and redundancy refer to how information is communicated (using different modalities in complementary ways, or presenting equivalent information through multiple modalities).

From a user perspective, much work on modalities has focused on how people integrate information received through different senses. Wickens and Hollands [17] present a multiple resource theory that considers cognitive capabilities and limitations in terms of perceptual channels (vision, hearing, touch, etc.), information form (of which the two most important for our purposes are lexical and symbolic) and stages of processing. They highlight limitations on sensory input (that multiple streams of information cannot be easily received through the same channel, such as eyes or ears, simultaneously) and on input, processing and action (that competing information in the same code, verbal or spatial, cannot be easily processed simultaneously). Other approaches that take a user focus include Barnard et al's work on Interacting Cognitive Subsystems [7], which considers the transformation and integration of sensory inputs through central processing to generate action, and Kieras et al's [12] work on Executive Process – Interaction Control (EPIC), which models human information processing in complex, multimodal tasks.

Since our concern is with assessing the usability of interactive systems, the capabilities and constraints on human processing, as well as those on system processing, have to be accommodated within any definition of a modality. Drawing on the insights from earlier work on modalities, we propose a definition: that a modality is a *temporally based instance of information perceived by a particular sensory channel.* This definition comprises three key elements, time, form and channel, which need some explanation.

Time refers to the static or dynamic way in which information is presented. This element is implicit in some other definitions of modality, e.g. in work on data fusion [15], but is essential for considering how both people and systems can integrate information from multiple sources over time. We distinguish three temporal forms: continuous (meaning that information remains available, in fixed form, over an extended period of time), discrete (information is communicated once, in a transient form) and dynamic (information is communicated over time, building up the message).

Information form is particularly important from a human perspective, in terms of how people express and comprehend information. Drawing on earlier work, we distinguish three important information forms: lexical, symbolic (e.g. graphical, with a meaning that can be inferred) and concrete (e.g. a scene, where no particular interpretation is intended).

For people, the primary sensory channels are visual, acoustic and haptic, though the set of possible channels might be extended to include olfactory (e.g. [2]). If the focus were on computer system input, then alternative input channels might be considered (e.g. keyboard input typically corresponds to lexical, haptic user output).

This definition of a modality, together with the extensible classification of possible values, is at the heart of the EMU method.

3   Overview of Original EMU Method

The original EMU method [10] drew on earlier task-oriented structured evaluation methods such as GOMS [4, 11] to develop a process-oriented analysis of user–system interaction modalities. The central idea behind the approach was that the analyst should work systematically through an interaction, taking account of the communications between user and system and also all other environmental interactions occurring in the situation. For example, when using an in-car navigation (or sat-nav) system, both user and system are also interacting with the car and the outside world, and the driver may also be interacting with passengers, which together constitute the environment. The core question is then whether all necessary information can be received, interpreted and integrated (by both user and system).

The analysis of modalities involves considering both input and output – for both user and system. This separate analysis is necessary to consider whether all information transmitted by one of the agents (user or system) is received and correctly interpreted by the other. As well as atomic modalities, there may also be composite ones, where some modalities depend on others; for example, tone of voice may communicate information that augments or contradicts the words spoken, or the colour of a sign may convey additional information.

Particular attention is paid to modality clashes. These may be physical (e.g. a user cannot look in multiple places at once, although attention may be caught by appropriately designed visual signals in peripheral vision).They may be temporal, in that multiple information inputs may be difficult to detect or interpret if they occur at the same time: an example would be the McGurk effect, where acoustic and visual information are slightly misaligned, making interpretation of speech difficult. One particular case of clashes that affects people is that, unless trained to do so in particular situations, people are unable to process two streams of lexical information simultaneously (e.g. reading while saying something different). They may also experience semantic clashes, of which an example would be the Stroop effect, where the colour of a word clashes with the meaning (e.g. the word "blue" written in red text). Hyde [10] also recognised that some interactions might be difficult for novices, but become easier with practice, such as changing gear in a car while negotiating a bend.

In the original version of EMU, analysis proceeds through eight stages:

1. The first stage, as in many analytical evaluation methodologies, is to define the task, or tasks, to be analysed.
2. The modalities used in the interaction are then listed, both descriptively (e.g. sat-nav gives voice direction) and in terms of the modality (e.g. system expresses acoustic-lexical-dynamic).
3. The third stage is to describe the user, system and environment in terms that might have an impact on the usability of the system.
4. A preliminary assessment of any modality issues should be performed.
5. A more complete and systematic analysis is performed, listing all steps of the interaction in terms of expressive and receptive modalities, to deliver a rich account of that interaction. This may include optionality (indicated by 'or') and simultaneous communications (indicated by 'and'); it should also include a note of any preconditions for communication (e.g. that a flashing light is within the visual field).
6. Clashes, as outlined above, are explicitly considered as the next step of analysis.
7. The penultimate step is to explicitly review the modalities used, considering usability issues that emerge (e.g. over-dependence on a single modality in a situation where large volumes of information need to be communicated).
8. Finally, Hyde [10] discusses the writing of the usability report, including conclusions and recommendations.

The method has been applied to the design of several systems, including a robotic arm for use by disabled people, a ticket machine and a central heating timer.

Two substantive tests of the EMU method have been conducted: one focusing on the usability and the other on the utility of the approach.

3.1 Usability Evaluation of EMU

The usability of the method was evaluated by teaching it to a group of 28 students with a background in HCI. They were asked to evaluate two systems using EMU, and their usability reports were assessed to establish how well they had understood the concepts and method, and whether they were able to apply it effectively. Following the test sessions, participants were invited to complete a questionnaire on their perceptions of applying EMU.

Details of this study are reported by Hyde [10]; here we summarise the main points of that study. The participants' detailed modality listings were compared to a model answer, and for most participants only minor errors were identified, indicating a good grasp of the core concepts. Participants experienced a little more difficulty in identifying modality clashes, and their ability to draw out usability insights from their analysis was variable. In questionnaire responses, most reported that the training had been clear, though some expressed doubts about their ability to apply the method correctly. There was, however, an overall concern that the application of the method was too time-consuming, and that an excessive attention to detail could, at times, divert attention from the broader usability issues that the analysis should have been highlighting.

The usability of any technique depends heavily on both the prior experience of the analyst and the quality of the training. As such, any single study will be inconclusive, as there are many variables that influence the outcome. Overall, the evaluation suggested that the approach could be understood and used effectively in a reasonable time, but that it should be made more lightweight where possible, without compromising the rigour of the technique.

3.2 Utility Evaluation of EMU

The utility of the method was evaluated by comparing the results of an EMU analysis against those of other evaluation techniques and also against empirical data. This study focused on the design of a robotic arm for use by people with limited movement. Seven other analytical evaluation approaches were applied to the same system (GOMS, Cognitive Walkthrough, Heuristic Evaluation, PUM, CASSM, and Z and STN representations). Empirical data of the arm in use was also analysed. A full account of this study is presented by Blandford et al [1]. In brief, the analysis showed that EMU occupies a useful niche in the repertoire of evaluation techniques. Z and STN were reasonably effective at supporting the identification of system-related problems such as the lack of an 'undo' facility, redundant operators, and long action sequences. GOMS supported the identification of many of the same issues as Z and STN, plus some concerning the synchronization of user actions with system behaviour. HE identified a range of issues, as defined by the particular set of heuristics applied. Most issues identified through Cognitive Walkthrough and PUM related to possible user misconceptions when interacting with the system. CASSM covered some of the same territory as CW and PUM, but also raised issues relating to the conceptual fit between how to operate the arm controller and what the user would want to do with the arm 'in the world' (e.g. concerning how easily the user could judge arm movements). EMU also covered some of the same territory as CW and PUM; in addition, it supported the identification of various issues relating to the modalities of interaction, as outlined below.

For the robotic arm and its interface, physical considerations were important. In particular, there was scope for system misinterpretation of user intentions so that the command issued by the user was not that received by the system. For example, the gestural input device had options scrolling across the screen, and the user had to nod when the required option was displayed to select it; this depended on the user's ability to synchronise their gesture with the system state. Consistent with the motivation for developing EMU to consider multimodal issues, this method proved the strongest for identifying these issues in the interaction.

EMU also proved effective in highlighting issues concerning the dual interactions with both the arm controller (which was located within the user's natural visual field) and the arm itself (which moved within a larger space beyond the controller).

Both the usability and the utility evaluations of EMU, as well as our own experience of applying it, indicate that it is understandable and useful, but that the original version of the method was rather cumbersome to use, and therefore needed streamlining and simplifying.

4   Simplified EMU Method

Following the evaluations, the EMU approach has been simplified in two ways: by reducing the number of formal stages in an EMU analysis and by de-emphasising the task analysis of the original step 5 (which typically duplicated findings of other task-oriented analysis techniques). The approach is still task-based, in that an interaction sequence, or a space of possible interaction sequences, is used as a basis for analysis, but the focus is on modalities, possible misinterpretations or breakdowns in communication, and modality clashes, considering interactions with the environment as well as with the system that is the focus of analysis.

The first stage is to select and describe a scenario of use, considering both a task sequence and the environment within which that task takes place. In order to make analysis efficient, it is important to focus attention on both representative and critical interaction sequences, but it is not necessary to consider repeated instances of the same modality configurations. When considering the environment, it is important to consider variability in the interactions; for example, in an office environment, a telephone might ring at unexpected times and distract the user, while on the road the environment provides many inputs and distractions that need to be integrated with information from the sat-nav as discussed below.

The second stage is to perform the modality analysis for selected interaction sequences. This involves considering every step, or phase, of the interaction in terms of five elements:

- *System, user* and *environment* modalities, remembering that these commonly occur in parallel (e.g. system receiving what user is expressing, or *vice versa*). In this context, we define the environment to be the broader context within which the user and system are interacting, including other technologies that are not the particular focus of the analysis.
- *Expressing* and *receiving*, noting which way the information is flowing.
- *Sensory channel*, considering for now the three possibilities of acoustic, visual and haptic, while recognising that the set of possible channels might be expanded.
- *Information form*, considering lexical, symbolic and concrete as the main forms.
- *Temporal form*, whether continuous, discrete or dynamic.
- The third stage is to consider interaction difficulties. These include:
- Potential mismatches between expressed and received modalities. These might include breakdowns where information is not received at all (e.g. discrete information presented visually, but not observed, or a user talking to a computer that is not set up to receive acoustic input at that moment). They can also include mismatches due to timing or interpretation problems, such as the example discussed above of timing and the gestural input device.
- Modality clashes, as discussed above.

- Integration difficulties of making sense of information received in different modalities or from different sources. From a system point of view, this might include data fusion difficulties; from a user perspective, it may include interpretation of information in the current (environmental) context.
- These stages are illustrated in the following example, where we present an outline analysis of an in-car navigation (or sat-nav) system.

5 Illustrative Example: In-Car Navigation

In this illustrative example, we base the analysis on a Garmin system, but aim to provide a description at a level of detail that generalises across various sat-nav systems, to draw out general points, rather than to focus on the details of implementation of this particular system. As well as the details of the sat-nav design, there might also be details concerning the car, how the sat-nav is fitted in the car, what other technologies (radios, MP3 players, etc.) might be available, whether there are passengers in the car, etc. The interaction will also be influenced by details of the route travelled, how familiar the driver is with that route, what signage is available, what the visibility is, etc.

One of the challenges in defining tasks is considering the level of detail and specificity with which it should be described. This is particularly so for devices such as sat-nav systems, which are intended to respond in a rich way according to the context of use. A very detailed description might yield valuable insights, particularly if details from an empirical study are also available: this would make it possible to consider issues such as the timing of instructions, the relationship to road signs, the visibility of the up-coming junction etc. However, such a rich account might not generalise well to other (similar but non-identical) situations. Therefore, we develop an abstract description of situations to illustrate a multi-modal analysis.

5.1 Stage 1: Defining the Scenario: Task and Environment

There are usually two key phases to interacting with a sat-nav system: set-up and use. For the purposes of illustration we consider one set-up task and an abstract in-use task.

Set-up typically starts with turning the sat-nav system on, then waiting for it to start up, identify its location and present the main options. The user then has to make a sequence of selections at the interface to define a destination; the model under consideration is a touch screen device, displaying both graphical icons and text, and with acoustic output. It would be possible to critique the sequence of action steps, or the labelling of options in terms of their textual or graphical clarity, but these issues are well covered by established evaluation approaches such as Cognitive Walkthrough [16], so for this analysis we check the consistency of interaction patterns across the sequence of steps and analyse one step in more detail. The environment for set-up might be the home, car or other starting place; it is unlikely to be changing rapidly, since the sat-nav should not be programmed while driving, but it might be dark or cold, or there might be glare from sunshine.

When the sat-nav is in use, at some abstract level we have a steady state, in which the sat-nav is delivering instructions which the user is following. The external visibility may be clear or poor (e.g. glare, low visibility or dark); the road conditions may be more or less demanding (e.g. heavy traffic); and there may be distractions (such as radio) or supports (such as a passenger to interpret sat-nav information and road signs). The driver should be interacting with the car controls, but not inputting information into the sat-nav.

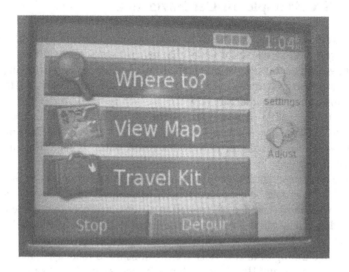

Fig. 1. Sat-nav menu

5.2 Set-Up: Modalities and Possible Interaction Difficulties

Next, we consider steps 2 and 3 for the first task. To turn the sat-nav on, it is necessary to press and hold the 'power' button until the display lights up. At this point, the user can release the button, and wait while a start-up message is displayed (accompanied by a multi-tone bleep); the user is asked to confirm that they agree to avoid interacting with the device while driving (at which point, the user is expected to press a soft-key on the display). Every soft-key press is accompanied by both a visual rendering and an audible 'beep'. Pressing illegal options (e.g. the 'up' key when it is not possible to scroll up) results in a two-tone beep: the usual 'button-press' beep followed by a lower pitch one. These modalities are summarised in Table 1; here, the modalities columns represent stage 2 of the EMU analysis and the 'notes' column highlights possible difficulties (stage 3). For start-up, we assume that the user's attention is focused on the device, and the only likely effects of the environment are it being cold or dark, or perhaps there being glare on the screen. If the device is fixed in the car, the user may have difficulty seeing the display while interacting with it.

Table 1. Interaction modalities and potential difficulties when initialising the sat-nav

Interaction event	User modalities	System modalities	Notes
User presses power button	Expresses haptic symbolic continuous	Receives haptic symbolic continuous	Users may have difficulties locating button in the dark, or pressing the button if their hands are cold or they are wearing gloves.
System displays start-up message and beeps	Receives visual symbolic continuous AND acoustic symbolic discrete	Expresses visual symbolic continuous AND acoustic symbolic discrete	This is assurance to the user that the device is functioning (but also signifying that it is not yet ready to be used).
System displays driving warning and on-screen acceptance button	Receives visual lexical continuous AND visual symbolic continuous	Expresses visual lexical continuous AND visual symbolic continuous	The user has to recognize the 'pressability' of a soft key.
User presses soft-key to confirm acceptance	Expresses haptic symbolic discrete	Receives haptic symbolic discrete	Touch screen may not accept input if user is wearing gloves. Screen may be hard to see if there is glare or user's hand obscures display.
System displays button 'depressed' and beeps, then displays main menu. See Fig 1.	Receives visual symbolic discrete AND acoustic symbolic discrete THEN visual lexical continuous AND visual symbolic continuous	Expresses visual symbolic discrete AND acoustic symbolic discrete THEN visual lexical continuous AND visual symbolic continuous	The initial system expressions are redundant, as the user can determine the effect of their action by seeing the menu.

The initial menu is shown in Figure 1. Whereas the earlier steps can be listed succinctly in a table, this display is much richer, and each element of it can be separately analysed to assess user interpretations. Here we interleave stages 2 and 3:

- There are five areas which are represented by soft key buttons, each of which has a lexical label (with or without an additional graphical label, which might be considered redundant). These are unlikely to be problematic.
- Two other areas ('settings' and 'adjust') are also clickable, but may not be recognised as such by a novice user.
- Two other areas, the 'battery' symbol and the time, display information about the state of the device, but cannot be interacted with.
- There is an additional area that the user can interact with: the top left-hand corner, if touched, will take the user to a new display showing "GPS is Off", together with a symbolic map of local GPS transmitters and their signal strength. This is unlikely to be discovered by most users.

- There are other controls (such as the power button) and connectors around the periphery of the device. In particular, at the back of the device (not shown in Figure 1) is a hinged, but unlabelled, component: the GPS antenna. If the user raises this antenna away from the body of the device, this is interpreted by the system as an instruction to turn GPS on; then a GPS signal indicator appears in the top-left corner of the screen, and if the user touches this area then a new display shows an estimate of the current GPS accuracy. The role of the antenna as an 'on/off' switch for the GPS is not immediately apparent, and has to be learnt.

In this section, we have outlined the steps of initializing the device, and highlighted some possible usability problems that emerge from a consideration of how the user is likely to interpret system output and also how the system interprets user actions. During set-up, in which interactions with the environment (whether at home or on the road) are likely to be minimal, we have focused on the user–system interaction. In our second example, we consider the broader interaction with the environment too, and possible variations of that situation.

5.3 Driving: Modalities and Possible Interaction Difficulties

While driving, we do not consider the task structure. The set of modalities in play is relatively static, and the issues concern how those modalities interact with each other. Stage 2 involves listing the modalities:

- The system receives input from GPS satellites from which it calculates its current position.
- If there are no passengers in the car, the system is unlikely to be receiving any other inputs.
- The system expresses visual, lexical and symbolic, dynamic modalities, as illustrated in Figure 2. It also gives verbal instructions intermittently (using an acoustic, lexical, dynamic modality).
- The environment includes the external world, which in turn includes the physical context (acoustic and visual, concrete, dynamic modalities) and signage (visual, lexical and symbolic, continuous modalities).
- The environment also includes the car itself, with which the user interacts via steering wheel, foot pedals and other controls. These controls receive input from the user via touch, and the user, in turn receives feedback from the controls by haptic (and also proprioceptive) feedback.
- The environment includes other devices, such as radio and dashboard displays, in the car. Dashboard displays may take various forms, most commonly visual, lexical and symbolic, continuous. (We consider the modality of the speedometer, for example, to be continuous rather than dynamic because it changes relatively slowly, and the user does not have to monitor it continually.) In some vehicles, dashboard displays may include acoustic output (lexical or symbolic).
- Radio output (or that of other entertainment systems) is typically acoustic, dynamic, and either lexical or symbolic. If the user adjusts the radio, the modalities include haptic, symbolic, discrete modalities (for making the adjustments) and visual, symbolic (or lexical), continuous modalities (for monitoring the new system state).

- The user expresses haptic modalities in interacting with both the vehicle controls and in-car systems (e.g. the radio). In some situations, the user may also talk – e.g. if using a car phone.
- The final consideration is of user receptive modalities. The user is likely to be receiving visual (lexical, symbolic and concrete) dynamic information from the environment, visual (lexical and symbolic) and acoustic (lexical) information from the sat-nav system, acoustic (lexical and symbolic) dynamic information from in-car entertainment systems, visual (lexical and symbolic) continuous information from the dashboard, and haptic, symbolic dynamic information from the car controls.

Laying out the modalities in this way does not immediately highlight possible problems, so stage 3 involves systematically working through the modalities and identifying possible clashes and other modality problems.

First, consider the sat-nav in its environment: it has to synchronise information from multiple satellites to calculate its current position and relate that to its database of geographical information. Depending on the location and quality of signal, this may be achieved with varying degrees of accuracy, which in turn determine the quality of information the device can deliver. In some situations, poor input information can result in "Lost satellite signal", with implications for the user as discussed below. Some sat-navs also derive information from the car telemetry system, which should increase the accuracy of available information, but we do not consider this possibility further.

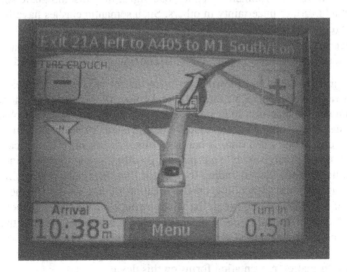

Fig. 2. An example sat-nav display while driving

Next we consider the sat-nav expressive modalities, and corresponding user receptive modalities. As shown in Figure 2, the device gives rich visual information, including a local route map (symbolic), the next instruction (lexical), estimated time of arrival (lexical) and distance to the next turning point (lexical). It also presents acoustic lexical information, intermittently. Systematically assessing these modalities:

- There are possible semantic clashes between acoustic and visual information from the sat-nav. The sat-nav may give an instruction such as "turn left" when the display indicates that there is still some distance to go before the turn: this information needs to be interpreted in the context of the current road situation.
- The acoustic information is, apart from the possible timing issue just noted, a subset of the visual information (in CARE terms, this is a redundant modality). If the driver only has access to the acoustic information, whether because of the location of the sat-nav in the car or because their visual attention is taken up elsewhere, the information available is relatively limited, and the meaning needs to be interpreted in the context of the external environment.
- In particular, there are possible semantic clashes between acoustic information from the sat-nav and visual information from the environment. A peculiar attribute of the auditory information from the particular sat-nav studied is that silence has a meaning – i.e. to go straight on. For example, a mini-roundabout might be regarded by the user as a roundabout, but not be represented as such within the system, so that if the user is expected to go straight across the roundabout then the system provides no acoustic instruction (which may be particularly confusing if the direction considered to be "straight" is not immediately obvious to the user). Similarly, if the main road bends to right or left, but there is a turning that goes straight ahead, the user may be unsure whether silence from the device means that they should go straight ahead or they should follow the road round the bend. Additional information in the environment, such as road signs, may disambiguate some situations, but add further uncertainty in others. Such semantic clashes have been noted by others (e.g. [6]).
- If the user is talking, or listening to other lexical information, the dynamic nature of the acoustic instructions may result in them being missed or misheard.

Focusing just on the visual information from the sat-nav, there are possible difficulties with various elements. The thickness and colour of the line (dependent modalities) that denotes the direction indicates the importance of the route, but obscures the corresponding information about the roads to be travelled (so visual information about whether the road to be turned onto is major or minor is absent). The lexical information is changing relatively slowly, so it may be possible for the user to glance at these information items while also attending to the road, but their relatively small size may make glancing difficult (depending on the location of the sat-nav in the car). The overlaying of some information (e.g. the white arrow over the "M25" label in Figure 2) and the placing of lexical items (e.g. "ters Crouch" in Figure 2) means that there is uninformative visual data on the screen. The display shown in Figure 2 is only one of several alternative displays: we use it for illustration purposes rather than evaluating all possible information presentation forms on this device.

Turning attention to the acoustic information alone, we note that it has various attributes: content (e.g. "turn left in 0.3 miles"), timing and tone. It has already been recognized (e.g. [3]) that the timing of instructions relative to the external environment is critical as the verbal information from the sat-nav needs to be interpreted in the context of the physical situation: for example, there may be ambiguity over which turning to take when there are several in quick succession. In EMU, the tone of voice is considered a dependent modality: for the sat-nav, it always sounds equally confident and reassuring. This may be at odds with actual degree of certainty (e.g. due to poor satellite information, or inaccuracy in underlying data), and consequently mislead the driver. We surmise that many incidents of people following sat-nav directions while ignoring warning signs in the environment are at least partly accounted for by the authoritative tone of voice employed in most sat-nav systems.

As noted above, most acoustic information is a replication of visual information. There are some exceptions, notably information about the state of the device. One example is implicit information that the driver has failed to follow directions – indicated by the acoustic information "recalculating". This contrasts with the information that a navigating passenger would typically provide, which would continue to refer to the navigation problem (e.g. telling the driver they have just gone the wrong way). Another example is "lost satellite signal", which leaves the user unsure how to interpret any subsequent directions, or leaves the user in an unknown place, with insufficient information to make decisions about where to go at junctions.

This second example illustrates some of the abstract issues that can be identified in a static analysis, focusing on the available modalities, the information that they communicate, and possible clashes and breakdowns in that communication.

6 Conclusions

Multimodal and ubiquitous systems are becoming widespread. Established analytical evaluation techniques are not well adapted to identifying the usability issues raised by the use of alternative or multiple modalities, or of assessing how systems are used within their broader environments. EMU is an approach that can complement more traditional evaluation techniques by focusing attention on information flows around an interactive system within its broader environment which will, itself, typically transmit and receive information that may augment, complement or interfere with that which passes between user and device.

We have illustrated the application of EMU to identifying some of the limitations of an exemplar sat-nav system. A satellite navigation system was chosen for this study because: the interaction between user and system is multimodal; the use of the system only makes sense within the broader environmental context (of the geographical region being traversed); and the system is safety-critical, making usability and user experience particularly important.

EMU focuses attention on the modalities of communications between user and system within the context of use. In particular, clashes between modalities, integration of information, and possible lost information can be identified through an EMU analysis. Earlier studies have shown that EMU is learnable [10] and that it occupies a particular niche within the space of analytical evaluation methods [1]. However, the initial study of EMU in use highlighted the fact that the process of conducting an analysis was unduly laborious. In this paper, we have presented a more lightweight approach, such that the costs of analysis are more appropriate to the benefits gained through conducting that analysis.

Acknowledgements

The development of the original EMU method was funded by a studentship from Middlesex University for Joanne Hyde. Recent work has been funded by EPSRC grants GR/S67494 and GR/S67500.

References

1. Blandford, A., Hyde, J.K., Green, T.R.G., Connell, I.: Scoping Usability Evaluation Methods: A Case Study. Human Computer Interaction Journal (to appear)
2. Brewster, S., McGookin, D., Miller, C.: Olfoto: designing a smell-based interaction. In: Proc. CHI 2006, pp. 653–662. ACM, New York (2006)
3. Burnett, G.E.: Usable vehicle navigation systems: Are we there yet? In: Vehicle Electronic Systems 2000 - European conference and exhibition, ERA Technology Ltd, June 29-30, 2000, pp. 3.1.1-3.1.11 (2000)
4. Card, S.K., Moran, T.P., Newell, A.: The Psychology of Human Computer Interaction. Lawrence Erlbaum, Hillsdale (1983)
5. Coutaz, J., Nigay, L., Salber, D., Blandford, A., May, J., Young., R.: Four easy pieces for assessing the usability of multimodal interaction: the CARE properties. In: Nordby, K., Helmersen, P., Gilmore, D.J., Arnesen, S. (eds.) Human-Computer Interaction: Interact 1995, pp. 115–120. Chapman and Hall, Boca Raton (1995)
6. Curzon, P., Blandford, A., Butterworth, R., Bhogal, R.: Interaction Design Issues for Car Navigation Systems. In: Sharp, Chalk, LePeuple, Rosbottom (eds.) Proc. HCI 2002 (short paper), vol. 2, pp. 38–41. BCS (2002)
7. Duke, D.J., Barnard, P.J., Duce, D.A., May, J.: Syndetic Modelling. Human-Computer Interaction 13, 337–394 (1998)
8. Elting, C., Zwickel, J., Malaka, R.: Device-dependant modality selection for user-interfaces: an empirical study. In: Proc. IUI 2002, pp. 55–62. ACM, New York (2002)
9. Fink, J., Kobsa, A.: Adaptable and Adaptive Information Provision for All Users, Including Disabled and Elderly People. New Review of Hypermedia and Multimedia 4, 163–188 (1998)
10. Hyde, J.K.: Multi-Modal Usability Evaluation. PhD thesis. Middlesex University (2001)
11. John, B., Kieras, D.E.: Using GOMS for user interface design and evaluation: which technique? ACM ToCHI 3.4, 287–319 (1996)
12. Kieras, D.E., Wood, S.D., Meyer, D.E.: Predictive Engineering Models Based on the EPIC Architecture for a Multimodal High-Performance Human-Computer Interaction Task. ACM Trans. Computer–Human Interaction 4, 230–275 (1997)
13. Lin, T., Imamiya, A.: Evaluating usability based on multimodal information: an empirical study. In: Proceedings of the 8th international Conference on Multimodal interfaces, ICMI 2006, Banff, Alberta, Canada, November 02 - 04, 2006, pp. 364–371. ACM, New York (2006)
14. Oviatt, S., Coulston, R., Lunsford, R.: When do we interact multimodally? Cognitive load and multimodal communication patterns. In: Proc. ACM International Conference on Multimodal Interfaces (ICMI), pp. 129–136 (2004)
15. Sun, Y., Chen, F., Shi, Y., Chung, V.: A novel method for multi-sensory data fusion in multimodal human computer interaction. In: Proc. OZCHI 2006, vol. 206, pp. 401–404. ACM, New York (2006)
16. Wharton, C., Rieman, J., Lewis, C., Polson, P.: The cognitive walkthrough method: A practitioner's guide. In: Nielsen, J., Mack, R. (eds.) Usability inspection methods, pp. 105–140. John Wiley, New York (1994)
17. Wickens, C.D., Hollands, J.G.: Engineering Psychology and Human Performance, 3rd edn. Prentice Hall International, London (2000)

Comparing Mixed Interactive Systems
for Navigating 3D Environments in Museums

Emmanuel Dubois, Cédric Bach, and Philippe Truillet

University of Toulouse, IRIT-IHCS, 31 062 Toulouse Cedex 9, France
{Emmanuel.Dubois, Cedric.Bach, Philippe.Truillet}@irit.fr

Abstract. This work aims at developing appropriate Mixed Interaction Systems
(MIS) for navigating 3D environments in a science centre context. Due to the
wide range and multi-disciplinary design aspects to consider in this context and
the lack of expertise in terms of MIS and public context evaluation, designing
and evaluating MIS is a complex task. Based on an integrated development
process, which combines a design model and a user-testing, this paper presents
the outcomes of the comparison of two MIS in terms of performance and satisfaction.

Keywords: User-centered design, user experiment, mixed interactive systems,
augmented reality, tangible UI, user-testing, design model.

1 Introduction

Technological and computational developments have pushed HCI beyond the traditional mouse / keyboard configuration, towards innovative and multiple display systems, multimodal interfaces, virtual and mixed reality and other "off-the-desktop"
interaction techniques. In the context of 3D environments [4], these evolutions contribute to a better support for navigating, exploring and visualizing 3D environments.
For the output, visualization techniques [27] or 3D displays are developed, such as
Head-Mounted Display, large/spherical screens. For the input, dedicated 3D devices
such as the Cubic Mouse [10] are developed, as well as "pen and tablets" techniques
[21], advanced forms of tracking mechanisms, speech and gesture-based interaction
[24], etc.

Faced with a museographic theme involving 3D representation of data, we wish to
explore and take advantages of these evolutions for creating an interactive experience:
we are seeking for a deeper involvement of the visitors during the visit. In this context, designing and evaluating the most appropriate interaction technique is not obvious because considerations from different domains must be merged.

In terms of design, 3D environment and science centre related aspects need to co-
exist. Among the large collection of advances in 3D user interface (UI) two interaction styles seem to be particularly appropriate for public experiences, because they
increase the system affordance. The first interaction style, **Modal behavior,** promotes
the use of a different interaction artifact for each available command: "pen and tablets" paradigms allow the clear representation on the tablet of widget-button representing commands. The second interaction style, the level of **input/output coupling**

T.C.N. Graham and P. Palanque (Eds.): DSVIS 2008, LNCS 5136, pp. 15–28, 2008.

reinforces the integration of the interaction artifacts with the targeted objects of inter-action: the Cubic Mouse [10] for example literally places visualized data in the user's hands. From the science centre perspective, **Mixed Interactive Systems** (MIS) such as tangible, augmented and mixed reality UI should be favored: indeed, they are more easily integrated in the museum architecture and adapted to different themes and they are able to hide technological devices, thus promoting the magical dimension of the experience and replacing objects at the centre of the user's visit of the science centre [26]. However, it is difficult to maintain the integration of 3D UI and science centre considerations all along a development process based on the most usual *ad hoc* or prototyping approaches.

In terms of evaluation, experience acquired from the design and evaluation of 3D UI in the literature often relies on niche applications in which performance is preva-lent; little place is left to 3D UI satisfaction analysis as defined in [16]. However satisfaction is becoming crucial when the task to perform is not clearly associated with a user's goal but allows creativity and exploration such as in science centre. In addition, "best practices" or expertise for supporting the evaluation of such interactive techniques do not exist yet.

Our goal is thus to compare mixed interaction techniques for navigating 3D envi-ronment in a science centre context: each of them combines one of the two interaction styles inferred by 3D UI experiences (modal behavior and input/output coupling) and science centre constraints. Our approach relies on an integrated development process involving 3 steps: 1) use of an existing design model to generate interactive solutions and ensure that 3D UI and science centre considerations are well combined, 2) im-plementation of the techniques on the basis of the design specifications, and 3) user testing including an assessment of performance and satisfaction aspects.

2   Mouse-Based and Mixed Interaction Techniques Design

Due to experimental requirements, a 3D interactive application that is robust, easy to understand and offering software API is required. We choose to use the part of the Google Earth (GE) free application [11] supporting the navigation onto satellite pic-tures of the Earth from a modifiable point of view. This application mimics our tar-geted museum application seeking to navigate over the Earth at different era. Next sections present how the set of selected commands are accessible with the mouse and the mixed interaction techniques that we developed.

2.1 GE Manipulation with a Mouse

A first set of commands is used to support translations of the displayed image of the earth: the **"go to" tasks**. For example, in order to visualize a region of the globe situ-ated to the left of the current screen, one must press the left mouse button, moves the mouse to the right and releases the mouse button: this results in a rotation of the globe from left to right (Figure 1, top). Likewise, translations of the mouse to the left, top or bottom result in displaying globe areas placed on the right, bottom or top of the cur-rent view, respectively. In addition, using the mouse wheel enables the user to modify the altitude of the birds-eye view: this corresponds to the definition of the zoom level on the images. The second set of commands considered in this experiment results in rotations of the displayed images: the **"turn around" tasks**. If the mouse cursor is in the upper part of the displayed globe area, pressing the mouse-wheel and then moving the mouse cursor horizontally to the left (resp. right), results in a counter-clockwise (resp. clockwise) rotation of the globe area as shown in Figure 1 (bottom): this corresponds to a modification of the orientation of the North direction, and this behavior is inverted if the mouse cursor is in the lower part of the screen. Finally pressing the scroll wheel and then vertically moving it down (resp. up), results in a diminution (resp. increase) of the angle between the point of view and the globe surface tangent (see Figure 1, bottom): this corresponds to a modification of the viewpoint, the **"tilt" tasks**.

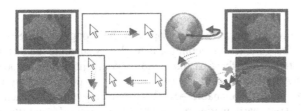

Fig. 1. Effect on GE of mouse translations while pressing left button (top) or wheel mouse (bottom)

In addition to the mouse-based interaction, we developed two mixed interaction techniques with the same basic commands. In order to support the combination of design considerations implied by 3D UI and science centre contexts, their design is based on the use of a design model specific to Mixed Interaction Techniques. We first briefly motivate the need for a specific design tool before using it for presenting the implemented techniques.

2.2 Design Approach

As already mentioned, science centre needs play in favor of mixed interaction techniques, i.e. interactive techniques involving a set of physical artifacts, devices, and digital resources. Such interaction techniques induce a multi-faceted interaction setting. To facilitate the reasoning about their design, physical artifacts have to be clearly identified and characterized, links between physical and digital resources must be expressed and the user's interaction within this complex interactive environment requires a clear description. Such a design-support should include task analysis considerations, domain object and dialog description, and should take into account the presence of physical objects.

However, until recently, mixed interactive system developments mostly consisted in the production of *ad hoc* prototypes, based on the use of new technologies. In order to face the rapid development of these systems, different design approaches emerge. TAC paradigm [22] and MCPrd [17] architecture describe the elements required in Tangible User Interfaces. More recently, some notations have been developed to support the exploration of Mixed Systems design space [6, 7, 23]: they are based on the identification of artifacts, entities, characteristics and tools relevant to a mixed system. Other work in mixed interactive systems study the link between design and implementation steps [15,20]. Among these design supports we choose to use the ASUR model because it offers a large set of characteristics [7], structured in an information flow oriented framework [8] useful for capturing the fundamental roles of the different artifacts in the mixed interaction. An ASUR model constitutes a formal and abstract specification of the interaction technique, which can be iteratively refined up to the identification of the technological devices to use. ASUR also provides a graphical editor based on an ASUR meta-model, thus allowing model transformations and interweaving with other models [5]. The next sections adopt this model to present the mixed interaction techniques we developed and how they incorporate interaction styles suggested by 3D UI experiences.

2.3 GE-Stick

The first interaction technique we developed is the Google-Earth Stick (GE-Stick). The goal of this first interaction technique is to clearly separate the different available commands: it is thus using the first interaction style identified in introduction: modal behavior. Using ASUR to reason about the design of a possible solution, lead to the identification of one distinguishable ASUR participating entity for each command. In the ASUR framework, participating entities can be of four different types: adapters (A component) bridging the gap between the computer system and the real world, digital resources managed by the computer system (S components), user interacting with the system, or physical artifacts of the real world (R components). Given our goal to design mixed interaction techniques for 3D navigation support, physical participating entities must be used to materialize the ten navigation commands: the ASUR model should thus involve ten physical entities. Inspired from the "Tangible Geospace" [25], the design solution described at this level could result in the use of ten different bricks with discriminating forms or colors. In the context of public spaces, too many artifacts may be hard to manage, given the risk of losing one of the ten bricks, and conflicts with classical ergonomics recommendations about capacity of short term memory (7 ± 2 chunks [18]).

To reduce this risk, the final ASUR model, presented in Figure 2, identifies only seven physical artifacts (R_{tool} components): six of them are used to materialize the four "cardinal" translations and two others represent the two directions for modifying the orientation of the point of view on the surface of the Earth; they are physically grouped together (*double-line ASUR relationship*) on the seventh artifact (R_{tool} component, Board) handled by the user (*double-line ASUR relationship*). To activate the command associated to one of them, a sensor (A_{in} component, RFID reader) is required to identify the physical artifact, when coming close to it (*double-line ASUR relationship*). The type of sensor can be further refined in the ASUR model by the "*medium*" property of the interaction channels 2x: it denotes the mean by which the information is transmitted and in this case the final model specifies radio-frequency on this channel. The command to apply is then transmitted along channel 5 to the database containing satellite images of Google Earth, a digital entity (S_{object} component, Google Map).

The four remaining commands are encoded through two adapters (A_{in} components, Slider and Potentiometer), i.e. captors directly linked to the computer system. They are used to sense changes to apply to the orientation to the north and the altitude.

Finally, an output adaptor (*component A_{out}*, Video projector) is required to provide the user with information in a visual way as specified by the "medium" of the channel 9. Every channel could be further refined by additional ASUR characteristics. This is however not relevant to the present work but is the purpose of [9] in which a complete and detailed modeling is presented.

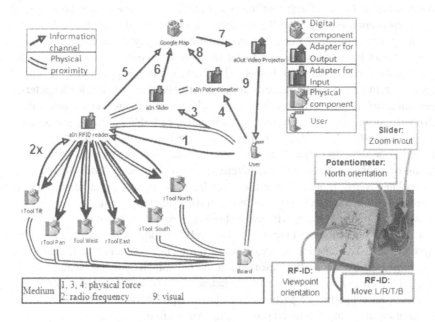

Fig. 2. ASUR modeling of the GE-Stick and actions a user can perform on it

Concretely, this interaction technique and its use are illustrated in Figure 2. It consists of a prop held in the user's hand and a board representing a compass rose. Six positions on the board are distinguishable: they correspond to the six physical participating entities identified in ASUR (R_{tool} *component*) and represent the six directions in which the Earth can be moved. These areas are equipped with a RF-ID tag. The lower part of the prop is equipped with a RF-ID reader: it corresponds to the sensor (the first A_{in} *component*) and the user has to bring the prop close to one of the six areas to detect the RF-ID tag and trigger the corresponding event.

The two remaining adapters (A_{in} *components*) identified to sense the changes to apply to the north orientation and the altitude are instantiated through two devices fixed on the prop: one is a potentiometer and can be turned with the thumb and forefinger to modify the orientation of the North axis; the second is a slider and can be slid up/down to change the zoom. In the specific and predefined "neutral zone", these buttons have no effect. Phidget sensors [19] are used for the implementation.

2.4 GE-Steering Board (GE-SB)

The second interaction technique developed is the Google-Earth Steering Board (GE-SB). The primary goal of this technique is to increase the coupling between the input interaction artifact and the navigated data (interaction style: input / output coupling). This coupling is reinforced to promote the homogeneity along three dimensions: *representations*, *scales* and *behaviors*.

Expressing the *representation* with the ASUR design model implies that one physical participating entity (R_{tool} component, Steering Board) must represent the manipulated data: Google Earth satellite images (S_{object} component, Google Map). The ASUR "*representation link*" fulfills this role and is expressed with the dashed arrow between a participating entity and its representation. The physical configuration of the physical artifact is identified by an adapter for input (A_{in} component, Camera), which is responsible for transmitting (channel 3) the command to apply onto the satellite images. To reinforce the homogeneity in terms of *behavior*, the ASUR characteristic "*representation*" is used to define the coding scheme used to encode the information. In channel 1, it must be "a set of discriminant and specifiable physical configurations of the artifact": the user will have to move this physical artifact (*channel 1*) to move away or in one direction, modify the orientation, etc. To strengthen the homogeneity in terms of *scaling*, the ASUR characteristic "*modification method*" of channel 2 specifies "hands/arm motions": the user will have to produce hand-gesture and not only small motions such as those required to move a mouse or joystick.

Finally, in a public context, wireless technologies and solutions that avoid any contact of the user with an electronic device are probably more suitable, at least to limit the risk of theft. This restriction is expressed in the "*medium*" characteristic of channel 2: the mean by which this information is transmitted will be "visual". Consequently, the "*sensing mechanism*" of this channel must be a "CCD and a recognition" algorithm. Characteristics of participating entities and interaction channels are summarized in Figure 3 and a detailed presentation can be found in [9].

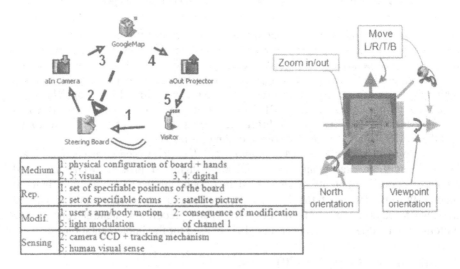

Fig. 3. ASUR modeling of the GE-SB and board motions that are recognizable by the system

Concretely, this interaction technique and its use are illustrated in Figure 3. A physical board is required and corresponds to the ASUR R_{tool} component. It represents the position of the point of view on the images. Moving the board results in moving the point of view on the satellite pictures accordingly: these motions are detected via the ASUR adapter identified (A_{in} component). Technically the GE-SB involves video-based tracking software [1] to localize the position of the reverse side of the board in the space. As illustrated in Figure 6 a camera for the detection of the board is positioned in front of the user. A neutral zone also exists in which only rotations can be triggered.

The model-based design approach has been enriched with an inspection based on Ergonomic Criteria dedicated to Virtual Environment [2]. Achieved by a MIS usability expert, it was used to detect problems that could have jeopardized user-testing and complicated results interpretation.

3 Experimental Settings

To compare the two mixed interaction techniques previously designed, an evaluation was carried out. It is based on user-testing and includes performance / satisfaction considerations. This experiment is a prospective attempt for comparing the effect of mixed interaction techniques in science centre contexts. In order to have sufficient control, it takes place in a usability lab and involved users who received "higher education" because, according to statistics of our science centre partner, they represent more than 60% of the visitors. Finally, the mouse is the reference technique, because it takes advantage of the user's habits and its use with Google Earth is feasible.

3.1 Users and Material

13 users were involved in this experiment, 8 males and 5 females (29.6 years old, SD=7.3). All of them have obtained a graduation degree and are well familiarized with mouse-based interaction with a computer but not especially accustomed to MIS and 3D UI. The version of Google Earth we used is 4.0.2416 and it was retro-projected on a screen 2.1 m wide, 1.5 m high (2.56 m in diagonal). Users stood in front of the screen, at approximately 2 m. A table was placed between them and the screen at 1.9 m. An area was defined on the table to represent the zone in which to manipulate the mouse; it also represented a vertical projection, onto the table, of the "neutral zone" defined for the GE-SB: this area is 0.3x0.25 m. A camcorder captured data displayed on the screen and the user's interaction (see Figure 4). On the other side of the screen, two observers measured the duration of each task accomplished by the user and took notes about misuses of the interaction techniques.

3.2 Procedure

Each user was involved in a 3 phases process: training, test and post-test interview. During the training phase, the goal was to teach to the user how to perform the ten different Google Earth commands involved in the experiment: six translations, including the zoom in and out, and 4 rotations. Users were informed that semi-automated zooming and moving with mouse are prohibited by experiment settings. Each user had to go through this training with the mouse first: it is the technique of our control group; users were then trained on the GE-Stick and GE-SB in a counterbalanced order. Finally, using the mouse only, cities involved in the measurement phase were visited (Paris, NY, Nouméa), to be sure that users could found these places during the test. Users had no time limit and were asked to confirm whenever they thought they perfectly understood and controlled how to trigger the commands before starting the test phase.

During the test phase, users were informed that the time to perform the following tasks would be now measured. This measurement phase was based on a predefined scenario. The scenario was made of seven steps involving the ten Google Earth commands previously taught to the user. Users were all starting from Paris and the first step asked the user to "reach New York (NY) at an altitude of 400 m". The following steps of the scenario were: tilt the Earth to observe the horizon, do the tour of the island, come back at the vertical of the Earth, go to Nouméa, tilt the Earth until observing the horizon and finally do the tour of Nouméa. This scenario thus includes three different types of tasks, namely "Go to", "Tilt" and "Turn around", each of them being performed twice during the scenario, in NY then in Nouméa. Each step of the scenario was stated by the experimenter who explicitly mentioned when to start carrying out each step. Each user had to perform the scenario three times, with the three different interaction techniques, in the same order taught in the training phase. For each scenario, 26 measures have been recorded: 13 users performed twice each type of tasks ("go to", "tilt", "turn around")

During the post-test interview, users were questioned about their qualitative experience with the applications, through a semi-guided interview.

4   Assessment Results

All experimental tasks were successfully performed by subjects except seven failures in the category of task "Turn around". All users had successfully achieved this task, with every interaction technique during the training phase but four failures were due to two users when using the mouse and three failures were due to two other users using the GE-SB. Most salient results are bolded in the following text.

4.1 Satisfaction Analysis

The semi-guided interview of the post-test phase was used to determine, the preferred interaction technique, their feelings about the discovery process, the three strongest and weakest points of each techniques, the most efficient and the most constraining techniques, and finally the physical workload. In this paper, we focus on the users' preferred interaction technique.

To identify preferred interaction technique, participants were asked to rank interaction techniques by preference order. A proportional score (range 0 to 20) was then computed by summing the scores given by the users to each interaction technique. According to this analysis the preferred interaction technique is the GE-SB (12.14) followed by the mouse (10.71) and GE-Stick (7.14). Preliminary interview analyses indicate that users prefer the GE-SB because it allows a good level of presence and a feeling of omnipotence. Preference for the mouse seemed to be based on familiarity arising from everyday uses (habit). Given that the input/output coupling interaction style has been embedded in the GE-SB design, this result highlights, in the present settings, the **impact of the level of coupling** of the interaction artifacts with the targeted interaction space on the user's interaction with a MIS.

4.2 Performance Analysis

4.2.1 Overall Performance Analysis

Means (M) and standard deviations (SD) of the overall durations of use (including the 7 steps of the scenario) are: mouse (M=5'19; SD=2'31); GE-Stick (M=6'48; SD=0'53); GE-SB (M=7'23; SD=2'13).

An analysis of variance (ANOVA) was performed. This analysis shows an effect [F (2,270)=3.0567; p=0.0487] of the interaction technique used to perform the scenario. Three complementary paired Student-Test reveals a significant difference between mouse and mixed interaction techniques (GE-SB vs. Mouse: p<0.001; GE-Stick vs. Mouse p=0.0259) but no significant effect between the mixed interaction techniques (GE-SB vs. GE-Stick: p=0.1887). These results show a better global performance of the control group using a mouse compared to MIS. It also illustrates that the performance order, based on the duration of use, is different from the preferred interaction technique order, i.e. user's satisfaction. This result highlights that in MIS context, like in traditional HCI context [16], performance and satisfaction are not necessarily correlated: as mentioned by [14], **performing a composite evaluation** (multi methods/dimensions/domains) is required to assess the quality of MIS.

Another straight performance result arises from the comparison of the SD of each interaction technique. The SD represents the level of variability between users' performance when interacting with an interaction technique: the smaller the variability, the more consistent the interaction technique in terms of stability of use among different users. Unexpectedly, it appears in the studied sample that the SD of the two mixed interaction techniques are equal (GE-SB) or smaller (GE-Stick) than the SD of the mouse (control group). Given that modal behavior interaction style has been embedded in the design of the GE-Stick, this result draws attention, in the present settings, to the **interest of the strong differentiation of each command** on the user's interaction with a MIS. More generally, stability of use is one of the major factors of transferability of an interaction technique to public spaces: indeed it positively affects consistency of use. This interesting result thus suggests that it is **worth further investigating mixed interaction techniques** in science centre context.

In order to better understand the differences among the interaction technique, performance results have been considered for each type of task.

4.2.2 Performance Analysis of "Go to" Tasks

A Multivariate Analysis of Variance (MANOVA) was performed to identify (1) the most efficient interaction technique to perform this task and (2) the difference between the realization of the first occurrence of the task ("Go from Paris to NY") and the second ("Go from NY to Nouméa"). Effects of the interaction technique [F (2,72)=117.87; p=1.95e-23], of the occurrence [F (1,72)=4.60; p=0.035] and of the interaction between this two main factors [F (2,72)=3.56; p=0.033] were revealed.

Table 1. Duration of realization of the task "Go to"

IT	Go to (s)	NY	Nouméa
	M.	51.31	60.00
Mouse	Var.	86.23	233.34
	M.	144.23	123.46
GE-SB	Var.	1122.52	145.93
	M.	160.54	138.23
GE-Stick	Var.	1206.27	545.52
Mean	M.	118.69	107.23

Fig. 4. Picture of the settings in front of the screen

Table 1 summarizes the mean (M) and variance (Var) of the performance of realization of the task "Go to" with each of the three techniques. Similarly to the overall performance analysis, **the better performance is accomplished with the mouse**. However, we noticed during the experiment that, with mouse use, the speed of the image translations was directly correlated with the speed of the user's movement of the mouse, while with the two other interaction techniques, the speed of the image translations is constant, even when user's movement are quicker or larger.

More interestingly, the effect of the occurrence shows that the control group spent more time to reach Nouméa from NY (2nd occurrence of the type of task "Go to") than to reach New York from Paris (1st occurrence): this is coherent because the distance between New York and Nouméa is twice the distance between Paris and New York. However, using the MIS, GE-SB or GE-Stick, it is more efficient to reach Nouméa (2nd occurrence) than New York (1st occurrence) (see table 1). In addition when considering the mean of the durations required to performed the "Go to" tasks with each interaction techniques separately, the mean of the second occurrence (going from NY to Nouméa) is significantly lower when using the MIS: GE-SB (p=0.026) and GE-Stick (p=0.032). This suggests that the participants continue to learn how to use MIS between Paris and New York and the result of this learning is the better performance to reach Nouméa from New York despite the double length of the trip. This result shows that along the experiment, users **improve their experience with the MIS**, which contribute to ensure a deeper involvement of the user.

4.2.3 Performance Analysis of "Tilt" Tasks

Another MANOVA was computed to explore the effects of "interaction technique" and "occurrence of the task" (NY vs. Nouméa) on "Tilt" tasks type. The results do not show any significant differences between interaction techniques [F (2,108)=0.868; p=0.422], occurrences of the task [F (2,108)=1.54; p=0.219] and interaction between these two factors [F (4,108)=1.44; p=0.224]. These interaction techniques thus appear to be equivalent to perform the "Tilt" task and are not especially associated with a learning effect (as opposed to the "Go to" task). However, one can note in Table 2 (left) an important and repeated dispersion of the users' performances on "Tilt" tasks, with the mouse: it confirms the overall stability of MIS identified in 4.2.1

Table 2. Duration of realization of the task "Tilt" (left) and "Turn around" (right)

IT	Time to (s)	Tilt (NY)	Untilt (NY)	Tilt Nouméa	Total	IT	Turn (s)	NY	Nouméa	Total
	M.	23.46	8.46	7.23	13.05		M.	64.92	53.69	59.31
Mouse	Var.	2127.7	56.43	15.35	75047	*Mouse*	Var.	4099.23	2864.24	3375.26
	M.	19.92	17.38	16.77	18.02		M.	60.38	24.61	42.50
GE-SB	Var.	27.24	49.09	104.52	59.02	*GE-SB*	Var.	7722.75	770.92	4409.62
	M.	14.92	13.31	19.77	16.00		M.	19.23	13.15	16.19
GE-Stick	Var.	12.41	6.23	130.02	54.68	*GE-Stick*	Var.	294.36	26.14	163.44

4.2.4 Performance Analysis of "Turn Around" Tasks

A last MANOVA was computed to explore the effects of "interaction technique" and "occurrence of the task" (NY vs. Nouméa) on "Turn around" tasks type. No significant effect can be observed regarding the occurrence of the task [F $(1.72)=2.32$; $p=0.132$] and the interaction between these factors [F $(2.72)=0.622$; $p=0.539$]: as opposed to the "Go to" task, no learning effect can be observed. More interestingly, a significant effect of the interaction technique exists [F $(2.72)=4.669$; $p=0.012$]. Three complementary student tests established that the **GE-Stick is significantly better to achieve the "Turn around" task** than the mouse ($p<0.001$) and GE-SB ($p=0.029$) (see Table 2): again this can be associated with the modal behavior interaction style, embedded in the GE-Stick. No significant difference is identified between the mouse and the GE-SB ($p=0.168$).

5 Discussion and Future Works

This paper presents a comparison of two mixed interaction techniques, useful for navigating 3D environments in a science centre context. Given the complex nature of this kind of environment and the relative lack of expertise in the evaluation of mixed interactive system, methodological and empirical results are required [3]. To address this issue, we selected a concrete use case, navigating Google Earth, and adopted a development process based on a design model and a user experiment.

The use of a design model dedicated to Mixed Interactive System (MIS), illustrates how different design considerations can be formally expressed in this model. We particularly focused on how to express two relevant 3D UI interaction styles ("modal behavior" and "input/output coupling"). Subsequently, additional science centre constraints and considerations have been introduced in the model, and final adjustments lead to the elicitation of two design solution of MIS, adapted to the considered settings.

The user testing included performance and satisfaction aspects and aimed at comparing three interaction techniques (IT): the two MIS, implemented on the basis of the model-based specifications and a mouse-based IT (control-group). The satisfaction analysis was based on a post-test interview and the performance analysis was based on 26 measures for each task supported by an IT. The rankings of these three IT according to the user preferences clearly differs from the ranking established according to the performance measurements. The first outcomes of this comparison thus confirm that satisfaction and performance are two complementary aspects to take into considerations when designing MIS for science centre contexts. Although the overall performance evaluation highlighted that the mouse is more efficient than the two MIS we developed, results obtain in these experimental settings also reveal that our MIS prototypes could well be transferred to public spaces: their overall inter-user performance stability is equal or better than the well known mouse and the user's appropriation of the MIS is significantly established on given tasks ("Go to" tasks type). These elements will contribute to reinforce the visitor's involvement in a science centre offering such interactive experience. Concerning the two interaction styles, each of them embedded in the design of one of the MIS, results show the importance of the "input / output coupling", especially on the satisfaction aspect of the evaluation. On the other hand the "modal behavior", by differentiating the commands, produces a positive implication on user involved in tasks that are hard to understand or perform, such as the "Turn around" tasks type.

Following this evaluation, problems with these MIS have also been identified. First, grasping the GE-Stick was not very easy because it was quite thick: rearranging the sensors or using the Nintendo Wii-mote for example will improve this limitation. Secondly, the speed of the translation was limited with the MIS, but a new Google Earth API will avoid this software limitation and allow the implementation of acceleration factors. Thirdly, finding the neutral area of the GE-SB was not immediate: solutions to this must be found.

Following this prospective work in terms of comparison of MIS, research perspectives have been identified. Firstly, the interaction styles considered raise the opportunity to refine the notion of interaction continuity. Indeed, each of them have a positive impact on different interaction dimensions either linked to performance or satisfaction: the input/output coupling present in the GE-SB increases the **scales compatibility** between the input and output, and the **significances of artifacts** involved; the modal behavior present in the GE-Stick increases the **consistency between user and MIS behavior**. These three dimensions might constitute three new relevant criteria for defining the notion of continuity in the context of MIS. Such criteria might even constitute a bridge to articulate HCI practices with furniture designer. Secondly, the design-test process adopted here establishes so far only to form of links between the models and the evaluation. The first link is based on the museum requirements (interaction styles and use of MIS): they are at the basis of the design models developed and they rationalize the experimental setting established to compare the techniques. The second link is in favor of an effective reengineering of interaction techniques: interesting results raised during an evaluation (*e.g. "turn around" is quicker with the GE-Stick than with the GE-SB*) can easily be linked to some parts of the ASUR model (*e.g. a user, the digital entity Google Map, an adapter for input and the three channels connecting them*); an iteration on the design-test process may thus bring a new solution build around this part of the model that has a positive impact on the interaction; alternatively, issues raised during the test can also be associated with specific parts of the model and constitute the main focus of the design of the next design iteration, while keeping other design considerations or constraints expressed elsewhere in the model in the first iterations. These kinds of links and impacts have to be further explored and could be further reinforced by the direct expression of a recommendation and criteria in terms of the design model: predictive evaluation would thus be supported by the design model. This anchor between design and evaluation also constitutes a promising basis to the deployment of replay based design steps. Finally, although we constituted our user sample with great care, it appears to be very hard to control its homogeneity because it involves individual capabilities of 3D navigation: in complement to [12] and [13], identifying difficulties, rules and method for supporting the recruitment process of participants, seems crucial.

To conclude, the work we reported has been in this paper could be considered as the outcomes of a first increment of the development of MIS in a museum context. This context was useful to establish a field of constraints and to experiment the design-test process in a concrete area. But we also believe that this approach might be applicable and valuable to any MIS development.

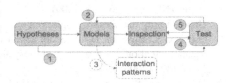

Fig. 5. Summary of the development process

This process (see figure 5), like any experimental process, is based on hypotheses. In our case, modeling is a step between hypotheses and the experimental step necessary to test these hypotheses (1) (e.g., test the interest to decoupling commands). The role of the modeling step is to support the generation and specify a possible MIS implementation of the hypothesis. Adding a retroactive loop (2) from the test to the model would be useful to relate empirical experiences to a model or part of it: this will improve the predictive power of the design model. Multiple iterations and experiments of this kind will feed a collection of mixed interactive systems patterns (3). Moreover, in our case the usability inspection successfully identified a set of usability problems (4). However, usability inspection missed some flaws observed in the test (e.g. form of the board). Adding a feedback loop (5) between test and inspection steps would constitute an opportunity to collect empirical experiences to enrich usability inspections and also their downstream utility [14]. In the long term, this empirical data could improve both usability methods and usability recommendations for MIS. Finally, this work has been done in the context of a museum.

References

1. ARToolkit: http://www.hitl.washington.edu/artoolkit
2. Bach, C., Scapin, D.L.: Adaptation of Ergonomic Criteria to Human-Virtual Environments Interactions. In: Conference proceedings of Interact 2003, Zurich, Switzerland, pp. 880–883. IOS Press, Amsterdam (2003)
3. Bach, C., Scapin, D.L.: Obstacles and perspectives for evaluating Mixed Reality Systems Usability. In: Int. Workshop MIXER 2004, Funchal, pp. 72–79. ACM Press, New York (2004)
4. Bowman, D.A., Kruijff, E., LaViola, J.J., Poupyrev, I.: 3D user Interafces: Theory and Practice. Addison-Wesley, Reading (2004)
5. Charfi, S., Dubois, E., Bastide, R.: Articulating Interaction and Task Models for the Design of Advanced Interactive Systems. In: Winckler, M., Johnson, H., Palanque, P. (eds.) TAMODIA 2007. LNCS, vol. 4849, pp. 70–84. Springer, Heidelberg (2007)
6. Coutrix, C., Nigay, L.: Mixed Reality: A Model of Mixed Interaction. In: Conference proceedings of AVI 2006, pp. 45–53. ACM Press, New York (2006)

7. Dubois, E., Gray, P.D., Nigay, L.: ASUR++: a Design Notation for Mobile Mixed Systems. In: Paterno, F. (ed.) Interacting With Computers, vol. 15, pp. 497–520 (2003)

8. Dubois, E., Gray, P.: A Design-Oriented Information-Flow Refinment of the ASUR Interaction Model. In: The IFIP conf. proc. of EIS 2007, Spain, p. 18 (2007)

9. Dubois, E., Gray, P., Ramsay, A.: A Model-Based Approach to Describing and Reasoning about the Physicality of Interaction. In: Proc. of Physicality 2007, UK, pp. 77–82 (2007)

10. Frölich, B., Plate, J.: The cubic mouse: a new device for 3D input. In: CHI 2000, The Hague (NL), pp. 526–531 (2000)

11. Google Earth: http://earth.google.com

12. Green, C.S., Bavelier, D.: Effect of action video games on the spatial distribution of visuospatial attention. J. of experimental psychology: Human perception and performance 32, 1465–1478 (2006)

13. Griffiths, G., Sharples, S., Wilson, J.R.: Performance of new participants in virtual environments: The Nottingham tool for assessment of interaction in virtual environments (NAIVE). Int. J. of Human-Computer Studies 64, 240–250 (2006)

14. Hartson, H.R., Andre, T.S., Williges, R.C.: Criteria for evaluating usability evaluation methods. International Journal of HCI 13, 373–410 (2001)

15. Hilliges, O., Sandor, C., Klinker, G.: Interaction Management for Ubiquitous Augmented Reality User Interfaces. Dipl. Thesis, TU München (2005)

16. International Standards Organisation, ISO 9241 - 11. Ergonomics requirements for office work with visual display terminals - Part 11: Guidance on usability. Genève: ISO (1997)

17. Ishii, H., Ullmer, B.: Emerging Frameworks for Tangible User Interfaces. IBM Systems Journal 39(3/4), 915–931 (2000)

18. Miller, G.A.: The magical number seven, plus or minus two: Some limits on our capacity for processing information. Psychological Review 63, 81–97 (1956)

19. Phidgets: http://www.phidgets.com/

20. Renevier, P., Nigay, L., Bouchet, J., Pasqualetti, L.: Generic interaction techniques for mobile collaborative mixed systems. In: Proc. of CADUI 2004, pp. 307–320. ACM, New York (2004)

21. Schmalstieg, D., Encarnaçao, M., Szalavari, Z.: Using Transparent Props for Interaction with Virtual Table. In: ACM conf. proc. of I3D 1999, pp. 147–154 (1999)

22. Shaer, O., Leland, N., Calvillo-Gamez, E.H., Jacob, R.J.K.: The TAC paradigm: specifying tangible user interfaces. In: Conf. proc. of PUC, pp. 359–369 (2004)

23. Trevisan, D.G., Vanderdonckt, J., Macq, B.: Conceptualising mixed spaces of interaction for designing continuous interaction. Virtual Reality 8(2), 83–95 (2005)

24. Tse, E., Shen, C., Greenberg, S., Forlines, C.: Enabling Interaction with Single User Applications through Speech and Gestures on a Multi-User Tabletop. In: Conf. proc. AVI 2006, Italy, pp. 336–334 (2006)

25. Ullmer, B., Ishii, H.: The metaDESK: models and prototypes for tangible user interfaces. In: Proceedings of the ACM symposium UIST 1997, Canada, pp. 223–232 (1997)

26. Wagensberg, J.: Food for Thought. Ecsite Newsletter, (44) Autumn 2000 (2000)

27. Ware, 2, Information Visualization: Perception for Design, p. 484. Morgan Kauffman, San Francisco (2000)

An Attentive Groupware Device to Mitigate Information Overload

Antonio Ferreira and Pedro Antunes

Department of Informatics, University of Lisbon
Campo Grande, 1749–016 Lisboa, Portugal
{asfe, paa}@di.fc.ul.pt

Abstract. We propose an attentive device for synchronous groupware systems to mitigate information overload. The opportunity seeker device leverages the users' natural alternation between doing individual work and attending to the group to dynamically manage the delivery timing and quantity of group aware-ness information that each user is exposed to. We describe how this device can be implemented on an electronic brainstorming tool and show its influence on the distribution of ideas to the users. Results from a laboratory experiment using this tool indicate that group performance increased 9.6% when compared to the immediate broadcast of ideas and a *post-hoc* analysis suggests that information overload was attenuated: users were subject to 44.1% less deliveries of ideas, which gave them 54.7% more uninterrupted time; users switched 18.8% faster from submitting an idea to start typing the next idea; and the time to write an idea was reduced by 16.3%.

1 Introduction

Attention management is increasingly important in our information-rich world as evidenced by the growing momentum of Attentive User Interfaces (AUI) in the field of Human-Computer Interaction (HCI) [1,2]. The prime motivation for AUI is the recognition that as the needs for information rise so do the costs of not paying atten-tion to it. So, instead of assuming the user is always focused on the entire computer display, AUI negotiate the users' attention by establishing priorities for presenting information.

Most AUI research is grounded on single-user work and assumes user performance degrades with the number of simultaneous requests for attention. Therefore, research-ers have enhanced input/output devices so that the user remains focused on a primary task without getting too much distracted by secondary—typically unrelated and unex-pected—tasks, e.g., by using eye-gaze and body orientation sensors [3], statistical models of interruptibility [4], and displays capable of showing information at various levels of detail [5].

Regarding multi-user work, the research is situated in video conferencing [6,7], making the study of AUI for groupware systems a largely unexplored area. We pre-sent three arguments to promote further investigations on this subject.

Firstly, the convergence of AUI and groupware systems poses new challenges to researchers due to differences in individual and group work:

T.C.N. Graham and P. Palanque (Eds.): DSVIS 2008, LNCS 5136, pp. 29–42, 2008.

- People working in a group are more occupied with requests for attention because they have to manage more information flows;
- Instead of doing a single extensive task, group members usually execute a series of intertwined tasks;
- Group members have to explicitly manage the trade-offs of attending to the group and doing individual work; and
- In group work the primary and secondary tasks are typically related and may both contribute to the shared goal.

Secondly, the current emphasis in AUI applied to groupware is still, to the best of our knowledge, on evaluating the enhanced input/output devices *per se*, e.g., the fluidity of movement or sudden brightness changes in videos [6], in contrast with determining the outcomes of using these devices in work settings.

Thirdly, groupware researchers are designing systems that provide ever greater awareness information about the presence and actions performed by users on a group through devices such as radar views, multi-user scrollbars, and telepointers [8,9]. However, a problem with this trend is that it fails to recognise that sometimes more is less due to the limitations in the human attentive capacity.

Given this situation, we must consider the group attention problem: as the needs for collaboration rise so do the costs of not paying attention and becoming overloaded with information.

We argue that this problem is inadequately addressed by existing groupware awareness devices because they are designed having into consideration hardware limitations, e.g., decorators for telepointers to attenuate jitter effects due to network latency [10], but do not make any assumptions regarding the human attentive capacity. Furthermore, these devices require manual control of the type and quantity of group awareness information, e.g., via filters, thus penalising individual performance. On the other hand, the devices restrict the amount of information displayed to the user, which mitigates information overload.

This trade-off between the benefits of limiting group awareness information and manual intervention by the user sets the stage for introducing a conceptual attentive device for groupware systems to automatically adjust awareness information based upon each user's predicted state of attention, which we present in Sect. 3. In Sect. 4 we explain how this device can be implemented on an attentive electronic brainstorming tool, and in Sect. 5 we describe a laboratory experiment to evaluate group performance with and without the attentive device, whose results are shown in Sect. 6. We conclude the paper in Sect. 7 with a summary of contributions and paths for future work.

2 Related Work

The study of AUI for groupware systems is, for the most part, an unexplored research area, with the exception of video conferencing. The GAZE-2 system was developed to facilitate the detection of who is talking to whom in remote meetings [6]. It works by displaying video images of the users' faces on the computer display, which can be automatically rotated by intervention of eye-trackers placed in front of each user, e.g., so that the faces appear to be staring at the user who is speaking. In this way, group turn taking may be more natural and require fewer interruptions to determine who will speak next.

Another feature of GAZE-2 is the automatic filtering of voices when multiple conversations are being held at the same time. Depending upon the user in focus, the respective audio stream is amplified, and the other streams are attenuated (but not eliminated). If the focus of interest suddenly changes, as sensed by the eye-tracker, the audio is again adjusted. Filters are also applied to the video images by decreasing their quality as the angle of rotation increases, to save network bandwidth.

eyeView explores the GAZE-2 ideas in the context of large meetings. It manipulates the size of video windows, arranged side-by-side, and the voice volumes of each user as a function of the current focus of attention [7].

These two groupware systems suggest that audio and video filters should be used to manipulate the amount of group awareness information that users are exposed to during electronic meetings. However, we found no evidence that group work benefited. Instead, the literature mentions technological evaluations through user questionnaires that measured the self-perception of eye-contact and distraction, as well as changes in colour and brightness during camera shifts [6]. A similar situation occurs with eyeView [7].

Some studies do address the evaluation of AUI from the perspective of task execution, but are restricted to single-user activity. One study measured the effects of interruptions on completion time, error rate, annoyance, and anxiety, and suggests that AUI should defer the presentation of peripheral information until task boundaries are reached [11]. In another study, the effectiveness and efficiency of users were evaluated as they performed two types of tasks under the exposure of four methods for coordinating interruption, and recommends that AUI should let users manually negotiate their own state of availability, except when response time for handling the interruptions is critical [12].

However, as we mentioned earlier, there are numerous differences in individual and group work, which opens an opportunity for doing research on AUI for groupware systems.

3 The Opportunity Seeker Device

To address the group attention problem that we stated in the introduction—highlighting the need to mitigate information overload during computer-mediated group work—we devised an attentive groupware device, called the opportunity seeker, to dynamically manage the *delivery timing* and *quantity* of group awareness information based upon each user's state of attention.

There is a trade-off in managing the timing and quantity of group awareness information, in that too few updates may give the wrong impression about what the group is doing, while too many may provide up-to-date information but be too distracting. We address this trade-off by leveraging the typical alternation between primary and secondary tasks in group work to find natural opportunities for interrupting the user. Following Bailey and Konstan [11], these opportunities should occur at the boundaries between consecutive tasks, i.e., for group work, at the transitions between the user doing individual work and paying attention to the group (see Fig. 1).

Fig. 1. Natural task switching during group work

Conceptually, the opportunity seeker has a queue for storing group awareness over time and this information should only displayed to the user when s/he is likely *not* doing individual work. Furthermore, a limit may be enforced to the quantity of information delivered at each opportunity if the rhythms of the user and the group differ too greatly, to avoid overloading the user.

4   An Attentive Brainstorming Tool

We implemented the opportunity seeker device on ABTool, a custom-made electronic brainstorming tool with built-in sensors of user performance, to dynamically manage the delivery timing and quantity of ideas displayed to each user over brainstorming sessions. In electronic brainstorming users can submit ideas in parallel and as the number of ideas increases, e.g., because the group is inspired or group size is large, users may no longer be able to process the flow of ideas, and may even become distracted by it, thus causing information overload.

A major challenge in applying the opportunity seeker to ABTool was to detect task switching during electronic brainstorming activity. Theoretically, the rules of brainstorming [13] encourage users to do two cognitive tasks: the first is to produce as many ideas as possible, because quantity is wanted; and the second is to read, or at least look at, the other users' ideas, because combination and improvement of ideas is sought. From a practical viewpoint, we analysed data from ABTool's logs of activity running with immediate broadcast of ideas (see sample and comments in Fig. 2), from which three patterns of user activity emerged:

- Users usually did not stop typing when they received ideas from the other users, thus, we assume they continued focused on the individual task of generating ideas;
- Users typically paused after putting forward an idea, presumably to keep up with the group; and
- We found numerous periods of time with no typing activity (not shown in Fig. 2).

Based upon this evidence, we hypothesise that a task boundary, i.e., an opportunity to display ideas from others, occurs when the user submits an idea to the group. In addition, new ideas should be delivered after a period of inactivity (currently, ten seconds), so that the user does not get the impression that the group is not producing ideas too.

Figure 3 shows the state transition diagram that models the behaviour of the user as assumed by the opportunity seeker on ABTool (also cf. Fig. 1): the user is either typing an idea (doing individual work) or reading other users' ideas (attending to the group).

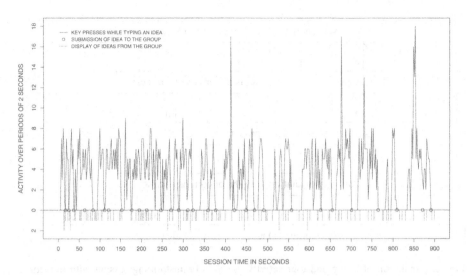

Fig. 2. User and group activity during a brainstorming session with ABTool, with instant broadcast of ideas to everyone on the group. Above the X-axis are aggregated counts of user key presses. The spikes occurred when the user pressed the delete or cursor keys. The circles on the X-axis show when the user submitted the idea s/he was typing to the group. Below the X-axis are the instants in time when the user received ideas from the other users.

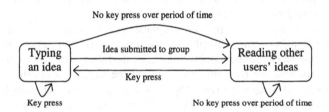

Fig. 3. Model of user behaviour assumed by the opportunity seeker on ABTool

Another feature of the opportunity seeker is that it imposes a limit on the number of ideas from others that can be displayed at once (currently, ten). This is to avoid over-loading the user, e.g., by filling up the entire computer screen with new ideas, when the user is working at a slower pace than the other group members.

Figure 4 shows a simulation that exemplifies the delivery of ideas with the opportunity seeker compared to the immediate broadcast of ideas.

Technically, ABTool is characterised by a client-server architecture, in which the server mediates the group information flows. The server also collects performance data, which are stored in an XML log. The purpose of the clients, one per user, is to receive input from the users and pass it on to the server, and to display new ideas as they become available from the server.

ABTool is written in C# and is built on top of the Microsoft .NET Framework 2.0. Communication between the clients and the server is done via TCP/IP sockets and all messages (ideas, key presses, users joining or retiring the group, sessions starting or

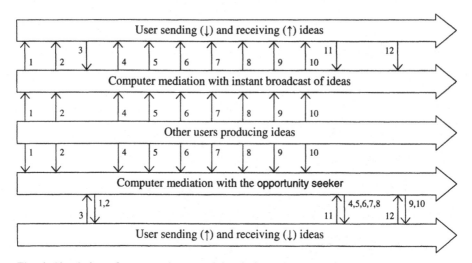

Fig. 4. Simulation of group and user activity during a brainstorming session with immediate broadcast of ideas (upper region) and with the opportunity seeker (lower region). In both cases the user produces three ideas (3, 11, and 12) but the exposure to the nine ideas s/he received from the other users is different. For illustration purposes, we do not show the propagation of ideas 3, 11, and 12 to the group, and limit the number of ideas delivered at once to five.

ending) are automatically serialised and de-serialised using BinaryFormatter objects attached to NetworkStream instances.

Within the client and server applications, messages are propagated using events, to which consumer objects can subscribe themselves. Given that almost all classes in ABTool handle message events, namely the user interfaces, the opportunity seeker, and the classes responsible for receiving and sending messages from/to the network, we defined an IHandlesMessages interface together with a default implementation for it, DefaultHandlesMessages, which relies on reflection to allow those classes to delegate the determination of the method to run as a function of the type of message associated with the event.

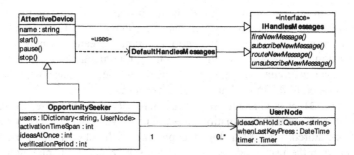

Fig. 5. Class diagram showing details of the opportunity seeker on ABTool

Figure 5 shows that the opportunity seeker on ABTool derives from the AttentiveDevice generalisation, which actually implements immediate delivery of ideas from the users to the group. The OpportunitySeeker class alters this default behaviour by maintaining separate queues, one per user, containing ideas that have been put forward by the other users on the group. The queue is stored in the UserNode, which also keeps a Timer object that every verificationPeriod milliseconds verifies the time of the most recent key press by the user, and if it was more than activationTimeSpan milliseconds ago, then it delivers up to ideasAtOnce ideas to the user.

The AttentiveDevice and OpportunitySeeker classes implement three methods: start() is run when a session starts or resumes; pause() is executed when, for some reason, the session needs to be paused; and stop() is run at the end of a session. Other methods handle the reception and forwarding of messages, but we omitted those for brevity.

To conclude the presentation of ABTool, we show in Fig. 6 two screen shots of the client application with the opportunity seeker running.

 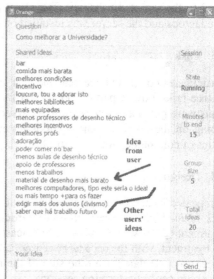

Fig. 6. Opportunity seeker managing the delivery of ideas on ABTool. Left: While typing an idea, the user receives no new ideas from the group. Right: When the user submits an idea to the group, new ideas from others are displayed.

5 Laboratory Experiment

We now describe a laboratory experiment that we set up using ABTool to test the hypothesis that group performance, measured as the number of ideas produced, improves when groups are exposed to the opportunity seeker device.

5.1 Participants

A total of 11 groups of 5 people, for a total of 55 volunteers (44 men and 11 women) participated in the experiment. The median age was 23 years (min. 20 and max. 29). 51 participants were students (40 undergraduate, 10 MSc, 1 PhD), and the remaining

4 comprised researchers, a software developer, and a translator. A convenience sampling was used to select participants, who were recruited from social contacts and posters on corridors at the University of Lisbon. No monetary reward was offered and the only information available was that the experiment would concern brainstorming.

5.2 Apparatus

The experiment was conducted in a laboratory room having five laptops with identical hardware (Intel Pentium M at 1.2 GHz, 1 GByte of RAM) and software specifications (Microsoft Windows XP SP2, .NET Framework 2.0), interconnected by a dedicated 100 Mbit/s Ethernet network. Keyboard sensitivity, desktop contents, display resolution, and brightness were controlled. Each computer had screen-recording software (ZD Soft Screen Recorder 1.4.3), and a web-camera (Creative WebCam Live!) affixed to the top of the display. The client application of ABTool was installed on the five laptops and the server was installed on an extra laptop.

5.3 Task

Participants completed practice and test tasks, both related to brainstorming. The practice task allowed participants to get familiar with ABTool. In the test task, participants were given a question and then asked to generate as many ideas as possible, by typing on the keyboard and by looking at the computer display. Speech and other forms of communication were disallowed.

5.4 Design

A repeated measures design was chosen for the experiment. The independent variable was *device type* and every group of participants was under the influence of a control treatment (CT)—with immediate broadcast of ideas to the group—and an experimental treatment, with the opportunity seeker (OS). The dependent variable, *group performance*, was calculated from the sum of the number of ideas produced by each user on the group per brainstorming session.

Table 1. Session order/brainstorming question per group and treatment. The questions were: A, how to preserve the environment; B, how to attract more tourists to Portugal; C, how to improve the university; and D, how to stimulate the practice of sports.

					Groups						
	1	2	3	4	5	6	7	8	9	10	11
CT	1/C	2/D	4/C	3/B	1/B	1/A	2/C	3/B	2/B	3/C	1/A
OS	3/B	1/A	2/B	4/C	3/C	2/B	3/A	1/C	1/C	2/A	3/B

The order of exposure to the treatments and the brainstorming questions are depicted in Table 1. We note that, sometimes, session order is greater than two and that four questions were used, because we are reporting here a part of a larger experiment with two additional treatments, involving similar brainstorming tasks.

5.5 Procedure

A trial started when a group of participants arrived at the laboratory room. An introduction to this research was given and participants were informed on their privacy rights and asked to sign a consent form. Next, participants filled in an entrance questionnaire about gender, age, and occupation. Written instructions on the rules of brainstorming and on the ABTool application were then handed in to all participants and read out loud by the experimenter.

Participants were asked to carry out the practice task for 5 minutes, after which questions about ABTool were answered. The group then performed the test tasks in succession, each lasting for 15 minutes, with a brief rest period in between. At the end of the trial, answers were given to the questions participants had about this research, comments were annotated, and the experimenter gave thanks in acknowledgement of their participation in the experiment.

6 Results

Results are organised in three parts: we begin with an analysis of overall group performance, which is central to our research hypothesis; we then decompose group performance in consecutive periods over a brainstorming session; finally, we show results from a *post-hoc* analysis based upon more fine-grained data.

6.1 Group Performance

Groups produced an average of 10.0 extra ideas per session ($SD = 17.2$), +9.6%, when under the exposure of the opportunity seeker (OS, $M = 113.7$, $SD = 60.8$) than under the control treatment (CT, $M = 103.7$, $SD = 62.0$). A total of 1251 ideas were put forward with the OS versus 1141 with the control device (see Table 2). Figure 7 further shows that the difference between treatment medians was 25 ideas per session (108 vs. 83).

Table 2. Number of ideas per group and treatment

	Groups											
	1	2	3	4	5	6	7	8	9	10	11	Total
CT	152	83	133	91	264	77	48	53	66	104	70	1141
OS	192	108	113	117	258	77	68	61	76	116	65	1251

The Shapiro-Wilk normality test indicated that both data distributions differed significantly from a normal distribution; therefore we applied the non-parametric Wilcoxon signed-ranks test, which revealed a significant 3.7% probability of chance explaining the difference in group performance, $W_+ = 45.5$, $W_- = 9.5$.

We also analysed possible confounding influences from the questions or session order on group performance to see if there was a bias introduced by popular questions or a learning effect due to the nature of the repeated measures design. We applied the Wilcoxon signed-ranks test to both scenarios, which found no significant influences: $p > 0.205$ and $p > 0.343$, respectively.

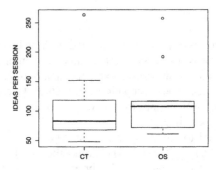

Fig. 7. Group performance under the control (CT) and experimental (OS) treatments

Given this evidence, we can accept the hypothesis that group performance improved when groups were exposed to the opportunity seeker device in electronic brainstorming tasks with ABTool. In other words, group performance can increase by managing the delivery timing and quantity of group awareness information displayed to the users.

6.2 Group Performance Over Time

Concerning the analysis of group performance through the duration of the brainstorming sessions, we broke down the 900 seconds that each session lasted into consecutive periods of 300, 150, and 30 seconds and counted the number of ideas put forward during each period.

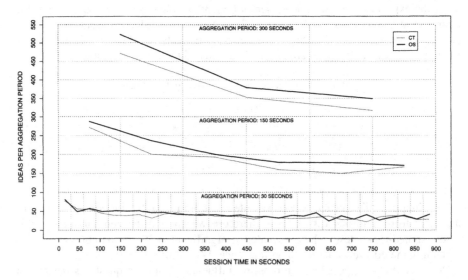

Fig. 8. Group performance through the duration of the brainstorming sessions under the control (CT) and experimental (OS) treatments. Top: number of ideas per period of 300 seconds. Middle and bottom: same, considering periods of 150 and 30 seconds, respectively.

By using this approach we intended to highlight specific periods when one of the devices would enable better group performance. For example, a brainstorming session may be divided into at the beginning (when users usually have plenty of ideas), at the middle, and at the end (when users are typically more passive). This division is actually depicted in the top region in Fig. 8, which shows that in all three periods of 300 seconds groups produced more ideas with the opportunity seeker than with the control device. This outcome is reinforced by similar results at the 150 seconds level of aggregation (see middle region in Fig. 8).

Finally, if we consider the count of ideas collected over consecutive periods of 30 seconds (see bottom region in Fig. 8), then group performance with the opportunity seeker is better in 21 out of 30 cases than with the control device.

We do not provide more statistics for this type of analysis because its meaning would be attached to the choice of periods, which depends on the context. Instead, we note that there seems to be no particular phase when results with the opportunity seeker could be considered worse than with the control device.

6.3 *Post-Hoc* Analysis

We also performed a *post-hoc* analysis comprising the influence of the opportunity seeker on the delivery of ideas to the users and a fine-grained study of user performance in terms of task switching time and individual work. As with the previous analysis of group performance, we also applied Wilcoxon signed-ranks tests to the data, but in this case we were interested in estimating the plausibility of chance explaining the differences, rather than doing null hypotheses significance testing, thus no family-wise corrections were made.

The opportunity seeker device reduced the number of deliveries of group ideas that reached a user in each session by 44.1% ($W_+ = 0$, $W_- = 1540$, $p = 0.000$), from an average of 82.7 ($SD = 48.1$) to 46.2 ($SD = 14.6$). Figure 9a shows more details. This was possible because each delivery comprised a batch 1.9 ideas on average ($SD = 1.2$), with up to 5 ideas per batch in 99% of the cases, unlike with the control device, in which new ideas were immediately broadcasted, one by one, to the group.

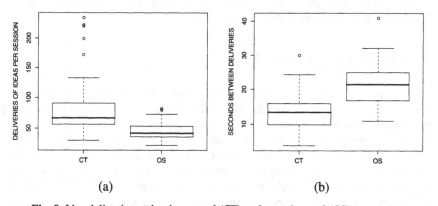

(a)   (b)

Fig. 9. Idea deliveries under the control (CT) and experimental (OS) treatments

Users also had 54.7% ($W_+ = 1540$, $W_- = 0$, $p = 0.000$) more time to think about and type ideas without receiving new ideas from others: an average of 21.2 seconds with the OS device ($SD = 6.1$) vs. 13.7 ($SD = 5.9$) with the CT device (see Fig. 9b).

The opportunity seeker trades up-to-date group awareness for less frequent deliveries of batches of information. This could have aggravated the alternation between doing individual work and attending to the group if, for instance, users had slowed down because of the apparent delays in group awareness updates or had become overloaded by the quantity of information in the batches.

In fact, users switched 18.8% ($W_+ = 469$, $W_- = 1071$, $p = 0.012$) more rapidly from submitting an idea to the group to start typing the next idea, presumably reading ideas from others in between: 27.7 seconds per idea ($SD = 19.2$) vs. 34.1 ($SD = 34.3$), on average (see Fig. 10a). We also found that, with the OS device, users needed an average of 21.5 seconds ($SD = 6.4$) versus 25.7 ($SD = 17.3$), −16.3% ($W_+ = 422$, $W_- = 1118$, $p = 0.004$) of time, to type an idea (see Fig. 10b).

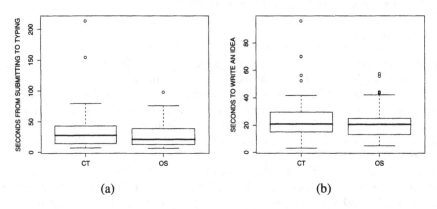

(a)   (b)

Fig. 10. Aspects of user performance under the control (CT) and experimental (OS) treatments

This evidence suggests that the opportunity seeker on ABTool mitigated information overload by leveraging the users' natural rhythms for doing individual work and attending to the group to manage the delivery of ideas.

7 Conclusions and Future Work

We highlighted the need to apply Attentive User Interfaces beyond single-user systems and to multi-user systems, e.g., due to the differences in individual and group work, and made contributions to address the group attention problem.

Firstly, we devised an attentive groupware device, the opportunity seeker, that acknowledges the users' natural alternation between doing individual work and attending to the group, and manipulates the delivery timing and quantity of group awareness based upon the user's predicted state of attention. Secondly, we showed how this device can be implemented on an electronic brainstorming tool and how task boundaries can be detected via keyboard activity. Thirdly, we provided evidence that the opportunity seeker device can increase the work done by groups, and that the improvement amounts to 9.6% in the number of ideas produced in electronic brainstorming tasks.

In addition, results from a *post-hoc* analysis show that the opportunity seeker reduced the number of deliveries of ideas by 44.1% by combining ideas in small batches and that this translated into 54.7% more time to think about and type ideas without receiving new ideas from others. In these conditions, users were 18.8% faster in alternating between generating an idea, which they did in 16.3% less time, and reading other users' ideas.

We believe that the attentive device we propose in this paper provides benefits for today's and tomorrow's demands: on the one hand, even if the users in our experiment were not overloaded with information, the number of ideas produced was, nonetheless, higher; on the other hand, the opportunity seeker facilitates the creation of electronic brainstorming sessions with larger group sizes because it ensures that each user will be exposed to new ideas from others at his or hers own natural rhythm, thus automatically mitigating information overload.

As for future work, we are considering several research paths: one is to re-evaluate the opportunity seeker in other types of computer-mediated group tasks, such as instant messaging or negotiation; another path is to analyse the quality of the ideas to determine, e.g., if there are more duplicates with the opportunity seeker; we are also considering doing a qualitative analysis based upon the videos we have captured with the screen recorder and the web-camera during the brainstorming sessions, to assess our assumptions about the users' focus of attention in this context, so far based solely upon activity logs; finally, we have plans to gather more fine-grained data (compared to video analysis) by introducing an eye-tracker in future experiments.

Acknowledgments

This work was supported by the Portuguese Foundation for Science and Technology, through projects PTDC/EIA/67589/2006 and POSC/EIA/57038/2004, and the Multiannual Funding Programme.

References

1. Vertegaal, R.: Attentive user interfaces: Introduction. Communications of the ACM 46(3), 30–33 (2003)
2. Roda, C., Thomas, J.: Attention aware systems: Introduction to special issue. Computers in Human Behavior 22(4), 555–556 (2006)
3. Vertegaal, R., Shell, J.S., Chen, D., Mamuji, A.: Designing for augmented attention: Towards a framework for attentive user interfaces. Computers in Human Behavior 22(4), 771–789 (2006)
4. Fogarty, J., Ko, A.J., Aung, H.H., Golden, E., Tang, K.P., Hudson, S.E.: Examining task engagement in sensor-based statistical models of human interruptibility. In: CHI 2005: Proceedings of the SIGCHI conference on Human factors in computing systems, pp. 331–340. ACM Press, New York (2005)
5. Baudisch, P., DeCarlo, D., Duchowski, A.T., Geisler, W.S.: Focusing on the essential: Considering attention in display design. Communications of the ACM 46(3), 60–66 (2003)

6. Vertegaal, R., Weevers, I., Sohn, C., Cheung, C.: GAZE-2: Conveying eye contact in group video conferencing using eye-controlled camera direction. In: CHI 2003: Proceedings of the SIGCHI conference on Human factors in computing systems, pp. 521–528. ACM Press, New York (2003)

7. Jenkin, T., McGeachie, J., Fono, D., Vertegaal, R.: eyeView: Focus+context views for large group video conferences. In: CHI 2005: Extended abstracts on Human factors in computing systems, pp. 1497–1500. ACM Press, New York (2005)

8. Raikundalia, G.K., Zhang, H.L.: Newly-discovered group awareness mechanisms for supporting real-time collaborative authoring. In: AUIC 2005: Proceedings of the Sixth Australasian conference on User interface, pp. 127–136. Australian Computer Society, Sydney, Australia (2005)

9. Gutwin, C., Greenberg, S.: A descriptive framework of workspace awareness for real-time groupware. Computer Supported Cooperative Work 11(3), 411–446 (2002)

10. Gutwin, C., Benford, S., Dyck, J., Fraser, M., Vaghi, I., Greenhalgh, C.: Revealing delay in collaborative environments. In: CHI 2004: Proceedings of the SIGCHI conference on Human factors in computing systems, pp. 503–510. ACM Press, New York (2004)

11. Bailey, B.P., Konstan, J.A.: On the need for attention-aware systems: Measuring effects of interruption on task performance, error rate, and affective state. Computers in Human Behavior 22(4), 685–708 (2006)

12. McFarlane, D.C.: Comparison of four primary methods for coordinating the interruption of people in human-computer interaction. Human-Computer Interaction 17(1), 63–139 (2002)

13. Osborn, A.F.: Applied imagination: Principles and procedures of creative problem-solving, 3rd edn. Scribner, New York (1963)

Multi-fidelity User Interface Specifications

Thomas Memmel[1], Jean Vanderdonckt[2], and Harald Reiterer[1]

[1] Human-Computer Interaction Group, University of Konstanz,
Universitätsstrasse 10, 78457 Konstanz, Germany
[2] Belgian Laboratory of Computer-Human Interaction, Université catholique de Louvain,
Place des Doyens, 1 – B-1348 Louvain-la-Neuve, Belgium
{memmel, reiterer}@inf.uni-konstanz.de,
jean.vanderdonckt@uclouvain.be

Abstract. Specifying user interfaces consists in a fundamental activity in the user interface development life cycle as it informs the subsequent steps. Good quality specifications could lead to a user interface that satisfies the user's needs. The user interface development life cycle typically involves multiple actors possessing all their own particular inputs of user interface artifacts expressed with their own formats, thus posing new constraints for integrating them into comprehensive and consistent specifications of a future user interface. This paper introduces a design technique where these actors can introduce their artifacts by sketching them in their respective input format so as to integrate them into one or multiple output formats. Each artifact can be introduced in a particular level of fidelity (ranging from low to high) and switched to an adjacent level of fidelity after appropriate refining. Refined artifacts are then captured in appropriate models stored in a model repository. In this way, co-evolutionary design of user interfaces is introduced, defined, and supported by a collaborative design tool allowing multiple inputs and multiple outputs. This design paradigm is exemplified on a case study and has been tested in an empirical study revealing how designers appreciate it.

Keywords: Collaborative design, formal and informal specifications, specification of interactive systems, usability requirements, user interface specifications.

1 Introduction and Motivations

Software practitioners and Human-Computer Interaction (HCI) specialists today concur that structured approaches are required to design, specify, and verify interactive systems [2,6,9,11,22] so as to obtain a high usability of their User Interface (UI) [19,21]. The design, the specification, and the verification of user-friendly and task-adequate UIs have become a success critical factor in many domains of activity.

In the German automotive industry for instance, a wide range of different interactive systems exists such as: in-car information systems supporting the driver while traveling, information visualization of navigation data and dynamic traffic data. Operating such systems must never compromise road safety, and the respective UIs must provide intuitive and easy-to-use navigation concepts to reduce driver's distraction to the lowest value possible. Both information visualization and navigation design are

T.C.N. Graham and P. Palanque (Eds.): DSVIS 2008, LNCS 5136, pp. 43–57, 2008.
© Springer-Verlag Berlin Heidelberg 2008

also important for corporate web sites and digital sales channels. Web applications, such as the car configuration, play an important role in the sales planning and disposal of extra equipment. In the car manufacturers we analyzed over the past three years (among them are Dr. Ing. h.c. F. Porsche AG and Daimler AG), UI design remains a too marginal activity that deserves more attention and HCI methods are not sufficiently implied in the overall development life cycle [17,18]. Most UI development tools are inappropriate for supporting actors from different disciplines in designing interactive systems. They all possess their own particular inputs of UI artifacts expressed with their own formats and these format are generally incompatible and heterogeneous. On the one hand, *formal* UI tools may prevent some actors from taking part in collaborative design if they these tools do not have an adequate knowledge of specific input formats and terminologies. On the other hand, *informal* UI tools may lead to misunderstanding and conflicts in communication across actors, particularly with programmers. In particular, some tools turn out to be more focused on requirements management than on providing support in extracting requirements from user needs and translating them into good UI design. After all, despite - or perhaps precisely because of - the vast functionality of many tools, the outcome is often unsatisfactory in terms of UI design. Due to the lack of appropriate tools, many actors tend instead to use tools they are familiar with and which can be categorized as being low threshold (for application) - low ceiling (of results), a phenomenon observed in [8]. Ultimately, we distinguish two different families of tool users:

1. *Client*: actors like business personnel, marketing people, domain experts, or HCI experts use office automation applications such as word processors and presentation software [18] to document user's needs and their contexts of use [7] in order to define the problem space. They will translate the needs as perceived from the real world, and their contextual conditions, into general usage requirements and evaluate their work at several quality stages. At this stage, responsibility is typically shared with, or completely passed on to, a supplier.
2. *Supplier*: actors with a sophisticated IT background (e.g., programmers or designers) translate usage requirements into UI and system requirements, deliver prototypes, and conclude the process in a UI specification. They prefer working with UI builders, and using more formal, precise and standardized notations, they narrow the solution space towards the final UI.

1.1   Shortcomings of, and Changes Desired in Current UI Specification Practice

The difference between these two categories of actors tends to result in a mixture of formats. This makes it difficult to promote concepts and creative thinking down the supply chain without media disruptions and loss of precision [16]. The following negative factors therefore contribute to UI development failure:

1. The lack of a common course of action and the use of inappropriate, incompatible terminologies and modeling languages [26] that prevent even the minimum levels of transparency, traceability and requirements-visualization that would be adequate for the problem.
2. The difficulty in switching between abstract and detailed models due to a lack of interconnectivity [8].

3. The difficulty of traveling from problem space to solution space, a difficulty that turns the overall UI development into a black-box process.
4. The burial of mission-critical information in documents that are difficult to research and have very awkward traceability. Experts are overruled when the UI design rationale is not universally available in the corresponding prototypes.
5. The perpetuation of unrecognized cross-purposes in client and supplier communication, which can lead to a premature change or reversal of UI design decisions, the implications of which will not be realized until later stages.
6. The resulting misconceptions that lead to costly change requests and iterations, which torpedo budgets and timeframes and endanger project goals.

Because of the immaturity of their UI development processes, industrial clients determine on a shift of responsibility and tend to change their UI specification practice:

1. Due to the strategic impact of most software, clients want to increase their UI-related competency in order to reflect corporate values by high UI quality [18].
2. Whereas conceptual modeling, prototyping or evaluation have always been undertaken by suppliers, the client himself now wants to work in the solution space and therefore needs to develop the UI specification in-house [16].
3. The role of the supplier becomes limited to programming the final system. The client can identify a timetable advantage from this change, and an important gain in flexibility in choosing his suppliers. Having an in-house competency in UI-related topics, the client becomes more independent and can avoid costly and time-consuming iterations with external suppliers.
4. It is nearly impossible to specify a UI with office-like applications. The existing actors, who are nevertheless accustomed to text-based artifacts, now require new approaches. The task of learning the required modeling languages and understanding how to apply these new tools must not be an unreasonably difficult one.

1.2 Tool Support That Is Adequate for the UI Design Problem

This cultural change must be supported by an integrating UI tool that allows the translation of needs into requirements and subsequently into good UI design (Table 1).

Table 1. Requirements for UI tools for interactive UI specification on the basis of [8,16]

Purpose/Added Value	Tool Requirement
Traceability of design rationale; transparency of translation of models into UI design	Switching back and forth between different (levels of) models
Smooth transition from problem-space concepts to solution space	Smooth progression between abstract and detailed representations
HCI experts can build abstract and detailed prototypes rapidly	Designing different versions of a UI is easy and quick, as is making changes to it
Support for design assistance and creative thinking for everybody; all kinds of actors can proactively take part in the UI specification	Concentration on a specific subset of modeling artifacts, which can be a UML-like notation or one that best leverages collaboration
The early detection of usability issues prevents costly late-cycle changes	Allowing an up-front usability evaluation of look and feel; providing feedback easily

In this paper we present both a set of models and a corresponding tool named IN-SPECTOR, which are designed to support interdisciplinary teams in gathering user needs, translating them into UI-related requirements, designing prototypes of different fidelity and linking the resulting artifacts to an *interactive UI specification*. The term *interactive* refers to the concept of making the process visually externalized to the greatest extent possible. This concerns both the artifacts and the medium of the UI specification itself. The latter should no longer be a text-based document, but a running simulation of how the UI should look *and* feel. Accordingly, we extend the meaning of UI prototypes to also include the provision of access to information items *below* the UI presentation layer. Being interactively connected, all of the ingredients result in a compilation of information items that are necessary to specify the UI (Table 2). In Section 2 we link our research to related work. Section 3 presents the common denominator in modeling that we developed. We explain how our tool, called INSPECTOR, will use the resulting interconnected hierarchy of notations. We illustrate how abstract and detailed designs can easily be created and also exported in machine-readable User Interface Description Language (UIDL) such as XAML or UsiXML. Section 4 presents the results of a first experimental evaluation that highlights the contribution of our approach. Section 5 gives a summary and an outlook.

Table 2. Main differences between prototypes and interactive UI specifications

Interactive UI Prototypes	Interactive UI Specifications
Vehicle for requirements analysis	Vehicle for requirements specification
Exclusively models the UI layer; may be inconsistent with specification and graphical notations	Allows drill down from UI to models; relates UI to requirements and vice versa
Either low-fidelity or high-fidelity	Abstract first, specification design later
Supplements text-based specification	Widely substitutes text-based specification
Design rationale saved in other documents	Incorporates design knowledge and rationale

2 Related Work

An early version of a model-driven UI specification method has been already presented [16]. With a separation of development concerns, different levels of abstraction and a simulation framework, we were able to establish an advanced UI modeling method. Although it was necessary to pre-define a domain-specific language (*high-threshold*), the results added significant value to a previously long-winded UI specification process (*high-ceiling*). But because the tool-chain was targeted towards the later stages of the process, office applications remained dominant during earlier phases. Moreover, the usage of a formal approach, targeted towards the generation of code from models, proved to be limiting in terms of freedom in creativity and promotion of innovative ideas. With INSPECTOR, we follow a model-based approach as our primary goal is not code generation, but the collaborative and interdisciplinary specification of non-standard UIs. However, our method and tool differ from other model-based solutions, such as the tools Vista [11], Mapper [13], and CanonSketch [8].

Vista [11] enables the designer to define mappings between four views of the same interactive system: a task model consisting of a recursive decomposition of the task into sub-tasks, a CUI model, specifications of the interaction written with the UAN notation, and specifications of the software architecture. Some of these relationships can be established and maintained semi-automatically by Vista. No logical definition of any underlying model is made explicit. Mapper [13] explicitly establishes mappings between models, either manually or automatically, the mappings being themselves governed by a common meta-model. This system does not allow any choice of using this or that model transformation and does not provide any visualization.

CanonSketch was the first tool that used canonical abstract prototypes and an UML-like notation, supplemented by a functioning HTML UI design layer. Task-Sketch [8] is a modeling tool that focuses on linking and tracing use cases, by means of which it significantly facilitates development tasks with an essential use-case notation. Altogether, TaskSketch provides three synchronized views: the participatory view uses a post-it notation to support communication with end-user and clients, the task-case view is targeted towards designers and is a digital version of index cards (well-known artifacts of user-centered or agile developers) and the UML activity diagram view is adequate for software engineers. As we will show in this paper, we closely concur with the concepts of these tools, but our approach differs in some important areas. Firstly, and in contrast to CanonSketch, we support detailed UI prototyping because we found that the high-fidelity externalization of design vision is especially important in corporate UI design processes. Secondly, we provide more ways of modeling (earlier text-based artifacts, task models and interaction diagrams).

DAMASK [14] and DENIM [21] both rely on a Zoomable User Interface (ZUI) approach for switching between different levels of fidelity through a visual drill-down process. Based on this experience and our own, we followed a consistent implementation of this technique and we chose to implement an electronic whiteboard metaphor for INSPECTOR. Whiteboards are commonly used because keeping the created artifacts visible to all actors enhances creativity, supports communication, makes it easier to achieve a common design vision and leads to faster decision-making. These tools also identified a need for supporting different levels of fidelity of requirements.

McCurdy et al. [15] identified five independent dimensions along which the level of fidelity could be more rigorously defined: the level of visual refinement, the breadth of functionality, the depth of functionality, the richness of interactivity, and the richness of the data model. In the remainder of this paper, the four first dimensions will be considered, the last one requiring a connection to a data model containing data. The level of fidelity is said to be *low* if the requirements representation only partially evokes the final UI without representing it in full details. Between high-fidelity (Hi-Fi) and low-fidelity (Lo-Fi), we can see *medium-fidelity* (Me-Fi). We usually observe that UI requirements only involve one representation type, i.e. one fidelity level at a time. But due to the variety of actors' inputs, several levels of fidelities could be combined together, thus leading to the concept of mixed-fidelity, such as in ProtoMixer [22]. Beyond mixed-fidelity, we introduce multi-fidelity [10] that is reached when UI requirements simultaneously involve elements belonging to different levels of fidelity, but only one level of fidelity is acted upon at a time, thus assuming that a transition is always possible between elements of different fidelity.

3   The Common Denominator in UI-Related Modeling

A sophisticated UI tool must be able to support all actors in actively participating in the UI specification process (Table 1). This requires it to deploy modeling techniques that can be used easily by everybody. We know that the Unified Modeling Language (UML) is a weak means of modeling the UIs of interactive systems [24]. As well as its shortcomings in describing user interactions with the UI, its notation also overwhelms most actors with too much (and mostly unnecessary) detail [1]. In most cases, moreover, designing UIs is an interdisciplinary assignment and many actors might be left behind due to the formality included in UML. Consequently, UML is like office-like artifacts in being inadequate for specifying the look *and* feel of interactive UIs. In our experience, the identification of adequate means of modeling for UI specification is very much related to the ongoing discussion on bridging the gaps between HCI and SE. This discussion is also propelled by the very difference in the way experts from both fields prefer to express themselves in terms of formality and visual externalization. HCI and SE are recognized as professions made up of very distinct populations. In the context of corporate UI specification processes as outlined in Section 1, modeling the UI also requires the integration of the discipline of Business-Process Modeling (BPM). The interaction layer - as interface between system and user - is the area where HCI, SE and BPM are required to collaborate in order to produce high quality UIs. As actors come from all three disciplines, the question is which modeling notations are adequate to extend and align their vocabulary.

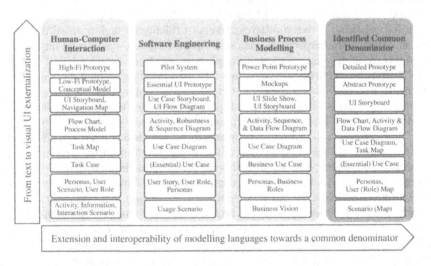

Fig. 1. Towards a common denominator in interdisciplinary modeling

As we found in our previous research, agile methods are close to HCI practice [17] and therefore represent a promising pathfinder for a course of action common to all three disciplines. Holt [12] presents a BPM approach that is based on UML class, activity, sequence and use-case notations. Ambler based his agile version of the Rational Unified Process (RUP) on a similar, but less formal, BPM approach [1]. In general, agile approaches already exist in HCI [17], BPM [1] and SE [3] and we can define a common denominator for all three disciplines (Fig. 1). Our goal is to keep this denominator as small as possible. We filter out models that are too difficult to be understood by every actor. We do not consider models that are more commonly used to support actual implementation or that have been identified as mostly unnecessary by Agile Modeling [1]. Despite an agile freedom in terms of formality, IT suppliers can nevertheless deduce the later structure of the UI much better from the resulting interactive UI specification than they can from Office-like documents. We integrate different levels of modeling abstraction to visualize the flow from initial abstract artifacts to detailed prototypes of the interaction layer. On the vertical axis in Fig. 1 we distinguish the models according to their level of abstraction (or level of fidelity). Models at the bottom are more abstract (i.e. text-based, pictorial), whereas those at upper levels become more detailed with regard to the specification of the UI. On the horizontal axis, we identify appropriate models for UI specification. Accordingly, we differentiate between the grade of formality of the models and their purpose and expressivity. The models with a comparable right to exist are arranged at the same level. At each stage we identify a common denominator for all three disciplines as a part of the interactive UI specification evolving thereby.

3.1 Text-Based Notations of Needs and Requirements: Personas and Scenarios

For describing users and their needs, HCI recognizes user profiles, (user) scenarios [23], role models [9], and personas [5]. Roles and personas are also known in SE and BPM and are therefore appropriate for initial user-needs modeling (see Fig. 1). As an interdisciplinary modeling language, research suggests scenarios [2] - known as user stories (light-weight scenarios) in agile development [3]. In SE, scenarios – as a sequence of events triggered by the user – are generally used for requirements gathering and for model checking. Such a scenario is used to identify a thread of usage for the system to be constructed and to provide a description of how the system will be used. HCI applies scenarios to describe in detail the software context, users, user roles, activities (i.e., tasks), and interaction for a certain use-case. BE uses scenario-like narrations to describe a business vision, i.e. a guess about users (customers), their activities and interests. Starting up INSPECTOR, the user can create a scenario map to relate all

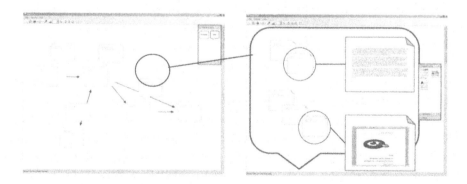

Fig. 2. Scenario map as entry stage to the modeling process (left); scenario info-bubble (right)

scenarios that will be modeled (Fig. 2, left). The user can first describe a single scenario in a bubble shape (Fig. 2, right): INSPECTOR provides a build-in text editor with appropriate templates and enables the direct integration of existing requirement documents into its repository. Later, the user will zoom-in and fill the scenario shape with graphical notations and UI design.

3.2   Graphical Notations: Requirements, Usage and Behavior Modeling

Entering this stage, INSPECTOR supports the important process of translating needs into requirements (see Fig. 1). Role maps [9] help to relate user roles to each other.

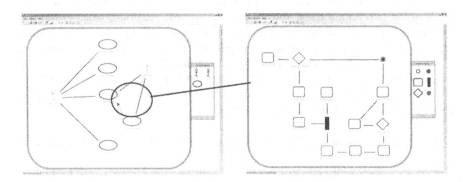

Fig. 3. Use-Case Diagram (left); Activity Diagram (right) with logic of single use case

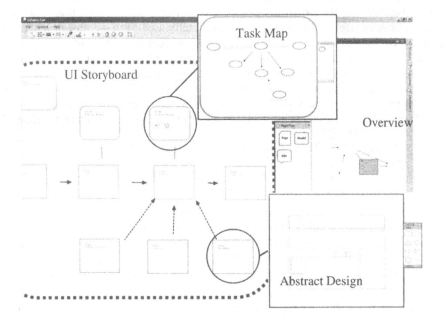

Fig. 4. UI storyboard with UI design and models (magnified areas for illustration)

Although different in name, task cases (HCI), essential-use cases (SE), and business-use cases (BPM) can all be expressed in a classical use-case notation (Fig. 3, left). Moreover, use-case diagrams (SE, BE) overlap with use-case and task maps (HCI) [9]. The latter also help to separate more general cases from more specialized (essential) sub-cases. We considered different models for task and process modeling and, following [1], we again selected related modeling languages (see Fig. 1). Activity diagrams (Fig. 3, right) are typically used for business-process modeling, for modeling the logic captured by a single use-case or usage scenario, or for modeling the detailed logic of a business rule. They are the object-oriented equivalent of flow charts and data-flow diagrams. They are more formal than the models HCI experts are usually familiar with, but they therefore extend the expert's competency in interdisciplinary modeling. Data-flow diagrams model the flow of data through the interactive system. With a data-flow diagram, actors can visualize how the UI will operate depending on external entities. Typical UI storyboards we know from HCI [18] serve as the interface layer between needs and requirement models and the UI design (Fig. 1, Fig. 4).

3.3 UI Prototyping and Simulation: Modeling Look and Feel

Prototypes are already established as a bridging technique for HCI and SE [6,24]. HCI mainly recognizes them as an artifact for iterative UI design. Avoiding risk when making decisions that are difficult to retract is a reason why prototyping is also important for business people. Accordingly, we chose prototypes as a vehicle for abstract UI modeling. They will help to design and evaluate the UI at early stages and they support traceability from models to design. Alternate and competing designs as well as revised ones can all be kept in the specification landscape for later reference and for a safe-keeping of the design rationale. The visually most expressive level is the high-fidelity UI prototyping layer (Fig. 5, left). It serves as the executable, interactive part of UI specification and makes the package complete (see Fig. 1). From here on, the actor can later explore, create and change models by drilling down to the relevant area of the UI specification. Moreover, programmers can pop-up the interactive UI specification to get guidance on the required UI properties.

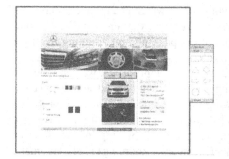 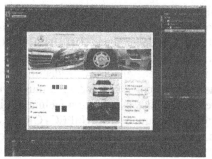

Fig. 5. INSPECTOR-made hi-fi UI design (left) in Microsoft Expression Blend (right)

Therefore, all created UI designs can be saved in two different UIDLs that are XML-compliant, thus demonstrating that INSPECTOR can accommodate any UIDL in theory. On the one hand, the XAML export guarantees the reusability of the specified UIs during the development by the supplier. The XAML code can, for example, be imported to Microsoft Expression Blend (Fig. 5, right). The XAML helps to provide simulations of the UI in a web browser such as Microsoft Internet Explorer. The links between pages that were created with INSPECTOR then also become links in the prototypical UI simulation. Equally important is the capability of INSPECTOR to export the results of the process in UsiXML (www.usixml.org) [13]. In this way, it can contribute to the early phases of needs analysis and requirements engineering: UI designs created can be exported from INSPECTOR and imported in any other UsiXML-compliant tool such as GrafiXML [20]. In the end, the means provided are platform- and implementation-independent, thus making INSPECTOR compliant with the Cameleon Reference Framework [7]. Other UIDLs could be used similarly.

3.4   Feedback and Review: Creating and Managing Annotations

In order to enable actors to attach notes to artifacts in the specification space, we have added a feedback and review component. It can be used by actors to review the models and UI designs. Annotations can thus either be attached to objects on the canvas freely or be linked to specific parts of a model or page (e.g., a widget). Consistent with the ZUI interaction paradigm, the annotations can be zoomed into and accordingly provide the opportunity for editing. The annotations can also be used for giving feedback on the UI specification. When actors execute the UI simulation and explore the underlying models, they can leave notes for the UI specification team. With color coding, we distinguish the feedback provided with different grades of severity, ranging from positive ratings (green) to critical ones (red). By summarizing the reviews of actors in a management console, we can visualize conflicting artefacts, inconsistencies and any revisions that may be needed, and we can easily support a jump zoom navigation to the relevant models or UI designs.

3.5   Zoom-Based Traveling through the UI Specification Space

INSPECTOR is based on the metaphor of a whiteboard, which is a quite common tool in collaborative design environments. Because of our own experience and that of others [14,21] in developing ZUIs, INSPECTOR offers panning and zooming as major interaction techniques. In this way, it supports the principle of focus+context principle: first, the general context is identified and when it is appropriate, we can focus on some relevant part of the context, thus giving rise to a new context and so forth. It therefore provides users with a feeling of diving into the information space of the UI specification whiteboard. INSPECTOR uses [4] and the appearance of its UI is based on a linear scaling of objects (geometric zooming) and on displaying information in a way that is dependent on the scale of the objects (semantic zooming) [25]. Automatic zooming automatically organizes selected objects on the UI. Animated zooming supports the user in exploring the topology of an information space and in understanding data relationships. For switching between models and UI designs, the user can manually zoom in and out and pan the canvas. Navigating between artifacts can be an extensive task, however, if objects are widespread in terms of being some distance along

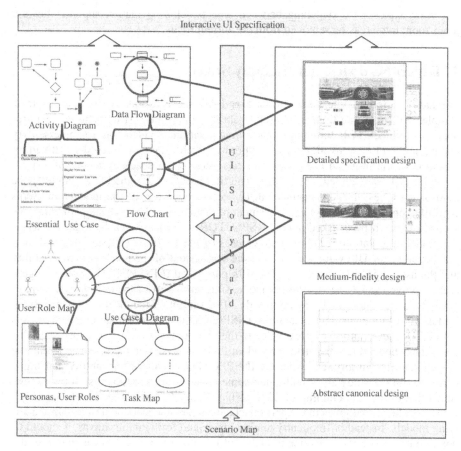

Fig. 7. Correlation of models and UI designs; exemplified modeling and design throughput

the three dimensions of the canvas (panning: x-axis, y-axis; zooming: z-axis). For a much faster change of focus as well as for traceability and transparency, INSPECTOR offers the possibility of creating links between models or elements of models (Fig. 7). Scenarios are the initial model, whereas the UI storyboard functions as the mediator between interconnected models and design. At early stages, for example, a user shape can be linked to and be part of user roles, personas, and use-cases. Zooming-in on a user shape reveals more details about the underlying personas. The use-case shapes can be part of a superordinate task map and can be linked accordingly. Moreover, zooming in a particular case could link to an essential use-case description and reveal more detail on user and system responsibilities. At this stage, activity and data-flow diagrams help to model the relationships of states, for example (Fig. 3). The user can link every model to UI designs of different fidelity and vice versa. During modeling, or while traversing relationships by panning and zooming, hints about the current zoom factor and the current position in the information space can be given in order to avoid disorientation. A common way of supporting the user's cognitive (i.e. spatial) map of the information space is an overview window (Fig. 4). In addition, INSPECTOR provides a tree-view explorer for switching between objects. This navigation support allows a jump zoom into areas far removed from the current focus.

4 Expert Feedback and Usability Study

We have started to interview software and UI specification experts (n=12) from Daimler AG in a questionnaire-based usability study. The participants were introduced to INSPECTOR through a short demonstration, a video and a supplementary text explaining the motivation for our approach. Each expert was provided with an installation of the tool and had two weeks to return his feedback by means of a questionnaire that was divided into 5 parts. The first part was designed to (1) identify the field of activities of every respondent, (2) get an overview of the models and tools typically applied, and (3) get an assessment of difficulties along the supply chain. The second to fourth parts asked about INSPECTOR in terms of (1) the applicability of the modeling notations, (2) the completeness of the UI design capabilities and their practicability for UI evaluation, and (3) the assessment of the tool's general usability and the user experience provided. The fifth part asked if INSPECTOR could, in general, improve the UI specification practice. Currently, half of the questionnaires have been completed (n=6) and we can provide a first outline of the most important results. So far, all respondents have stated that INSPECTOR, as a tool that combines models with UI Design, contributes great value to their work style (average 4.83 pts; scale 1-5 pts). The added value was particularly identified in terms of an increased coherence of models and design artifacts, whereby INSPECTOR enhances traceability and transparency. But the study also highlighted some conceptual shortcomings. Some experts stated that during the building of a UI design, INSPECTOR could be enhanced by a contextual layer that gives the expert the chance to cross-check the design with underlying models. Instead of frequently jumping back and forth on the canvas, it should be possible to temporarily visualize models and UI concurrently. We have started to develop such a preview feature in order to further enhance the traceability of artefacts.

Other usability issues concerned the general interaction with the tool and were similar to those found during a diary study. For the latter, we used INSPECTOR in an interaction design lecture. Three groups of computer science and HCI students (n=8) were asked to use the tool during a Volkswagen use-case study on the specification of rear-seat entertainment systems. For a period of three weeks, every student wrote his own diary to give insight into (1) the kind of models created, (2) additional tools that were applied, (3) problems that occurred, (4) ratings of the user experience, (5) general issues and opinions about the tool. We decided for the diary study in order to be able to evaluate INSPECTOR over a longer period of time. Because we were interested in how the empirical results change with the duration and intensity of usage, we preferred a long-term study to classical usability tests. In weekly workshops, we discussed the intermediary results and recorded the issues for subsequent correction. By means of the diary study, we e.g. found that objects on the ZUI canvas occasionally behaved inconsistently after the tool was used for several hours and an extended amount of zoom operations had been performed. Students also reported issues with integrated external documents (PDF, Word, etc.), when they repeatedly saved and opened their projects. This led to an intensifying disarrangement of the XML structure in saved project files and significantly prevented a fluent and enduring work style. It would have been mere chance if we had identified these problems in a much shorter lab-based usability study. That way, we were able to solve these issues quickly. Moreover, we found that some participants firstly preferred to create the first abstract prototypes with paper and pencil. We realized that the use of the built-in sketching mechanism increased as soon as we provided a pen tablet as input device; like in [10]. Students were initially also not comfortable with all the notations provided and required assistance on their proper application. We addressed this issue by making a start on including a help feature that guides users through the UI specification process by explaining notations as well as their scope of application. In addition, we enhanced the affordance of templates for e.g. personas or essential-use cases to ease the understanding of the artifacts. After all, the diary study and the upgrades resulted in an improvement of the feedback on the tool usability: rated with an average of 1.75pts (std. 0.46) (on a 5-point Likert scale) after the first week and 3pts (std. 0.00) after the second, participants reviewed INSPECTOR with an average of 4.25pts (std. 0.46) at the end of the study. A repeated-measure ANOVA revealed a significant main effect for the rating across the weeks ($F(2,14)=105.00$, $p<0.001$). Furthermore the differences between each week are also very significant statistically (week 1 vs. week 2: $F(1,7)=58.33$, $p<0.001$; week 2 vs. week 3: $F(1,7)=58.33$, $p<0.001$).

5   Summary and Outlook

In this paper, we have introduced INSPECTOR, a collaborative design tool for sharing UI designs at various levels of fidelity in order to match the requirements that multiple actors may rely on various inputs and formats. The notion of multi-fidelity has already been proved feasible in UI prototyping [10] and is then extended to UI requirements here in a ZUI. Based on our experience in UI specification and design, we have come to the conclusion that the typical methods and tools available are not adequate. UI tools must support not only the "hard" aspects, but also the "soft" aspects of UI development to support the delivery of usable and innovative systems in the future [8]. These include support for creativity and improvisation. With our experimental tool-support, actors are supported in applying informal models they are familiar with, and are given the opportunity of UI prototyping with different fidelities. Being logically linked, transitions from abstract to detailed artifacts increase the transparency of design decisions and enhance the traceability of dependencies. This improves communication, consistency, and lastly, the necessary understanding of the overall problem space that has to be made accessible through an innovative UI. Based on a ZUI approach, our INSPECTOR tool integrates and innovatively interconnects the required artifacts in an interactive UI specification that serves as a living repository of the design rationale. With our approach, we focus on actors in charge of the conceptualization, and particularly the specification, of UIs. We therefore do not support the automatic generation of the final UI like in [7], but the exchangeability of the overall specification as well as the sophisticated UI designs in machine-readable format. We will continue to enhance our tool in order to make it a fully capable and scalable alternative to the tool-landscape applied in current industrial practice.

References

1. Ambler, S.W.: Agile Modeling. John Wiley & Sons, New York (2002)
2. Barbosa, S.D.J., Paula, M.G.: Interaction Modelling as a Binding Thread in the Software Development Process. In: Proc. of the ICSE 2003 Workshop on bridging the gaps between software engineering and human-computer interaction SEHCI 2003, IFIP, May 3-4, 2003, pp. 84–91 (2003)
3. Beck, K.: Extreme Programming Explained. Addison-Wesley, Reading (1999)
4. Bederson, B.B., Grosjean, J., Meyer, J.: Toolkit Design for Interactive Structured Graphics. IEEE Transactions on Software Engineering 30(8), 535–546 (2004)
5. Beyer, H., Holtzblatt, K.: Contextual Design: Defining Customer-Centered Systems. Morgan Kaufmann, San Francisco (1998)
6. Blomkvist, S.: Towards a model for bridging agile development and user-centered design. In: Seffah, A., Gulliksen, J., Desmarais, M.C. (eds.) Human-centered software engineering – Integrating usability in the development process. Human-computer Interaction Seires, pp. 219–244. Springer, Berlin (2005)
7. Calvary, G., Coutaz, J., Thevenin, D., Limbourg, Q., Bouillon, L., Vanderdonckt, J.: A Unifying Reference Framework for Multi-Target User Interfaces. Interacting with Computers 15(3), 289–308 (2003)
8. Campos, P., Nunes, N.: Towards useful and usable interaction design tools: CanonSketch. Interacting with Computers 19(5-6), 597–613 (2007)
9. Constantine, L.L., Lockwood, L.A.D.: Software for Use: A Practical Guide to Models and Methods of Usage-Centered Design. Addison-Wesley, Reading (1999)
10. Coyette, A., Kieffer, S., Vanderdonckt, J.: Multi-Fidelity Prototyping of User Interfaces. In: Baranauskas, C., Palanque, P., Abascal, J., Barbosa, S.D.J. (eds.) INTERACT 2007. LNCS, vol. 4663, pp. 149–162. Springer, Heidelberg (2007)
11. Elnaffar, S., Graham, N.C.: Semi-Automated Linking of User Interface Design Artifacts. In: Proc. of 3rd Int. Conf. CADUI 1999, pp. 127–138. Kluwer Academic Publisher, Dordrecht (1999)
12. Holt, J.: A Pragmatic Guide to Business Process Modelling. British Computer Society, United Kingdom (2005)
13. Limbourg, Q., Vanderdonckt, J.: Addressing the Mapping Problem in User Interface Design with UsiXML. In: Proc. of 3rd Int. Workshop on Task Models and Diagrams for user interface design TAMODIA 2004, pp. 155–163. ACM Press, New York (2004)
14. Lin, J., Landay, J.A.: Damask: A Tool for Early-Stage Design and Prototyping of Multi-Device User Interfaces. In: Proc. of the 8th Int. Conf. on Distributed Multimedia Systems, San Francisco, pp. 573–580 (2002)
15. McCurdy, M., Connors, C., Pyrzak, G., Kanefsky, B., Vera, A.: Breaking the Fidelity Barrier: An Examination of our Current Characterization of Prototypes and an Example of a Mixed-Fidelity Success. In: Proc. of CHI 2006, pp. 1233–1242. ACM Press, New York (2006)
16. Memmel, T., Bock, C., Reiterer, H.: Model-driven prototyping for corporate software specification. In: Harning, M.B., Gulliksen, J. (eds.) Proc. of the Engineering Interactive Systems Conference EIS 2007, Salamanca, March 22-24, 2007. Springer, Berlin (2007)
17. Memmel, T., Gundelsweiler, F., Reiterer, H.: Agile Human-Centered Software Engineering. In: Proc. of the 21st BCS Conf. on Human-Computer Interaction HCI 2007, pp. 167–175 (2007)

18. Memmel, T., Reiterer, H., Ziegler, H., Oed, R.: Visual Specification as Enhancement of Client Authority in Designing Interactive Systems. In: Roese, K., Brau, H. (eds.) Proc. of the 5th Workshop of the German Chapter of the Usability Professionals Association, pp. 99–104. Frauenhofer IRB Verlag, Stuttgart (2007)
19. Metzker, E., Reiterer, H.: Evidence-Based Usability Engineering. In: Proc. of the 4th Int. Conf. on Computer-Aided Design of UIs CADUI 2002, pp. 323–336. Kluwer Acad., Dordrecht (2002)
20. Michotte, B., Vanderdonckt, J.: GrafiXML, A Multi-Target User Interface Builder based on UsiXML. In: Proc. of 4th Int. Conf. on Autonomic and Autonomous Systems ICAS 2008, Gosier, March 16-21, 2008. IEEE Comp. Soc. Press, Los Alamitos (2008)
21. Newman, N.W., Jason, J.L., Hong, I., Landay, J.A.: DENIM: An Informal Web Site Design Tool Inspired by Observations of Practice. J. Human-Comp. Int. 18(3), 259–324 (2003)
22. Petrie, J.N., Schneider, K.A.: Mixed-fidelity Prototyping of User Interfaces. In: Proc. of DSV-IS 2006, pp. 199–212. Springer, Heidelberg (2006)
23. Rosson, M.B., Carroll, J.M.: Usability Engineering: scenario-based development of human computer interaction. Morgan Kaufmann, San Francisco (2002)
24. Sutcliffe, A.G.: Convergence or competition between software engineering and human computer interaction. In: Seffah, A., Gulliksen, J., Desmarais, M.C. (eds.) Human-centered software engineering – Integrating usability in the development process. Human-Computer Interaction Series, pp. 71–84. Springer, Berlin (2005)
25. Ware, C.: Information Visualization: Perception for Design. Morgan Kaufmann, San Francisco (2004)
26. Zave, P., Jackson, M.: Four Dark Corners of Requirements Engineering. ACM Transactions on Software Engineering and Methodology 6(1), 1–30 (1997)

HOPS: A Prototypical Specification Tool for Interactive Systems

Anke Dittmar, Toralf Hübner, and Peter Forbrig

Rostock University, 18055 Rostock, Germany
{anke.dittmar,toralf.huebner,peter.forbrig}@uni-rostock.de

Abstract. This article suggests higher-order processes as a formal framework to model interactive systems and supplies a corresponding prototypical specification tool (HOPS). Processes and their components reflect the recursive nature of interaction. Each component is an independent process itself. Though higher-level processes specify the interaction between their components they do not fully control them. HOPS offers a unified description of behavioral and structural aspects. Structured sets of sub-processes (e.g. hierarchies) serve to represent specific domains of interest within a process. Operations are the smallest units for analyzing and designing behavior. However, they can be unfolded to processes and vice versa. This supports an understanding of interactive systems as open and nonmonotonic systems. Their composition/ decomposition may exhibit unpredictable behavior. It is shown that the approach follows the interaction paradigm more closely than existing modeling approaches in HCI. Possible usage scenarios are given.

1 Introduction

Systems serve to analyze behavior that exists and can be experienced by senses as well as to establish such behavior. We know ecosystems, economic systems, computing systems, cognitive systems and so on. In our approach, a system is seen as consisting of interacting parts which can be characterized as interactive systems themselves. Due to this recursive nature, sub-systems can exist independently and have similar properties as the whole system but in a simpler form. According to Wegner, "interactive systems interact with an external environment they cannot control" [1]. Hence, the interaction paradigm supports the idea of openness and nonmonotonicity. A decomposition may create unpredictable sub-systems. A composition of sub-systems may produce noninteractive behavior [1]. It may also produce new behavior at a higher level of organization.

This paper introduces HOPS as a prototypical tool to describe and animate interactive systems. HOPS stands for *H*igher-*O*rder *P*rocesses *S*pecification formalism. It is based on preliminary work presented in [2]. The concept of higher-order processes facilitates a unified behavioral and structural description of interactive systems as requested e.g. in [3]. Sub-systems are specified by lower-level processes which constitute the components of higher-level ones. However, an enclosing process does not fully control the specific behavior of its environment but focuses on those aspects that seem to be relevant for the interaction between its components. This and the fluid

T.C.N. Graham and P. Palanque (Eds.): DSVIS 2008, LNCS 5136, pp. 58–71, 2008.
© Springer-Verlag Berlin Heidelberg 2008

boundary between processes and operations as smallest units to analyze and design behavior support the description of open systems and acknowledge incomplete and not necessarily consistent descriptions as they are typical for the interaction paradigm. In addition, a process is characterized by its set of sub-processes allowing a shift of focus. Sub-processes mainly serve two purposes. First, they are used to specify changes in the environment caused by operations. Second, they facilitate the elaboration and description of specialized sub-structures or particular domains of interest.

In the next section, the application of HOPS is illustrated by a small example. Sect. 3.1 introduces the conceptual framework to model interaction. In Sect. 3.2, HOPS is proposed as supporting specification mechanism. It is shown that it facilitates different specification styles. Sect. 4 is about influences on the suggested approach. In Sect. 5, possible usage scenarios are sketched, and Sect. 6 draws some conclusions and proposes directions for future work.

2 A Motivating Example

Listing 1 shows the HOPS-specification of a basic process *Bool*. It has no components but two operations *true* and *false* (lines 3, 4). Line 6 says that the process either behaves like sub-process *T* or like *F*. Generally, the behavior is described by a collection of alternative sequences of operations. Here, *T* is characterized by one infinite sequence: $\langle false,true,false,true,false,...\rangle$. *F* behaves similarly but starts with *true* (lines 7, 8). The basic process *Entry_1* in Listing 2 defines operations *init*, *edit*, and *finish*. The equation in line 7 specifies the set $\{\langle init,finish\rangle,\ \langle init,edit,finish\rangle,$ $\langle init,edit,edit,finish\rangle,...\}$ as the focused behavior of *Entry_1*.

Listing 1. Bool.pr   **Listing 2.** Entry_1.pr

```
1  PROCESS Bool
2  OPS
3      true,
4      false
5  SUB PROCESSES
6      Bool = T XOR F,
7          T = false; F,
8          F = true; T
9  END PROCESS
```

```
1  PROCESS Entry_1
2  OPS
3      init,
4      edit,
5      finish
6  SUB PROCESSES
7      Entry_1 = init ; edit* ; finish
8  END PROCESS
```

Let us continue with the more complex specification in Listing 3. Process *Space* has two components called *visible* and *icon* (lines 5, 6). Both are *Bool* processes. Furthermore, *Space* defines a number of new operations: *init*, *add*, *remove*, *finish*, *show*, *hide*, *iconify*, *deiconify*, *action* (lines 8-21). The definition of an operation can include a pre and post-condition as well as an operationalization part:

   op_name: <{*precondition*},{*post condition*}> = *operationalization*.

Conditions are state descriptions of components of the actual process. For example, sub-process *T* of *Bool* represents a state 'True' (denoted as *T(Bool)*) while *F(Bool)* represents a state 'False'. The precondition in line 21 says that *action* is enabled if *visible* is in state 'True' and *icon* in 'False'. As another example, operation *deiconify* is executable if the space is visible but an icon (line 19).

Listing 3. Space.pr

```
 1 PROCESS Space
 2 USES "widgets_java"
 3
 4 BASIC COMPS
 5     visible: Bool,
 6        icon: Bool
 7 OPS
 8   init
 9      = <<visible.false ; icon.false ; fCall([this],space_init(this))>>,
10   add,
11   remove,
12   finish  = <<fCall([this],space_finish(this))>>,
13   show: <{visible: F(Bool)}, {}>
14      = <<visible.true ; fCall([this],space_show(this))>>,
15   hide: <{visible: T(Bool)}, {}>
16      = <<visible.false ; fCall([this],space_hide(this))>>,
17   iconify: <{visible: T(Bool), icon: F(Bool)}, {}>
18      = <<icon.true ; fCall([this],space_iconify(this))>>,
19   deiconify: <{icon: T(Bool), visible: T(Bool)}, {}>
20      = <<icon.false ; fCall([this],space_deiconify(this))>>,
21   action: <{visible: T(Bool), icon: F(Bool)}, {}>
22
23 SUB PROCESSES
24   Space = init ;
25      (add [] remove [] show [] hide [] iconify [] deiconify [] action)*
26         ; finish
27 END PROCESS
```

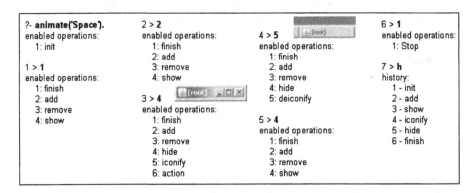

Fig. 1. An interactive animation of process *Space*: ⟨*init,add,show,iconify,hide,finish*⟩

Operations and partial equations describe the interaction between components. In Listing 3, all operations of the components are bound in operationalization parts of new defined operations. The equation in lines 24-26 specifies valid sequences of operations (with ';' as sequential operator, '[]' for alternatives, and '*' for iterations). However, some of them are excluded by preconditions. Though ⟨*init,iconify,finish*⟩ is valid according to the equation it violates the precondition of *iconify* because component *visible* would be in state *F(Bool)*.

In addition, operationalization parts of operations can contain 'foreign code' (denoted by 'fCall'). In this example, methods of a Java-class *PSpace* are used to create a

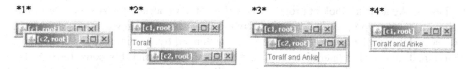

Fig. 2. Process *Pres*: two spaces *c1* and *c2* and one entry moving between them

frame in operation *init*, to show it, to hide it (lines 9, 14, 16), and so on. A command-line interactive animation of the process is depicted in Fig. 1. In each step, the user is given a set of enabled operations where they can choose from. For convenience, the animation run is represented in four columns and user inputs are in bold. Some side effects of foreign calls are indicated. By entering 'h', the user can see the actual sequence of operations (step 7).

Now, let us imagine how two spaces and one entry process could interact in a 'reasonable' way. Entries serve to enter and display text. However, they need to be located in a space in order to be editable. As described above, spaces can be created, shown, hidden, iconified, and deiconified. They are able to 'host' entities like entries (by operations *add* and *remove*). If they are visible and not presented as an icon they allow actions (by operation *action*). This understanding may be illustrated in Fig. 2. It represents side effects of the following animation run of process *Pres* with components *c1*, *c2*, *e* (Listing 4):

⟨*init, c1.show, c2.show, *1* add_to_c1, edit_in_c1, *2* move_to_c2,*
*move_to_c2, edit_in_c2, *3* c2.hide, move_to_c1, *4* finish*⟩

1, *2*,... are reference points to the situations depicted in the figure.

Listing 4. Pres.pr

```
 1  PROCESS Pres
 2  USES "widgets_java"
 3
 4  BASIC COMPS
 5          e: Entry,
 6         c1: Space,
 7         c2: Space,
 8      in_c1: Bool
 9
10  OPS
11      init  =  <<e.init ; c1.init ; c2.init>>,
12      add_to_c1
13          = <<c1.add ; in_c1.true ; fCall([c1,e],space_add(c1,e))>>,
14      move_to_c1: <{in_c1:F(Bool)}, {in_c1:T(Bool)}>
15          = <<c2.remove;c1.add;in_c1.true; fCall([c2,e],space_remove(c2,e))
16            ; fCall([c1,e],space_add(c1,e))>>,
17      move_to_c2: <{in_c1:T(Bool)}, {in_c1:F(Bool)}>
18          = <<c1.remove; c2.add;in_c1.false; fCall([c1,e],space_remove(c1,e))
19            ; fCall([c2,e],space_add(c2,e))>>,
20      finish =  <<e.finish ; c1.finish ; c2.finish>>,
21      edit_in_c1: <{in_c1:T(Bool)}, {}>  =  <<e.edit ; c1.action>>,
22      edit_in_c2: <{in_c1:F(Bool)}, {}>  =  <<e.edit ; c2.action>>
23
24  SUB PROCESSES
25      Pres = init ; add_to_c1
26             ; (move_to_c1 [] move_to_c2 [] edit_in_c1 [] edit_in_c2)*
27             ; finish
28  END PROCESS
```

Let us take a closer look at process *Pres*. First, it is important to note that the initial behavior of every process is determined by the concurrent running of its components. (*Entry* is defined like *Entry_1* in Listing 2 but extended by 'foreign code'.) As already mentioned, interactive operations and partial equations restrict this behavior (e.g. by coordination). Operation *init* is an operationalization of a sequence of *init*-operations of components *e*, *c1*, *c2* (denoted by '<<...>>', line 11). That is to say, this sequence happens without interruption. However, it also says that the appropriate components must be in a state that enables their *init*-operations. As another example, *edit_in_c1* can only be performed if entry *e* is able to perform operation *edit* and operation *action* is enabled by component *c1*. In addition, the precondition of *edit_in_c1* must be satisfied: component *in_c1* must be in state 'True' (line 21). Process *Pres* knows the following operations of its components:

   e: *init, edit, finish*,
   c1,c2: *init, finish, add, remove, action*,
   in_c1: *true, false*.

All of them are bound in operationalization parts. However, the process does not know the operations *show*, *hide*, *iconify*, and *deiconify* of *c1* and *c2*. Their execution is not constrained. To illustrate this point, we assume that *init* has already been performed in a running animation. Now, we have the following situation:

   enabled operations: *add_to_c1*, *c1.show*, *c2.show*.

Operation *add_to_c1* is enabled according to line 25 in Listing 4. However, the execution of operation *init* included the execution of *c1.init* and *c2.init*. This enables operations *c1.show* and *c2.show* (see Listing 3) though they are not in the focus of process *Pres*. Just to make it more clear, we continue the animation. After performing *add_to_c1* and *c1.show* we get the situation:

   enabled operations: *move_to_c2*, *edit_in_c1*, *finish*, *c1.hide*, *c1.iconify*, *c2.show*.

It becomes apparent that process *Pres* concentrates on describing how to move the entry between both spaces and how to make it editable in a space. However, a possible hiding or iconifying of a space is not considered anymore at this level.

3 Modeling Interaction

"Whenever we capture the complexity of the real world in formal structures, whether language, social structures, or computer systems, we are creating discrete tokens for continuous and fluid phenomena." [4]

3.1 Conceptual Basis of HOPS: Higher-Order Processes

Operations and Processes Operations are names to refer to phenomena.[1] They do not explain how changes occur. They have no inner structure but are seen as 'atomic', as happening without interruption. *Processes* are abstractions over operations. They have a structure and interruption is inherent to them. In the simplest case, a process defines one operation *o* and the focused behavior can be described by the sequence $\langle o \rangle$. Such

---

[1] *Interaction* may be a more appropriate term. We chose *operation* in order not to interfere with the name the underlying paradigm.

processes represent the transition from operations to processes and vice versa. Higher-level processes contain *components* which are processes themselves. On the one hand, an enclosing process describes the interaction of its components. On the other hand, they constitute its environment. A higher-order process only focuses on those operations which seem to be relevant for the interaction. It can define new operations and operationalize sequences of operations of components. Again, the behavior a process concentrates on is given by a collection of alternative sequences of operations known to it. Pre- and post-conditions assigned to interactive operations can constrain the behavior. They specify the state of the environment before and after an operation occurs. A condition is expressed as a set of sub-processes of components.

Sub-Processes Let P be a process with an initial focus on the set Ops_P of operations and the set $Beh_P \subseteq Ops_P^*$ of alternative sequences. A process S with corresponding Ops_S and $Beh_S \subseteq Ops_S^*$ is a sub-process of P if [2]

- $Ops_P \subseteq Ops_S$
- $\forall\ seq_S \in Beh_S\ \exists\ seq_P \in Beh_P\text{:}\ \ seq_S \restriction Ops_P = seq_P$

Take note that each process is a sub-process of itself. In the sequel, a sub-process S of a process P is denoted by $S(P)$. It has two main characteristics.

- It describes a partial behavior of P.
- It introduces operations which were not in the focus of P.

We use these features for two purposes: for describing states and their manipulation by operations, and for embedding a set of processes in a common context or in a domain of interest.

- We say a process P is in state $S_1(P)$ if it currently allows the partial behavior specified by $S_1(P)$. An operation can change this state by enabling another partial behavior $S_2(P)$.
- A process P can work as context of processes $S_1,...,S_n$ ($n \in Nat$) if it abstracts from specific operations of S_i ($i=1,...,n$) but concentrates on their common behavior and structure. Then, $S_1,...,S_n$ become sub-processes of P. A common context could be a context of use as in the example in the next section.

The following definition makes a distinction between basic and additional components to support the specification of structured sets of sub-processes.

Definition 1 (higher-order process - intensional description)

A process P is a 5-tuple (C_b, C_{add}, Ops, Sub, Beh) with

- $C_b \cup C_{add}$ is the finite set of *components* of P ($C_b \cap C_{add} = \varnothing$).

  - Each component $c_i\text{:}P_i$ consists of an identifier c_i and a sub-process P_i.
  - C_b is the set of *basic components*.
  - C_{add} is the set of *additional components*.

- $Ops = Ops_b \cup Ops_{add} \cup Ops_n$ is the set of operations known to P where

---

[2] Restriction: $seq \restriction Ops$ is the sequence of operations one gets by omitting all operations from seq which are not in Ops, e.g. $\langle a,b,a,c,b,d,c \rangle \restriction \{a,c\} = \langle a,a,c,c \rangle$.

- $Ops_b = \{c_i.op_{i_j} \mid c_i{:}P_i \in C_b \ \wedge \ op_{i_j} \in Ops_{P_i}\}$ is the set of operations of basic components which are in the initial focus of P.
- $Ops_{add} = \{c_i.op_{i_j} \mid c_i{:}P_i \in C_{add} \ \wedge \ op_{i_j} \in Ops_{P_i}\}$ is the set of operations of additional components introduced by sub-processes of P.
- Ops_n is the set of operations defined by P. An operation is a 4-tuple $(op, PreCond, PostCond, OpSeq)$ with

    - op is the identifier of the operation.
    - The pre- and post-condition *PreCond* and *PostCond* are possibly empty sets of components in restricted forms. A restricted form of $c_i{:}P_i$ is a pair $c_i{:}S(P_i)$ with $S(P_i)$ is a sub-process of P_i.
    - $OpSeq \in (Ops_b \cup Ops_{add})^*$ is the *operationalization part*.

- *Sub* is the set of *sub-processes* of P. The following conditions must be satisfied for each $S : (C_b{}^S, C_{add}{}^S, Ops^S, Sub^S, Beh^S) \in Sub$.

    - Each component $c_i{:}P_i \in C_b$ occurs in $C_b{}^S$ in a possibly restricted form.
    - Each component of $C_b{}^S$ is a possibly restricted form of a component of $C_b \cup C_{add}$.
    - $Ops^S \subseteq Ops$ is the set of operations known to S.

- *Beh* $\subseteq Ops^*$ is the set of alternative sequences of operations of P.

A process P describes a behavior by a set *Beh* of alternative sequences of operations known to it. For simplicity, we refer to *Beh* as the behavior of P. However, take note that processes do not know all operations of their components. Furthermore, we already mentioned that a fluent boundary between processes and operations is assumed. Processes can be folded to operations by appropriate operationalizations. The other way around, operations can be unfolded to processes to explore them more deeply. The assumption that a process can only be a focused description of certain aspects of a phenomenon implies that a more thorough analysis (or design) of operations and lower-level descriptions can exhibit unexpected behavior. The same might be true if processes are seen as interacting parts of an enclosing process. This idea is reflected to a certain extent in the following extensional description of higher-order processes. A process partly knows its components to describe their interaction but otherwise has no influence on any kind of behavior.

Definition 2 (higher-order process - extensional description)

Let $P = (C_b, C_{add}, Ops, Sub, Beh)$ be a process. The extensional description of P comprises each sequence *seq* of operations with $seq \upharpoonright Ops \in Beh$.

3.2 The Specification Formalism HOPS

HOPS is a prototypical implementation of higher-order processes. It allows text-based specifications and their animation. Throughout this section we use a second example for illustration. Specifications consist of a process identifier and possibly empty lists of basic components, additional components, operation definitions, and partial equations. For brevity, EBNF-rules below show a simplified syntax. They ignore e.g. separators and priorities of operators in equations.

```
Process := PROCESS Id2 [USES FSource*][BASIC COMPS Comp*]
            [ADDITIONAL COMPS  Comp*]        [OPS Op*]
            [SUB PROCESSES   PartEqu*]     END PROCESS ;
Comp    := Id : SubProc ;
Op      := Id : < { Comp* } , { Comp* } > [ = OpDef ] ;
OpDef   := Instr    |    << Instr* >> ;
Instr   := Id . Id    |    ForeignCall ;
PartEqu := Id2 = Expr ;
Expr    := [NOT] Factor [ * | + ]   |   Expr BinOp Expr ;
Factor  := [ Expr ] | ( Expr ) | Id (. Id)* | Id2 ;
BinOp   := [] | ||| | ; | XOR | AND | OR ;
SubProc := Id2 [ ( Id2 ) ]
```

Initial behaviour Initially, the behavior of a process is implicitly determined by the concurrent (uncoordinated) composition of the basic components. Listing 6 shows process *Vehicle_1* with three basic components and an additional one. Process Engine is defined in Listing 5. Component doors knows operations *open and close*. It behaves similarly to Bool processes as mentioned in Sect. 2. The initial behavior may be illustrated by the animation run in Fig. 3. Animations concentrate on operations of basic components only. They abstract from the occurrence of any other operations including those of additional components. Theoretically, such operations could happen at each animation step (see Def. 2).

Listing 5. Engine.pr

```
1 PROCESS Engine
2 OPS    start,
3        stop
4 SUB PROCESSES
5    Engine = (Off ; On)*,
6    On = stop,
7    Off = start
8 END PROCESS
```

Listing 6. Vehicle_1.pr

```
1 PROCESS Vehicle_1
2 BASIC COMPS
3    running: Bool,
4    doors: Doors,
5    motor:  Engine
6 ADDITIONAL COMPS
7    has_power: Bool
8 END PROCESS
```

```
?- animate('Vehicle_1').
enabled operations:   enabled operations:   enabled operations:   enabled operations:
  1: Stop               1: Stop               1: Stop               1: Stop
  2: motor.start        2: motor.start        2: motor.start        2: motor.start
  3: doors.close        3: running.false      3: doors.open         3: running.false
  4: doors.open         4: running.true       4: running.false      4: doors.close
  5: running.false      5: doors.open
  6: running.true                             3 > 3                 4 > ...
                        2 > 4
1 > 3
```

Fig. 3. An animation of Vehicle_1: ⟨doors.close,running.true,doors.open,...⟩

Partial equations and operations Partial equations help to describe structures of sub-processes like hierarchies more conveniently. The name of the sub-process is given on the left-hand side of an equation. The expression on the right-hand side consists of sub-processes, operations and predefined operators. A process implicitly knows all operations of its components which either occur in operationalization parts or in partial equations. While Vehicle in Listing 7 knows all operations of its components, process Pres in the introductory example focuses on some only. Operations and partial equations influence the initial behavior.

- Operationalizations require uninterrupted sub-sequences of operations.
- Preconditions of operations reject some formerly valid sequences.
- Operators in partial equations restrict a behavior in two ways:

    - behavioral operators *compose* valid sequences,
    - structural operators *combine* different sets of valid sequences.

Listing 7. Part of Vehicle.pr

```
 1 PROCESS Vehicle
 2 // components -> see Vehicle_1.pr
 3 OPS
 4     ring,
 5     honk,
 6     start: <{motor: On(Motor), doors: Closed(Doors), running: F(Bool)},
 7             {running: T(Bool)}> = running.true,
 8     stop: <{running: T(Bool)}, {running: F(Bool)}> = running.false,
 9     collector_up: <{has_power: F(Bool)}, {has_power: T(Bool)}>
10         = <<has_power.true ; motor.start>>,
11     collector_down: <{has_power: T(Bool)}, {has_power: F(Bool)}>
12         = <<has_power.false ; motor.stop>>,
13     open_doors: <{running: F(Bool), doors: Closed(Doors)},
14             {doors: Opened(Doors)}> = doors.open,
15     close_doors: <{doors: Opened(Doors)},
16             {doors: Closed(Doors)}> = doors.close,
17     park: <{motor: Off(Motor)}, {}>
18
19 SUB PROCESSES
20     Vehicle = Tram XOR Bus,
21     GeneralBeh = ((start ; stop)* ||| (open_doors ; close_doors)*); park,
22     Tram = GeneralBeh AND TramBeh,
23     Bus = GeneralBeh AND BusBeh,
24     TramBeh = (collector_up ; ring* ; collector_down)*,
25     BusBeh = (motor.start ; motor.stop)* ||| honk*
26 END PROCESS
```

In the following, E, E_1, E_2 are expressions in partial equations of P with known operations $Ops_E...$ and behaviours $Beh_E...$, $^{\wedge}/2$ is the concatenation operator.

Behavioral operators:

sequence: $Beh_{(E_1 ; E_2)} = \{ s_1 {}^{\wedge} s_2 \mid (s_1 \in Beh_{E_1}) \wedge (s_2 \in Beh_{E_2}) \}$

concurrency: $Beh_{(E_1 ||| E_2)} = \{ s_{1_1} {}^{\wedge} s_{2_1} {}^{\wedge} s_{1_2} {}^{\wedge}...{}^{\wedge} s_{1_n} {}^{\wedge} s_{2_n} \mid$
$(s_{1_1} {}^{\wedge} s_{1_2} {}^{\wedge}...{}^{\wedge} s_{1_n} \in Beh_{E_1}) \wedge (s_{2_1} {}^{\wedge} s_{2_2} {}^{\wedge}...{}^{\wedge} s_{2_n} \in Beh_{E_2}) \}$

alternative: $Beh_{(E_1 [ ] E_2)} = \{ s \mid s \in Beh_{E_1} \vee s \in Beh_{E_2} \}$

iteration: $E^* = (E ; E^*) [] Done$

option: $[E] = E [] Done$

Structural operators:

AND: $Beh_{(E_1 \text{ AND } E_2)} = \{ s \mid s \in (Ops_{E_1} \cup Ops_{E_2})^* \wedge (s \mathbin{\wr} Ops_{E_1} \in Beh_{E_1})$
$\wedge (s \mathbin{\wr} Ops_{E_2} \in Beh_{E_2}) \}$

OR: $Beh_{(E_1 \text{ OR } E_2)} = \{ s \mid s \in (Ops_{E_1} \cup Ops_{E_2})^* \wedge ((s \mathbin{\wr} Ops_{E_1} \in Beh_{E_1})$
$\vee (s \mathbin{\wr} Ops_{E_2} \in Beh_{E_2})) \}$

XOR: E_1 XOR E_2 = E_1 [ ] E_2

NOT: $Beh_{(NOT\ E)} = \{\ s\ |\ s \in Beh_P \wedge \neg (s \mid Ops_E \in Beh_E)\ \}$

In the example, the general behavior of vehicles is characterized by sequences ⟨*park*⟩, ⟨*start,stop,park*⟩, ⟨*start,stop,open_door,close_door,park*⟩... (line 21). Preconditions exclude some sequences. For example, the precondition of *open_door* would be violated by sequences ⟨*start, open_door,...*⟩. Vehicles are described more precisely by the equation in line 20. They are either trams or busses, and hence also show some specific behavior. Trams perform operations *collector_up*, *collector_down*, and *ring* in orders as described in line 24 and so on. Again, preconditions exclude some sequences which would be valid according to the partial equations only.

Foreign code HOPS allows to perform 'foreign code' within the execution of operations. Since the interpreter is implemented in SWI-Prolog, we have so far experimented with Java (by using JPL) and Prolog.[3] A foreign call has two parameters: the list of interacting components, and the call itself (see e.g. Listings 3, 4). A mapping between HOPS components and Java objects is implemented. This may be illustrated in Fig. 2. The spaces c1 and c2 of the root process are mapped to Java containers with the component identifiers as titles. Foreign code is not considered in Sect. 3.1, but there are several 'pragmatic' reasons to include it into HOPS.

- Foreign code can represent parts of a system we abstract from by HOPS-operations. Post-conditions of HOPS operations can describe (expected) effects of foreign calls. Hence, HOPS-specifications could help to analyze and develop applications in a structured but at the same time experimental way.

- Foreign code supports a richer illustration of and richer interaction with animations of HOPS-specifications as indicated in Fig. 1 and 2.

- It helps to convey our understanding of interactive systems as open systems.

Supported modeling styles The HOPS notation supports top-down as well as bottom-up thinking. The initial behavior of a process constrains the behavior of sub-processes (top down). However, the way sub-processes are composed and combined also influences the behavior of the whole process and extends its focus (bottom up). A vehicle is either a tram or a bus (a combination). Hence, a vehicle can ring or honk but it cannot do both (Listing 7). A person could first be a child and then an adult (a composition: Person=Child ; Adult) and so on. Sub-processes allow to build specialized structures like hierarchies.

Furthermore, HOPS-specifications are hybrid in the sense that they allow to express structural and behavioral knowledge in a unified way. This knowledge does not need to be consistent. It can happen that the behavior of a process P is empty ($Beh_P=\varnothing$) if conditions of operations exclude all valid sequences derived by the partial equations of P. However, human knowledge is never 'fully consistent' and needs to be constantly reconsidered. Yet, a hybrid notation leads to more concise and probably more 'natural' descriptions than pure state or temporal notations as we have pointed out in [5] at the example of TaOSpec.

---

[3] http://www.swi-prolog.org, http://www.swi-prolog.org/packages/jpl/

4 Influences on This Work

The paper is to be seen in the context of the author's previous work (e.g. [6], [5], [7]). It is rooted in task analysis and modeling (e.g. TKS [8], CTT [9], GTA [10]) and in the specification of interactive systems (from formalisms like [11], [12], [13] to model-based approaches as in [14], [15], [16]). It is based on process algebras (CSP [17], CCS [18]) and their use in hybrid notations as well as on object-oriented ideas. However, this work is also rooted in a broader review of HCI literature about interaction and about human activity ([19], [20], [21] to name a few sources). Though the focus is on a formal description of interaction and corresponding specification tools the authors are conscious of the limitations of this approach. For example, one will never fully understand the fluid boundaries between planned human (inter-)actions and sub-conscious habits. And yet, the proposed folding and unfolding of processes and operations may be a reflection. Like any other artifact, formal frameworks allow us to see 'things' in the world we wouldn't see otherwise. Appropriate tools allow us to act accordingly. It is, perhaps, more a question of not to be 'caught in an artifact' but to be open to enrich it and to see limitations in its applicability.

A thought in [22] had much influence on our way to describe interaction. It is certainly expressed by other authors as well. Vygotski pointed out that there are mainly two ways to analyze phenomena. One can decompose a whole system into *elements*, or one can look for smallest *units* of analysis which can exist independently and can be combined. Elements in the first approach have a different quality than the whole. Hence, all properties of the system can only be explained by 'artificial' associative links between sub-parts. In contrast, units already have all characteristics of the whole but at a lower level of organization. Vygotski uses water for a comparison. Why does water extinguishes fire? If we decompose water into the elements oxygen and hydrogen we hardly find an answer. Hydrogen burns and oxygen facilitates burning. But if we look at the molecules and their interaction (molecular movement) we might be more successful.

In the analysis and the design of interactive systems we find both approaches. Architectural models like the Seeheim model or the arch model deal with specialized sub-structures which cannot exist independently. Almost all task-based design approaches distinguish between task models, dialog models, presentation models, application models etc. and consider associations between model elements. Interactors ([13] as an example already mentioned above) are, perhaps, one of those approaches which look for autonomous units. According to [3], the behavior of interactors "can, in principle, be mathematically described in terms of the lower order interactors of which...[they] are composed". Higher-order processes can be considered as interactors. However, they follow the interaction paradigm more closely as shown in the next section.

The suggested approach supports both a thinking in units, and in elements. Operations are the smallest units of analysis and synthesis. They refer to uninterrupted parts of behavior over time. Processes are abstractions over operations and are characterized by interruption. The proposed intensional and extensional process definitions and the concept of de-/operationalization support the idea of fluid boundaries between processes and operations, and so the idea of open, nonmonotonic systems.[4] Hence, HOPS has a quite different semantics than specification formalisms mentioned above. Even though sub-processes are specified in a similar style. To deal with focused behavior is not the same as to deal with hidden behavior (like in process algebras). To hide 'something' means that one has to know it, but a focus on 'something' says nothing about the rest. Interacting components may be seen as partly independent, 'active' attributes of processes. We believe that the suggested approach supports the extension, refinement, and adaptation of processes as inherently incomplete descriptions of interactive systems whether used for analysis or synthesis purposes.

5 Elaboration of Usage Patterns

Barnard et al ask for a stronger integration of HCI theories of different sub-domains and propose the development of generic representations of 'systems of interactors' [3]. Their abstract view on such representations is depicted in Fig. 4. Interactors represent Type 1-theories (knowledge in a specific sub-domain). They are hierarchically organized from the higher-order assembly (A), to basic

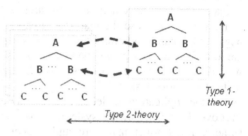

Fig. 4. Systems of interactors, suggested in [3]

units of meaning (B), down to the level of constituent interactors (C). So called Type 2-theories are introduced to describe the interaction between different sub-systems. They are seen as "mapping from the macrotheory of one level of explanation into the microtheory of another and vice versa" [3]. Such mappings are indicated in Fig. 4 by dashed arcs between interactors at different levels of abstraction. In our approach, higher-order processes describe both Type 1- and Type 2-theories. Their components represent the interactive sub-systems. Hence, Type 2-theories fit the interaction paradigm and are not mere links between elements of Type 1-theories.

Fig. 5 exemplarily shows our idea. Three processes are sketched: a task model to describe user tasks, an application model to describe the functional core of a software application, and a UI model to describe the interaction between the users and the application. Hierarchies of sub-processes are used to structure each model. In the example, we assume that sub-task (sub-process) $T2$ is supported by the application, or, more precisely, by a part of the functional core which is described by sub-process $F1$. Hence, the UI process contains two components $tm:T2(T)$ and $am:F1(F)$ and

---

[4] According to [1], a decomposition of nonmonotonic systems may create interactive unpredictable systems while a composition may produce noninteractive algorithms. A simple example in HOPS would be a process R with two components $c1:P$, $c2:Q$, an operation $r = <<c1.p1;$ $c1.p2; c2.q>>$ and the partial equation $R=r$. P and Q are assumed to be basic processes with $P = (p1 [] p2)*$ and $Q = q*$. While R embodies an algorithm (operation r), an isolated running of P or Q exhibits interactive behavior.

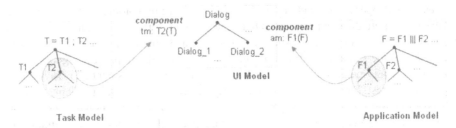

Fig. 5. Dynamic relation between tasks and functions

models the interaction between a user who wants to accomplish sub-task *T2* and the technical system. Of course, further differentiation is possible. For instance, separate processes could describe knowledge about presentation aspects or about control aspects of dialogues. This could help to follow architectural patterns like the PAC model [23].

However, we chose the example situation in Fig. 5 to draw attention to the often neglected dynamic relation between tasks and functions of an application. It is a truism that the way how people perform tasks is evolving, sometimes in an unpredictable way. (Interaction means openness!) What happens, for example, if people get a deeper understanding of task *T2*? They may wish a more subtle support by the application, and so the application model and the UI model need to be refined or even modified to improve the quality of the system. However, most modeling approaches in HCI assume a fixed functional core and concentrate on problems like multiple representations, distributed interfaces etc.

6 Conclusions and Future Work

This paper introduces the prototypical specification tool HOPS and its conceptual basis as means to analyze and design systems according to the interaction paradigm. The suggested approach offers a unified description of behavioral and structural aspects. This was illustrated through a couple of examples. It acknowledges the openness of interactive systems and supports the idea of design as an ongoing intervention process.

So far, HOPS served as a tool to explore and experiment with the idea of higher-order processes and to elaborate first usage patterns. In the future, we would like to prove the applicability of the approach to the analysis and the design of systems more deeply. Chatty requires in [24] that architectural issues of interactive software are already addressed at the level of programming languages. It may be interesting to investigate which specifications styles for describing architectural and implementational decisions can be supported by HOPS. Further versions of the tool might include reasoning mechanisms for detecting inconsistencies in parts of specifications, more elaborated operationalization mechanisms, and a parameter concept.

References

1. Wegner, P.: Why interaction is more powerful than algorithms. Comm. ACM 40(5) (1997)
2. Dittmar, A., Forbrig, P.: A unified description formalism for complex HCI-systems. In: Proc. of SEFM 2005. IEEE Computer Society, Los Alamitos (2005)

3. Barnard, P., May, J., Duke, D., Duce, D.: Systems, Interactions and Macrotheory. ACM Transactions on Human-Computer Interaction 7, 222–262 (2000)
4. Dix, A.: Upside-Down ∀s and Algorithms - Computational Formalisms and Theory. In: Carroll, J. (ed.) HCI Models, Theories, and Frameworks - Toward a Multidisciplinary Science, Morgan Kaufmann, San Francisco (2003)
5. Dittmar, A., Forbrig, P.: The Influence of Improved Task Models on Dialogues. In: Proc. of CADUI 2004. Kluwer Academic Publishers, Dordrecht (2004)
6. Dittmar, A., Forbrig, P.: Higher-Order Task Models. In: Jorge, J.A., Jardim Nunes, N., Falcão e Cunha, J. (eds.) DSV-IS 2003. LNCS, vol. 2844. Springer, Heidelberg (2003)
7. Dittmar, A., Gellendin, A., Forbrig, P.: Requirements Elicitation and Elaboration in Task-Based Design Needs More Than Task Modelling: A Case Study. In: Coninx, K., Luyten, K., Schneider, K.A. (eds.) TAMODIA 2006. LNCS, vol. 4385. Springer, Heidelberg (2007)
8. Johnson, P.: Human computer interaction: psychology, task analysis, and software engineering. McGraw-Hill Book Company, New York (1992)
9. Paterno, F., Mancini, C., Meniconi, S.: ConcurTaskTrees: A notation for specifying task models. In: Proc. of INTERACT 1997 (1997)
10. Veer, G.C., van der Lenting, B.F., Bergevoet, B.A.J.: GTA: Groupware Task Analysis - Modeling Complexity. Acta Psychologica 91, 297–322 (1996)
11. Alexander, H.: Executable Specifications as an Aid to Dialogue Design. In: Proc. of INTERACT 1987. Elsevier, Amsterdam (1987)
12. Sufrin, B., He, J.: Specification, analysis and refinement of interactive processes. In: Harrison, M.D., Thimbleby, H. (eds.) Formal Methods in Human-Computer Interaction. Cambridge University Press, Cambridge (1990)
13. Abowd, G.D.: Formal Aspects of Human-Computer Interaction. PhD thesis, Oxford University Computing Laboratory (1991)
14. Paterno, F.: Model-Based Design and Evaluation of Interactive Applications. Springer, Heidelberg (2000)
15. Luyten, K., Clerckx, T., Coninx, K., Vanderdonckt, J.: Derivation of a Dialog Model from a Tasl Model by Activity Chain Extraction. In: Jorge, J.A., Jardim Nunes, N., Falcão e Cunha, J. (eds.) DSV-IS 2003. LNCS, vol. 2844. Springer, Heidelberg (2003)
16. Calvary, G., Coutaz, J., Thevenin, D.: A Unifying Reference Framework for the Development of Plastic User Interfaces. In: Nigay, L., Little, M.R. (eds.) EHCI 2001. LNCS, vol. 2254. Springer, Heidelberg (2001)
17. Hoare, C.A.R.: Communicating Sequential Processes. Prentice-Hall, Englewood Cliffs (1985)
18. Milner, R.: Communication and Concurrency. Prentice-Hall, Englewood Cliffs (1989)
19. Engeström, Y.: Learning by Expanding: An Activity-Theoretical Approach to Development Research. PhD thesis, Orienta-Konsultit Oy, Helsinki (1987)
20. Dourish, P.: Where the Action Is. MIT Press, Cambridge (2001)
21. Kaptelinin, V., Nardi, B.A.: Acting with technology: activity theory and interaction design. MIT Press, Cambridge (2006)
22. Vygotsky, L.: Thought and Language. The MIT Press, Cambridge (1934/1986)
23. Coutaz, J.: PAC: An Object Oriented Model For Implementing User Interfaces. SIGCHI Bull. 19(2) (1987)
24. Chatty, S.: Programs = data + algorithms + architecture: Consequences for interactive software. In: Proc. of the 2007 joint conference on Engineering Interactive Software. Springer, Heidelberg (2007)

Systematic Analysis of Control Panel Interfaces Using Formal Tools

J. Creissac Campos[1] and M. D. Harrison[2]

[1] Department of Informatics/CCTC, Universidade do Minho, Braga, Portugal
Jose.Campos@di.uminho.pt
[2] School of Computing Science, Newcastle University, UK
Michael.Harrison@ncl.ac.uk

Abstract. The paper explores the role that formal modeling may play in aiding the visualization and implementation of usability requirements of a control panel. We propose that this form of analysis should become a systematic and routine aspect of the development of such interfaces. We use a notation for describing the interface that is convenient to use by software engineers, and describe a set of tools designed to make the process systematic and exhaustive.

1 Introduction

Applying formal techniques to analyze interactive systems makes possible a more systematic approach to the evaluation of the usability of a new design. Formal techniques can provide an incisive analysis that is effective in uncovering potential unforeseen interaction problems which can then be explored from a usability perspective. The paper demonstrates how a collection of tool supported property patterns (akin to those described in [12]) can be used to make this process more systematic. The interface under analysis is specified using Modal Action Logic (MAL) which focuses on the meaning and effect of action. The approach is illustrated by analyzing the air conditioning system for a family car. In addition to potential usability problems, the patterns help discover discrepancies between assumed meanings based on the user manual and meanings derived by experimenting with the system.

The proposed techniques are similar in aim to those of [5] and [14]. MAUI [9] is a comparable tool supported technique for analyzing control panel systems. The work presented here differs by (1) supporting a textual design specification notation and (2) supporting the systematic analysis of a set of standard interface properties. There is no space in this paper to do full justice to a comparison between these techniques and to compare the range of other techniques that have been developed recently, see for example [11] for a review. The focus here is to demonstrate how formal techniques can be made more routine and systematic through a real example. The example illustrates techniques that fit naturally with the programmer's view of the system while at the same time triggering a usability perspective. The paper describes:

1. a notation that clearly and simply captures characteristics of interactive devices
2. a set of properties that can be systematically checked of the interactive system
3. a tool that pulls together the means of specification and the means of checking, that is accessible to appropriate developers.

T.C.N. Graham and P. Palanque (Eds.): DSVIS 2008, LNCS 5136, pp. 72–85, 2008.
© Springer-Verlag Berlin Heidelberg 2008

Finally, discovery tools are required to explore the consequences of the problems uncovered by these techniques. The systematic approach is supported by the IVY tool developed to check MAL specifications. The paper explains the characteristics of the tool and comments on how the formal approach can be complemented by a more user focussed analysis.

2 The Example

The example is the automatic air conditioning panel of the Toyota Corolla (2001 European version). The actions of the air conditioning system concern setting temperature and altering the rate and direction of the flow of air. While the actions associated with temperature and rate of flow are relatively straightforward, complications involve the number of modes that deal with the direction of flow. The complete set of actions and displays is identified below.

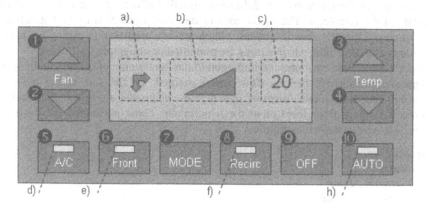

Fig. 1. The air-conditioning control panel

Figure 1 shows what the control panel looks like. The panel has ten buttons (these are enumerated in the figure) and there are seven display features that can change through use of the air conditioning system ((a)-(h)). These elements are first identified before describing them in more detail through the specification. The buttons correspond to actions in the model, the names of the actions are as follows: (1) increase fan speed (*fanspeedup*); (2) decrease fan speed (*fanspeeddown*); (3) increase target temperature (*tempup*); (4) decrease target temperature (*tempdown*); (5) select air conditioning mode (*ackey*); (6) select windscreen (front) flow mode (*frontkey*); (7) select flow mode (*modekey*); (8) select air intake mode (*airintakekey*); (9) off (*off*); (10) select automatic mode (*autokey*).

The displayed indicators are perceivable attributes of the state. These are identified in the model by the names in brackets in the following list: (a) flow mode (*airflow*); (b) fan speed (*fanspeed*); (c) target temperature (*settemp*); (d) air-conditioning on/off (*ac*); (e) wind screen (front) flow mode on/off (*front*); (f) recirculation air intake mode (*airintakefresh*); (g) automatic mode on/off (*auto*).

3 The Modeling Notation

A MAL specification is produced focusing on relevant actions and attributes of the state. The semantics of MAL is discussed in more detail in [6,1]. This set of actions and attributes may be modified as additional assumptions about the specification are identified through experimenting with the system or exploring properties of the specification. The specification is structured using hierarchical interface components (called interactors). In the example one interactor describes all the actions and visible attributes of the state of the system. No assumptions are made in this analysis about other properties that may be important from a usability point of view. For example, a user may feel or hear the effect of changes in the temperature, fan speed and where the air is flowing. These additional modalities are ignored. Context effects, for example whether the car windows are open or not, are also ignored. In practice these aspects of the system could be considered additionally if appropriate.

There are three types of MAL axioms. *Propositional axioms* describe invariants over the state of the interactor. *Modal axioms* describe effects of an action in terms of the state of the interactor. The modal axioms describe production rules that define a state machine. Finally *deontic axioms,* which are not used in this example, capture conditions that determine when actions are permitted or obligatory.

Three visible state attributes are important to the functioning of the air conditioning system: temperature (*settemp*), flow speed defined by the fan speed indicator (*fanspeed*) and flow mode (*airflow*) that defines where the air flows, for example dashboard level or floor level or to the windscreen. These attributes, see (a)-(c) in Figure 1, can be described as follows:

interactor *main*
   attributes
   [vis] *settemp* : *Temp*
   [vis] *airflow* : *AirFlow*
   [vis] *fanspeed* : *FanSpeed*

The specification consists of one interactor named *main*. The modality [vis] of each attribute is "visible". These attributes of the states are changed by three sets of buttons: *settemp* by [*tempup*] (3) and [*tempdown*] (4); *fanspeed* by [*fanspeedup*] (1) and [*fanspeeddown*] (2); the flow mode is controlled by a more complicated set of buttons. While the manual provided an initial explanation of how the controls are used, this information was updated in the light of analysis and experimentation.

[*tempup*] (*settemp* < *MAXHOT* → *settemp'* = *settemp* + 1)
$\qquad\qquad\qquad$ ∧ (*settemp* = *MAXHOT* → *keep*(*settemp*))
[*tempdown*] (*settemp* > *MAXCOLD* → *settemp'* = *settemp* − 1)
$\qquad\qquad\qquad$ ∧ (*settemp* = *MAXCOLD* → *keep*(*settemp*))

Normal logical operators are used in the specification; actions appear in square brackets. The expression to the right of the action describes how the state attributes are changed. In the case of [*tempup*] if temperature is lower than the maximum possible (*MAXHOT*) it is incremented. The new state of *settemp* is indicated by priming the attribute, hence (*settemp'*) becomes the previous plus one. If temperature is already equal to *MAXHOT*, then its value does not change: (*keep(settemp)*). If an attribute does not appear in the keep list and its behaviour is not defined by the axioms, then it assumes a random value. [*tempdown*], [*fanspeedup*] and [*fanspeeddown*] have similar definitions. More axioms are required for actions associated with where the air flows. Possible air flow modes are defined by the set:

AirFlow = {*panel, double, floor, floorws, wsclear*}.

Whether the air conditioning system (temperature, fan and airflow) is switched on or off is not yet captured in these axioms. The fact that this aspect of the design is not clearly visible in the system is the reason for this omission. The only possible indicator is the fan speed (see indicator (b) in Figure 1), but this is an indirect and not very salient association. This omission raises an issue for the designer as to whether this aspect of the design should be made more clear.

The air conditioning mode selector key (5) is defined when the system is on and when it is off. When off, pressing the button has no effect on the state attributes, when on the mode key simply changes the *ac* attribute, toggling its value.

on → [*ackey*] *ac'* = ¬*ac* ∧ *keep(auto, airintake, settemp, on, front, airflow, fanspeed)*
¬*on* → [*ackey*] *keep(auto, airintake, settemp, on, front, airflow, fanspeed, ac)*

The windscreen (*flow*) mode selection button [*frontkey*] has the following axioms:

on → [*frontkey*] *on'* ∧ *front'* = ¬*front* ∧ *keep(settemp)*
¬*on* → [*frontkey*] *on'* ∧ *front'* ∧ *keep(settemp)*
[*frontkey*] *front'* → (¬*auto'* ∧ ¬*airintake'* ∧ *ac'*)
front ↔ *airflow* = *wsclear*

Hence when the system is on, pressing the front button will toggle the front attribute, and when switched off the button will switch it on (*on'* asserts the new value of *on* is *true*). The final axiom specifies an invariant, namely when the front mode is set the airflow is always in windscreen clear mode. The *modekey* and *airintakekey* are specified as follows:

[*modekey*] ¬*auto'* ∧ *front'* ∧ *keep(airintake, settemp, on, fanspeed)*
¬*front* → [*modekey*] (*airflow* = *panel* → *airflow'* = *double*)
    ∧ (*airflow* = *double* → *airflow'* = *floor*)
    ∧ (*airflow* = *floor* → *airflow'* = *floorws*)
    ∧ (*airflow* = *floorws* → *airflow'* = *panel*) ∧ *keep(ac)*
[*airintakekey*] *airintake'* = ¬*airintake*
    ∧ *keep(auto, settemp, on, front, airflow, fanspeed, ac)*

It was difficult to produce an unambiguous and accurate specification of this system based on *both* the manual and use of the system because: (a) the manual is not clear in places – e.g., "When the Front key is pressed, air flows mainly through the windscreen vents, and the FRESH air intake mode is automatically set" is only true when the front mode is off; (b) the manual is incomplete - e.g., the fact that pressing the mode key in auto mode turns the mode indicator off is not described in the manual; (c) the manual is inconsistent with the device - e.g., references to the A/C button being depressed are not consistent with the actual user interface where buttons do not have a depressed state; (d) descriptions within the manual are mutually inconsistent - e.g., "press the MODE key to switch off AUTO mode" and "in AUTO mode you do not have to use the MODE key, unless you want a different flux mode"; (e) assumptions are omitted - e.g., the manual descriptions only describe changes produced by the buttons and assume that what is unmentioned remains unchanged which is as already stated not what is assumed in MAL. Appendix A provides a set of axioms that combine the results derived from reading the manual with observations from use of the system.

4 Systematic Analysis

Analysis is first concerned with the credibility of the system, exploring those properties that should be true in terms of a plausible mental model of the system. For example:

$$AG(auto \rightarrow on) \tag{1}$$

The property is described in CTL (Computational Tree Logic, see for example, [4]) and asserts that auto mode can only be armed if the system is on. This property is not true in the version of the system specification based on the manual. A counterexample shows that the air intake key arms the automatic mode without switching the system. A new specification in which the previous state of the system could be recovered even though the system had been switched off fixes the problem. Exploration of other properties indicates that when switching between modes (for example from auto mode to front mode and back) the system keeps a memory of the state in each mode. In the specification a variable $acmem$ is used to define the state of the ac mode. This and further exploration of system actions produces further changes to the specification (see Appendix A).

The axioms that relate to $acmem$ are as follows:

$[ackey]\ acmem' = ac'$
$[a :-\{ackey\}]\ keep(acmem)$
$front \rightarrow [modekey]\ ac' = acmem$
$\neg on \rightarrow [a :\{fanspeedup, fanspeeddown\}]\ ac' = acmem$
$[frontkey]\ \neg front' \rightarrow ac' = acmem$

When $ackey$ is pressed, $acmem$ stores the new value of ac (first axiom), all other actions do not change its value (second axiom – note use of $a:-\{ackey\}$ which defines actions a not including $ackey$); pressing $modekey$ when the front mode is on, puts the air conditioning mode in the state stored in memory (third axiom), and the same happens when $fanspeedup$ or $fanspeeddown$ are pressed while the system is off (fourth axiom), or if pressing $frontkey$ leaves the front mode on (fifth axiom). Property 1 is true in this new model.

Standard patterns were developed for the systematic analysis of interactive systems. Due to space constraints, only minimal information on the patterns is provided, presenting basic (no concurrency) formulations only. The patterns use a number of notational assumptions. s is the valuation of the attributes in the current state (S), $c \subseteq dom(\rho)$ (with ρ: $Attributes \rightarrow Presentation$ defining the presentation modalities) a subset of perceivable attributes, $=_*$ is equality distributed over attributes in the state, a

an action, $AX_a\ p$ a shorthand for $AX(a \rightarrow p)$ (i.e., in all next states arrived at by a, p holds), $\neq_*$means at least one attribute must be different, and *pred*an optional predicate used to constrain the analysis to a sub-set of states. The patterns are formulated in a CTL like logic that is transformed into correct CTL by the IVY tool (described in Section 5).

Feedback is a key property of a good user interface that helps the user gain confidence in the effect of actions. It helps create an appropriate mental model of the system. Feedback properties can be verified with the following pattern:

Property Pattern: *Feedback*
Intent: To verify that a given action provides feedback.
Formulation: $AG(pred(s) \wedge c =_* x \rightarrow AX_a\ (c \neq_* x))$ Under the defined condition (*pred*), the action (*a*) will always cause a change in some perceivable attribute (in *c*).

If the mode key is instantiated in the pattern, i.e., $a \equiv modekey$ and feedback is provided by the airflow indicator (indicator (a) in figure 1), the property can be expressed as:

$$AG(airflow = x \rightarrow AX_{modekey}(airflow \neq x)) \tag{2}$$

The IVY tool instantiates the pattern, generating five properties, one for each flow mode action. These all hold, suggesting that the airflow indicator provides adequate feedback and therefore mode change is clear. Instantiation of the property with *fanspeedup* and associated indicator *fanspeed* (see indicator (b) in figure 1) produces

$$AG(fanspeed = x \rightarrow AX_{fanspeedup}(fanspeed \neq x)) \tag{3}$$

The property fails when the fan speed is at maximum (10) and the button does not change speed (or indicator). In practice failure of a property may not be significant. While no other indicator is clear at this limit, this may not be a problem for the user.

Consistency of action is another characteristic of a system that facilitates predictability and learning. Consistency can be internal (between different parts of the system) or external (with other systems). Four buttons which act as on/off switches (A/C, Auto, Mode and Front) look the same and should be internally consistent.

Property Pattern: *Behavioural consistency*
Intent: To verify that a given action causes consistent effect.
Formulation: $AG(pred(s) \wedge s =_* x \rightarrow AX_{ac}(effect(x,s)))$ with *effect* : $2^{(S \times S)}$ characterising the effect the action should have in the state.

This generalization of the Feedback pattern states that the action must always cause the same effect in the user interface. The candidates for test are buttons *ackey, frontkey, airintakekey* and *autokey*, the relevant state is the status of each button (*ac, front, airintake* and *auto*, respectively), and the desired effect is the toggling of that status. In the case of *ackey*, the pattern gives:

$$AG(ac = x \rightarrow AX_{ackey}(ac = \neg x)) \tag{4}$$

All the instantiated properties hold when the system is switched on except [*auto-key*]. In the case of [*autokey*] the button only turns the mode on, it does not turn it off. One of the interesting features of this design is that when the system is off there are a number of unexpected side effects of pressing some of these buttons that cause changes to subsequent behavior.

Although one form of undo has been analyzed already (for the on/off switches), another relevant pattern is whether there are actions that can undo the effect of other actions.

Property Pattern: *Undo*

Intent: To check whether the effect of an action can be undone.

Formulation (any action): $AG(s =_* x \rightarrow AX_{a1}EX(s =_* x))$
with a_1 the action whose effect we want to undo, any action required to undo.

Formulation (specific action): $AG(s =_* x \rightarrow AX_{a1}(EX(a_2) \wedge AX_{a2}(s =_* x))$
a_2 the action that should undo a_1; the action availability test ($EX(a_2)$) is optional.

Property Pattern: *Reversibility*

Intent: To check whether the effect of an action can be eventually reversed/undone.

Formulation: $AG(s =_* x \rightarrow AX_{a1}EF(s =_* x))$

For the mode button this pattern checks whether there is another action that can be identified as performing its undo. Focussing on the airflow indicator:

$$AG(airflow = x \rightarrow AX_{modekey}AX_{xaction}(airflow = x)) \tag{5}$$

Attempting the verification for x_{action} = *autokey* fails for all properties, except when *airflow* = *floorws*. It fails because *modekey* does not have a symmetric action that undoes its effect (on the airflow mode). Exploring why it holds in the one case leads to the unexpected conclusion that the *modekey* action is unavailable when the air flow mode is *floorws*. The mode key action should always be available to allow the flow mode to be changed. The model has been specified so that the user can always press the buttons but this does not imply that pressing a button always has an effect. The problem is that the cyclic behaviour 'implemented' by the mode button includes *wsclear* but this mode should only be accessible by using the Front key. Whether the *modekey* can always be undone by some means leads to a positive answer.

$$AG(airflow = x \rightarrow AX_{modekey}EF(airflow = x)) \tag{6}$$

5 Checking Patterns Using IVY

The IVY tool supports the patterns described in the previous section. Its architecture is given in Figure 2. The tool has four components: a *model editor* designed to support MAL interactor development; a *property editor* designed to support the formulation of relevant usability related properties; a *translator* (i2smv) that transforms interactor models into the model checker's input language; a *trace visualizer/analyzer* that helps analyze any traces produced by the model checker.

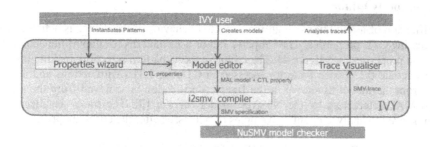

Fig. 2. IVY Architecture

5.1 The Model Editor

The editor supports the structure and syntax of MAL [1] interactors in two editing modes indicated in the two windows of figure 3. In graphical mode the overall structure of the model can be viewed and manipulated while at the same time providing an individual edit capability. The textual mode involves the usual editing facilities: cut and paste, undo and redo etc. This mode supports direct editing and fine tuning. The interactor in graphical mode is based on UML class diagrams [13].

Interactor aggregation and specialization uses an approach consistent with UML to make it easier for designers to understand a model's representation. A number of inspectors are provided in graphical mode to make it possible to edit the different aspects of the model (types, attributes, actions and axioms of the selected interactor, and so on). Textual mode allows direct editing of the text of the model thus enabling experienced users to edit the model more quickly. Aspects of the text can be changed directly instead of using the inspector panels of the graphical mode. Less expert users may choose more guidance through the graphical mode.

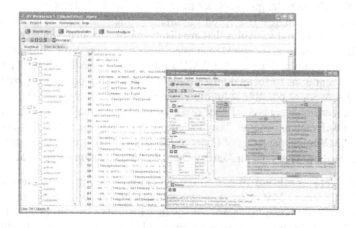

Fig. 3. IVY Model Editor

5.2 Property Editor

Verification of assumptions about the expected behavior of the device is achieved by expressing CTL properties. The Property Editor uses patterns to support the choice of specific properties (see figure 4). The editor supports pattern selection, making it easy to instantiate the chosen pattern expressed in CTL (or LTL) with actions and attributes from the model as shown in the figure. Verification is achieved from the translated MAL interactors by the NuSMV model checker [3]. The trace visualizer can then be used to analyze counter-examples or witnesses after the checking process.

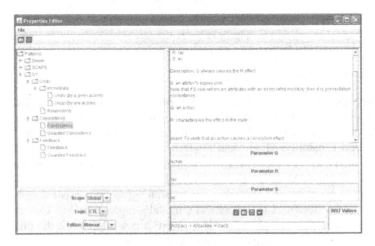

Fig. 4. Expressing properties using patterns

5.3 Trace Visualization

Traces are expressed in terms of the variables and states generated through the translation into SMV's input language. Since the SMV model includes some state artifacts that were created through this step an important element in trace visualization is to ensure that the states and variables that are displayed for the analyst are only in terms of the original interactors. A typical example of this reversion is the elimination of the attribute 'action', annotations used in SMV to distinguish MAL actions. The visualization component aims to focus on the problem that is being pointed out by the trace to support discovery of possible solutions reducing the cost of the analysis.

The visualizer implements a number of alternative representations to explore the acceptability of different approaches. They include: a tabular representation that is similar to the existing SMV implementation of Cadence Labs (www.cadence.com); a graphical representation based on states; and an Activity Diagram representation based on actions [7].

The tabular representation (figure 5) presents information in a table similar to that generated by Cadence SMV or by [12]. Column headings show state numbers. The beginning of a cycle is shown by an asterisk. Cells with darker backgrounds indicate that the attribute's value in the current state has changed since the previous state otherwise a lighter background is used. This idea, adopted from [12], shows quickly when the interactor's attributes change state.

main.ac	1	2	3
acmem	0	0	0
action	0	0	0
action	airintakekey	autokey	fanspeedup
airflow	wsclear	floorws	floorws
airflowmem	wsclear	wsclear	wsclear
airintake	0	0	0
airintakemem	0	0	0
auto	0	1	0
automem	0	1	1
fanspeed	0	10	10
front	1	0	0
on	0	1	1
settemp	15	15	15

Fig. 5. Tabular representation: no feedback for *fanspeedup*

The state based representation (see figure 6, left) represents each interactor in a column showing evolution of interactor states (attributes are listed against each state). The global state (including all interactor variables) is represented separately to serve as an index to the states of the individual interactors. A green arrow indicates the beginning and end of loops in this state. Alternatively a pop-up option toggles attribute representation to provide a more compact view (as shown in figure 6). While attributes are not represented in the diagram they can be consulted by placing the mouse over each state, thereby reducing information and making it easier to discover the problem highlighted by the trace. Actions are shown as labels in the arrows between two consecutive states if a transition exists. A second variant of this diagram represents the (physical) states of the SMV modules generated from the model.

The Activity Diagram representation follows the notation of UML 2.0 for activity diagrams (right hand side, figure 6). Activities are represented by one rectangle with rounded corners. The small rectangles associated with the activities represent the state of the interactor before and after an activity occurs. As this representation clearly focuses on actions, interactor attributes appear as pop-ups. The attribute values can be consulted through one pop-up, placing the mouse on the rectangles of the states.

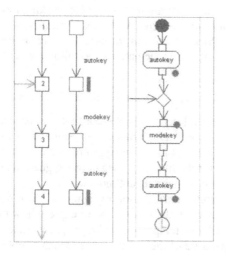

Fig. 6. Counter example representations (state based/activity diagram)

5.4 Exploring the Traces

The visualizer (in all modes) makes it possible to mark states depending on criteria defined over the state attributes. Criteria are defined by relations (=, >, <) between attribute pairs or between attributes and values. To each criterion is associated a color. All the states that verify a given criterion are annotated with the specified color. In the case of figure 6 states marked are states where *airflow = panel*.

In the case of comparison of attributes, two half-circles of the chosen color are drawn near each one of the relevant attributes. In the case of comparison between attributes and values, filled circles are drawn, with the chosen color. If the pop-ups option is enabled the condition represented by each marker can be revealed by placing the mouse over it.

6 Extending the Analysis

Mode complexity is a fundamental issue in interactive system design and is particularly susceptible to model checking analysis. In [8] two types of modes are identified: action modes and indicator modes. Problems might arise when two modes are similar but not the same (leading users to believe the system is in a mode that it is not). Other problems arise through the evolution of modes (for example, actions might cause undesirable/incorrect mode changes) rendering the effect of action unpredictable.

A step beyond the toggling behavior of buttons would be to analyze whether the buttons, when pressed twice, leave the overall mode of the system in the same state. Consider, for example, the front key. If the system is off it always turns the system on. Further investigation could explore a broader concept of "working mode" (a set of state attributes that are related by mode). For example testing whether it is the case that when the system is on, the effect of turning the air flow on and off is to leave the system in the same working mode as it was in initially. For this case the Undo pattern can be used with the specific action formulation, making a_1 and a_2 equal to the *frontkey*. In this case the attributes that are relevant to the working mode include the attributes *auto, on, ac, airintake* and *airflow*. Attributes *settemp, fanspeed* and *front* are not relevant to the analysis. Since the action *frontkey* has already been exhaustively analyzed it shall be ignored. Applying the pattern, the following property is produced:

$AG((auto, on, ac, airintake) =_* x \rightarrow$

$AX_{frontkey}(EX(frontkey) \wedge AX_{frontkey}((auto, on, ac, airintake) =_* x))))$

Action modes may be explored using the consistency pattern. When the effect is different from the one expected, action modes can be identified. Alternatively a guard can be used to identify a relevant mode making it possible to check whether the action has the correct behavior for the mode (or, negating the guard and checking whether it has that same behavior outside the relevant mode).

The above analysis limits consideration by ignoring the function of the panel. In the style of [2] an alternative strategy would be to explore how the device enables the environment to reach a desired temperature. This property relates to the context of use of the device, the temperature of the environment, which is not present in the model. There is no space in the paper to present a relevant analysis.

7 Conclusion

For formal techniques to become a widely used approach to the analysis of interactive systems two developments are necessary. The first is to make the analysis commonplace and systematic for developers. The second is to allow reuse of similar specifications to reduce the work necessary to perform the analysis. The work described in this paper addresses both these developments. The use of IVY and patterns provides real promise that systematic techniques are now available for a class of control panel systems. Consideration has been limited to control panel interfaces because the specification of dynamically changing nested actions becomes relatively cumbersome in MAL. The variety and number of such systems that are currently under analysis is growing substantially. The same small set of examples is no longer the focus of attention. Combining tools like IVY with repositories of specifications such as that envisaged by Thimbleby using XML standards (see, for example [9]) will provide an invaluable resource for interactive system developers. The issue of reuse is also being addressed. Patterns provide significant support for developers when they face new designs. Further work is required to explore generic interactors, similar to that discussed in the broader context of smart environments [10].

Acknowledgments. We acknowledge with thanks EPSRC grant EP/F01404X/1 and FCT/FEDER grant POSC/EIA/56646/2004. Michael Harrison is grateful to colleagues in the ReSIST NoE (www.resit-noe.org), José Campos to Nuno Sousa for work in IVY.

References

1. Campos, J.C., Harrison, M.D.: Model checking interactor specifications. Automated Software Engineering 8, 275–310 (2001)
2. Campos, J.C., Harrison, M.D.: Considering context and users in interactive systems analysis. In: van de Veer, G., Palanque, P., Wesson, J. (eds.) Engineering Interactive Systems (accepted for publication, 2007)
3. Cimatti, A., Roveri, M., Olivetti, E., Keighren, G., Pistore, M., Roveri, M., Semprini, S., Tchaltsev, A.: NuSMV 2.3 user manual. Technical report, ITC-IRST, Trento, Italy (2007)
4. Clarke, E.M., Grumberg, O., Peled, D.A.: Model Checking. MIT Press, Cambridge (1999)
5. Degani, A.: Taming HAL: designing interfaces beyond 2001. Macmillan, Palgrave (2003)
6. Duke, D.J., Harrison, M.D.: Abstract interaction objects. Computer Graphics Forum 12(3), 25–36 (1993)
7. Fowler, M.: UML Distilled: a brief guide to the standard object modelling language, 3rd edn. Addison-Wesley, Reading (2004)
8. Gow, J., Thimbleby, H., Cairns, P.: Automatic critiques of interface modes. In: Gilroy, S.W., Harrison, M.D. (eds.) DSV-IS 2005. LNCS, vol. 3941, pp. 201–212. Springer, Heidelberg (2006)
9. Gow, J., Thimbleby, H.W.: MAUI: An interface design tool based on matrix algebra. In: Jacob, R.J.K., Limbourg, Q., Vanderdonckt, J. (eds.) Computer Aided Design of User Interfaces IV, CADUI 2004, pp. 81–94 (2004)

10. Harrison, M.D., Kray, C., Campos, J.C.: Exploring an option space to engineer a ubiquitous computing system. Electr. Notes in Theoretical Computer Science 208C, 41–55 (2008)
11. Heymann, M., Degani, A.: Formal analysis and automatic generation of user interfaces: Approach, methodology, and an algorithm. Human Factors: The Journal of the Human Factors and Ergonomics Society 49(2), 311–330 (2007)
12. Loer, K., Harrison, M.D.: An integrated framework for the analysis of dependable interactive systems (IFADIS): its tool support and evaluation. Automated Software Engineering 13(4), 469–496 (2006)
13. Rumbaugh, J., Jacobson, I., Booch, G.: The Unified Modeling Language Reference Manual (UML). Addison-Wesley, Reading (1999)
14. Thimbleby, H.W.: Press on: principles of interaction programming. MIT Press, Cambridge (2007)

Appendix A System Definition

defines
 MAXCOLD = 15
 MAXHOT = 30
 MAXFANSPEED = 10
types
 Temp = MAXCOLD .. MAXHOT
 AirFlow = {panel, double, floor, floorws, wsclear}
 FanSpeed = 0..MAXFANSPEED

interactor main
 attributes
  [vis] *auto, on, front, ac*: boolean
  [vis] *airintake: boolean*   # *true: fresh / false: recirc*
  automem, acmem, airintakemem: boolean
  [vis] *settemp: Temp*
  [vis] *airflow: AirFlow*
  airflowmem: AirFlow
  [vis] *fanspeed: FanSpeed*
 actions
  autokey off modekey fanspeedup fanspeeddown tempup tempdown frontkey ackey airintakekey
 axioms
  [*autokey*] *auto' ∧ on' ∧ ¬front' ∧ keep(airintake, settemp)*
  [*off*] *¬auto' ∧ ¬on' ∧ fanspeed'=0 ∧ ¬ac' ∧ keep(airintake,settemp,front,airflow)*
  [*modekey*] *¬auto' ∧ ¬front' ∧ keep(airintake,settemp,on,fanspeed)*
  ¬front → [modekey] (airflow=panel → airflow'=double) ∧ (airflow=double → airflow'=floor)
     ∧ (airflow=floor → airflow'=floorws) ∧ (airflow=floorws → airflow'=panel) ∧ keep(ac)
  [*fanspeedup*] *¬auto' ∧ on' ∧ keep(airintake, settemp, front, airflow)*
  on → [fanspeedup] (fanspeed<MAXFANSPEED → fanspeed'=fanspeed+1)
             ∧ (fanspeed=MAXFANSPEED → fanspeed'=fanspeed) ∧ keep(ac)
  ¬on → [fanspeedup] fanspeed'=1
  [*fanspeeddown*] *¬auto' ∧ on' ∧ keep(airintake, settemp, front, airflow, ac)*
  (on ∧ auto) → [fanspeeddown] keep(fanspeed, ac)
  (on ∧ ¬auto) → [fanspeeddown] (fanspeed >0 → fanspeed'=fanspeed -1)
             ∧ (fanspeed =0 → fanspeed'=fanspeed) ∧ keep(ac)
  ¬on → [fanspeeddown] fanspeed'=1
  on → [tempup] (settemp<MAXHOT → settemp'=settemp +1)
         ∧ (settemp=MAXHOT → settemp'=settemp) ∧ keep(auto,airintake,on,front,ac)
  ¬on → [tempup] keep(auto,airintake,settemp,on,front,airflow,fanspeed,ac)
  on → [tempdown] (settemp>MAXCOLD → settemp'=settemp -1)
         ∧ (settemp=MAXCOLD → settemp'=settemp) ∧ keep(auto,airintake,on,front,ac)

¬on → [tempdown] keep(auto,airintake,settemp,on,front,airflow,fanspeed,ac)
on → [frontkey] on' ∧ front'=¬front ∧ keep(settemp)
¬on → [frontkey] on' ∧ front' ∧ keep(settemp)
[frontkey] front' → (¬auto' ∧ ¬airintake' ∧ ac')
front ↔ airflow=wsclear
on → [ackey] ac'=¬ac ∧ keep(auto,airintake,settemp,on,front,airflow,fanspeed)
¬on → [ackey] keep(auto,airintake,settemp,on,front,airflow,fanspeed,ac)
[airintakekey] airintake'=¬airintake ∧ keep(auto,settemp,on,front,airflow,fanspeed,ac)
[] ¬auto ∧ ¬on ∧ fanspeed=0 ∧ ¬ac
airflow
¬front → [frontkey] airflowmem'=airflow
front → [ac:-{frontkey, modekey}] keep(airflowmem)
front → [modekey] airflow'=airflowmem
(on ∧ front) → [frontkey] airflow'=airflowmem
(¬on ∧ front) → [frontkey] keep(airflowmem)
airintake
¬front → [frontkey] airintakemem'=airintake
front → [ac:-{ffrontkey, airintakekeyg}] keep(airintakemem)
front → [airintakekey] airintakemem'=airintake'
(on ∧ front) → [frontkey] airintake'=airintakemem
(¬on ∧ front) → [frontkey] keep(airintakemem)
ac
[ackey] acmem'=ac'
[ac:-{ackey}] keep(acmem)
(front ∧ on) → [modekey] ac'=acmem
(front ∧ ¬on) → [modekey] keep(ac)
¬on → [ac:{fanspeedup,fanspeeddown}] ac'=acmem
[frontkey] ¬front' → ac'=acmem
[autokey] ac'=acmem
auto
[ac:{autokey,modekey}] automem'=auto'
[ac:-{autokey,modekey,frontkey}] keep(automem)
¬on → [frontkey] keep(automem)
on → [frontkey] automem'=auto
[frontkey] ¬front' → auto'=automem

Investigating System Navigation Ergonomics through Model Verification

Alexandre Scaico[1], Maria de F. Q. Vieira[1], Markson R. F. de Sousa[1],
and Charles Santoni[2]

[1] LIHM DEE CEEI UFCG
Caixa Postal 10105 - Campina Grande - Paraíba - Brazil
{scaico,fatima,marckson}@dee.ufcg.edu.br
[2] LSIS-UMR 6168
Av. Escadrille Normandie Niemen
13397 Marseille Cedex 20 France
charles.santoni@lsis.org

Abstract. This paper discusses the use of formal models in the process of investigating the ergonomics of the navigation component in interactive systems. The investigation is based upon model analysis and a set of navigation properties. The formalism employed on this work was Coloured Petri Nets. The paper illustrates how the set of ergonomic properties was mapped into the model properties with the support of the formalism tools and specific functions developed to support the interface designer during model analysis. The context chosen as the basis for discussion is the operation of automated systems in the electricity industry; and a case study is presented to illustrate the analysis.

Keywords: Model based design, safety critical interfaces, CPN.

1 Introduction

The adoption of formal methods has been an approach growing in acceptance among human interface designers in order to validate alternative choices in the early stages of design. In this modelling context one can use various formalisms, which in turn support different kinds of analysis. The formalism employed on this work was Coloured Petri Nets (CPN) [3]. This choice of formalism was based on the availability of a graphic notation and tools to support simulation and formal analysis such as property verification.

On this paper one will explore modelling and analyzing the navigation component of human interfaces, in the context of industrial automated systems; more precisely in the electricity industry. The case study developed during this work is based on a real installation that belongs to one of the biggest electricity companies in Brazil.

Electric systems are currently operated through different levels of automation. One of those levels concerns the use of supervisory software, which integrates the plant's resources, supporting the operator on his supervision and control task. During this study one of this system's substation was modelled from the viewpoint of its supervisory software human interface. Studying the company's human error reports it was

T.C.N. Graham and P. Palanque (Eds.): DSVIS 2008, LNCS 5136, pp. 86–91, 2008.

found that a high incidence of errors is related to the operator altering the task sequence in relation to the prescribed one. This finding motivated the study of the navigation component of the human interface in order to analyze the alternatives given to the user and adjust them to prevent those errors.

This paper is organized as follows. Section 2 presents the proposed navigation CPN model. Section 3 presents the usability properties. Section 4 discusses the case study model analysis and illustrates the functions which were built to support the analysis. Section 5 presents discusses the analyses results and proposes future steps.

2 Modelling and Analyzing the Navigation Component of Human Interfaces

The interface navigation model was built as a modular structure to allow, through minor modifications, its adaptation to different installations within the application context; acting as a framework for building other models. The Navigation model represents the navigation possibilities between windows in typical supervision software, such as: operator's login, plant synoptic, trend graphs, variable's history, event and alarm, and help. The windows display the interaction objects available to the operator to perform the plant's supervision and control tasks.

In the case study, the navigation model was instantiated to represent the supervisory system at the substation as well as the interaction objects typically available in the electric system such as: relays switch, switch breakers, command switches, and the toggle switch local/remote command. An object model library was built that represents the devices typically found in the electricity company substation installations. This library together with the navigation model simplified the representation of other similar installations within the same company.

3 Model Properties

A set of navigation properties was proposed to reflect desirable features from the ergonomic point of view, which can be verified through model analysis [4]. It follows a brief description of these, which are classed as validity properties [2].

(1) *Reversibility* is related to the user ability of returning to a previous point in the interaction; while cancelling previous operations. This property can be verified by means of the CPN model property *reachability*. (2) The *Existence of access paths between specific points of the interaction ensures* the access to specific states of the system. This property can be verified through the analysis of the CPN markings; checking the reachability of a state M_j from an initial state M_k. (3) *Reinitialization* is the possibility of returning to the initial point of the interaction, and can be verified through the analysis of the CPN net markings. If the initial state is in the list of the model's *home marking*, this property is verified. (4) *Access to Exit* is the possibility of exiting the system from various strategic points. To detect the exit points in the model's state space one checks if all the dead markings listed in the Occ report correspond to an exit point. A model with this property will have the markings corresponding to exit states in the list of the dead markings as well as in the list of home markings.

(5) The *Existence of alternative navigation paths when performing a specific task* ensures efficiency in task performance and interaction flexibility; thus allowing for different levels of user experience and profiles. To investigate this property, the *All-Path* [5] function was developed to search the model state space for all the existing paths between two states. Other functions were also developed to be combined with the *AllPath* function for this search.

4 Model Analysis

The model analyses focus on the verification of usability properties in the model's state space. The CPN formalism offers Design/CPN [1] as a supporting tool to model building, simulation and verification. Using this tool, one can obtain the model's Occurrence graph (Occ) and a standard report on the model properties. Some of the model properties can be verified directly on the tool's standard report, while others demand the functions developed specifically for the purpose of investigating alternative navigation paths between states.

The navigation paths analysis allows investigating alternative ways of performing a task in the modelled system. As a result the designer can anticipate interaction problems related to the existence of paths which: (a) allow the operator to perform forbidden or inappropriate actions, (b) take the operator to the end of the task without having completed it, (c) change the prescribed order of actions. Anticipating these problems can lead into a more ergonomic and safer interaction.

In order to analyze the navigation paths it is necessary to perform three steps: (1) determine the initial and final state of the interaction related to the task; (2) identify in the state space all the possible paths between those states and (3) analyze the actions that constitute each state, looking for potential flaws that could lead into errors.

Determining, in the model state space, the task's initial and end states that comply with a specific search criteria is non-trivial, since the search parameters vary according to the intended precision of the search result. It implies searching for all the navigation paths that include a specific subset of the interface elements (such as switches, buttons, etc), which can vary from just a few to all of the objects present in the model. This translates into finding all the places in the CPN model which have their tokens in predefined states. To help the designer, functions were written to return all the states that satisfy a specified predicate. The function *Def_est* returns a list with all the states that comply with a specific predicate.

The *AllPath* function was developed to identify in the model's state space all the possible paths between states, overcoming the analysis limits of the Design/CPN tool. This function was rewritten to overcome its original restriction of applying only to models with 100 to 200 states. This was achieved by discarding the paths of no interest and limiting the number of interactions. This function's parameters are: the initial state, the final state, the path size and the number of iterations. The path size determines the number of navigation steps to be considered in the search. It means that it will return all the navigation paths up to the specified number of steps found within the specified number of iterations, and the information on having reached or not the entire space state.

Having found and listed all the possible paths between two states, these must be analyzed in terms of the actions that can be performed when the user follows them. Design/CPN allows verifying the model markings for a specific model state using the function *DisplayNodes*. To analyze the navigation path between states one must analyze each node of interest and compare it with the subsequent one. This means comparing places to determine the changes between model states. The node comparison task, performed manually, is tedious, subject to errors and can be unfeasible depending on the number of paths and the number of nodes in each path. To simplify it, a function was written that compares two nodes in the space state and returns only the places with different markings. Its output is similar to the function *DisplayNodes* in Design/CPN, highlighting the difference between two nodes. It follows an example of its application to the case study:

```
Difference between node 169 and node 296 is:
Login'Allow_Nav 1: 1`nav_perm --- Login'Allow_Nav 1: empty
```

On this example there was a change in one place (*Allow_Nav*) in the model page *Login*. The place *Allow_Nav*, in node 169, had 1 token of type *nav_perm,* and in node 296 had no token left. Analyzing the change, given the inexistence of tokens in the place *Allow_Nav* models "no navigation allowed", one concludes that an action blocked the user navigation.

4.1   Case Study Analysis

Initially the analysis was performed on the tool's standard report, focusing on the model's home properties; then it progressed into the verification of the model navigation properties. From the CPN tool standard report it was concluded that the Occ generation was full; therefore the properties' verification could be performed in all of the model's state space. From the report it was found. That no home markings implied the inexistence of dead markings which represented the interface exit points. Removing the exit points from the model and recalculating the state space, the new report showed that all the states became home markings. This result implies that the system operator can reach any state from any point of the interface. This is a desirable situation since dead markings, other than the exit points, would imply "dead ends" in the interface navigation which would prevent the operator from performing the task.

From the navigation property verification the results obtained were: the *Reinitialization* property was verified; the *Reversibility* was also verified and the property *Access to Exit points* does not apply to the context of supervisory systems, for safety reasons.

For the case study the interaction scenario analyzed consisted of closing the voltage line TL01Y3 at the substation using the supervisory software. It follows the description of the analysis three steps.

The first step consisted in finding the interaction's initial and end state. During this step the function *def_est* was employed with its parameters related to the line's switch break and switch gear states. Initially the line was in the open state followed by a closed state. The function returned only one state matching the specified condition:

```
Line TL01Y3 open - 267
Line TL01Y3 closed - 1
```

The second step consisted in applying the function AllPath to identify all the possible paths that connect the initial and final states, found in the previous step. Knowing that there are three elements involved in the interaction, one concludes that the number of intermediate states during the interaction was seven (the initial state, plus two states for each element). Therefore, the path length to be researched by the function in the state space was up to seven states. To limit the AllPath function's processing time, the iterations were limited to 5000000.

Function call: `AllPath(267,1,7,5000000);`

Result:

```
List:
[ 267, 631, 824, 1737, 268, 637, 1 ]
[ 267, 631, 824, 1736, 272, 663, 1 ]
[ 267, 630, 66, 176, 268, 637, 1 ]
[ 267, 630, 66, 174, 10, 32, 1 ]
[ 267, 629, 67, 184, 272, 663, 1 ]
[ 267, 629, 67, 182, 10, 32, 1 ]
List Size: 6
AllPath finished - Iterations: 3924
val it = () : unit
```

The third step in the case study analysis, consisted in verifying, for each navigation path, the progressive changes between the model states. The function *cnodes* compares two consecutive states in the navigation sequence, searching for differences between them and returns a list of places with different markings. Then the function was employed to compare pairs of nodes, within the six navigation paths obtained in the previous step. It follows this function's calls related to the third navigation path `[267, 630, 66, 176, 268, 637, 1]` in the previous list:

```
cnodes(267,630);
cnodes(630,66);
cnodes(66,176);
cnodes(176,268);
cnodes(268,637);
cnodes(637,1);
```

and the *cnodes* function's output:

```
Difference between node 267 and node 630 is:
Loc_Rem'Allow_Nav 1: 1`allow_nav --- Loc_Rem'Allow_Nav 1: empty
Switchgear'SG_Open 1: 1`(TL01Y3,SG31Y34)++ 1`(TL01Y3,SG31Y35) ---
    Switchgear'SG_Open 1: 1`(TL01Y3,SG31Y35)
Switchgear'Wait_Conf_Close 1: empty --- Switchgear'Wait_Conf_Close 1:
    1`(TL01Y3,SG31Y34)
val it = () : unit
```

The results indicate that the places **Loc_Rem'Allow_Nav, Switchgear'SG_Open** and **Switchgear'Wait_Conf_Close,** had their markings changed; meaning that the switchgear SG31Y34 was closed. Analyzing all six navigation paths it was possible to anticipate potential interaction errors such as performing the task in a wrong sequence of steps. Having identified the potential errors due to: changes in the prescribed sequence of actions, missing or non-pertinent actions; the designer can introduce mechanisms such as warnings and navigation restrictions during the interaction.

5 Final Considerations and Future Directions

Since most industrial incidents are related to human procedures, it is assumed that improving system's ergonomics will reduce the human error. As discussed in this paper, user interface model analysis helps to eradicate flaws that may induce human errors. This paper has presented a CPN navigation model and its application to a case study related to the use of supervisory software in the electricity industry. To ensure the feasibility of the analysis procedures, and reduce the manual efforts involved, functions were developed to help the interface designer search the model's state space.

From the preliminary results the authors are confident that the adoption of the proposed properties along with function's support during model analysis can bring considerable gains to the design of human interfaces, in the chosen context. Knowing alternative navigation paths, between two interface states, during task performance is essential to design more effective and safe interactive systems.

Several prospects are envisaged to complement and deepen this research work in terms of the analysis approach. Initially it is proposed to refine the AllPath function to account for the reversibility of actions. This will allow for a simplification in the alternative path analysis. In addition it is intended to add behavioural characteristics to the objects' models such as faulty behaviour, and to expand it to represent new objects. Representing material faults will widen the scope of the analysis. It is also planned to parameterize the objects´ models in order to turn the navigation model into a framework capable of representing a variety of human interface designs found in the industrial electricity sector. This framework will simplify the designer modelling task.

References

1. Design/CPN, http://www.daimi.au.dk/designCPN/
2. Hussey, A., MacColl, I., Carrington, D.: Assessing Usability from Formal User-Interface Designs. software Verification Research Centre TR00-15, The University of Queensland (May 2000)
3. Jensen, K.: Coloured Petri Nets. Basic Concepts, Analysis Methods and Practical Use. Monographs in Theoretical Computer Science, vol. 1. Springer, Heidelberg (1992)
4. Sousa, M.R.F., Turnell, M.F.Q.V.: User Interface Based on Coloured Petri Nets Modeling and Analysis. In: Proceedings of the 1998 IEEE International Conference on Systems Man and Cybernetics, San Diego, USA (1998)
5. Turnell, M.F.Q.V., Scaico, A., Sousa, M.R.F., Perkusich, A.: Industrial User Interface Evaluation Based On Coloured Petri Nets Modelling and Analysis. In: Johnson, C. (ed.) DSV-IS 2001. LNCS, vol. 2220, pp. 69–87. Springer, Heidelberg (2001)

Tool Support for Representing Task Models, Dialog Models and User-Interface Specifications

D. Reichart, A. Dittmar, P. Forbrig, and M. Wurdel

University of Rostock, Department of Computer Science,
Chair in Software Engineering,
Albert-Einstein Str. 21,
18059 Rostock, Germany
daniel.reichart@uni-rostock.de

Abstract. This paper focuses on the visualization of task models. Models in general can be presented in different ways. We focus on tool support for different editors working on the same instance of a task model.

1 Introduction

During the last years a lot of tools for task models have been developed and proven to be especially useful for requirements specification. Nevertheless, it was recognized that in the HCI community well established notations like CTT [3] cause some problems in other communities. This might be especially the case since task diagrams are not part of the Unified Modeling Language [10].

In [2] we already discussed some relations between task models and activity diagrams. In the following we briefly demonstrate tools for different task representation. It is assumed that the reader is familiar with task models.

2 Task-Model Representation

We already mentioned that CTT is some kind of standard in the HCI community to represent task models. Originally our task models were presented in a slightly different form because we attached roles, artifacts, tools and devices to tasks. Of course these models can be presented in a CCT-like style as well. We developed an Eclipse [4] plugin for this purpose. The visualization of a task model can be seen in figure 1.

Fig. 1. Task model for writing mails in a CTT-like presentation

T.C.N. Graham and P. Palanque (Eds.): DSVIS 2008, LNCS 5136, pp. 92–95, 2008.

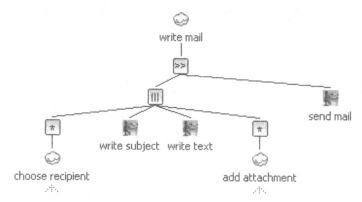

Fig. 2. Task model for writing mails in an operator-centric

To understand the model of figure 1 one has to know the priorities of the temporal relations. With another presentation this can be avoided. In figure 2 it is quit clear what has to be done before "send mail" can be executed.

We already mentioned that Task models are not part of UML. Therefore, it seems to be wise to offer software engineers an opportunity to get a presentation of a task model as activity diagram, a first citizen of UML.

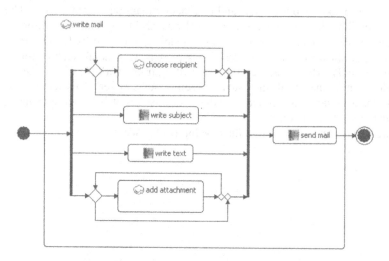

Fig. 3. Task model for writing mails as activity diagram

Based on these task models that already can be animated, dialog graphs are specified that allow to generate canonical abstract prototypes that later are refined to concrete user interfaces [11]. Figure 4 gives an impression how the graph specification looks like. During the demonstration animated specifications, animated canonical abstract prototypes and animated concrete prototypes will be shown.

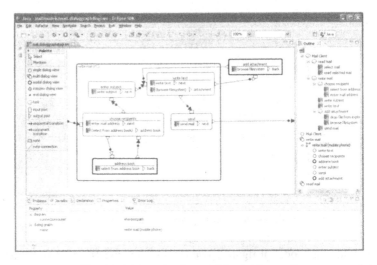

Fig. 4. Dialog and task model for writing mails

3   Model-Based Development of Tool Support

After several years of individual software development we recently used the MDA approach [8] to specify our models and to generate main parts of our tools. The technology offered by the eclipse environment [4] was used to develop our editors.

Based on Meta models and the eclipse modeling frameworks [5] editors can be generated that allow the manipulation of task models. In general, such editors are not very user friendly. However, the graphical editing framework [6] offers a technology to develop editors that fulfill the usability requirements better. These editors work on the same data mode as the generated editor. In this way it is possible to manipulate model daty by different editors.

Figure 4 gives an impression of the development process.

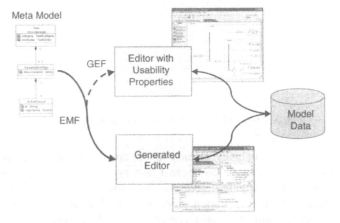

Fig. 5. General approach for model-based development in the object-oriented world

4 Summary and Outlook

Concepts were discussed how task model can be made more attractive for different communities by presenting them in different ways. Based on one single internal model different editors with different presentations and interactions can be use.

Temporal relations available in task models but missing in UML can be represented by stereotypes. This was not discussed in this paper but will be demonstrated.

During the demonstration it will also be shown how modules can be introduced into dialog specification and how this helps to specify user interfaces for different platforms.

References

1. Berti, S., Correani, F., Mori, G., Paternò, F., Santoro, C.: A transformation-based environment for designing multi-device interactive applications. In: Proceedings of the 9th international conference on Intelligent user interfaces, Funchal (January 2004)
2. Brüning, J., Dittmar, A., Forbrig, P., Reichart, D.: Getting SW Engineers on Board: Task Modelling with Activity Diagrams. In: Proc. of EIS 2007, Salamanca, Spain (March 2007)
3. CTTE, http://giove.cnuce.cnr.it/ctte.html (visited: 20.02.08)
4. Eclipse, http://www.eclipse.org/ (visited: 20.02.08)
5. EMF, http://www.eclipse.org/emf/ (visited: 20.02.08)
6. GEF, http://www.eclipse.org/gef/ (visited: 20.02.08)
7. GMF, http://www.eclipse.org/gmf/ (visited: 20.02.08)
8. MDA, http://www.omg.org/mda/ (visited: 20.02.08)
9. Mori, G., Paternò, F., Santoro, C.: Design and Development of Multidevice User Interfaces through MultipleLogical Descriptions. IEEE Transactions on Software Engineering, 507–520 (2004)
10. UML, http://www.uml.org (visited: 20.02.08)
11. Wolff, A., Forbrig, P., Dittmar, A., Reichart, D.: Tool Support for an Evolutionary Design Process using Patterns. In: Proc. of the Workshop: Multi-channel Adaptive Context-sensitive (MAC) Systems: Building Links Between Research Communities, Glasgow (2006)

Towards a Library of Workflow User Interface Patterns

Josefina Guerrero García[1], Jean Vanderdonckt[1], Juan Manuel González Calleros[1],
and Marco Winckler[1,2]

[1]Université catholique de Louvain, Belgian Laboratory of Computer-Human Interaction,
Place des Doyens, 1 – B-1348 Louvain-la-Neuve, Belgium
[2] IHCS-IRIT, Université Paul Sabatier, 118 route de Narbonne, Toulouse F-31062, France
{josefina.guerrero, juan.gonzalez}@student.uclouvain.be,
jean.vanderdonckt@uclouvain.be, winckler@irit.fr

Abstract. A collection of user interface design patterns for workflow information systems is presented. Each Workflow User Interface Pattern (WUIP) is
characterized by properties expressed in the PLML markup language for expressing patterns and augmented by additional attributes and models attached to
the pattern: the abstract user interface and the corresponding task model. These
models are specified in a User Interface Description Language. All WUIPs are
stored in a library and can be retrieved within a workflow editor that links each
workflow pattern to its corresponding WUIP, thus giving rise to a user interface
for each workflow pattern. The software then gathers these UIs and the ones
corresponding to workflow tasks into a user interface flow, a new concept introduced for specifying the intertwining of interfaces used by workers and the
workflow manager in a single workflow.

Keywords: design pattern, user interface description language, user interface
flow, workflow information system, workflow model editor, WUIP.

1 Introduction

Workflow is defined as the automation of business process. It allows better alignment
of Information Technology (IT) with business because organization applications can
be expressed in a way that makes sense to business users. Business users are the organization's resources who are performing work, accomplishing business goals. Assigning tasks to resources is complicated due to the different levels of skills they have,
for instance: experience or availability to do the task. To address the allocation problem, a collection of workflow resource patterns [9] has been identified that provide
the manner in which tasks are allocated or offered to resources. Generally a resource
needs an agenda to handle their tasks, and a manager needs to control the way tasks
are assigned and their progress. A Workflow Information System (WfIS) is a system
that defines, creates and manages the execution of workflows through the use of software; the users of a WfIS interact with it through its user interfaces (UIs).

Developing UIs for WfIS represents new challenges today, not only for its diversity
but also because user interaction takes place in two different logical levels synchro-
nously. Interaction at the higher level means the manager specifying and designing the
system, for that purpose UIs for workflow resource patterns are needed; in addition,

T.C.N. Graham and P. Palanque (Eds.): DSVIS 2008, LNCS 5136, pp. 96–101, 2008.
© Springer-Verlag Berlin Heidelberg 2008

managers needs a UI monitoring workflow execution. Interaction at the lower level, resources are carrying out (UIs are needed for the actual execution of tasks) their allocated tasks (UIs with users agendas) whose current status is then communicated to the manager.

This paper aims to define a library of UI patterns for WfIS addressing the aforementioned challenges; the library is intended to represent the largest collection as possible of UI design patterns that are applicable to workflow resources patterns in a WfIS. The paper is organized as follows: Section 2 reports the state of the art, Section 3 describes the methodology for creating *workflow UI patterns* (WUIP), Section 4 explains how these WUIP could be then interpreted in terms of a WfIS. Section 5 presents how to link the UIs generated. Section 6 presents a conclusion of this work and some future avenues.

2 State of the Art

A *pattern* is referred to as "the abstraction from a concrete form which keeps recurring in specific non-arbitrary contexts" [8]. A *design pattern* systematically names, motivates, and explains a general design that addresses a recurring design problem in object-oriented systems [2]. A UI design pattern is a particular instantiation of the pattern concepts in Human-Computer Interaction (HCI). According to the Pattern Language Markup Language (PLML) that resulted from two ACM CHI workshops aimed at defining a common format for UI patterns, a pattern is typically characterized by: a meaningful short name, an alternate name (alias), a general description of the problem, and the solution. It also gives implementation hints and examples. Many interesting works have been achieved that resulted in UI pattern collections (www.cs.kent.ac.uk/people/staff/saf/patterns/plml.html). In HCI, UIs have been subject to the pattern-based approach [10], but also other aspects such as domain, task, dialog, and abstract UI patterns have been considered successfully [7,10,14].

Workflow patterns refer specifically to recurrent problems and proven solutions related to the development of WfIS in particular, and more broadly, of process-oriented applications. On the one hand, several languages have been proposed for designing, specifying, and verifying workflow processes and patterns, and on the other hand, there are many commercial workflow management systems where control-flow and data-flow are well addressed. Workflow resource patterns have been identified that capture the different manners in which resources are presented and used in workflows [9]. The rationale for identifying these patterns was the need to master the many ways according which work can be distributed. The researchers have developed a web site (http://www. workflowpatterns.com/patterns/resource/) that contains descriptions and examples of theses patterns, along with supporting tool (YAWL), papers and evaluations of how workflow products support the patterns. However, not all considers mechanisms for resource handling and they all lack from UI generation from workflow specifications.

In order to structure the development cycle of a workflow UI, we are relying on FlowiXML [4], a structured method for developing UIs of a WfIS that advocates the automation of business processes according to a model-driven engineering approach based on the requirements and processes of the organization. Model-driven UI design [1, 5, 6] is intended to assist designers to obtain UIs with a formal method, preferably one that is computer-supported. Several works have addressed the specific need for modeling UI for workflows [11, 12], all of them adopting a model-based approach but none of them generating UIs.

3 Developing User Interfaces for Workflow Information Systems

The methodology is applicable: i) to integrate human and machines based activities, in particular those involving interaction with IT applications and tools; and ii) to identify how tasks are structured, who perform them, what their relative order is, how they are offered or assigned, how tasks are tracked.

In this section, only an overview of this method is provided, for the complete definition of the semantics and the syntax, we refer to [4, 13]. The underlying conceptual model is composed of four models: *workflow*, *process*, *task*, and *organization*. The workflow model is recursively decomposed into processes which are in turn decomposed into tasks. A *process model* indicates the ordering of processes in time, space, and resources. Each process gives rise to a process model structured and ordered with process operators. Process operators determine whether the flow of work is sequential, parallel split, exclusive choice or multiple choices, with the corresponding merger operators, synchronization and simple merge. A *task model* represents a decomposition of tasks into sub-tasks linked with task relationships. Transformations are applied in cascade through the workflow layers using a mapping model. In order to support the mapping between the layers, predefined relationships were used: reification, decomposition, isExecutedIn, etc. [13].

By exploiting task models description, different solution scenarios can be modeled [4]. Each scenario represents a particular sequence of actions to be performed. Task models do not impose any particular implementation so that user tasks can be better analyzed without implementation constraints; it is, even possible to analyze user activities. Finally, the UI is derived from scenarios extracted from task models using a transformational approach [3]. FlowiXML is compliant with the Cameleon Reference Framework [1] for developing multi-target UIs.

4 Workflow User Interface Patterns

After having defined the methodological context in the previous section, this section will introduce, define, and explore the original concept of Workflow User Interface Pattern (WUIP).

We adopted the following methodology for defining the WUIPs:

1. *Augmented UI pattern definition*: from each workflow resource pattern a WUIP is created and consistently described through PLML attributes. In addition to those attributes, we also introduced the following fields that we believed that were missing from the version 1.1 of PLML: strengths, weaknesses, opportunities, and threads (according to a SWOT analysis that is missing because PLML only incorporates forces), a category, an evidence scale (from 0=no evidence supports the pattern to 5=two or more experiments support the pattern), a taxonomy of links between patterns (e.g., X uses Y in its solution, X is a variant of Pattern Y, X has a similar problem as Y, X is related in the related patterns section to Y, X specializes Y, X connects to Y), bibliographic reference, domains of human activity.

2. *Incorporation in the model-driven engineering method*: for each initial pattern definition resulting from the previous step, a task model has been specified using CTT notation [6]. This task model may serve as task patterns for WfIS like they serve in related work [7, 14].

3. *Final WUIPs*: from the task model resulting from the previous steps, an abstract UI and, consequently, a concrete UI have been defined in terms of the User Interface Description Language (here, UsiXML) so as to form corresponding abstract and concrete UI models. These two pairs of models have then been attached to the current pattern definition to finally obtain a complete WUIP. Each aspect of the abstract or concrete UI that tackles some concept incorporated in the model-driven engineering method can now be expressed in terms of the expanded UIDL.

Applying the above methodology resulted in 43 WUIPs [3]. We give below only a snapshot of some of these patterns for facilitating the understanding and for illustration purpose. Also, to support the application of the 43 WUIPs, a special module has been developed in Java and incorporated in our workflow model editor, see Fig. 1. This module B) enables the designer, while modeling the general workflow, to retrieve any WUIP from the library, to configure it, and to automatically incorporate it in the current model. Therefore, instead of redefining the complete pattern in terms of model elements found in the model editor (the workflow is defined by Petri nets), the application of a WUIP automatically includes the corresponding definition in the model and generates the corresponding UsiXML files for the UI that has been predefined for each WUIP and for defining the workflow (being itself entirely described in UsiXML).

Deferred allocation pattern – The ability to defer specifying the identity of the resource that will execute a task until runtime. Fig. 1 B reproduces how the pattern is retrieved from the library at design-time and precisely defined in the workflow editor (Fig, 1 A).

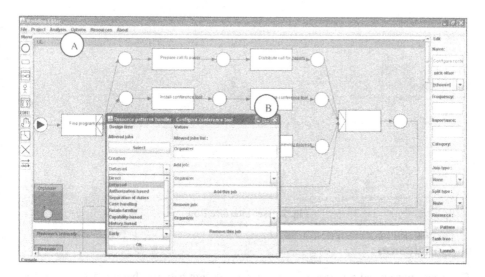

Fig. 1. Workflow resource pattern in design phase of workflow

5 Linking All User Interfaces

After having defined the UIs corresponding to the workflow patterns through the WUIP mechanism, we still need to produce UIs corresponding to tasks found in the process. These UIs can be produced by any appropriate method, such as [5, 6]. After that, we need now to link all the UIs: the ones for the workflow management and the ones for the workflow tasks. This will be achieved thanks to a new concept introduced in this paper; the *user Interface flow*. During the execution of work, information passes from one resource to another as tasks are finished or delegated; in our method we use an agenda assigned to each resource to manage the tasks that are allocated/offered to her/him, and a work list that allows to workflow manager views and manages the tasks that are assigned to resources. By linking UIs we expect to solve the problem of synchronizing the communication among them.

A *User Interface Flow* is defined as an octuple UIF (A, Σ, U, T, δ, ω, ai, ao) where (Fig. 2 depicts it graphically):

➤ A is a nonnegative finite set of Abstract Containers (AC).
➤ Σ is a set of input events [set of events occurring in AC].
➤ U is a nonnegative set of user stereotypes, such that $\forall$ a $\in$ A: $\exists$! u $\in$ U † is used by (a,u) [unique] or $\exists$ u_1, u_2... u_n $\in$ U † is used by {a, u_1, u_2... u_n} [a is shared among u_1, u_2... u_n].
➤ T is a set of output transitions [output transitions means a navigation from starting AC to a final one, we do not want to commit ourselves to a particular type or representation].
➤ δ is a transition function, δ : A x Σ $\rightarrow$ A [a transition is AC + abstract event occurring in one AC]
➤ ω is an output function, ω : A $\rightarrow$ T
➤ a_i is the initial AC [a_i $\in$ A], a_o is the final AC [a_o $\in$ A, $a_o \neq a_i$]

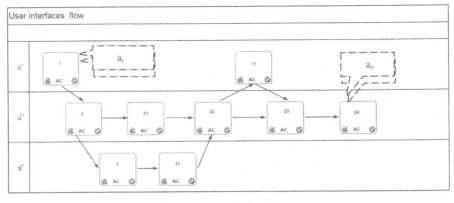

Fig. 2. User interface flow

6 Conclusion

This paper introduced a library of user interface design patterns that are particularly applicable to user interfaces of workflow information systems. Each pattern is compatible with the literature and has been integrated in a workflow model editor. Designers are able now to specificity resource allocation patterns using UIs that fits: both at design-time (when everything is clear) and at run-time (when design decisions were postponed and manager must decide how to allocate the task), considering constraints imposed by mutually excluded patterns (for instance, once a task has been directed allocated it can not be defined as deferred). Of course, these specifications can be edited before producing the system code. The results of the modeling phase with respect to the UI viewpoint introduces a the concept of user interface flow we have formally defined and illustrated including how various users involved in the workflow will collaborate and their corresponding user interface. Finally, from our previous work, we are benefit from its capability to automatically generate UIs from specifications for both the workflow model (in this way, it is no longer needed to redraw the definition of the pattern in terms of places and transitions) and the user interface model (in this way, it is no longer needed to specify again the UI supporting the workflow pattern).

References

1. Calvary, G., Coutaz, J., Thevenin, D., Limbourg, Q., Bouillon, L., Vanderdonckt, J.: A Unifying Reference Framework for Multi-Target User Interfaces. Interacting with Computers 15(3), 289–308 (2003)
2. Gamma, E., Helm, R., Johnson, R., Vlissides, J.: Design Patterns: Elements of Reusable Object-Oriented Software. Addison-Wesley, Reading (1994)
3. Guerrero, J., Vanderdonckt, J.: Workflow user interfaces patterns. Working Paper IAG 08/08, Université catholique de Louvain, Louvain-la-Neuve (2008)
4. Guerrero, J., Vanderdonckt, J.: FlowiXML: a Step towards Designing Workflow Management Systems. Journal of Web Engineering 4(2) (2008)
5. Kristiansen, R., Trætteberg, H.: Model-Based User Interface Design in the Context of Workflow Models. In: Proc. of Tamodia 2007, pp. 227–239. Springer, Berlin (2007)
6. Paternò, F.: Model-based design and evaluation of interactive applications. Applied Computing. Springer, Berlin (1999)
7. Radeke, F., Forbrig, P., Seffah, A., Sinnig, D.: PIM Tool: Support for Pattern-Driven and Model-Based UI Development. In: Proc. of Tamodia 2006, pp. 82–96. Springer, Heidelberg (2006)
8. Riehle, D., Züllighoven, H.: Understanding and Using Patterns in Software Development. Theory and Practice of Object Systems 2(1), 3–13 (1996)
9. Russell, N., van der Aalst, W.M.P., ter Hofstede, A.H.M., Edmond, D.: Workflow Resource Patterns: Identification, Representation and Tool Support. In: Pastor, Ó., Falcão e Cunha, J. (eds.) CAiSE 2005. LNCS, vol. 3520, pp. 216–232. Springer, Berlin (2005)
10. Seffah, A., Gaffar, A.: Model-based user interface engineering with design patterns. Journal of Systems and Software 80(8), 1408–1422 (2007)
11. Stavness, N., Schneider, K.A.: Supporting Flexible Business Processes with a Progression Model. In: Proc. of MBUI 2004. CEUR Workshop, January 13, 2004, vol. 103 (2004)
12. Stolze, M.: Riand, Ph., Wallace, M., Heath, T.: Agile Development of Workflow Applications with Interpreted Task Models. In: Proc. of Tamodia 2007, pp. 2–14. Springer, Heidelberg (2007)
13. UsiXML, http://www.usixml.org
14. Wurdel, M., Forbrig, P., Radhakrishnan, T., Sinnig, D.: Patterns for Task- and Dialog-Modeling. In: Proc. of HCI International 2007, vol. 1, pp. 1226–1235 (2007)

Specification and Verification of Multi-agent Systems Interaction Protocols Using a Combination of AUML and Event B

Leila Jemni Ben Ayed and Fatma Siala

UTIC : Research Unit of Technologies of Information and Communication ESSTT, 5, Avenue Taha Hussein, P.B. : 56, Bab Menara, 1008 Tunis, Tunisia
leila.jemni@fsegt.rnu.tn, fatma.siala@gnet.tn

Abstract. In this paper, we present a specification and verification technique for interaction protocols in multi-agent systems using a combination of Agent Unified Modeling Language (AUML) and the Event B method. The objective is to improve the semi-formal representation of agents, their precedence relation and protocol states as well as the formal analysis of safety and liveliness. The interaction protocol is initially modeled using the AUML protocol diagram. Then, the resulting model is translated into Event B and enriched with required interaction protocols properties to be verified using a B powerful support tool: B4free. In this paper, we focus on the translation process of AUML protocol diagrams into Event B and we illustrate our technique by an example of multi-agent systems interaction protocol.

Keywords: Multi-Agent System, specification, verification, AUML, Event B.

1 Introduction

Multi-Agent Systems (MAS) [6] are characterized by a complex behavior linked to abundant interaction between distributed entities which exchange data and coordinate their activities in order to achieve common goals. They require a high level of safety and reliability. To reduce the complexity and reach a necessary degree of reliability and safety, it would be quite interesting to lay out a specification approach which simplifies the requirement description and deals with mathematical notations inducing verification.

In the past few years, many research efforts have focused on the specification and the verification of the MAS. Agent UML [9], has been proved useful for the specification of multi-agent systems. AUML extends different diagrams of UML to model MAS in four views, agents, environment, interaction and organization. In particular, class diagrams in AUML model the organization and represent different agent roles and the relations between them, statechart diagrams represent agents behaviors, protocol diagrams, which extend sequence diagrams, model the agents interactions. Other diagrams are proposed [9] to model the indeterminism in MAS. AUML with its new diagrams provides many advantages to agent systems design, such as simplified training and unified communication between development teams. However, AUML lacks a precise semantic and in consequence, it does not allow verification of required

T.C.N. Graham and P. Palanque (Eds.): DSVIS 2008, LNCS 5136, pp. 102–107, 2008.

properties of interaction protocols. On the other hand, formal methods are the mathematical foundation for software. They increase the quality of applications development and perform their reliability. Several solutions have been proposed for the specification of MAS using formal methods. Bakam [3] proposed to model protocol interactions in MAS with coloured petri networks. This formalism is limited by the space explosion which requires some simplification of the model. Another work has been proposed in [10] by Regayeg et al. to define a new language based on the Z notation and the linear temporal logic LTL allowing specifications of the internal part of agents and interaction protocol (communications) between agents. The use of Z supporting tools allows to verify the specifications, but the proposed patterns/formalisms do not deal with dynamics of physical worlds. Another problem in using this solution is related to combinatorial explosion in state number in the modelled system. Thought formal methods led to better precision than semi formal ones, they are still difficult to learn and to use. This is why we need a graphical representation of such notations. As pointed out in the literature [8], an appropriate combination of semi-formal techniques and formal methods can give rise to a practical and rigorous Multi-Agent interaction protocol development method.

In this context, we propose in this paper a new specification and a verification technique for Multi-Agent Systems interaction protocols using AUML protocol diagram which give readable models and the Event B method which allows verification of required properties related to relation between agents and protocols states. The proposed translation gives a formal semantic for the AUML protocol diagrams using the Event B. Then, we can rigorously verify AUML by analyzing derived B specifications also some elements can be represented in the Event B model to verify deadlock non existence and precedence relations. In the proposed technique, the MAS interaction protocols are initially modeled with AUML protocol diagrams. After that, the resulting graphical and readable model is translated into Event B in incremental development. This resulting model is enriched by relevant properties (safety (deadlock-inexistence), liveliness (precedence relation), strong fairness, etc) which will be proved using a B powerful tool, like B4free [4]. Other works proposed the use of semi-formal and formal methods for the design of interaction protocols in MAS. Hilaire et al. [7] proposed a general framework for modelling MAS that focuses on organisational aspects. Authors define OZS as a formal notation combining Object-Z and statecharts, in order to represent agents, their behaviors and their interactions. However this model does not address dynamical aspects of MAS. Fadil and Koning [5] proposed a solution combining AUML with B AMN (Abstract Machine Notation) [1]. Our work, which combines the use of AUML and Event B, is near to the one of [5]. However, we propose translation rules for the concepts of AUML into the notation of the Event B [2] which is more adapted than the B AMN to the specification of MAS as reactive systems. Also, there is a semantic equivalence between messages and interactions in AUML protocol diagram and events in Event B which does not exists with operations in B AMN because operations may be called by the environment. Each agent reacts following an event which can be for example a received message. In this paper, we present the proposed technique using the combination of AUML protocol diagrams and Event B, a sub set of rules translating messages, agents and relations between messages into Event B. By an example of a Contract-Net protocol [9], we illustrate our approach.

construction of the B machine dynamic part and the generation of the invariants describing required properties. These invariants will be verified at the third step with a B tool by proving that the initialization verifies invariants and that every event, if it holds, it preserves invariants.

Construction of the static part: The basic units of the static part are agents, messages and roles.

Rule1. This rule is applied to generate the B machine static part (Fig. 3):

1. From agents, their messages and roles we generate three sets *AGENTS* which corresponds to agent's roles, *MESSAGES* which corresponds to all messages and *STATES_E* which ccorresponds to different states of the system.
2. We add three types of variables: *exchanged_msg, hand_name_event* and *ett. exchanged_msg* describes the exchanged messages between agents. It takes the *(sender, message, receiver)* form. For each system state, identified by the event name, we generate a new variable *hand_name_event*. This variable takes the value 1 when the event holds and 0 in the other case. The variable *ett* represents system states.
3. We initialize the variable *exchanged_msg* to an empty set, each variable *hand_name_event* to 0 and the variable *ett* to *event_begin* in the INITIALISATION clause. For the example in Fig 2.b, we obtain the specification in Fig. 3.

MODEL MCnetprotocol
SETS AGENTS = {initiator, participant};
    MESSAGES ={cfp ,propose, refuse, n_understood, reject, accept, inform, failure} ;
    STATES_E={evt_cfp, evt_d_prn, evt_prn, evt_p, evt_r, evt_n, evt_d_ra, evt_ra, evt_d_if, evt_if, evt_i,
    evt_f, evt_d_evt, evt_a, evt_b, evt_c, evt_t, evt_end, evt_begin};
VARIABLES
    Exchanged_msg, protocol, hand_cfp, hand_d_prn, hand_prn, hand_p, hand_d_ra, hand_ra, hand_d_if,
    hand_if, hand_i, hand_d_e, hand_a, hand_b, hand_c, hand_t, ett
INVARIANTS
    exchanged_msg $\in$ AGENTS $\leftrightarrow$ (MESSAGES$\leftrightarrow$AGENTS)|| hand_cfp $\in$N || hand_d_prn $\in$N ||
    hand_prn $\in$ N || hand_p$\in$ N ||hand_d_ra $\in$ N || hand_ra $\in$ N || hand_d_if $\in$ N || hand_if $\in$N ||
    hand_i$\in$N || hand_d_e$\in$N || hand_a $\in$ N || hand_b $\in$N || hand_c $\in$ N ||hand_t $\in$ N || ett$\in$ STATES_E
INITIALISATION
    Exchanged_msg := $\emptyset$ || hand_cfp:=0 || hand_d_prn:=0 || hand_prn:=0 || hand_p:=0 || hand_d_ra:=0 ||
    hand_ra:=0 || hand_d_if:=0 || hand_if:=0 || hand_i:=0 || hand_d_e:=0|| hand_a:=0|| hand_b:=0||
    hand_c:=0|| hand_t:=0|| ett:=evt_begin

Fig. 3. The static part of the Event B model

Construction of the dynamic part: The dynamic part is derived from simple or complex messages and protocol states. The result appears in the clause EVENTS.

Rule 2. The simple messages: Each message is added as an event. The result for the case of the CFP (Call For proposal) is given in Fig. 4. The guard of this event is the system state (using *ett*) and its action adds to the variable *exchanged_msg*, the new message and changes the value of the system state.

Rule 3. Event occurrence: For each new event *name_event* we generate a new variable *hand_name_event*. This variable takes the value 1 if the event occurs and 0 in the other case.

> **event_cfp** = SELECT ett=evt_begin THEN Exchanged_msg:=exchanged_msg ∪
> {initiator ↦ {cfp ↦ participant}} ‖ ett:= evt_cfp END ;

Fig. 4. Translation of a simple message

Rule 4. Complex messages: AUML contains three complex messages types: XOR, AND and OR. For each message XOR, which generates $M1, M2,...,Mn$ messages, we add two events, the first event *Detect_M1_.._Mn* detects one of the messages. For our example, *Detect_propose_r_n* is the detection event (Fig. 5). The second event *event_M1_...._Mn* send the selected message (*event_propose_refuse_nunderstood* (Fig. 5).

For each message, we assume that the protocol passes through four states: end; active; error and wait. We add a new set (STATES_P = {end, active, error, wait}) and a variable *protocol* modeling protocol states. The action of the event associated to this message will be updated by adding *(protocol:=v)* where v ∈ STATES_P. The variable *protocol* takes the value *active* since the negotiation messages (Call For Proposal, inform,...); *end* on the receipt of a refuse, cancel or agree message; *error* on the receipt of failure message and *wait* in the case of an XOR message where each elementary message makes the protocol in different states. As shown in Fig. 5, CFP is a negotiation message then we update *event_cfp*, by adding *(protocol:= active)*.

> **Detect_propose_r_n** = SELECT hand_cfp=1 ∧ hand_d_prn=0 ∧ ett=evt_cfp
>   THEN ANY ee WHERE ee∈ {propose,refuse, n_understood} THEN msg3:=ee END‖
>   hand_d_prn:=1‖ ett:= evt_d_prn END ;
> **event_propose_refuse_nunderstood** = SELECT hand_d_prn=1 ∧ hand_prn=0 ∧ ett=evt_d_prn
>   THEN Exchanged_msg:=exchanged ∪ {participant ↦ {msg3 ↦ initiator}} ‖
>   hand_prn:=1 ‖ protocol:=wait ‖ ett:=evt_prn END ;
> **event_propose** = SELECT hand_prn=1 ∧ hand_p=0 ∧ ett=evt_prn ∧
>   exchanged_msg(participant)={propose ↦initiator}
>   THEN protocol:=active ‖ hand_p:=1 ‖ ett:= evt_p END;
> **event_refuse** = SELECT hand_prn=1 ∧ hand_p=0 ∧ ett=evt_prn ∧
>   exchanged_msg(participant) = {refuse ↦ initiator}
>   THEN protocol:=end ‖ hand_p:=1 ‖ ett:= evt_r END;
> **event_n_understood** = SELECT hand_prn=1∧ hand_p=0 ∧ ett=evt_prn ∧
>   exchanged_msg(participant) ={n_understood ↦ initiator}
>   THEN protocol:=error ‖ ett:=evt_n ‖ hand_p:=1 END ;

Fig. 5. Translation of the protocol states with a complex message

Fig. 5 shows the translation of the XOR message *event_propose_refuse_nunderstood* which detects one of its elementary messages: *propose, refuse* and *not_understood*.

Rule5. The Deadlock: When no event can be triggered, the system is blocked. That is the deadlock problem. Especially the situation holds when the two conditions: protocol is active and *(time >= time_out)* are verified. To solve this problem, we add a

> **OFF**= SELECT protocol=active ∧ (time ≥ time_out) THEN protocol:=end ‖ ett:=evt_fin END;
> **ON**= SELECT protocol=end ∧ time< time_out THEN protocol:=active ‖ ett:=evt_begin END

Fig. 6. Added events to avoid deadlock

new event OFF, which puts the protocol to *end* under these conditions and the event ON to ensure the resumption of protocol. Fig. 6 shows the result for the example.

Fill up the system with properties: In this step, we enrich the model with invariants describing properties. One of them could express that whenever the system is in a considered state, the protocol takes a certain value. For example, if the system is in CFP state then the protocol is active: *(ett=evt_cfp) ⇒ (protocol= active)*.

3 Conclusion and Perspectives

In this paper, we have proposed a specification and verification technique translating AUML protocol diagrams into Event B. This allows one to rigorously verify AUML models by analyzing derived Event B specifications and to prove that the modeled protocol respects all safety and liveliness constraints. We have presented some of the proposed translation rules for AUML protocol diagrams into Event B and we have illustrated them over the Contract-Net Protocol example. Our future focus shall consists of considering more dynamic properties, proving the correctness of the set of translation rules and developing a tool supporting proposed technique to ensure the systematic verification of required properties.

References

1. Abrial, J.-R.: The B book: Assigning Programs to Meanings. Cambridge University Press, Cambridge (1996)
2. Abrial, J.-R.: Extending B without changing it (for developing distributed systems). In: First B Conference, Putting Into Practice Methods and Tools for Information System Design, France, p. 21 (1996)
3. Bakam, I., Kordon, F., L-Page, C., Bousquet, F.: Formalization of a specialized multi-agent system using coloured petri nets for the study of a hunting management system. In: Rash, J.L., Rouff, C.A., Truszkowski, W., Gordon, D.F., Hinchey, M.G. (eds.) FAABS 2000. LNCS (LNAI), vol. 1871, pp. 123–132. Springer, Heidelberg (2001)
4. Clearsy, http://www.b4free.com/download.htm
5. Fadil, H., Koning, J.-L.: Vers une spécification formelle des protocoles d'interaction des systèmes multi-agents en B. In: 6eConfrence Francophone de MOdlisation et SIMulation; MOSI 2006, Maroc (2006)
6. Ferber, J.: Multi-Agent Systems: An Introduction to Distributed Artificial Intelligence. Addison-wesley Professional, Reading (1999)
7. Hilaire, V., Koukam, A., Gruer, P., Muller, J.-P.: Formal specification and prototyping of multi-agent systems. ESAW000. In: Proceedings of the First International Workshop on Engineering Societies in the Agent World, London, pp. 114–127 (2000)
8. Jemni Ben Ayed, L., Hlaoui Ben Daly, Y.: Translating Graphical Conceptual Model from STATEMATE to FNLOG. In: IEEM 2007: IEEE International Conference on Industrial Engineering and Engineering Management, Singapore (2007)
9. Odell, J., Van Dyke Parunak, H., Bauer, B.: Extending UML for agents. In: Proceedings of the Agent-Oriented Information Systems Workshop at the 17th National conference on Artificial Intelligence. ICue Publishing, Texas (2000)
10. Regayeg, A., Kacem, A.-H., Jmaiel, M.: Specification and verification of multiagent applications using temporal Z. In: Intelligent Agent Technology Conference (IAT 2004), pp. 260–266. IEEE Computer Society, China (2004)

Pattern Languages as Tool for Discount Usability Engineering

Elbert-Jan Hennipman, Evert-Jan Oppelaar, and Gerrit van der Veer

Open Universiteit, School of Computer Science, Valkenburgerweg 177,
6419 AT Heerlen, The Netherlands
ehn@ou.nl, oppelaar@gmail.com, gvv@ou.nl

Abstract. Despite growing pattern collections in the field of Human-Computer Interaction (HCI), both on the Internet [1-3] and in books [4, 5], these collections have usability problems when being used by those software engineers, who lack expertise in human-centered design. In this paper we report on the development of a tool that is intended to improve accessibility and usability of HCI design patterns for engineers. We aim at a tool that is simple and safe to be used without expert knowledge. Such a tool can be used in what could be labeled "discount usability engineering". A new type of HCI pattern language combined with a supportive tool is intended to overcome some of the gaps these engineers have in HCI-background.

Keywords: Discount usability engineering, design pattern languages, HCI.

1 Introduction

"A design pattern is a structured textual and graphical description of a proven solution to a recurring design problem" [6 (p. 7)]. Considering that definition, it can be stated that using design patterns supports making *good design decisions*. It is important to note that *a proven solution* only means that the solution *works*; it does not guarantee that it is *the best solution*. A single design problem may have different solutions depending on a given context [4, 6].

HCI design patterns are a specific case of proven design knowledge. Different from other types of patterns, HCI design patterns can be considered solutions for end-user problems, which are in fact only indirectly problems of the designer [4, 7-9].

At the Interact '99 patterns workshop the purpose of using HCI design patterns was formulated as follows (we inserted the italics to stress the distinction): 'The goals of HCI design pattern languages are

- to share successful HCI design solutions among *HCI professionals*
- to provide a common language for HCI design to *anyone* involved in the design, development, evaluation, or use of interactive systems' [10]

While "sharing" includes the discovery or development of patterns as well as its use, the second bullet points to use in practice of established patterns specifically. We aim at the second group of stakeholders for HCI patterns - *anyone involved in the design, development, evaluation or use of interactive systems*. This broad group of stakeholders

T.C.N. Graham and P. Palanque (Eds.): DSVIS 2008, LNCS 5136, pp. 108–120, 2008.

should be able to use these pattern languages as well. This group includes professional programmer-designers, who often in fact are novices in HCI. They will often be found in small ICT companies and in larger companies with a small ICT department. Currently these companies have a problem: the software engineers and programmers they employ happen to be responsible for Interaction Design and User Interface Design, mostly without adequate specialized education for this. Sometimes, the management of these companies does not even value user-centered design or mistakes this for 'visual design' [11], and, in most cases, no budget is (made) available for usability engineering. These professional programmer-designers should be enabled to make responsible use of pattern languages.

This group of stakeholders needs a tool that supports design decisions. Borchers and Thomas [12] hint in this direction with their question for the discussion panel at CHI 2001 '*Who are HCI design patterns for*, and what should they be used for – as *Design Rationale*, to replace standards or guidelines, or for training in industry and academia?'

Contrary to the goal of HCI design patterns, Seffah and Javahery [13] found that *software developers* 'experience difficulty when attempting to understand, master and apply a specific pattern in their context'. Segerståhl and Jokela [9] found usability problems when pattern collections were used by engineers.

Our project has the flavor of discount usability, but the effect will be different from the approach of Nielsen [14]. Where his approach takes care of saving costs of different usability evaluation steps, our approach is to improve the design decisions of non-experts in usability design.

2 Background

Johnson [11] indicates that usability is often addressed very late in the development stage, shortly before release. Frequently, software engineers find themselves responsible for the Interaction Design during the development, doing 'the best they can under *adverse circumstances*' that 'are created by their management' [11]. We don't advocate the idea of software-engineers being responsible for Interaction Design, but, considering the fact that this is still common practice, they can use all the help they can get.

The use of patterns is becoming common in many engineering domains, including both Software Engineering and HCI. We expect that software engineers will be able to make better Interaction Design decisions if they can use HCI design patterns effectively. The existing usability issues with usability patterns need to be taken care of to make that possible.

2.1 Rationale for the Use of Patterns

There are multiple reasons to choose design patterns for transferring design knowledge:

- using patterns is a familiar activity for software engineers, because patterns have been around and in use in Software Engineering (SE) since about 1995 [15]
- the use of HCI design patterns was found 'highly beneficial' by software developers in an empirical study by Seffah and Javahery [13]

- HCI design patterns are considered to be more effective in transferring knowledge than guidelines, because of the structural way in which problem, context, solution and rationale are connected and discussed [16]. Guidelines have usability issues because they often describe do's as well as don'ts [17]. Patterns formulate examples of good design.
- a volume of practical design knowledge is publicly available and accessible in pattern collections online [1-3] and in books [4-6]. There is a critical mass of knowledge waiting to be used
- relations between patterns make it possible to dynamically create different views on patterns for different tasks and domains, as well as to structure these patterns around a certain problem or in a certain hierarchy

2.2 Usability of Usability Patterns

The usability of HCI design patterns (or usability patterns - there is a mixed use of terminology) has been studied by Seffah and Javahery [13], who identified three main issues that need to be addressed:

1. there is no universally accepted standard for describing HCI design patterns, and the narrative character makes them ambiguous and abstract (as are guidelines)
2. there is no tool support for usability patterns engineering
3. software developers have trouble translating the patterns between different platforms (such as handheld, web and software interfaces)

Segerståhl and Jokela [9] did an empirical evaluation of the usability of HCI design patterns, resulting in a detailed list and in recommendations for improvement. We decided to add the issues identified by Segerståhl and Jokela:

4. none of the existing pattern collections covered all their problem cases
5. existing pattern collections focus on different levels of the design process, such as task (search) or representation (visual design)
6. the naming of HCI design patterns was in some cases inconsistent and difficult to learn
7. a standard way of organizing, grouping and categorizing HCI design patterns is still lacking
8. the same patterns appears with different name when described for a different platform

Fincher et al. [18] indicate that "*little is understood about the activities involved in both creating and using patterns*". One such activity is formulating a problem statement, and according to Borchers [6 (p. 68)] "*it turns out that this part is often the most difficult one to write in a pattern*". For the engineers we focus on, it is even more difficult to formulate a problem statement in the field of HCI, because that is not their expertise. Therefore we add three more usability issues:

9. there is little to no explicit knowledge about the activities involved in *creating* and integrating HCI design patterns in current pattern tools
10. there is little to no explicit knowledge about the activities involved in *using* patterns
11. it is hard for engineers to formulate a problem statement with the end-user in mind

2.3 Relevant Questions

Summarizing the usability issues mentioned above, there are several questions that need answering. When designing and creating a tool meant for knowledge transfer from usability design experts to engineers who are novices in HCI, it is important to externalize the relevant internal knowledge of the experts, resulting in the following questions for the experts:

1. What are the activities involved in the *creation* of patterns, how does this relate to the approach and focus of the pattern?
2. How can we externalize the internal knowledge HCI-experts apply when *using* HCI design patterns, in terms of problem statement and search behavior?

To create a pattern management and exploring tool where experts can create new HCI design patterns and HCI experts and Software Engineers alike can use them consistently, there are questions for an interchangeable pattern format:

3. What is the best way to standardize pattern formatting in terms of organizing, grouping, categorizing, structuring, naming and describing a pattern?
4. Are HCI design patterns platform-specific (e.g. considering target systems with small-screen vs. big-screen, mobile vs. desktop) and if so, how should this be addressed?

We envision a final answer resulting in a decision support tool that uses HCI design patterns to guide problem analysis, problem formulation and problem solving.

3 HCI Design Patterns

There is no strictly defined use of the terms interaction design patterns, user interface design patterns, usability patterns, HCI design patterns and variations of these [19]. What all these terms have in common is that they describe design patterns that are relevant in HCI.

There are several 'living' pattern collections in the field of HCI, some of which have the construct of a pattern language. We define a *pattern collection* as any set of patterns, often with some categorization. A *pattern language* is an interconnected set of patterns [20], organized and structured in a meaningful way from the point of view of the user of the set [21]. If there are enough means to interconnect patterns, a single pattern could be part of different pattern languages. Over the past few years the effectiveness of pattern languages in their current format have been discussed, and suggestions for extension and improvement have been made [7, 22].

Certain aspects of patterns are relevant for answering the questions formulated in section 2, mainly the different approaches to HCI design patterns, pattern language markup language, the relation of HCI patterns to Software Engineering and the existence of anti-patterns. We will deal with each of these aspects in this section.

3.1 Approaches to Patterns

There is no universally accepted classification for HCI design patterns. Consequently, different collections each have their own approach [9].

The approach or view that is most appropriate for the task at hand is determined by the Interaction Designer when searching and browsing through the pattern collection [23]. Though not explicitly defined, some approaches can be identified.

Layered approach

Some HCI pattern collections are based on a view of the user interface (or Human-computer interaction) comprising layers [24-26]:

Task Layer. This relates to task-description patterns. These patterns describe solutions conceptually. An example would be the 'multi-level undo'-task [1].

Semantic Layer. Bridging patterns relate strongly to this layer [19]. A bridging pattern describes the needed assets in software engineering to accommodate a certain user-task. The patterns in this level describe a solution in terms of entities and possible operations on these entities.

Syntactic Layer. This relates to action-description patterns. These patterns describe solutions on a lower level, in terms of dialogues like form filling, wizard, and pull down menus. These are found in several pattern collections [2, 3].

Representation Layer. This considers visual representations, choice of labels, design of icons, etc. We will not consider patterns on this level in our project, though they do exist (e.g. in the designing interfaces collection [3]).

Perspective-based approach

Another approach is perspective-related, making a primary distinction between user initiated actions and system initiated actions [23]:

End-user initiated action. Patterns in this category are about enabling the end-user to do something or to avoid something. E.g., the *Language Selector* [2] pattern, describing the end-users' need to select a preferred language and a solution to that problem.

System initiated action. Patterns in this category are about a problem in the communication of the system to the end-user. The user needs to perceive, understand or know something, and this pattern describes a way of doing that for the given situation and context. E.g., the *progress indicator* [3] pattern, describes the solution to 'how to show the progress of the system on a time-consuming operation'.

In some patterns these two orientations are merged, e.g. the *autocomplete* [4] pattern. The *autocomplete* pattern describes the situation in which an end-user problem (uncertainty in filling forms) and a system problem (preventing input of incorrect information) merge.

Context of design approach

In this approach, patterns are grouped according to their use in a certain context, such as a specific domain (e.g. the *museum pattern* [5]) or with a specific purpose (e.g. the *community building pattern* [6]).

---

[1] http://www.designinginterfaces.com/Multi-Level_Undo
[2] http://www.welie.com/patterns/showPattern.php?patternID=language-selector
[3] http://www.designinginterfaces.com/Progress_Indicator
[4] http://www.welie.com/patterns/showPattern.php?patternID=autocomplete
[5] http://www.welie.com/patterns/showPattern.php?patternID=museum
[6] http://www.welie.com/patterns/showPattern.php?patternID=community-building

Functionality based approach
In this approach patterns are grouped according to their functionality. Each group contains related patterns in the same functional area, such as 'showing complex data' or 'getting around'. This approach is found in the designing interfaces collection by Tidwell [3].

Different approaches work in different situations. Consequently Van Welie and Van der Veer [21, 23] suggest not to choose a specific approach, but to enable multiple approaches. When patterns are interconnected correctly, each approach becomes a pattern language in itself, because of the internal coherence and meaningful structure and organization.

Pattern languages support a more problem oriented way of browsing and searching than pattern collections as such, and, hence allow more efficient problem solving.

3.2 PLML

In an effort to create more unified, accessible pattern languages, the Pattern Language Markup Language (PLML) was introduced in 2003 [27]. The online pattern collection of Welie [2] uses PLML v1.1. PLML is becoming the most universally accepted format to describe HCI patterns. The use of XML makes them relatively easy to exchange. There are disadvantages as well:

- PLML has very few mandatory elements, what makes it flexible, but does not encourage structured pattern creation
- Patterns described in PLML are still highly narrative, which sometimes causes usability problems [13]
- There is little semantics in the area of pattern relations (only three types of relations are defined). This makes the patterns harder to search and filter systematically. Several additional types of relations have been identified that could be relevant, such as '*equivalent, superordinate, subordinate, competitor, and neighboring*' [13].

An extended version of PLML (PLMLx) has been proposed by Bienhaus [28] but Fincher [29] addressed concerns dealing with too many elements becoming mandatory. More recently Deng et al. [30] proposed PLML v1.2. This newer version enables a richer description of patterns and pattern-attributes (most importantly forces and changelogs), to be used with the pattern management tool *MUIP*. PLML v1.2 has not been adopted broadly yet.

PLML is a good candidate answer to our question 3 in section 2.3 '*What is the best way to standardize pattern formatting in terms of organizing, grouping, categorizing, structuring, naming and describing a pattern?*', though not in its current form. We will adapt the newer PLML version to our needs.

3.3 Relating HCI Patterns to SE

A study by Bass and John [31] reveals that some interaction concepts have dependencies in software architecture. They have analyzed these using a scenario-based approach. The same issue was found by Folmer, Van Welie and Bosch [19]. Their solution to closing the gap between interaction concepts and software engineering is introducing bridging patterns. These patterns describe the minimal essential software architecture to accommodate certain user tasks (such as '*multilevel undo*'). From our point of view, this is an interesting addition, considering the background of our target group. This explicit combination will appeal to the software engineer, because the implications of interaction design decisions for the software architecture become clear instantly.

These patterns are also useful in the layered approach at semantic level, describing the problem in terms of entities and operations on these entities.

3.4 Use of Anti-patterns

Biljon et al. [17] have investigated the use of anti-patterns. The intention of anti-patterns is to avoid common pitfalls, but the conclusion of Biljon et al. [17] is that anti-patterns can actually create pitfalls. The cognitive processing of anti-patterns has to deal with negation. They strongly argue not to use anti-patterns, unless the positive pattern has been firmly established. Taking into account that we will be developing for engineers - professionals, but not in HCI - the use of anti-patterns is not considered useful in our project.

4   Pattern Design and Management

Managing and maintaining patterns and pattern collections is especially relevant for patterns that are published on the Internet. Online knowledge can easily be maintained, preventing it from getting stale and being outdated. The Internet has the affordance of being up to date. This is a blessing and a curse: there needs to be commitment to keep the pattern-base up to date, because it is expected to be. Our project is meant to be maintained (by the Dutch Open University that will consider our product a standard part of Computer Science public domain adult education) and validated by HCI experts (the program board of our sponsoring foundation), and relies partly on the commitment of that community.

Pattern design faces several problems, e.g., (4.1.) how to provide characteristic and explaining names for the engineer to choose from [9]; (4.2) how to identify and describe forces and context [6]; (4.3) how to formulate the problem statement [6]; and (4.4) how to create meaningful relations to other patterns [13].

We will demonstrate the difficulties of developing patterns with examples from the Interaction Design Patterns collection by Welie [2].

4.1   Labeling Patterns: Externalizing and Formalizing Problems

Novices in HCI will encounter difficulties to externalize and formalize their ideas of interface problems into a problem statement that fits the pattern collection used. Current HCI design patterns are often titled by the *solution* and not the problem. Patterns are usually indexed or listed by their title, therefore defeating part of their purpose.

In figure 1 the title *autocomplete* does not give away anything about the problem that is being solved, but refers to the solution. Using the *alias*-element in PLML, both making the problem recognizable, and revealing the solution, can be realized. E.g. the alias 'user uncertainty' adds problem-related meaning to the title.

Title: Autocomplete

Problem: The user wants to enter a label that is part of a large set

Solution: Suggest possible label names as users are typing ...

Fig. 1. An excerpt from the *autocomplete pattern* [7] illustrating a bad choice for a pattern title

4.2 Conditions for Pattern Matching: Analysis of Context and Forces

A problem can have different solutions in different contexts. Sometimes alternative solutions for a single problem are in fact patterns on their own. In fact the context has both a *recurring part* and a *differentiating part*. These patterns are not really a single pattern.

In figure 2 we see that 'dozens of ways' are indicated and the three most common solutions are presented. This is a typical case of the narrative character of patterns standing in the way of clear semantics and relations. All three (or even "dozens") solutions should be presented as separate patterns, related to the aggregate pattern by means of an '*is-a*' relationship.

In the same way, each solution will have a different impact on "conflicting forces" [32]. Forces are arguments in favor or against a certain solution. Borchers [6 (p. 68)] labels them 'conflicting interests'. A specific solution has consequences in geometrical layout (screen size), usability (a visual cue when new email arrives is of no use for visually impaired end-users), cognitive aspects (fit to the user's mental model), and system performance (processor load). The use of forces is an answer to our question 4 in section 2.3. Different platforms have different forces, and defining these forces correctly will enable identifying a pattern that fits the platform.

Title: Main Navigation

Problem: Users need to know where they can find what they are looking for.

Solution: Place an always visible menu at a fixed position on the page. Support this main menu with additional navigation tools

Context: All sites need some form of main navigation

How: There are <u>dozens of ways</u> to design the main navigation for your site. However, the most common ones are the *Horizontal Menu* and *Vertical Menu* or *Inverted L Menu*. The choice (...) must be based on the information architecture for the site (*...other constraints mentioned...*)

Fig. 2. An excerpt from the *Main Navigation pattern* [8] illustrating the need for greater pattern separation

4.3 Formulating Problem Statements

As Borchers [6] indicated, formulating the problem statement is one of the most difficult parts in creating a pattern.

---

[7] http://www.welie.com/patterns/showPattern.php?patternID=autocomplete
[8] http://www.welie.com/patterns/showPattern.php?patternID=main-navigation

Title: Fly-out Menu
> *Problem:* Users need to have direct access to sub-navigation but the amount of screen estate for navigation is limited
> *Solution:* Combine horizontal navigation with a sub-menu that flies-out when the users hovers over the main menu-item

Fig. 3. An excerpt from the *Fly-out Menu pattern* [9] illustrating how problems and forces are intertwined

In figure 3 we see an example of a problem statement that consists of two parts: a problem statement (*users need to have direct access to sub-navigation*), and one of the active forces (*the amount of screen estate for navigation is limited*). Separating these two (problem statement and forces) will improve browsing and searching patterns.

4.4 Creating Meaningful and Relevant Relations between Patterns

The pattern collection by Welie [2] is interconnected by means of pattern-links. The previously mentioned Main-Navigation pattern links to the Fly-out Menu pattern, but not vise-versa. These links have no specific meaning, other than 'there is some kind of relation between these patterns'. Often patterns are only linked one-way.

Creating a construct to describe meaningful relations will improve both creating and using patterns, as was found by Seffah and Javahery in the UPADE project [13].

4.5 Putting It Together

This suggested restructuring, formalization, and categorization of patterns will help our target audience of novice HCI designers to identify, as well as understand, the relevant patterns based on *target end-user group (relevant knowledge, skill, experience, and culture), targeted experience, available system resources*, and *available screen size*.

These are now usually implicitly noted in the textual description of context, or even left out if considered trivial (to HCI experts).

5 Requirements

Ultimately, we will combine our efforts in improving HCI pattern usability into a platform (website) where HCI patterns are presented in such a way that they are:

- Manageable by experts (to make sure only validated patterns appear)
- Public domain
- Usable as tools in usability engineering for software engineers
- Guide the engineers in making the right design decisions:
  - Guiding in problem analysis
  - Guiding in problem formulation
  - Guiding in problem solving

---

[9] http://www.welie.com/patterns/showPattern.php?patternID=fly-out-menu

- Accommodate different approaches, as proposed by Van Welie and Van der Veer [21, 23]
- Inviting to software engineers

This aims at a better end-user-experience of the products (websites, applications) being created [7].

6 Project Phases

Our research is a continuation of Van Welie, Van der Veer and Eliëns [16], and seeks to involve model-based user interface (UI) engineering using design patterns as advocated by Ahmed and Ashraf [22]. Both these sources focus on the end-user and apply a task based approach, and so will our project.

Our project is three-tiered. First we need to externalize knowledge that HCI experts have on creating and using HCI patterns. Secondly, we need to create a solid pattern base and a tool to use and maintain these patterns. Thirdly, we need to evaluate, improve and extend the pattern base and tool, by adding more domains.

6.1 Externalizing Expert Knowledge

Both creation and use of design patterns is common practice amongst HCI experts. The implicit knowledge of HCI experts needs to be externalized to become useful for software engineers. We will do this by asking some HCI experts to create a pattern and describe their thoughts and actions using a think aloud protocol. The same approach will be taken to externalize knowledge on the use of HCI patterns. That is the first phase of our project, and will answer questions 1 and 2 from section 2.3. Our aim is mainly to capture the essence and conceptual model behind creation and use of design patterns, and to integrate this in a tool.

6.2 Development of a Single-Domain Based Tool

In the second phase, we will develop a design guidance tool that provides a solid pattern base and the necessary functionality. The tool will use the findings of the first phase to guide software engineers in the use of HCI patterns. Initially we will focus on one domain for which a pattern language is publicly available. In our case this is the museum website domain [33, 34], and our focus will be galleries and smaller museums.

The tool will also have the ability to manage patterns in a guided way, to make sure that the result is usable. The tool will be designed in an iterative way with repeated evaluation of the prototype by engineers with, as well as without, HCI expertise. During this iterative development, evaluation of the prototype will be done through well established usability analysis techniques (e.g. observations, interviews, heuristic evaluations, and usability tests with the System Usability Scale [35, 36]). The software development will be based on the Agile method [37] to incorporate direct feedback and multiple iterations.

6.3 Broadening the Scope

The final step will be to broaden the scope of our project, and introduce more domains. In this phase, the project will be made available in the public domain, and iteratively improved to being used in the wild.

We will present this tool in Q1 of 2009.

7 Summary

In this paper we address the need for ready-to-use design knowledge for those software engineers who lack expertise in human-centered design. That was one of the original goals of HCI design pattern languages, but several studies and our experience learn that this goal has not been achieved (yet). In 2.3 we elicited four main questions about the creation of HCI design pattern languages, and about the use of these pattern languages.

The first two questions address the need to externalize expert knowledge in use as well as creation of patterns. In paragraph 6.1 we describe the use of a think aloud protocol to elicit this "internal" knowledge.

Question 3 addresses the need of pattern standardization and relevant pattern languages, to enable the systematic use thereof. In paragraph 3.2 we introduce PLML as an approach to this question.

Question 4 addresses the need of a platform independent use of HCI design patterns. In paragraph 4.2 we find that *forces* can be used to describe platform-specific characteristics and enables pattern creators to specify platform specific as well as platform independent patterns.

Acknowledgements

This research has been supported by SenterNovem, an agency of the Dutch Ministry of Economic Affairs.

References

1. Yahoo! Design Pattern Library, http://developer.yahoo.com/ypatterns/
2. Patterns in Interaction Design, http://www.welie.com/
3. Designing Interfaces, http://www.designinginterfaces.com/
4. Tidwell, J.: Designing Interfaces. O'Reilly Media, Inc, Sebastopol (2005)
5. Van Duyne, D.K., Landay, J.A., Hong, J.I.: The Design of Sites: Patterns, Principles, and Processes for Crafting a Customer-centered Web Experience. Addison-Wesley Professiona, Reading (2003)
6. Borchers, J.: A Pattern Approach to Interaction Design. John Wiley & Sons, Chichester (2001)
7. van Welie, M., Trætteberg, H.: Interaction Patterns in User Interfaces. In: PLoP 2000 conference (2000)
8. Buschmann, F.: Series Foreword, pp. xiii-xv. John Wiley & Sons, Chichester (2001)

9. Segerståhl, K., Jokela, T.: Usability of interaction patterns. In: Conference on Human Factors in Computing Systems, pp. 1301–1306 (2006)

10. Borchers, J.O., Fincher, S., Griffiths, R., Pemberton, L., Siemon, E.: Usability pattern language: Creating a community. AI & Society 15, 377–385 (2001)

11. Johnson, J.: GUI Bloopers 2.0 Common User Interface Design Don'ts and Dos. Morgan Kaufmann Publishers, San Francisco (2008)

12. Borchers, J.O., Thomas, J.C.: Patterns: what's in it for HCI? In: Conference on Human Factors in Computing Systems, pp. 225–226 (2001)

13. Seffah, A., Javahery, H.: On the Usability of Usability Patterns. In: Workshop entitled Patterns in Practice, CHI (2002)

14. Nielsen, J.: Guerrilla HCI: Using Discount Usability Engineering to Penetrate the Intimidation Barrier. Cost-Justifying Usability, 245-272 (1994)

15. Gamma, E., Helm, R., Johnson, R., Vlissides, J.: Design Patterns: Elements of Reusable Object-Oriented Software. Addison-Wesley, Reading (1995)

16. van Welie, M., van der Veer, G.C., Eliëns, A.: Patterns as Tools for User Interface Design. Tools for Working with Guidelines: Annual Meeting of the Special Interest Group, 313-324 (2000)

17. Van Biljon, J., Kotzé, P., Renaud, K., McGee, M., Seffah, A.: The use of anti-patterns in human computer interaction: wise or Ill-advised? In: Proceedings of the 2004 annual research conference of the South African institute of computer scientists and information technologists on IT research in developing countries, pp. 176–185 (2004)

18. Fincher, S., Finlay, J., Greene, S., Jones, L., Matchen, P., Thomas, J., Molina, P.J.: Perspectives on HCI patterns: concepts and tools. In: Conference on Human Factors in Computing Systems, pp. 1044–1045 (2003)

19. Folmer, E., Welie, M., Bosch, J.: Bridging patterns: An approach to bridge gaps between SE and HCI. Information and Software Technology 48, 69–89 (2006)

20. Schummer, T., Borchers, J., Thomas, J.C., Zdun, U.: Human-computer-human interaction patterns: workshop on the human role in HCI patterns. In: Conference on Human Factors in Computing Systems, pp. 1721–1722 (2004)

21. van Welie, M., van der Veer, G.C.: Pattern Languages in Interaction Design: Structure and Organization. Proceedings of Interact 3, 1–5 (2003)

22. Ahmed, S., Ashraf, G.: Model-based user interface engineering with design patterns. Journal of Systems and Software 80, 1408–1422 (2007)

23. Van Welie, M.: Personal communication, Amsterdam (February 2008)

24. Moran, T.P.: Command Language Grammar: A Representation for the User Interface of Interactive Computer Systems. INT. J. MAN-MACH. STUDIES 15, 3–50 (1981)

25. Norman, D.A.: The design of everyday things. Doubleday, New York (1990)

26. Rohr, G., Tauber, M.: Representational framework and models for human-computer interfaces. In: van der Veer, et al. (eds.) Readings on Cognitive Ergonomics-Mind and Computer. Springer, Heidelberg (1984)

27. Fincher, S.: Perspectives on HCI patterns: concepts and tools (introducing PLML). Interfaces 56, 26–28 (2003)

28. Bienhaus, D.: PLMLx Doc. (2004),
http://www.cs.kent.ac.uk/people/staff/saf/patterns/plml.html

29. Fincher, S.: PLML extensions: concerns (2004),
http://www.cs.kent.ac.uk/people/staff/saf/patterns/concerns.html

30. Deng, J., Kemp, E., Todd, E.G.: Focusing on a standard pattern form: the development and evaluation of MUIP. In: Proceedings of the 6th ACM SIGCHI New Zealand chapter's international conference on Computer-human interaction: design centered HCI, pp. 83–90 (2006)

31. Bass, L., John, B.E.: Linking usability to software architecture patterns through general scenarios. The Journal of Systems & Software 66, 187–197 (2003)
32. Alexander, C.: The Timeless Way of Building. Oxford University Press, Oxford (1979)
33. Coepijn, C.: The new Van Gogh Museum Website. Vrije Universiteit, Amsterdam (2005)
34. Van Welie, M., Klaassen, B.: Evaluating museum websites using design patterns. Technical Report: IR-IMSE (2004)
35. Brooke, J.: SUS-A quick and dirty usability scale (1996)
36. Tullis, T.S., Stetson, J.N.: A comparison of questionnaires for assessing website usability (2004)
37. Alliance, A.: Manifesto for Agile Software Development , http://www.agilemanifesto.org/

Cascading Dialog Modeling with UsiXML

Marco Winckler[1,2], Jean Vanderdonckt[2], Adrian Stanciulescu[2],
and Francisco Trindade[3]

[1] IRIT, Université Toulouse 3, France, 118 route de Narbonne,
F-31062 Toulouse cedex 9 (France),
winckler@irit.fr, http://liihs.irit.fr/winckler/
[2] Belgian Lab. of Computer-Human Interaction, Louvain School of Management,
Université catholique de Louvain, Place des Doyens,
1 – B-1348 Louvain-la-Neuve (Belgium)
jean.vanderdonckt@uclouvain.be, http://www.isys.ucl.ac.be/bchi
[3] Federal University of Rio Grande do Sul (UFRGS), Caixa Postal 15064,
91501970 Porto Alegre (Brazil)
fmtrindade@inf.ufrgs.br

Abstract. This paper discusses multi-level dialog specifications for user interfaces of multi-target interactive systems and it proposes a step-wise method that
combines a transformational approach for model-to-model derivation and an interactive editing of dialog models for tailoring the derived models. This method
provides a synthesis of existing solutions for dialog modeling using a XML-
based User Interface Description Language, UsiXML, along with State-
WebCharts notation for expressing the dialog at a high level of abstraction. Our
aim is to push forward the design and reuse of dialog specifications throughout
several levels of abstraction ranging from task and domain models until the final user interface thanks to a mechanism based on cascading style sheets. In this
way, it is expected that the dialog properties are not only inherited from one
level to another but also are made much more reusable than in the past.

Keywords: cascading style sheet, dialog modeling, multi-target user interfaces,
StateWebCharts, user interface description language, UsiXML.

1 Introduction

The large variety of computing systems available nowadays (e.g., low-weight desk-
top/notebook computers, cell phone, Personal Digital Assistant - PDA, Smartphone)
have created a milestone for cost-effective development and fast delivery of multi-
target interactive systems [21]. Multi-target user interfaces should be adapted to device's constraints such as screen resolution and preferred interaction techniques (e.g.
text, graphical, voice-based, gesture) which requires the inclusion of the notion of
plasticity in the development process [3]. Quite often, it is required the development
multiples versions of the same applications. The availability of many computing devices creates problems for ensuring cross-consistent execution of the software along
different platforms and it will ultimately increase the costs and time required for software construction and maintenance.

T.C.N. Graham and P. Palanque (Eds.): DSVIS 2008, LNCS 5136, pp. 121–135, 2008.
© Springer-Verlag Berlin Heidelberg 2008

In the last years User Interface Description Languages (UIDL) appeared as a suitable solution for developing multi-target user interfaces. By applying appropriate model transformations, specifications of User Interfaces (UI) created with UIDLs can be reused and adapted according to constraints imposed by input/output devices, different contexts of use, or specific user preference. For example, UIDLs such as UIML [1], XIML [15], XUL [20], UMLi [7], among many others, have been successfully used for this purpose. In this scenario, the Cameleon reference framework [5] introduced a fresh perspective for the development of User Interface Description Languages (UIDL) by proposing 4 abstraction levels for the specification of user interface (i.e., task models, abstract UI, concrete UI and final UI). Such as multi-layer specification aims at giving more flexibility for specifying variations of the UI design, which is often required to generate the best solution according different contexts of the use. By successive transformations of abstract models, the specification of the UIs is completed and refined to more concrete specifications until it features executable device-platform-modality dependent specifications.

We assume that an UIDL must cover three different aspects of the UI: the static structure of the user interfaces (i.e. including the description of user interface elements - e.g., widgets - and their composition), the dynamic behavior (i.e., the dialog part, describing the dynamic relationships between components including event, actions, and behavioral constraints) and the presentation attributes (i.e., look & feel properties of UI elements). However, this is not always the case as many UIDLs do not provide full modeling support for all theses aspects. In particular, dialog model is one of the most difficult to exploit and it is often misunderstood [11].

Dialog models play a major role on UI design by capturing the dynamic aspects of the user interaction with the system which includes the specification of: relationship between presentation units (e.g., transitions between windows) as well as between UI elements (e.g., activate/deactivate buttons), events chain (i.e., including fusion/fission of events when multimodal interaction is involved) and integration with the functional core which requires mapping of events to actions according to predefined constraints enabling/disabling actions at runtime.

In this paper, we analyze the specification of the dialog part when using a multi-layer description language. In particular, it presents a method that combines transformational approaches and interactive (i.e., manual) edition of dialog models. The remainder of this paper is structured as follows: Section 2 defines the concepts that are useful for understand our approach which is presented in Section 3, and illustrate how they have been implemented in a case study (here, a car rental system) in Section 4. Section 5 discusses the related work. Section 6 summarizes the benefits and discusses some future avenues to this work.

2   Basic Concepts

This section describes the basic concepts about modeling the dialog aspect of multi-target applications.

2.1 The Architecture of Dialog Arch

The basic assumption on dialog modeling is that it must describe the behavior of input and output devices, the general dialogue between the user and the application and the logical interaction provided by the interaction technique. These requirements for dialog modeling can be decomposed in layers as proposed by architecture Arch [2] which describes the various architectural components of an interactive application and the relationships between them as show in Fig. 1. For the purpose of this paper, the left hand side of the Arch (which concerns the functional core of the application) is not relevant. The steps that are considered in a complete dialog between the user and the system, from the physical input to the physical output (presentation rendering) are the following:

1) Low-level events (physical events) are generated by the physical devices and received by the Physical Interaction component;
2) Low-level events are transformed into logical events that independent of the employed input device;
3) Logical events are treated by the dialog controller which coordinate the sequence of events and the connection the functional core of the application;
4) Changes in the system state generates abstract rendering events;
5) Rendering events are reified into more concrete events offering a concrete rendering of the physical output.

Fig. 1. The architecture Arch

According to the Arch architecture above the dialog model (step 3) can be isolated from technical details concerning the physical input events and rendering output. So that, changing the input/output devices (e.g., mouse x touch screen) would not affect the specification of the dialog itself (this is true when considering the same interaction technique, ex. pointing). Conversely, different dialog models would be applied to different contexts of the use (ex. guided interaction through sequential screens or all-at-one interaction on a single screen) without a major impact on the input and/or output devices. Moreover, the same dialog model would be suited to different modalities with similar results. The dynamic adaptation of the dialog should be flexible enough in order to support any modification of the presentation, however the method allowing the adaptation are out of the scope of this paper.

2.2 Levels of Abstraction of User Interfaces

The Cameleon Reference Framework [5] proposes to describe user interfaces according four levels of abstractions: *task models, abstract user interfaces (AUI), concrete user interface (CUI)* and *final user interface (FUI)*. By appropriate tool support it is possible to refine abstract user interface elements into more concrete specifications. According to the step considered, user interface specifications include more or less details about the user interface behavior, which lead designers to treat different dialog components (ex. state, condition, transitions, actions, etc) as exemplified in Table 1.

Table 1. Abstraction levels on dialog modeling

UI Abstraction level	Concepts	Dialog Components
Task Model (TM)	Interactive tasks carried out by the end user & domain objects	Tasks and dependencies between tasks
Abstract User Interface (AUI)	UI definition independent of any modality of interaction	Relationship between logical presentation units (e.g. transition between windows), logical events, abstract actions
Concrete User Interface (CUI)	Concretizes AUI into CIOs (widget sets found in popular graphical and vocal toolkits)	States, (concrete) events, parameters, actions, controls, changes on UI dialog according to events, *generic* method calls, etc
Final User Interface (FUI)	operational UI that runs on a particular platform either by interpretation or by execution	"Physical" signature of events, platform specific method calls, etc

2.3 Specifying User Interface Dialogs

There are a large number of notations and techniques for describing the dialog aspect of the user interface. A review on the advances of dialog notations can be found in [11]. Hereafter we focus on some few, but representative, UIDLs which are presented in Table 2. Some notations are devoted to the dialog aspect of the user interface (for example, ICO [3], SCXML [18] and SWC [21]), while other UIDLs might also cover the structure and the presentation aspects. Is some cases the description of the dialog is supported by an external language (e.g., XUL), however, quite often, the dialog is embedded into the UIDL, such as is the case of UsiXML, XUL and UIML.

Currently only UsiXML [10] and TERESA XML [12] have 4 levels of abstraction as proposed by the Cameleon Reference Framework. XUL and UIML's dialog specification are oriented to implementation, which corresponds to the level CUI and FUI in the framework Cameleon.

As UIDLs must capture the intended dialog behavior, the specification of complex relationship between widgets quite often requires some kind of formal description technique such as Lotus, Petri Nets or Statecharts. However, this not avoids having some UIDLs implementing specific notations. It is noteworthy that UIDLs based on Petri Nets (such as ICO [3]) or based on StateCharts (SCXML[18] and SWC [21]) should also be considered as *generic* languages which can be employed at different levels of abstract of the user interface design.

UIDLs might include many mechanisms for specifying dynamic behavior such as the *UI changes* (corresponding to the local dialog changing properties of individual user interface components, ex. widgets), *method calls* (facilitating the integrating with the application's functional core), *events*, explicitly representation of current system

Table 2. Support for Dialog Modeling of some User Interface Description Languages

Language	Aspects described	Specification	Levels of abstraction	Formalism/ Notation language	Dynamic behavior described	Data exchange	Control (conditions)
USIXML	Presentation, Dialog, Structure	Embedded	Task Model, AUI, CUI, FUI	Specific notation for every abstraction level	transition, method call, ui change	parameters	Yes
XUL	Presentation, Dialog, Structure	XBL Xul binding language	CUI, FUI	Specific notation	transition, method calls	parameters	Yes
ICO	Dialog	Embedded	Generic	Petri Net	ui changes method call, event, transition	reference	Yes
SCXML	Dialog	Embedded	Generic	Statecharts	event, method call, transition, state	parameter, reference	Yes
TERESA-XML	Presentation, Dialog, Structure	Embedded	Task model, AUI, CUI, FUI	Lotus	event, ui changes, transition	Parameters	Yes
UIML	Presentation, Dialog, Structure	Embedded	CUI, FUI	Specific notation	ui changes method call, event, transition	parameters, reference	Yes
SWC	Dialog	Embedded	Generic	Statecharts	ui changes method call, event, transition, state	Parameters	Yes

state and explicitly representation of *transitions* changing the state of the system. *Date exchange* can be done via passage of *parameters* along transitions, by *reference* to objects or both. All notations surveyed consider some kind of control for specifying constraints (i.e. conditions) during the execution of the dialog.

3 A Method for Dealing with Multi-level Dialog Specification

The proposed method is based on the following shortcomings:

- *Autonomy of the dialog* with respect to the structure and the presentation of the UI which implies that for any UI model describing the user interface components must have at least one dialog model supporting each design options. The separation of the dialog might lead to the reusability of some specifications and improve readability.

- *Use of formal description technique* for reducing the ambiguity of specification; This requirement is also important for implementing tool support;

- *Use of some graphical representation for the dialog.* This is an important requirement for improving the readability of specifications;

- *Combined use of automated and manual transformations* of abstract UI specification into more concrete UI. Automated transformations might improve productivity but designer should be able to modify the dialog afterwards;

- *No imposed start point for dialog specifications.* It is advisable to start by task models. However, some designers would prefer to start with more concrete dialog models and then refine them until the implementation; conversely, abstractions can be defined after deep analysis of existing concrete models.

3.1 Notations

The method proposed relies on UIDLs able to cover different level of abstraction and independence of dialog towards the user interface. For the purpose of this paper we employ two notations: UsiXML [10] to describe the structure and the presentation aspects of the user interface, and SWC [21] to describe the dialog.

UsiXML (USer Interface eXtensible Markup Language) is defined in a set of XML schemas. Each schema corresponds to one of the models in the scope of the language. UsiXML consists of a User Interface Description Language (UIDL) that is a declarative language capturing the essence of what a UI is or should be independently of physical characteristics. It describes at a high level of abstraction the constituting elements of the UI of an application: widgets, controls, containers, modalities, interaction techniques, etc. Several tools exist for editing specification using UsiXML at different level of abstraction. The interest on UsiXML is the fact that it supports all fours levels of abstraction considered in this paper. Despite of that, UsiXML do not impose any particular development process so that designers are free to choose the abstract level the most appropriate to start their projects.

StateWebCharts notation (SWC) was originally proposed to specify dynamic behavior of Web applications. SWC is a formal description technique based on Harel's StateCharts. States in SWC are represented according to their function in the modeling: they can be static, dynamic, transient or external. Additionally, SWC transitions explicitly represent the agent activating it (e.g. user actions are graphically drawn as continuous arrows while transitions triggered by system or completion events are drawn as dashed arrows). The interest on SWC for this paper remains on the full support to describe events and the notion of containers associate to states which can be easily mapped to UsiXML containers. Further information about these notations and the proper mapping between then is given along the case study on section 4.

3.2 Step-Wise Method

The method presented in this section proposes the combined use of transformational approaches and interactive (i.e. manual) edition of dialog models. The name "cascade" is a reference for the fact that, similar to other user interface models, dialog models can be derive from abstract to more concrete specification. The general reification schema is presented by Fig. 2.

The reification schema presented is composed of the following steps: 1) a task model is produced; 2) an Abstract Dialog Model can be generated automatically from task models using transformation rules. In this case, the dialog at this level is limited to the relationship that can be inferred from task models. Designers must create dialog specifications using external tools. Abstract UI can also be created manually in the absence of task models. Appropriate mapping is required to connect the Abstract UI and the Abstract Dialog. 3) A Concrete Dialog Model will be generated from the

Abstract Dialog Model based on transformation rules. More Concrete Dialog Components will be added manually according to design choices. 4) The Final UI Dialog Control is generated from Concrete Dialog Control to copy with the target platform.

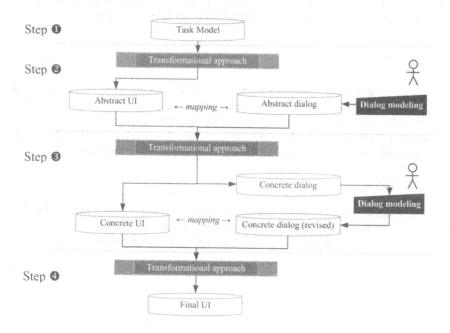

Fig. 2. Dialog reification schema

Table 3. Mapping scheme between UsiXML and SWC constructs

Abstraction level of UI	UsiXML Construct	SWC Constructs	Description of Constructs
Task Model	*Task*	-	User tasks
(TM)	Relationships (e.g. *enabling*)	-	Relationships between tasks
Abstract	*abstractContainer*	*compound states*	*High level containers for UI components*
User Inter-	*abstractIndividualComponent*	*basic states*	*UI containers (ex. presentation units)*
face	*control*	*transitions*	*Relationships between containers*
(AUI)			
Concrete	*window*	basic state	UI components featuring containers
User Inter-	*behavior*	transition	Definition of relationships between containers
face (CUI)	*event*	event	Events raising
	action	action	Behavior associated to events
	methodCall / transition / uichange	action type	Action executed when event is triggered
	-	condition	Pre-condition associated to actions
	parameters	parameters	Data exchange format
	-	user transitions	User initiated actions
	-	system transitions	System initiated actions (ex. timed transitions)
	-	transient states	Non-deterministic behavior of functional core
	-	history states	Memory for recent states
	-	end states	Notification of end of system execution

Designers could start working the dialog at any step of the abstraction levels presented by Fig. 2 by reusing specifications produced via a transformational approach or creating specification for both UI components and dialog at each level. The mapping of between the dialog specification with SWC and others components of the user interface in UsiXML is ensured by mapping tables as presented in Table 3.

4 Case Study

The case study concerns a simple car rental system allowing users to choose a car, book and pay a reservation and print a receipt. The detailed case study can be found in [16] (pp. 140-164). The next sections present the car rental system featuring 3 levels of abstraction (task model, AUI and CUI); the level FUI is similar to the CUI (refining dialog primitives to target platforms) so, it will not be described hereafter.

4.1 Task Model

The task model considered for the car rental application is presented in Fig. 3.a. The sequence for execution of sub-tasks could follow different orders thus originating different scenarios. We limit our discussion to a single scenario presented in Fig. 3.b.

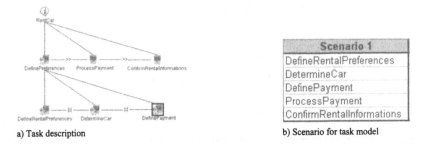

a) Task description   b) Scenario for task model

Fig. 3. Specification of task models: a) task model using IdealXML; b) a scenario

In Fig. 4 we present the task model according to the UsiXML syntax as it is generated by the tool IdealXML. One might notice that all relationships and dependencies among tasks are preserved at this level (see lines 14 and 26 for enabling tasks and 18 and 22 for undetermined choices) so that many scenarios can be extracted.

4.2 Abstract User Interface (AUI)

Once we have defined the task models, it is possible to generate the abstract model for the user interface. Fig. 5 presents the corresponding abstract user interface (only abstract containers - e.g. abstract windows – are shown) for the task model. The abstract model provides definitions for user interfaces that are independent of any modality of interaction. By using appropriate transformation rules, it possible to generate *abstract containers* from task definitions as presented in Fig. 6. Abstract containers correspond to the static part of the user interface.

```
1.    <?xml version="1.0" encoding="UTF-8"?>
2.    <!--Tasks-->
3.    <taskmodel>
4.      <task id="st0task0" name="RentCar" type="abstraction">
5.        <task id="st0task2" name="DefinePreferences" type="interaction">
6.          <task id="st0task3" name="DefineRentalPreferences" type="interaction"/>
7.          <task id="st0task4" name="DetermineCar" type="interaction"/>
8.          <task id="st0task5" name="DefinePayment" type="interaction"/>
9.        </task>
10.       <task id="st0task6" name="ProcessPayment" type="application"/>
11.       <task id="st0task7" name="ConfirmRentalInformations" type="application"/>
12.     </task>
13.     <!--Tasks relationships-->
14.     <enabling>
15.       <source sourceId="st0task2"/>
16.       <target targetId="st0task6"/>
17.     </enabling>
18.     <undeterministicChoice>
19.       <source sourceId="st0task3"/>
20.       <target targetId="st0task4"/>
21.     </undeterministicChoice>
22.     <undeterministicChoice>
23.       <source sourceId="st0task4"/>
24.       <target targetId="st0task5"/>
25.     </undeterministicChoice>
26.     <enabling>
27.       <source sourceId="st0task6"/>
28.       <target targetId="st0task7"/>
29.     </enabling>
30.   </taskmodel>
```

Fig. 4. UsiXML specification of task models for a car rental system

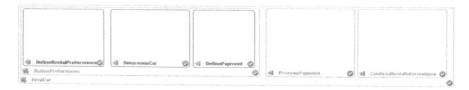

Fig. 5. Abstract User Interface as depicted by IdealXML

```
1.    <?xml version="1.0" encoding="UTF-8"?>
2.    <auimodel>
3.      <abstractContainer id="idaio00" name="RentCar">
4.        <abstractContainer id="idaio01" name="DefinePreferences">
5.          <abstractIndividualComponent id="idaio02" name="DefineRentalPreferences">
6.            <abstractIndividualComponent id="idaio03" name="idaio03">
7.              <control id="idaio04" name="idaio04" actionType="interaction" ac-
tion="dialog.defineRentalPreferences" />
8.            </abstractIndividualComponent>
9.          </abstractIndividualComponent>
10.         <abstractIndividualComponent id="idaio05" name="DetermineCar">
11.           <abstractIndividualComponent id="idaio06" name=" idaio06">
12.             <control id="idaio07" name="idaio07" actionType="interaction" action="dialog.determineCar" />
13.           </abstractIndividualComponent>
14.         </abstractIndividualComponent>
15.         <abstractIndividualComponent id="idaio08" name="DefinePayment">
16.           <abstractIndividualComponent id="idaio09" name="idaio09">
17.             <control id="idaio10" name="idaio10" actionType="interaction" action="dialog.definePayment" />
18.           </abstractIndividualComponent>
19.         </abstractIndividualComponent>
20.       </abstractContainer>
21.       <abstractIndividualComponent id="idaio11" name="ProcessPayment">
22.         <abstractIndividualComponent id="idaio12" name="idaio12">
23.           <control id="idaio13" name="idaio13" actionType="application" ac-
tion="dialog.processPayment" />
24.         </abstractIndividualComponent>
25.       </abstractIndividualComponent>
26.       <abstractIndividualComponent id="idaio14" name="ConfirmRentalInformations">
27.         <abstractIndividualComponent id="idaio15" name="idaio15">
28.           <control id="idaio16" name="idaio16" actionType="application" action="dialog.confirmRentalInformations" />
29.         </abstractIndividualComponent>
30.       </abstractIndividualComponent>
31.     </abstractContainer>
32.   </auimodel>
```

Fig. 6. UsiXML specification of abstract models for a car rental system

At this step one must identify two common dynamic behaviors: transitions between different presentation units, the so called *interaction* (Fig. 6, line 7); or the so called *application* which will be refined to *method calls* in the concrete user interface (Fig. 6, line 23). The so called *interaction* behavior corresponds to local dialog control; its implementation is very simple as it just proceeds to the next presentation unit. The so called *Interaction* behavior has a strong impact on the dialog of the application as their execution might affect the sequencing of the next task. For example, the execution of the task *ProcessPayment* might return at least two possible states for the systems: *successful payment* or *payment fail*. Such as dynamic behavior is described in the dialog model presented by Fig. 7. In Fig. 7, continuous lines on transitions (i.e. t4 and t5) correspond to interactive tasks which can be automatically refined by successive transformation of task models whilst dashed lines (i.e. t6) correspond to a behavior that should be defined manually by the designer.

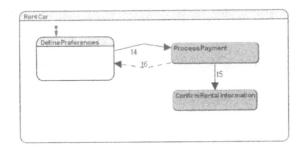

Fig. 7. Abstract Dialog modeling with SWC for a car rental system

It is noteworthy that the dialog at this step is also independent of the platform. Further refinement is required in order to complete the integration with the functional core of the application. The mapping between states and transitions of SWC to UsiXML components is made manually by choosing from the UsiXML specification the components that fits the best to the purpose of the dialog. In the example presented at Fig. 7, the state *DefinePreferences* is mapped to the *abstractContainer* named *DefinePreferences* (see line 4 of Fig. 6).

4.3 Concrete User Interface (CUI)

At this step some modality constraints can be added into the design. There are many possible scenarios for developing dialog models according to the modality chosen. Due to space reasons we limited a single scenario but that could have 2 possible dialog models. The first case considers a dialog model for interactions on a single presentation unit. For the second case, user interaction is supported along three different presentation units. The first scenario (i.e. a single presentation unit) would be suitable for large displays where users can freely choose the order of filling in the forms whilst the second scenario (i.e. several presentation units) is suitable for small displays (e.g. PDA) or to context of use where users need to be more guided during interaction (e.g. vocal interaction on cell phones).

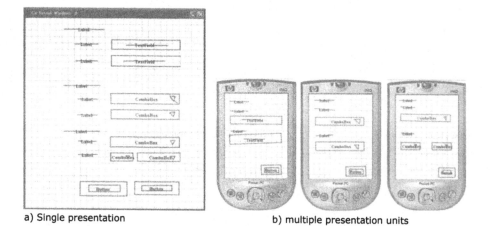

a) Single presentation   b) multiple presentation units

Fig. 8. Concrete User Interface Specification using SketchiXML

Fig. 9 presents the corresponding CUI specification in UsiXML for the single presentation unit depicted in Fig. 8.a.

```
1.    <?xml version="1.0" encoding="UTF-8"?>
2.      <uiModel id="Car_Rental" _ >
3.        <head>
4.          <version modifDate="2007-12-19T15:45:21.031-02:00"/>
5.          <authorName>SketchiXML</authorName>
6.        </head>
7.        <cuiModel id="Car_Rental-cui" name="Car_Rental-cui">
8.          <window id="window_0" name="window_0" … >
...
9.              <comboBox id="ComboBox_0" name="ComboBox_0"…>
10.             <behavior>
11.               <event id="evt_0" eventType="change" eventContext="Button_0"/>
12.               <action id="act_0" name="act_0">
13.                 <methodCall methodName="dialog.carTypeChange">
14.                 <action>
15.             </behavior>
16.             </comboBox>
...
17.             <button id="Button_1" name="Button_1">
18.             <behavior>
19.               <event id="evt_1" eventType="click" eventContext="Button_1"/>
20.               <action id="act_1" name="act_1">
21.                 <methodCall methodName="dialog.defineRentalPreferences">
22.                 <methodCall methodName="dialog.determineCar">
23.                 <methodCall methodName="dialog.definePayment">
24.                 <action>
25.             </behavior>
26.             </button>
...
27.          </window>
28.      </cuiModel>
```

Fig. 9. UsiXML Concrete User Interface Specification for a single presentation unit

In Fig. 10 we propose four design options for the concrete dialog. The option a) (*single presentation unit*) corresponds to the dialog modeling for the single presentation depicted in Fig. 8.a. The mappings for connecting the SWC specification with the other components of the UsiXML description are in bold face. The operational execution of the model Fig. 10.a is the following: once the state *DefinePreferences* is reached, all user interface components in the mapping are shown in a single presentation unit. The transitions in SWC are implemented according to events, actions and method calls mapped from UsiXML controls (ex. Fig. 9, line 11, 12 and 13).

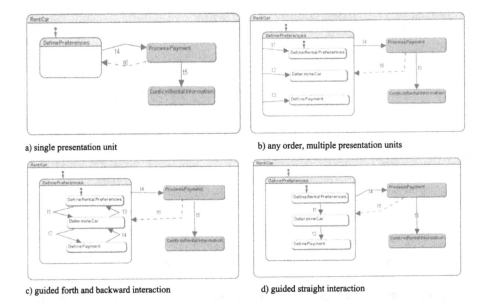

a) single presentation unit   b) any order, multiple presentation units

c) guided forth and backward interaction   d) guided straight interaction

Fig. 10. Design option for dialog at the level Concrete Specification of the User Interface

Fig. 10.b, c and d, propose alternative interaction behavior for the multiple presentation units depicted in Fig. 8.b. In all these examples, the mapping to concrete components also include the sub set of containers named *definePreferences, determine-Car,*and *definePayment*, which were previously identified at the step AUI (see section 4.2). The most important differences concerns how the states are connected to each other. It noteworthy that these design options only affect the specification of the dialog and the UsiXML remain the same. As a consequence, a dialog model does not imply a specific modality as any of the design options are suitable for rendering the user interface via different channels.

5   Related Work

Several works have been done on the design and specification of the dialog aspect of the user interfaces. Considering the organization of complex dialog structures, one should mention the hierarchical events proposed by Kosbie [9] which demonstrates how high level events can be identified and reified to low-level events triggered by user interface devices. Important improvements have also been done towards formal description techniques for the specification of complex dialog behavior. In this respect, it is noteworthy the ICO formalism [3], based on Petri Nets, allows more expressive and modular dialog specifications than the earlier attempts on formal methods for describing fusion/fission of complex events as they occurs in multimodal interaction techniques [13]. The organization of dialog models toward independent, modular and self-contained dialog structures have been a main target for developing complex interactive systems [8]. These previous work have mainly address the case of the organization of the dialog according to a single implementation.

As far as multi-target user interfaces is a concerns, only a few work have considered multi-level dialog specification. Book and Gruhn [4] have proposed the use of external dialogs for treating different presentation channels for multimodal Web applications. Their approach is based on a formal description technique called Dialog Flow Notation (DFN) that provides constructs for the design of modular navigation models for multimodal Web applications. Mori, Paterno and Santoro [12] have proposed a design method and tool called TERESA for dealing with the progressive transformation of abstract description of the user interface to final implementations whilst try to preserve the usability and plasticity of the user interface. Similarly, Luyten et al. [11] have proposed a transformational approach for derive final user interface dialog from task models. These solutions are based on top-down approach of development with little flexibility for implementing design options.

6 Conclusion and Future Work

This paper discussed several issues related to multi-level dialog specifications for multi-target user interface User Interface Description Languages. Additionally it proposes a design method combining two currently available UIDLs: UsiXML and SWC. This work tried to demonstrate that transformational approaches and manual dialog specification can be combined to promote the reification of abstract user interface into more concrete user interfaces. The approach presented is duly based on the clear separation of the dialog aspect of the other components of the user interface. Such as separation presents several advantages such as it improves the readability of models, it supports reuse of specifications and it might help the management of versions according different design choices. This method is clearly based on open standards like UsiXML which make possible to assemble UI elements built with different tools (for instance, IdealXML, SketchiXML, GrafiXML, see www.usixml.org) and couple them with external dialog specifications (for example, SWC). The advantage of such as an approach is that one can reuse knowledge and tools for dealing with dialog models and study the limits of dialog specification at different levels of abstraction. Dialog models created with SWC can be simulated by the SWCEditor [23] so that, the behavior of the application can be inspected at any time.

The current work is limited to dialog specified produced with the SWC notation. However, we suggest that it could be generalized for other dialog description techniques with similar expressive power. Another limitation is the fact no complex multimodal interaction techniques requiring fission/fusion of events, for example, has been taken into account. Such as situation will be investigated in future work.

References

1. Ali, M.F., Pérez-Quiñones, M.A., Abrams, M.: Building Multi-Platform User Interfaces with UIML. In: Seffah, A., Javahery, H. (eds.) Multiple User Interfaces: Engineering and Application Framework. John Wiley and Sons, New York (2003)
2. Bass, L., Pellegrino, R., Reed, S., Seacord, R., Sheppard, R., Szezur, M.R.: The Arch model: Seeheim revisited. In: User Interface Developer's workshop version 1.0 (1991)

3. Bastide, R., Palanque, P.: A Visual and Formal Glue Between Application and Interaction. Journal of Visual Language and Computing 10(5), 481–507 (1999)

4. Book, M., Gruhn, V.: Efficient Modeling of Hierarchical Dialog Flows for Multi-Channel Web Applications. In: Proc. of 30th Annual Int. Computer Software and Applications Conference COMPSAC 2006, Chicago, September 17-21, 2006, pp. 161–168. IEEE Computer Society, Los Alamitos (2006)

5. Calvary, G., Coutaz, J., Thevenin, D., Limbourg, Q., Bouillon, L., Vanderdonckt, J.: A Unifying Reference Framework for Multi-Target User Interfaces. Interacting With Computers 15(3), 289–308 (2003)

6. Collignon, B., Vanderdonckt, J., Calvary, G.: An Intelligent Editor for Multi-Presentation User Interfaces. In: Proc. of 23rd Annual ACM Symposium on Applied Computing SAC 2008, March 16-20, 2008, pp. 1634–1641. ACM Press, New York (2008)

7. da Silva, P.P., Paton, N.W.: User Interface Modeling in UMLi. IEEE Software 20(4), 62–69 (2003)

8. Conversy, S., Eric, B., Navarre, D., Philippe, P.: Improving modularity of interactive software with the MDPC architecture. In: Proc. of Engineering Interactive Systems 2007 (IFIP WG2.7/13.4 10th Conference on Engineering Human Computer Interaction jointly organized with IFIP WG 13.2 1st Conference on Human Centred Software Engineering and DSVIS - 14th Conference on Design Specification and Verification of Interactive Systems) EIS 2007, Salamanca, March 22-24, 2007. Springer, Heidelberg (2007)

9. Kosbie, D.S.: Hierarchical events in graphical user interfaces. In: Proc. of ACM Conf. on Human factors in computing systems CHI 1994, Boston, April 1994, pp. 131–132. ACM Press, New York (2004)

10. Limbourg, Q., Vanderdonckt, J.: UsiXML: A User Interface Description Language Supporting Multiple Levels of Independence. In: Matera, M., Comai, S. (eds.) Engineering Advanced Web Applications, pp. 325–338. Rinton Press, Paramus (2004)

11. Luyten, K., Clerckx, T., Coninx, K., Vanderdonckt, J.: Derivation of a Dialog Model from a Task Model by Activity Chain Extraction. In: Jorge, J.A., Jardim Nunes, N., Falcão e Cunha, J. (eds.) DSV-IS 2003. LNCS, vol. 2844, pp. 203–217. Springer, Heidelberg (2003)

12. Mori, G., Paternò, F., Santoro, C.: Design and Development of Multidevice User Interfaces through Multiple Logical Descriptions. IEEE Transactions on Software Engineering 30(8), 507–520 (2004)

13. Navarre, D., Palanque, P., Bastide, R., Schyn, A., Winckler, M., Nedel, L., Freitas, C.M.D.S.: A Formal Description of Multimodal Interaction Techniques for Immersive Virtual Reality Applications. In: Costabile, M.F., Paternó, F. (eds.) INTERACT 2005. LNCS, vol. 3585, pp. 170–183. Springer, Heidelberg (2005)

14. Palanque, P., Bastide, R., Winckler, M.: Automatic Generation of Interactive Systems: Why A Task Model is not Enough. In: Proc. of 10th Int. Conf. on Human-Computer Interaction HCI International 2003, Heraklion, June 22-27, 2003, pp. 198–202. Lawrence Erlbaum Associates, Mahwah (2003)

15. Puerta, A., Eisenstein, J.: XIML: A Common Representation for Interaction Data. In: Proc. of 6th ACM Int. Conf. on Intelligent User Interfaces Conference IUI 2002, San Francisco, January 13-16, 2002, pp. 216–217. ACM Press, New York (2002)

16. Stanciulescu, A., Vanderdonckt, J.: Design Options for Multimodal Web Applications. In: Proc. of 6th Int. Conf. on Computer-Aided Design of User Interfaces CADUI 2006, Bucharest, June 6-8, 2006, pp. 41–56. Springer, Heidelberg (2006)

17. Stanciulescu, A., Limbourg, Q., Vanderdonckt, J., Michotte, B., Montero, F.: A Transformational Approach for Multimodal Web User Interfaces based on UsiXML. In: Proc. of 7th ACM Int. Conf. on Multimodal Interfaces ICMI 2005, Trento, October 4-6, 2005, pp. 259–266. ACM Press, New York (2005)
18. State Chart XML (SCXML): State Machine Notation for Control Abstraction. W3C Working Draft, February 21 (2007), http://www.w3.org/TR/scxml/
19. Trindade, F.M., Pimenta, M.S.: RenderXML – A Multi-platform Software Development Tool. In: Winckler, M., Johnson, H., Palanque, P. (eds.) TAMODIA 2007. LNCS, vol. 4849, pp. 292–297. Springer, Heidelberg (2007)
20. XML User Interface Language (XUL), Mozilla Foundation (January 2008), http://www.mozilla.org/projects/xul/
21. Weiser, M.: The world is not a desktop. Interactions 1(1), 7–8 (1994)
22. Winckler, M., Palanque, P.: StateWebCharts: a Formal Description Technique Dedicated to Navigation Modelling of Web Applications. In: Jorge, J.A., Jardim Nunes, N., Falcão e Cunha, J. (eds.) DSV-IS 2003. LNCS, vol. 2844, pp. 61–76. Springer, Heidelberg (2003)
23. Winckler, M., Barboni, E., Farenc, C., Palanque, P.: SWCEditor: a Model-Based Tool for Interactive Modelling of Web Navigation. In: Proc. of 4th Int. Conf. on Computer-Aided Design of User Interfaces CADUI 2004, Funchal, January 14-16, 2004, pp. 55–66. Kluwer, Dordrecht (2005)

Designing Graphical Elements for Cognitively Demanding Activities: An Account on Fine-Tuning for Colors

Gilles Tabart[1,3], Stéphane Conversy[1,3], Jean-Luc Vinot[2],
and Sylvie Athènes[4]

[1] LII ENAC, 7, avenue Edouard Belin, BP 54005, 31055 Toulouse, Cedex 4, France
[2] DSNA, DTI R&D 7, avenue Edouard Belin, BP 54005, 31055 Toulouse, Cedex 4, France
[3] IHCS IRIT, 118, route de Narbonne, 31062 Toulouse Cedex 9, France
[4] EURISCO International, 23, avenue E. Belin, BP 44013 31028 Toulouse Cedex, France
`tabart@cena.fr, stephane.conversy@enac.fr, vinot@cena.fr,`
`sylvie.athenes@eurisco.org`

Abstract. Interactive systems evolve: during their lifetime, new functions are added, and hardware or software parts are changed, which can impact graphical rendering. Tools and methods to design, justify, and validate user interfaces at the level of graphical rendering are still lacking. This not only hinders the design process, but can also lead to misinterpretation from users. This article is an account of our work as designers of colors for graphical elements. Though a number of tools support such design activities, we found that they were not suited for designing the subtle but important details of an interface used in cognitively demanding activities. We report the problems we encountered and solved during three design tasks. We then infer implications for designing tools and methods suitable to such graphical design activities.

Keywords: User interface, graphical rendering, graphical design, color design, design study, critical systems.

1 Introduction

Visualizations of rich graphical interactive systems are composed of a great amount of graphical elements. Perception of graphical elements is highly dependent on multiple interactions between visual dimensions such as color, area, shape etc. and display context such as type of screens and surrounding luminosity. Understanding these interactions involves multidisciplinary knowledge: psychophysics, human computer interaction, and graphical design. How can visualization designers make sure that they minimize the risk of confusion? How can they be sure that any modification done on a 20 years old system will not hinder the perception, and hence the activity, of the users? How to convince users and stakeholders? In general, how can they design, validate, check, assess, and justify their design?

This kind of questions has been addressed at the level of the design process for the functional core, with methods such as Rational Unified Process or with Design Rationale

T.C.N. Graham and P. Palanque (Eds.): DSVIS 2008, LNCS 5136, pp. 136–148, 2008.
© Springer-Verlag Berlin Heidelberg 2008

tools [9], or at the level of code, using tools based on formal description of interaction, such as Petri Nets [1]. However, tools and methods to design, justify, and validate user interfaces at the level of graphical rendering are still lacking. A number of past studies addressed this problem, but their results did not quite apply to the specific kind of user interfaces we design: those that contain multiple, overlapping elements, the perception of which are very dependent on subtle details, and that users scrutinize during long periods of time in a demanding cognitive context. Good examples are the latest generation of jetliners, in which pilots interact with graphical elements on liquid crystal displays (LCD) to manage the flight, or air traffic controllers who rely mostly on radar views with multiple graphical elements, to space aircraft within safety distance. As these interactive systems are used in critical situation, the need for sensible, justified, and verified design is even more important.

In order to design such tools and methods, one must identify the relevant dimensions of the activity that they are supposed to support. This paper is a report of graphical design activities for interactive systems. We present our experience as designers during various design activities we conducted. We then discuss important considerations one has to take into account during such activities, or if one wants to design tools and methods to support it.

2 Related Work

Graphical design issues have been studied by organizations like W3C [16], FAA [7] and NASA [13]. They have established a batch of guidelines about UI graphical design and recommendations about common visual perception issues. Researchers in information visualization worked on efficient representations [5,17]. Graphical semiology introduced visual variables (size, value, color, granularity, orientation and shape) together with their ability to present nominative, ordered or quantitative data [2]. Brewer [3] proposed tools to help design harmonized color palettes for cartography visualizations. Lyons and Moretti analyzed current color design tools [11], and designed a tool for creating structured, harmonious color palettes [10]. We extensively used guidelines from NASA and Lyons & Moretti molecules approach. They help guide the design process, and help structure the colors used. However, NASA guidelines are short on precise guidelines with subtle but important rendering problems. In addition, the molecules tool does not provide much help for the kind of constraints and needs we had during the process.

3 Studies and Experience Feedback

In this section, we present three design tasks that we conducted. We redesigned interactive systems that support air traffic controllers. In order to understand the design process, we first set the context by briefly presenting air traffic control (ATC) and the three tasks we had to accomplish as designers. We then report on our experience.

3.1 Air Traffic Control Activity

All our tasks dealt with graphical design issues pertaining to the main French radar screen software used by the air traffic controllers. The software main goal is to display three-dimensional aircraft positions as if seen from above. The air space is divided into "sectors": complex three-dimensional airspaces criss-crossed with various routes. Each sector is managed by a team of 2 controllers: the tactical controller, who monitors aircraft through the radar screen and give vocal orders to pilots through a radio link, and the planning controller who organizes flights arriving from neighboring sectors. Controllers rely on flight plans, requests by pilots, requests from other sectors, current weather and traffic conditions to manage the air traffic, making judgments about the most efficient and safe way for aircraft to proceed through the air space while keeping within safe distance from each other. Each controller faces a radar screen displaying the sector under his/her responsibility. Each aircraft is represented as an icon showing its current position and smaller icons showing a few of its past positions. The current position is linked to a label with the flight identifier, current speed and flight level. In accordance with the controller's preferred settings, each screen might have a different configuration (zoom level, pan, visible layers, etc).

In ATC, the graphical information displayed has a high level of criticality. A controller may hold the fates of several thousand people during his work shift and his judgment is based on well-established work practice, his experience, and his perception of the displayed information. Therefore, all information has to be coherently displayed, in a very accessible but not intrusive fashion in order to spare the cognitive resources.

3.2 Design Process

As the tasks are mostly concerned with designing colors, we present the approach we used in terms of color model, tools, and methods.

Color models, calibration, and tool

RGB is the color model used in graphic computer-cards for encoding color. RGB is based on additive syntheses of colors using 3 primaries: red, green and blue. Software developers often use this model to specify color. RGB is a "machine-based" model: it is difficult to manipulate, and hinders the structuring of color choices. Other color spaces, such as models proposed by the Commission internationale de l'éclairage (CIE, International Commission on Illumination) and specially CIE LCH(ab) are "human perception-based" model. We used the LCH color space for two reasons. As LCH is a mostly linear perceptual model, it allows predictable manipulations. Furthermore, the L (luminosity), C (saturation), and H (hue) dimensions are semantically known color dimensions which further structured design: it helps organize colors (and hence conceptual entities) with three mostly orthogonal dimensions. In the remaining of the paper, we call "color" the perceptual phenomena referring to a particular LCH or RGB combination (and not simply the hue). We applied a calibration process on each monitor we used, so as to minimize the effects of bad rendering chain settings. Furthermore, we defined a reference ICC profile [8], and used it while designing colors, so as to maximize consistency between design sessions.

During our tasks, we designed and used our own tool to choose and modify colors. The tool can import a set of colors, sort colors into group, and display them around a hue circle using the LCH model and the reference ICC profile. It also allows to express constraints with "molecules" of color [10], or to modify directly their hue, their level of saturation, or their level of luminosity (Fig. 1). We will not describe further this tool, as it is not the purpose of this paper and is only a draft of what should

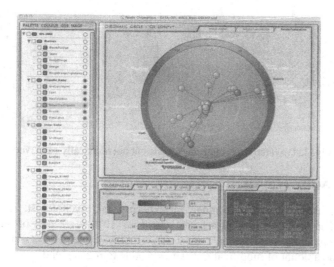

Fig. 1. The ad hoc tool with the color palette, color wheel, color spaces and color samples

become a genuine instrument. However, it helped us identify relevant aspects about the design activity and about desirable features of an efficient tool.

Context of the design

During the first task, we designed colors directly in the control room. We had to work on specific displays that were installed in control centers in order to design with real activity conditions in mind. In addition, we had to take the controllers' opinions into account and iterate with them to reach an agreement and validate our work. As previously said, a control position comprises two screens. We kept an image of the old configuration on one display and applied modifications to the other so that we could compare the results of the transformation and discuss them with the controllers. We also displayed the old configuration on the old CRT monitors to compare between color renderings. Using an actual configuration also allowed us to check if looking at the screen from different visual angles did not influence too much color perception.

The colors were then translated to RGB and inserted in the radar view configuration file, in which color names are matched with their RGB hexadecimal code, e.g. (name "*Orange*") (value 0xd08c00). When drawing a graphical element, the software refers to colors by their name e.g. ConflitEtiquette#N_Foreground: MC#*Orange*#NColorModel. Using this indirection, designers can share the same color between different elements. For example, when an alarm has to be applied both to a radar track and to an information panel (Fig. 2}, a designer can tag these two elements with the named color *orange*. Thus, if the hexadecimal value of orange color is modified, all orange elements will be changed. The configuration scheme is a way for the designers to structure color-coding. As such, it makes the task of configuring the radar view easy, and enables the system to accommodate unexpected changes or important security fixes. For the two other tasks, we worked on our computer on which we imported the palette to be changed.

Fig. 2. Two elements: same color code but not identically perceived

3.3 Design Activities Study

Our team includes a graphic designer, an experimental psychologist, and two HCI specialists. The tasks we present are real-world tasks: they are part of an industrial process, as changing such systems must follow precise steps. We were then constrained in the amount of modifications we were able to recommend.

First task: updating a global color design
Our task was to adapt the color settings of the main radar view software. presents the interface: the control panel on the left side, the main radar view in the middle, and the flight lists on the right side. The left panel present manifold options for choosing pan and zoom level or slices/layers of the sector to displayed, for example. On the main view, different areas are represented in the background with different colors, while 1 pixel wide lines represent flight routes. Flights current and past positions are represented by 3 to 5 pixel wide squares. A tag with textual information about the flight (callsign, level, speed etc.) is linked to the shape with a 1 pixel wide line. The right panel is reserved for alarms and a list of flights. Selected flight information is displayed at the bottom of this panel.

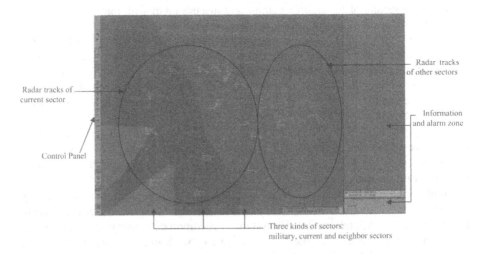

Fig. 3. The main visualization for air traffic control

We had to adapt the color settings because the system evolved both technologically and functionally. The CRT displays on which the application runs have been replaced with LCD displays. Color rendering on LCD differs from CRT: they are more saturated, while the beam is narrower. The difference in rendering completely changes the overall appearance of the visualization. Furthermore, the CRT displays are square while LCD displays have a 16:10 ratio, which changes the proportional amount of the different graphical elements. Beside hardware evolution, the activity regularly evolves, with the addition of new functionalities, new control procedures or new sector arrangements. This results in stacked modification, with no real global design.

On the one hand, we had to hold the perceived color constant while moving from CRT and LCD display. On the other hand, we had to harmonize color palettes between configurations from five air traffic control centers. Each one has its own color palette, due among others to traffic particularities. This specific task may seem trivial (changing colors); but to achieve it, we had to modify almost all colors of the application, and a lot of questions and problems were raised.

Second task: organizing flights into categories
The second task was to add new colors to an existing color palette. This requirement came from a new need in approach control activity. Controllers doing "approach control" regulate air traffic around airport areas. They needed to distinguish three categories of flights around Paris, those concerning Orly airport, those concerning Roissy airport, and in transit flights. They also needed to separate flights into two flows, e.g. Orly or "Orly-associated" airports. Together with users, a team of engineers had previously designed and installed a palette with three named colors ("green", "pink", "blue"). We had to harmonize the palette, while keeping identifiable colors.

Third task: redesign of an interface
The third task consisted in the entire redesign of the prototype of a future radar view. We were less constraint by historical constraints, and freer to test original configurations. Even though this task is still in progress, it has brought some valuable information.

3.4 Design Accomplishment and Teaching

This section presents a description of our work as designers. The description is organized around the similar issues we encountered during the three tasks. For each issue, we describe our goals, the constraints driving our choices and the solutions we eventually chose.

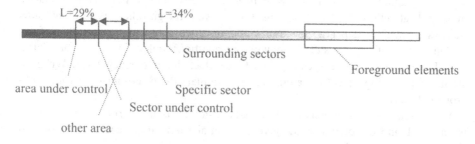

Fig. 4. Representation of the graphical elements' luminosity

Information visibility, luminosity and background
The first issue concerns information visibility (am I able to see an entity?), discriminability (am I able to differentiate between two entities?), identifiability (am I able to identify an entity among a known set of entities?) and legibility (how easily read is the text?). We first worked on luminosity. All the colors we designed are achromatic: there is no perceptible hue information. In the LHC model, it is implemented by setting color saturation to null.

Luminosity difference enables separation of juxtaposed and layered objects. Sectors are large, uniform surface juxtaposed on the background. Controllers must discriminate and identify them so as to see if a flight is about to enter or leave their controlled sector. Layered objects include sectors (background), routes, beacons, and flights (foreground). Routes and beacons must be visible, while flights must pop out and be legible.

We first designed sectors luminosities, since they end up acting as the background for most objects, and foreground colors can only be set according to the background. Fig. 4 shows the resulting distribution of the gray luminosities of the different sectors: a gray for the controlled sector, another gray for the surrounding sectors, and a last gray for a special area. The sector under control is the darkest: this sector is the most important for the controllers, and flights should be maximally visible here. The surrounding sectors are thus lighter. In bi-layered sector, controllers have to distinguish between two areas in the sector under control. We spread apart two grays around the gray of the sector under control. The second area luminosity is farther from the controlled area luminosity than the surrounding sector luminosity because it is more important to identify the controlled area than the others. However, the second layer gray must also be different enough from the surrounding sector gray. The four grays are very close in luminosity (range L=5%).

This example highlighted a problem with the possibilities of choosing a color in a relatively small range. This issue comes from imposed constraints about gray and from the fact that the 8bit-per-channel RGB color space used by the system is poor; it does not contain enough values to express all the shades of a color range. On a machine color model, grays are made by mixing equally R, G and B. Thus, between white and black there are only 254 possible grays. Furthermore, we precisely tuned the set of grays by incrementing or decrementing RGB values one by one, as the conversion between LCH and RGB was not precise enough. We had to work with the system color space instead of the perceptual color space.

Some graphical objects must be more than simply visible. For example, alarms must grab attention when they are displayed. Even though other visual dimensions such as animation help grab the user's attention, we chose to separate them from background or others grays elements with one additional color dimension, the saturation. Indeed, alarms have specific hues that reflect the emergency level. We gave alarms object a high level of saturation to accentuate the discrimination from background objects.

Some areas, such as military zone, can be considered as an "alarming" area. To differentiate them from civil area and give them an alarming appearance, we decided to slightly color them with a reddish gray.

Confidence and comfort

The global image must be harmonious: even if it is difficult to formally quantify it, the satisfaction resulting from using a good-looking image nevertheless matters. Moreover, it improves the controllers' confidence into the system. For example, the planning controller typically configures the zoom level to have a global view of future flights arriving in his sector. However, for narrower sectors, a lot of gray flights not under this controller's responsibility become visible on both sides of the current sector, because the new screen has a 16/10 ratio. These flights tend to raise the object density of the image too much. The global scene perception is spoiled and controllers are less confident in their ability to analyze the image. This resulted in uncomfortable situations, where controllers were afraid to miss an important event, and felt obliged to constantly check the image. This issue never arose with square screens.

Global comfort of the scene is also an issue when designing alarms. On the one hand, alarms must interrupt the user and be remembered, so they are intrinsically not comfortable. On the other hand, if an alarm comes to persist on the screen (e.g. the controllers have seen the alarm but they have to finish some other actions first, or because no action allows the controllers to get rid of them), it should not hinder the controllers'activity. In order to increase comfort with such persistent alarms, we had to decrease their saturation level, and make them less "flashy".

Categorizing and ordering graphical objects

One important point in the design process is categorizing and ordering objects. In the second task, we had to group flights in categories and flows. The three main categories had color hues that had been decided in a past design: green, pink and blue. The controllers proposed a separation into two sub-flows. They designed a solution by using various color dimensions, which resulted in heterogeneous colors. We worked with the LCH color space in order to homogenize the design choices. We set apart the three hue angles by 120 degrees and we distributed the sub-flows around each main hue. In order to see the results and finely tune the design, we built an image containing 6 examples of the exact shapes to be colored. We embedded this image in the tools we used, as can be seen at the bottom left of Fig. 1.

We tried to match the conceptual hierarchy with the perceptual hierarchy. For example, the two kinds of flights displayed match their relative importance for the controller. Flights that the controller has currently in his charge are represented in a bright color and others, controlled by neighboring sectors, are in a darker gray.

Alarms are also graduated: according to their importance, they have a certain hue and saturation level. We had to conform to alarm hierarchy and cultural color habits (such as red for danger).

Surface does matter: perception and software design limitation

We observed that surface influences perception: according to the surface on which a color is applied, the perception of this color is different. For example, we designed a color for small/medium size military sectors. The color is a gray with a hint of red (which name is "lie de vin"). We later used the color palette in another control center, embedding a larger military zone. When this same color was applied to this surface, the reddish gray seemed too saturated (i.e. too red). We had to decrease the saturation in order to make sectors look grayer when they are big, but still keep a distinctly reddish nuance when they are smaller. Fig. 2 shows a second example with two elements displayed with the same alarm color code. The first element is a 1 pixel wide text; the second one is the background of an information panel. Due to surface and/or pixel arrangement, the same orange color applied to both these graphical elements does not appear to be the same when a text or a background.

We have been able to accommodate the problem in the first example with a single color. But it proved to be impossible in the second example: we had to design two colors. It follows that the configuration file is not as structured any longer: if one decides to change the orange in the future, one has to change two colors instead of one. This matter is linked to the use of the indirect method for coding colors that we presented above. With a simple indirect color-coding scheme, there is no means to accommodate for differences in color perception due to the amount of surface. This example shows that the coding method can hinder the controller's activity: there is a risk that a color is not identified as corresponding to a particular state, or that two elements cannot be associated through their color.

Another issue concerns very small elements like one pixel-wide lines or glyphs. When we applied low saturated colors to such elements, their hues did not come out very well. These observations can be explained by the fact that, with this kind of small elements, some pixels may end up being isolated on a background color. They are thus "eaten" by background colors and lose some of their properties [14].

Human subjectivity: naming color, acceptability opinions.
The next issue is about color perception properties. In the LCH color space we used to organize colors. L, C and H dimensions are supposed to be orthogonal, i.e. if a designer changes a color along a single dimension, the perception of the other dimensions should not change. However, if some colors can be modified in saturation or luminosity without losing their essence (think of light or dark blue), some colors cannot be easily modified without impacting perception of hue. Red for example is identified as such only for a medium luminosity level, otherwise it is identified as ochre/brown with low luminosity, and pink with high luminosity. We experienced this problem when we tried to lower the saturation of alarms, because they were too sharp: when we applied the modification, the element was not perceived as red any longer, but as ochre, which completely disabled its identification as an alarm. We had to change both saturation and hue to keep a color identifiable as red. This phenomenon shows that colors cannot be modified automatically, or at least without precaution.

A related issue concerns the naming of colors. In their activity, controllers use color name so as to identify graphical elements. For example, they use the name of the color to refer to a particular flight status instead of referring to the status itself, as in "can you check the bathroom green airway?". In such circumstances, if a color has to be modified, it must be kept recognizable and identified as the same named color to accommodate historical use.

Human subjectivity is also an issue. For example, there is a large diversity of opinions about the saturation thresholds between a comfortable color and an uncomfortable one. This depends on human perception and sensation but also on the hue value. Furthermore, opinions vary in time, because of habituation or fatigue: the same person can disagree with a design choice at some time, and then agree with it later.

Display context

The perception of colors is dependent on the type of monitor. Nowadays, controllers use multiple screens: a radar view, but also a list of flights view, displayed on an almost horizontal screen under the radar view. The colors used on this screen must match the colors used on the radar view, as some of them allow elements to be grouped. However, even after calibration, it proved to be difficult to get exactly the same colors on both screen. For example, there were situations where up to four different blues were displayed on the screen. All four colors were very close in terms of LCH. The problem was worse when we took into account the second screen: we had to spread apart further the hue of each blue so as to allow recognition and association within the two screens. However, we did not explore further the problem, as our assignment was only to work on the main radar view. Fortunately, there are other contextual information that allow the controllers to discriminate between the status reflected by the colors. Nevertheless, this problem should not be overlooked.

The temperature of the display also influences perception. For example, we changed the saturation and hue of a slightly colored gray from $C=3\%$ to $C=2.92\%$ and from $H=156°$ to $H=206°$ to make the values coherent with other colors. We did it offline, and to our surprise, when users saw the new result, they said it was too colored. We learned three things. First, a $50°$ modification of hue with saturation as low as 3% is noticeable (and hindering). Second, offline modifications are harmful, even if based on sensible reflection made by an experienced graphical designer. Third, this is another example that shows that specifying a gray with $R=G=B$ is harmful, because it does not take into account every parameter that influences color rendering and perception.

A lasting, iterative activity

Even though it is possible to roughly describe the workflow we used (design luminosity first, then saturation, then small objects), the actual activity was done in an iterative manner. Besides, as any design activity, the tasks took us some time to accomplish.

First, we had to fix problems introduced by our own new settings: it was difficult to know the impact of a modification, to remember the dependencies between constraints, and to check every possible problem all along the process. Furthermore, we had to explore several configurations, going back and forth between intermediate solutions, which was not an easy task to do with the tools we were using. Besides, designing needs maturation and understanding of the context, for both the designers and the users. For example, designing the right warning orange required the designer to really integrate the conditions of apparition and the context of use of such orange. Regular discussions around the examples and the tools really helped designers and users to achieve a successful result. Finally, designing a color palette is highly subjective. This is not to say that users do not know what they want, but diversity between users, fatigue due to hours of design, changing context conditions etc. make the design subject to unexpected modifications, at best local, at worst global. As designers, we had to react accordingly. For example, in the first task, we worked with users so as to get their feedback and fix problems as soon as possible. After one day of designing, we had a new palette that was satisfying to both the users and the designers. When we came back the following day, the users found that the new configuration made the image too uncomfortable because it was too luminous. We had to lower the luminosity of each color one by one to fix this problem.

4 Implication for Design

In this section, we sum up the experience we gained during our tasks. We identify the relevant dimensions to take care of, when designing tools and methods to support graphical elements design.

Design with actual, controllable examples
Actual color design tools allow control of color dimensions and checking of the results on a square displaying the resulting color [11]. However, to really design a color, we had to configure the application with the newly designed color, and check it in an actual scene, in our case a radar view. This takes time and prevents an efficient iteration loop. In our ad-hoc tools, we tried to solve this problem by embedding a sample of the flights that were supposed to be organized in flows and sub-flows. This allowed us not only to check the results, but also to completely change the way we handled designing, as we could test multiple solutions quickly, and adjust swiftly and precisely each color. In fact, color-design tools should use an imaging model, not a color model as they do today [6].

Design with multiple examples at once
An object may be involved in multiple situations. For example, when designing the color of a flight, we had to take into account all the backgrounds over which it could be displayed. This forced us to go back and forth between different configurations of the application. Thus, a color tool should not only embed controllable examples, but it should also allow an easy switching between examples (either by juxtaposing them, or progressively disclosing them).

The global scene is important
We highlighted the importance of designing on real scene samples. However, it is important to keep in mind that these samples are only parts of a global graphical scene. All individual elements build up the perception of the global scene, and global rendering is the only mean to check the global comfort of the UI. Inversely, the global scene influences the perception of a single element. In order to experience these interactions, a designer must work on real scenes, and not just approximate or simplistic ones.

Foster explorative design
Making a design successful requires exploring and comparing alternative solutions. Our tools hinder exploration, as they require to save the configuration and to relaunch the application, to compare with early designs. Fortunately, we could use two screens to compare our designs with the configuration currently in use in control centers: this scheme must be generalized to any intermediary configuration, whether it concerns a single element, or a set of elements. Sideviews is an example of such style of design [15].

Foster constraints expression
We also noticed the importance of expressing constraints and reifying them. During the design phases, remembering all constraints is difficult. Actually, color molecules implement a kind of constraints, enforced with graphical interactions [10]. Such graphical constraints would have made group settings easier: it would have allowed us to lower

the luminosities of several elements at once. In addition, constraints expressed with formulas would check that a change of a parameter does not violate a previously fulfilled constraint. However it is sometimes difficult to express constraints, either graphically, or even prosaically: the constraints between the sectors gray are complex, and a tool that would enforce them would be too cumbersome to use.

Expressing and structuring colors
The LCH model, together with calibrated displays, is the right tool to express color. The LCH color space allows for predictable manipulations and structured design. However, when designing very precise values, the resolution of the machine color model hinders tuning. We were obliged to tune the final RGB values to find the right set of gray level for background. A right tool would facilitate expressing and manipulating the structured relationships between colors while at the same time allowing small adaptations using the final color model.

Even if based on the perceptual system, the LCH model is not perfect. The dimensions are mostly orthogonal, but not perfectly orthogonal. The LCH model does not allow for modifications that would guarantee that a named color is still perceived as the same. Color expression and constraints must take into account the specificities of named colors, and provide suitable interaction to help designers manipulate them.

Not just about design: integrate all purposes
During our design activities, we found that our task was not only to reach a final palette, but also to help users express their needs, to help us justify our choices and convince users, and to help accept the new settings. In the justification phase, by giving quantitative arguments, constraints would enable to argument for the choice eventually made. A list of constraints would also act as a proof that criterions required by a specification document are respected, and would help define an experimental plan to experimentally assess the design choices [12].

A tool to help designing should not be used only once, but also as an instrument that would accompany the configured system all along its lifetime. Actually, the tool itself would play the role of the configuration file of the target application. Such a tool would reify the design choices and justifications and help designers understand and respect past constraints that led to a particular design. As such, it would serve as a design rationale tool, and would extend the notion of active design documents [9, 4].

5 Conclusion and Perspectives

In this paper, we reported about our experience as designers of colors for graphical elements. We showed that interaction between visual dimensions and display context makes the design very dependent on small details. We reported how we handled various technical, cultural, and perceptual constraints. Based on this experience, we devised a set of implications for designing future instruments to support graphical design activities.

Notwithstanding the specificity of cognitively demanding ATC activities where even the smallest detail is important, the set of implications for design we devised should be of interest in other contexts. For example, web design requires defining a palette, but for a design to be coherent and harmonious, the same concerns that we expressed here should be taken into account. The features of the tool we envision would be of the same usefulness, whether as a design tool, as a design rationale tool, or as an evaluation tool.

References

1. Barboni, E., Navarre, D., Palanque, P., Bazalgette, D.: PetShop: A Model-Based Tool for the Formal Modelling and Simulation of Interactive Safety Critical Embedded Systems. In: Proceedings of HCI aero conference, Seatle, USA (2006)
2. Bertin, J.: Sémiologie graphique: Les diagrammes -Les réseaux - Les cartes (Broché) 1070 pages Editeur: Editions de l'Ecole des Hautes Etudes en Sciences janvier 31 (1999)
3. Brewer, C.A.: Color Use Guidelines for Mappingand Visualization. In: MacEachren, A.M., Taylor, D.R.F. (eds.) Visualization in Modern Cartography, ch. 7, pp. 123–147. Elsevier Science, Tarrytown (1994)
4. Boy, G.A.: Active design documents. In: proceedings of the 2nd Conf. on Designing interactive Systems: Processes, Practices, Methods, and Techniques. Amsterdam (1997)
5. Card, S., Mackinlay, J., Shneiderman, B.: Information Visualization Readings in Information Visualization:Using Vision to Think, pp. 1–34. Morgan Kaufman, San Francisco (1998)
6. A Colour Appearance Model for Colour Management Systems: CIE CAM 2002, CIE 159, 2004 (2004)
7. Federal Aviation Administration (FAA). Human factors design standard (HFDS), HF-STD-001 (March 2008), http://hf.tc.faa.gov/hfds
8. Specification ICC.1:2004-10 (Profile version 4.2.0.0) Image technology colour management : Architecture, profile format, and data structure, International Color Consortium (2004)
9. Lacaze, X., Palanque, P., Barboni, E., Navarre, D.: Design Rationale for Increasing Profitability of Interactive Systems Development., Rationale Management in Software Engineering, pp.182-197 (2005)
10. Lyons, P., Moretti, G.: Incorporating Groups into a Mathematical Model of Color Harmony for Generating Color Schemes for Computer Interfaces. In: Proceedings of the 2005 IEEE conference on Virtual Environments, Human-Computer Interfaces, and Measurement Systems, 18-20 July 2005, pp. 80–85 (2005)
11. Lyons, P., Moretti, G.: Nine tools for generating Harmonious Colour Shemes. In: Masoodian, M., Jones, S., Rogers, B. (eds.) APCHI 2004. LNCS, vol. 3101. Springer, Heidelberg (2004)
12. Mackay, E.W., Appert, C., Beaudouin-Lafon, M., Chapuis, O., Du, Y., Fekete, J.D., Guiard, Y.: Touchstone: exploratory design of experiments. In: Conference on Human Factors in Computing Systems, pp. 1425–1434 (2007)
13. NASA Color Usage (2004) (March 2008), http://colorusage.arc.nasa.gov
14. Tabart, G., Athènes, S., Conversy, S., Vinot, J.L., Effets des Paramètres Graphiques sur la Perception Visuelle : Expérimentations sur la Forme, la Surface, l'Orientation des Objets et la Définition des Ecrans. In: IHM 2007 (2007)
15. Terry, M., Mynatt, D.E.: Supporting experimentation with Side-Views. Communications of the ACM 45(45), 1006–1008 (2002)
16. Techniques For Accessibility Evaluation And Repair Tools, W3C workink draft (2000), http://www.w3.org/TR/AERT#color-contrast
17. Ware, C.: Information Visualization: Perception for Design, December 2004, 435 pages, 2nd edn. Morgan Kaufmann, San Francisco (2004)

Lightweight Coding of Structurally Varying Dialogs

Michael Dunlavey

Pharsight Corporation, 276 Harris Ave., Needham, MA 02492, USA
mdunlavey@pharsight.com
781-449-2719 (home office) 781-974-7833 (cell)

Abstract. A non-language-specific technique is given for programming of user interface (UI) dialogs. It allows the model (application data) to be pure (containing no UI-specific code). It requires no writing of callbacks or event handler functions. It allows editing of arbitrary data structures, with dynamic structural variation. This is achieved with a paradigm in which the UI specification code need not overtly name or store objects. Object management is performed automatically, facilitated by an incremental control structure. Volume of source code is reduced by about an order of magnitude compared to common UI toolkits. It has been implemented several times and used extensively in industry.

Keywords: Differential execution, Incremental computation.

1 Introduction

We present a practical technique called Dynamic Dialogs(DD) for programming user interface dialogs in commonly used languages, with about an order of magnitude less source code and coding errors compared to other methods. It allows real-time update with arbitrary structural variation.

The brevity arises from automatic management of objects and events. Only a procedure in the form of one to create the display at a point in time is written (plus some action code). The same procedure is incrementally re-executed to update the display in real time, under a control structure called Differential Execution (DE)[1]. While the procedure is imperative in style, it has the declarative property that it specifies *what* the dialog should contain at the time it is executed, not *how* to change it from a prior state. The technique does require a certain programmer discipline – to ignore UI objects and let the mechanism handle them.

The correctness proof, literature review, and wider discussion, not possible to include in this brief paper format, will be gladly provided to interested readers.

2 A Minimal Implementation

Understanding DE involves two key concepts, that we address in order. The first is the simple idea of storing data and objects in a FIFO (not in instance variables) so they can be re-visited upon re-execution. The second is how to accomplish structural variation. To explain these, we exhibit a minimal implementation in C++ (so as to be

T.C.N. Graham and P. Palanque (Eds.): DSVIS 2008, LNCS 5136, pp. 149–154, 2008.

very clear about how it works), while asserting that industrial-strength proprietary versions have been in use for a long time, and a useful one is public-domain[2].

Incremental execution techniques require some sort of cache, and this technique uses a FIFO queue. For the implementation below (lines 1-28) there is a queue called **q**, and two mode booleans, **r** and **w**. **r** means reading from the queue is enabled, and **w** means writing is enabled. (We apologize for the anachronistic coding of boolean values as integers.) Line 3 is a macro called **P** whose use is explained below. Routine **deGetPut** (lines 4-7) is a general routine to read an integer, write an integer, or both, depending on mode. (Note that reading happens before writing, allowing long-term storage.) Lines 8-15 implement the **IF-END** statement and its helper function **ifUtil** used for structural variation. (We understand the use of macros may be controversial.) Lines 16-25 define a primitive routine **deLabel**, that maintains a label object in the UI. Lines 26-28 give the control routines **Show**, **Update**, and **Erase** used by the application program (not shown) to drive the UI.

```
1  queue q;
2  BOOL r = 0, w = 0;
3  #define P(x)(w ? (x) : 0)
4  void deGetPut(int& oldval, int& newval){
5    if (r) oldval = q.get();
6    if (w) q.put(newval);
7  }
8  #define IF(t) {BOOL rsv = r, wsv = w; if(ifUtil(P(t))){
9  #define END   } r = rsv; w = wsv;}
10 BOOL ifUtil(BOOL t){
11   BOOL tOld; deGetPut(tOld, t);
12   r &= tOld;
13   w &= t;
14   return (r || w);
15 }
16 void deLabel(int x, int y, int wid, int hei, string str){
17   int id = 0;
18   if (!r && w) id = MakeANewLabel(x, y, wid, hei, str);
19   deGetPut(id, id); // long-term memory of id
20   if (r && !w) DestroyLabel(id);
21   if (r && w){
22     // if position, size, or contents of Label
23     // not equal x, y, wid, hei, or str, then update it
24   }
25 }
26 void Show()   {r = 0; w = 1; deContents();}
27 void Update(){r = 1; w = 1; deContents();}
28 void Erase()  {r = 1; w = 0; deContents();}
29
30 int x, y;
31 void deContents(){
32   time_t time = P(Time());
33   P((x = 0, y = 0));
34   deLabel(x, y, 100, 20, "First Label");   P(y += 20);
35   deLabel(x, y, 100, 20, time.ToString()); P(y += 20);
36   deLabel(x, y, 100, 20, "Last Label");    P(y += 20);
37 }
```

Lines 30-37 give the specific user interface definition **deContents**, consisting (in this example) of three text labels arrayed vertically, with the center label showing the current time. The application program calls **Show** to create the display, then calls **Update** repeatedly, incrementally updating it each time, and finally calls **Erase** to clear it. At all times, the queue contains the ids of the visible labels, and the label objects themselves remember their position, size, and contents.

Now, to demonstrate structural variation, suppose the center label is only to exist when the time in seconds is odd. It can be wrapped in an **IF-END** statement, like this:

```
IF(Odd(time.Seconds()))
    deLabel(x, y, 100, 20, time.ToString()); P(y += 20);
END
```

If **Update** is called often enough, multiple times per second, the center label will be seen to blink in and out of existence, only showing when the seconds are odd, while the last label moves up and down to make room for it. **IF-END** works by saving its test value in the queue, and when that value changes, the enclosed objects are created or deleted by temporarily turning off **r** or **w**, respectively. The programmer (of **de-Contents**) need not (and must not) write code to effect these changes.

We hope this gives the flavor of the technique, and now we briefly explain how it is generalized.

1. The primitive routine **deLabel** is a stand-in for any routine that manages the lifetime of a control, widget, or any kind of object. Such a routine, when it reads from the queue, has to read the same number of values as it writes when it writes.

2. A sequence of statements, as in **deContents**, can be any length, as long as it only calls primitive routines like **deLabel**, conditional statements like **IF-END**, or any subroutine that follows the same rules. Any subroutine that follows these rules is conventionally given the prefix "**de**" standing for "differential execution". The routine **deContents** is so named because it defines the contents of the UI, and it is the routine called from **Show**, **Update**, and **Erase**.

3. There are many variations on the **IF** statement, of which useful ones, easily implemented, are **ELSE**, **ELSEIF**, **FOR**, **WHILE**, and **SWITCH**. The statements in the body of such a statement follow rule (2), implying that arbitrary nesting is allowed.

4. Other computations can also be included, as long as they do not interrupt flow of control, and as long as they are prevented from executing when **w** is false. We call this the *erase-mode rule*, and the **P** macro (protect) enforces it. Notice in the example above that this allows the last label to move up and down as necessary because **(y += 20)** only executes when **w** is true. It also implies that arguments to subroutines should be protected (but not necessary if they are only simple constants or global variables). Note that rules (2), (3), and (4) define a sub-language that is Turing universal, so that arbitrarily complex displays can be maintained, within resource limits.

5. The combined values of **r** and **w** constitute global modes, called **SHOW**, **UP-DATE**, and **ERASE**. Further modes can be added. For example, we can add a mode called **EVENT**, the purpose of which is to handle user input events such as clicking a button or typing into a text edit field.

An example of an industrial dynamic dialog is shown in Figure 1.

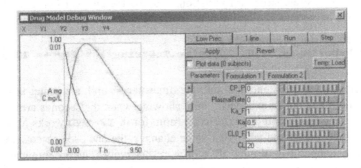

Fig. 1. A typical dynamic dialog. All components and structural variation are updated in real time

3 Reduced Source Code

The reduction in source code is demonstrated by a small example. In Java Swing, there is an example of how to create simple dialogs, called TextInputDemo[3], shown on the left in Figure 2. Not counting extraneous code, it is 270 lines.

Fig. 2. TextInputDemo - 270 lines of code vs. 60

On the right is a similar dialog written with DD, available on-line[2]. It is 60 lines of code, 4.5 times smaller.

4 A Realistic Example

Following is a more realistic example showing how DD can be used in practice[2]. A dialog is given to edit structurally varying application data. It is included to show 1) how the application data is unmodified for the UI (1-6), 2) how a complex dialog is built with 33 lines of code, 3) how one line of code (41,42,45) can manage the lifetime of an input control (and not easily get it wrong), 4) how a repeated group can be created with just two lines of code (14,16), and 5) how action code is attached to button controls with an **if** statement (18,36).

The application data is an array of health-care patients:

```
1  class Patient {public:
2    String name;
3    double age;
4    bool smoker; // smoker only relevant if age >= 50
5  };
6  vector< Patient* > patients;
```

deContents specifies a label, followed by the controls for each patient, followed by a button that can add a patient. By default, controls are laid out vertically.

```
10 void deContents(){ int i;
11   // first, have a label
12   deLabel(200, 20, "Patient name, age, smoker:");
13   // for each patient, have a row of controls
14   FOR(i=0, i<patients.Count(), i++)
15     deEditOnePatient( P( patients[i] ) );
16   END
17   // have a button to add a patient
18   if (deButton(50, 20, "Add")){
19     // when the button is clicked add the patient
20     patients.Add(new Patient);
21     DD_THROW;
22   }
23 }
```

deEditOnePatient is the routine that specifies the controls for one patient, in a horizontal layout. The controls are a button to remove the patient, an edit control for the name, an edit control for the age, and a checkbox for the smoker boolean. The latter control only exists if the age is 50 or more..

```
30 void deEditOnePatient(Patient* p){
31   // determine field widths
32   int w = (Width()-50)/3;
33   // controls are laid out horizontally
34   deStartHorizontal();
35     // have a button to remove this patient
36     if (deButton(50, 20, "Remove")){
37       patients.Remove(p);
37       DD_THROW;
39     }
40     // edit fields for name and age
41     deEdit(w, 20, P(&p->name));
42     deEdit(w, 20, P(&p->age));
43     // if age >= 50 have a checkbox for smoker boolean
44     IF(p->age >= 50)
45       deCheckBox(w, 20, "Smoker?", P(&p->smoker));
46     END
47   deEndHorizontal(20);
48 }
```

Figure 3 shows the dialog in operation.

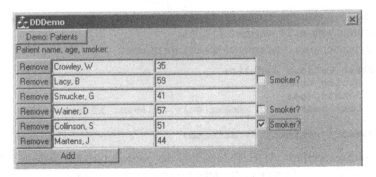

Fig. 3. A dialog with dynamic structural variation

5 Performance

Time and memory to perform an update is $O(N)$ where N is the number of visible controls. Updates are performed on every keystroke and mouse click (and on a timer if desired). An update of Figure 3 (N=24) takes 62ns on a 1.6ghz laptop in the case of no state change. State changes, of course, incur the additional cost of altering the controls.

6 Conclusion

Dynamic Dialogs, used for many years in industry, uses a FIFO-based incremental computation technique to allow dialogs with real-time structural variation to be programmed with minimal source code and bugs.

References

1. Dunlavey, M.: Differential Evaluation: A Cache-Based Technique for Incremental Update of Graphical Displays of Structures. Software Practice and Experience 23, 871–893 (1993)
2. Dunlavey, M.: Project DynDlgDemo (2007), http://sourceforge.net/
3. TextInputDemo,
   http://java.sun.com/docs/books/tutorial/uiswing/examples/components/TextInputDemoProject/src/components/TextInputDemo.java

ReWiRe: Designing Reactive Systems for Pervasive Environments

Geert Vanderhulst, Kris Luyten, and Karin Coninx

Hasselt University – transnationale Universiteit Limburg – IBBT
Expertise Centre for Digital Media Wetenschapspark 2,
3590 Diepenbeek, Belgium
{geert.vanderhulst,kris.luyten,karin.coninx}@uhasselt.be

Abstract. The design of interactive software that populates an ambient space is a complex and ad-hoc process with traditional software development approaches. In an ambient space, important building blocks can be both physical objects within the user's reach and software objects accessible from within that space. However, putting many heterogeneous resources together to create a single system mostly requires writing a large amount of glue code before such a system is operational. Besides, users all have their own needs and preferences to interact with various kinds of environments which often means that the system behavior should adapt to a specific context of use while the system is being used. In this paper we present a methodology to orchestrate resources on an abstract level and hence configure a pervasive computing environment. We use a semantic layer to model behavior and illustrate its use in an application.

1 Introduction

Although pervasive computing environments have gained much importance over the last years, they remain among the most complex environments to develop interactive software for. Generic development environments that explicitly target ambient spaces are scarce because of several reasons:

Lack of engineering approaches: most pervasive applications are ad-hoc coded and hence are only applicable in just one situation [5].
New middleware requirements: middleware is required to abstract hardware, deal with distributed computing resources, steer the migration of user interfaces, etc [7].
Support for situation-aware human-computer interaction: the context in which tasks are executed affects the user's interaction with the system [2].

In this paper we report on the *ReWiRe* framework [8] which supports the dynamic composition and adaptation of behavior rules in a pervasive environment. With services and devices that enter and leave the user's environment, the ability to support the dynamic composition of the interactive system is a strong requirement. Our approach relies on a semantic layer that captures the context of the entire environment (its users, devices, services, etc) and uses this information to configure the behavior of resources (section 3). Since orchestration is performed at an abstract level, we can mask the underlying service technologies (section 4). To accomplish this, we have underpinned our framework with semantic Web frameworks such as RDF, OWL and

T.C.N. Graham and P. Palanque (Eds.): DSVIS 2008, LNCS 5136, pp. 155–160, 2008.

OWL-S [8]. We demonstrate our approach by means of a test-bed that illustrates how services can be orchestrated and (re)wired at runtime to take advantage of changes in the environment configuration (section 5).

2 Related Work

The emergence of Web services has lead to different solutions to coordinate distributed business processes, e.g. BPEL [1]. Pervasive services demand for similar orchestration tools that take into account the full environment context. This goes beyond dealing with preconfigured service compositions, but also involves runtime adaptation of the environment configuration whilst users are interacting with it. Muñoz et al. [5] propose a model-driven approach for the development of pervasive systems. A domain specific language (PervML) is used to specify the system using conceptual primitives suitable for the target domain.

Mokhtar et al. [4] also study highly dynamic pervasive computing environments where users need to perform tasks anytime anywhere, using the available functionality of the pervasive environment. Grimm [3] identified three requirements that should be fulfilled by systems that support these dynamic interactive pervasive environments: support for a continuously changing context of execution and make this explicit in the system design, support for ad-hoc composition of devices and services and collaboration among users should be supported out-of-the-box. With *ReWiRe* we tackle exactly these requirements.

3 Environment and Behavior Model

We use a semantic layer to describe the context of use of an interactive software system during its lifetime. This layer includes both an environment and a behavior model which are described by an ontology. Several (domain-specific) ontologies can be merged at runtime and offer a dynamic schema that evolves when new software components become available. The system's configuration is linked with an instance of these ontologies. Figure 1 presents the environment and behavior ontology together with the OWL-S ontologies. The OWL-S ontology describes a service in terms of what it does (*profile*), how it is used (*model*) and how to interact with it (*grounding*). Although OWL-S services are usually considered to be semantically enriched Web services, a service can be any arbitrary piece of functionality that can be used in the environment. With OWL-S one can describe a service (e.g. its inputs and outputs) in a uniform way and define a custom grounding that provides details on how to invoke that service. We use OWL-S service descriptions to attach functionality to 'resources' in the environment model. A resource represents everything that can be included in this model, e.g. users who interact with the surroundings, devices that offer computing power, storage and input modalities, etc. Domain-specific ontologies that introduce new concepts such as light resources are merged with an upper environment ontology at runtime. The environment ontology defines 'sensors' and 'actions' to interact with these resources:

- **Sensor**: A Sensor publishes context events that occur in a resource in the environment. In other words, a sensor provides remote context events to interested resources in the environment.
- **Action**: An Action has a one-to-one correspondence with an OWL-S service. We introduce the term 'Action' to differentiate between the definition of a service in the environment model and an OWL-S service. For example, 'DoSearch' and 'DoSpellingSuggestion' are two OWL-S services (i.e. actions) that belong to the service 'GoogleService'.

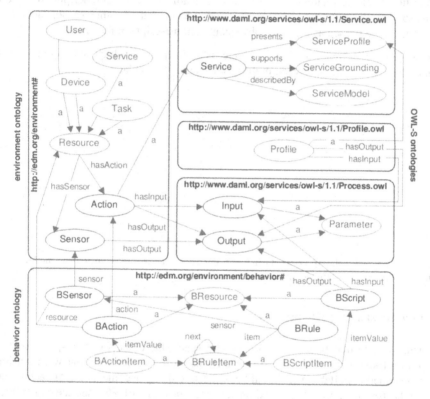

Fig. 1. The environment and its behavior are described using ontologies

While sensors and actions allow interaction with resources, their output data often lacks context w.r.t. other resources. Consider for example a 'LocationService' that triggers a sensor each time the location of a tracked object changes. This sensor outputs plain coordinates which have few meaning to other resources. Hence we introduce context-aware sensors and actions in the behavior model, such as a 'NearWhiteboard' sensor that is triggered when a tracked object approaches the whiteboard in a room. This sensor interprets coordinates produced by the location sensor and thus adds a concrete meaning to this data. Semantically enriched sensors and actions act as building blocks to compose Event-Condition-Action (ECA) rules and are defined in the behavior ontology. We distinguish the following concepts in this ontology:

- **BSensor**: A BSensor represents a resource/sensor pair, optionally linked with a script that acts as a filter on the base sensor: only if certain conditions are met, the behavior sensor is triggered (e.g. a script could check if the sensor's output parameters match certain values).
- **BAction**: A BAction represents a resource/action pair.
- **BScript**: A BScript encapsulates script code (e.g. JavaScript) that is dynamically interpreted. Scripts also have input and output parameters that are read and set using dedicated variables ($in, $out).
- **BRule**: A BRule relates a BSensor with a chain of actions and scripts. When the sensor is triggered, this chain is executed. The output of either sensor, action or script can be passed as input to subsequent actions/scripts in the chain.

Consider for example the behavior rule listed in figure 2 which will automatically turn on the light in the hall when motion is detected at this place.

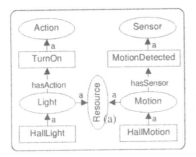 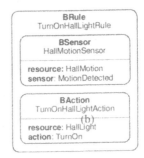

Fig. 2. A behavior rule (b) connects independent resources in the environment model (a): a light is automatically switched on when motion is sensed

4 Orchestrating Resources

To achieve a desired behavior in an ambient space, the objects in this space need to adapt to a (new) context of use. Hence different software services that were not initially designed to collaborate, should be orchestrated and become aware of each other. Our orchestration approach is based on semantic matching of Web service capabilities [6]. Semantic matching is a key element to establish late binding and a service-oriented architecture (SOA) has proven to be useful for this purpose in highly dynamic pervasive environments [4].

In *ReWiRe* the behavior of the environment is described by a set of rules $R_0,...,R_n$ that all contain a reference to a behavior sensor S and a set of executable items $I_0,...,I_n$ with I_i either a behavior action or a behavior script. When a rule's sensor is triggered, its behavior items are executed one by one in the specified order, consuming and producing data. The inputs and outputs of behavior resources are described by OWL-S parameters in a similar way as the parameters of a semantic Web service are described. OWL classes and OWL's built-in XML schema types (xsd:string, xsd:integer, ...) describe a parameter's datatype. Parameter p_1 matches parameter p_2 if both parameter types are equivalent or if the parameter type of p_1 subsumes the parameter type of p_2. In other words, the parameter type of p_2 is either an exact match of the parameter type of p_1 or it is a 'super class' (in terms of OWL class equivalence) of p_1. A service is only invoked if all input parameters that have no (default) value are set. Otherwise a service call will usually lead to a malfunction.

5 Collaborative Paint Application

A proof-of-concept application built using our framework aims to improve the experience of painting in the digital world. We try to mimic a real-world multi-user painting setup by supporting heterogeneous federations of devices. For example, figure 3 shows a user painting on a canvas projected on a touch-sensitive whiteboard, using a PDA to select and mix colors. The whiteboard represents the painter's easel while the PDA acts as his mobile color palette. Users can use their own devices or make use of the resources already present in the environment (e.g. tabletop device, tablet interface, . . .) to participate in the painting process.

Fig. 3. A user is creating a painting on the whiteboard using his PDA as a mobile palette, whilst another user is painting using a tablet interface

While this application could be realized using traditional development approaches, this would involve a lot of ad-hoc coding. Using our framework, one has to provide a functional core ('PaintService') along with user interface components leveraging this functionality and a set of behavior rules to orchestrate paint resources in the environment. Note that legacy paint applications can be (re)used as a functional core in our framework and benefit from *ReWiRe*'s distribution capabilities. By differentiating between an engineering and a modeling step, we promote code reuse whilst being able to alter the behavior of resources at runtime. In an exemplary scenario, we linked a sensor that is triggered when a new device enters the environment (discovered by the middleware) with a distribution request for the paint canvas interface, provided that the target-device is capable of running this component. Besides, we installed an RFID tag near the whiteboard that triggers a 'PaletteTagScanned' sensor when it is scanned (through a 'RFIDService'). A behavior rule that is invoked when this sensor provides new data, executes an action that migrates a user interface for the color palette to the device that scanned the tag (e.g. a PDA). This allows a user to move his PDA (equipped with an RFID reader) near the RFID tag to have a palette distributed to it.

6 Conclusion

In this paper we presented a model-driven approach to coordinate the behavior of a pervasive application. Our future work includes improving the behavior model and its tool support. While the behavior rules are currently composed as a linear list of orchestrated actions/scripts, more complex behavior rules require a more advanced structure, e.g. to model conditional tests on output values. A remaining challenge is to integrate this system-oriented orchestration with a more user-oriented task modeling approach.

Acknowledgments. Part of the research at EDM is funded by EFRO (European Fund for Regional Development) and the Flemish Government. Funding for this research was also provided by the Research Foundation – Flanders (F.W.O. Vlaanderen, project number G.0461.05).

References

1. Barreto, C., et al.: Web Services Business Process Execution Language Version 2.0 (2007), http://docs.oasis-open.org/wsbpel/2.0/wsbpel-v2.0.pdf
2. Encarnaçãao, J.L., Kirste, T.: Ambient Intelligence: Towards Smart Appliance Ensembles. In: From Integrated Publication and Information Systems to Virtual Information and Knowledge Environments, pp. 261–270 (2005)
3. Grimm, R.: One.world: Experiences with a Pervasive Computing Architecture. IEEE Pervasive Computing 03(3), 22–30 (2004)
4. Mokhtar, S.B., Georgantas, N., Issarny, V.: COCOA: COnversation-based service COmposition in pervAsive computing environments with QoS support. J. Syst. Softw. 80(12) (2007)
5. Muñoz, J., Pelechano, V., Cetina, C.: Software Engineering for Pervasive Systems. Applying Models, Frameworks and Transformations. In: Int. Workshop on Software Engineering for Pervasive Services (SEPS 2006) (2006)
6. Paolucci, M., Kawamura, T., Payne, T.R., Sycara, K.P.: Semantic Matching of Web Services Capabilities. In: Horrocks, I., Hendler, J. (eds.) ISWC 2002. LNCS, vol. 2342, pp. 333–347. Springer, Heidelberg (2002)
7. Vanderhulst, G., Luyten, K., Coninx, K.: Middleware for Ubiquitous Service-Oriented Spaces on the Web. In: Proc. of the 21st Int. Conf. on Advanced Information Networking and Applications Workshops (AINAW 2007), pp. 1001–1006 (2007)
8. Vanderhulst, G., Luyten, K., Coninx, K.: ReWiRe: Creating Interactive Pervasive Systems that cope with Changing Environments by Rewiring. In: Proc. of the 4th IET Int. Conf. on Intelligent Environments (IE 2008) (to appear, 2008)

Toward Multi-disciplinary Model-Based (Re)Design of Sustainable User Interfaces

Jan Van den Bergh, Mieke Haesen, Kris Luyten,
Sofie Notelaers, and Karin Coninx

Hasselt University - tUL - IBBT, Expertise Centre for Digital Media,
Wetenschapspark 2, 3590 Diepenbeek, Belgium
{jan.vandenbergh,mieke.haesen,kris.luyten,sofie.notelaers,
karin.coninx}@uhasselt.be

Abstract. This paper reports on our experience in using the MuiCSer process framework for the redesign of the user interface for operating an industrial digital printing system. MuiCSer is created to support the user-centered interface design of new *and* legacy systems by a multi-disciplinary team. The process framework is created to enhance increased flexibility, usability and sustainability of the designed user interfaces. Resulting user interfaces are decoupled from the application logic, but still help to maintain consistency with the available functionality even when this changes over time. This report focuses on the usage of the task model during the analysis of the current user interface, the creation of user interface prototypes at various fidelity levels and the still ongoing realization of a flexible user interface management system to support future changes of the deployed user interfaces.

1 Introduction

In contrast with traditional design efforts, our challenge is to create a new design that can evolve together with the rest of the application: a sustainable user interface. The purpose is to reduce the cost of further improvements to the software that will be applied after the design has finished. It is very likely that a complex industrial application such as the one we are targeting, will be updated regularly (as evidenced by the history of the redesigned software). Because of the extreme complexity of such an application, the efforts of updating application logic as well as the related user interface have a high cost.

Furthermore, in terms of user interface complexity, we are dealing with a user interface that surpasses the complexity of most user interfaces a regular user has to deal with. The user interface of such a high-end digital printing system can easily contain hundreds of different windows (tabs are counted as a separate window) although this amount can vary depending on the needs of the specific user. It is easy to loose track of both the overview and the important details when only traditional design methodologies (e.g. card sorting and paper prototypes) are used to steer the redesign.

A model-based approach allows capturing these inter- and intra-window relationships and link window sequences with tasks that need to be supported using e.g. a task

T.C.N. Graham and P. Palanque (Eds.): DSVIS 2008, LNCS 5136, pp. 161–166, 2008.
© Springer-Verlag Berlin Heidelberg 2008

model. It is however equally important to be able to trace the individual components in the final user interface back to the tasks they support. When dealing with the redesign of such complex user interfaces in combination with new as well as changing requirements, a fully automated transformational approach is not an option. To support these goals we used a new software engineering process framework, *Multidisciplinary user-Centered Software engineering (MuiCSer)*, that is visible for the customer, has some degree of agility and allows more easy updates once a design is deployed as the final user interface [1]. This approach is based on our experience with model-based approaches, user-centered user interface design and software engineering processes to provide a solution that supports user-centered interface redesign for complex evolving systems.

MuiCSer does not stop at first delivery of the system and thus the necessary tools and runtime environment need to be provided to support further evolution of the system. Therefore we ensured that existing commercially supported tools can be used to further develop the system, while custom tools are provided to keep track of the model relations. In this paper, we discuss our first results of this approach to redesign the user interface of a complex industrial application into a sustainable user interface.

2 MuiCSer

The usability of a system can be improved by using a User-Centered Design approach as described in ISO 13407 [2]. When a redesign concerns the user interface of a complex system, it is also important not to loose track of the functionality offered by the application logic. Model-based approaches can help us to preserve the link between the user interface and the application logic. We use the MuiCSer process framework [1] to provide a smooth integration between user interface design and software development and to support the involvement of a multi-disciplinary team.

The MuiCSer process, shown in Fig. 1, starts with a user and task analysis to learn about the tasks end users carry out with the existing interface. Other behavioral aspects of the end-user operating the interface are also captured by observations and contextual inquiries. Narrative reports, personas [5] and scenarios typically result from a user and task analysis, while a sensible and correct redesign of a system requires more structured models about the user requirements and the application logic. Existing manuals are also examined to complete the task analysis; these provide a clear overview of what functionality is available and how the supported functionality is communicated to the end-users. It also allows us to filter out the most important workflow patterns supported by the system.

The results of the analysis, obtained in the first stage, are used to progress towards system interaction models and presentation models. We label this stage the structured interaction analysis stage. Models support a combination of user requirements and functional requirements in order to keep track of the application logic during the design and the development of the user interface. These models contribute to low-fidelity prototypes which evolve into high-fidelity prototypes and the final user interface. Both low- and high-fidelity prototypes are often created by designers, thus tool support is required that checks for consistency with other models, such as the task model while creating the prototypes.

MuiCSer supports the iterative development of systems, including several evaluations, verifications and validations of the artifacts. For the development of complex systems we propose to use a central repository that keeps pace with changes of several artifacts and maintains and labels relationships between artifacts.

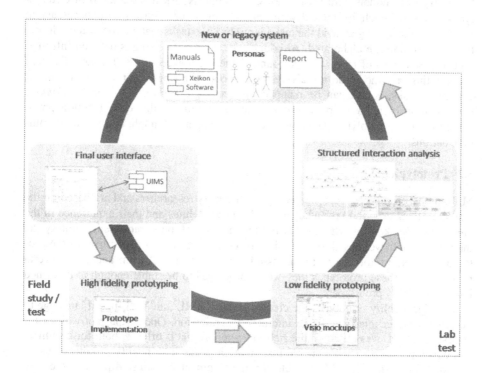

Fig. 1. The MuiCSer framework illustrated using artifacts as they were created in the Warhol project. Note that the visualization of the prototypes and final user interface are intermediate results and do not reflect the actual interfaces.[1]

3 Applying MuiCSer : UI Redesign of a Complex System

The digital printing system being redesigned can be managed using two different applications. Since these applications were extended with new functionality over several years, a redesign of the user interfaces became required to obtain one single coherent user interface and to improve the usability. The redesign cycle started with usability researchers who carried out a user and task analysis. This resulted in a report including findings on the observations, a set of personas and a high-level Hierarchical Task Analysis. In this section we describe the path we take to progress from this report toward a more detailed task model, and how this model was and is being used to redesign the user interfaces.

---

[1] The usability researchers opted for mid-fidelity instead of low-fidelity prototypes.

3.1 Creating the Task Model

Based on the report of the usability researchers and the existing software and manuals, detailed task models were created. We use the ConcurTaskTrees (CTT) notation to specify task models with CTTE [3]. CTT supports task hierarchies with different types of tasks, which are related with temporal operators. Since it is unnecessary to detail all the tasks (e.g. extend the task hierarchy), the tasks that are focused on during the first iteration are elaborated. Although the task model contains detailed information of a selection of tasks, a task count of the CTT exceeds 1850 tasks[2]. The leaf tasks in this task model do not always correspond to a single user action. In case of command tasks, a task can be mapped onto a single action. E.g. a task "*Confirm configuration changes*" corresponds to a single action; in this case a button press. Whenever a task involves changing or selecting data, a task might correspond to multiple actions.

3.2 Prototyping

Mid-fidelity prototypes were created by the usability researchers and are based on the results of their user and task analysis, usability guidelines and their experience in the creation of this kind of artifacts. During the creation of these mid-fidelity prototypes, the CTT models were used to determine the completeness and correctness of the prototypes. These prototypes were discussed within the project team and after several reifications of these prototypes they were considered to be stable enough to be turned into high-fidelity prototypes.

The high-fidelity prototypes are created using XAML[3], an XML-based language to describe the user interface for an interactive application. One of the motivations for choosing XAML was based on the rich tool support that is offered, both for designers and developers. These tools enable fast creation of the high-fidelity prototypes using drag-and-drop when possible and custom development for selected parts of the user interface.

To ensure that the created prototypes are consistent and complete with respect to the task model, the XAML describing the user interface controls is enhanced with structured annotations which indicate the corresponding task model. Annotations are inserted in the XAML code that link the parts of the user interface description (subtrees because of the XML-language) with tasks from the task model. Our approach can be used with other XML-based user interface description languages such as XForms[4], UIML[5] and UsiXML[6].

With these simple links in place, we can build tools that support developers and designers to maintain consistency and correctness between the task model and high-level prototypes. For example, we created a tool that automatically verifies whether the user interface is complete with respect to the tasks from the task model. I.e. all

---

[2] These tasks are spread over more than 20 separate CTT files to deal with the complexity and limitations of the tools.

[3] http://msdn2.microsoft.com/en-us/library/ms752059.aspx

[4] http://www.w3.org/MarkUp/Forms/

[5] http://www.oasis-open.org/committees/uiml/

[6] http://www.usixml.org

tasks that need to be explicitly presented to the user have a corresponding user interface part in the prototypes. Referring back to Fig. 1, this is one example of information that is maintained throughout the different stages in our process.

4 Toward a Runtime System Supporting Evolution

Because the final user interface will be used by users that have divergent skillsets and that need to perform other tasks, the user interface should be tailored according to the user role. Furthermore, the user interface has to be able to smoothly evolve together with the capabilities of the printing system as well as the changing preferences of the user. One of the challenges is to support this evolution in the systems' user interface and to support changes in design while maintaining consistency and correctness of the user interface. We created a user interface management system (UIMS) that exploits the relationships between the tasks and the user interface descriptions that are created during design. A single XAML-file, stored in the UIMS, describes the contents of a single window (we count each tab as a separate window) and can be linked to multiple tasks. The latter indicates a single window can be used to perform multiple tasks.

The availability of the tasks within a single window as well as the organization and availability of the windows within the user interface of the application is determined by a task model that is associated to a specific user. The concrete visualization of the window structure will be determined by the project team, based on the most appropriate user interface patterns, such as those described by Van Welie [7], and the results of user tests and integrated in the user interface management system.

A user-specific task model will be created in a similar manner as the creation of multi-device user interfaces based on a single task model [4]. One will start from a task model that describes the complete capabilities of the digital printing system that are exposed through the user interface. Tasks that are not relevant for a specific user (or group of users) can be omitted from this task model and will consequently be hidden from the user interface.

Extending the system can then be done by a simple two or three step process; by adding a task to the task model and adding the necessary XAML-file (fragments) and optionally updating the user profiles when the added functionality is not desired for a specific user. The system then takes care of the changes in the user interface structure implied by these additions.

Task model relationships specified between the tasks can be used to see the impact of changes in the user interface due to changes in the user profile or offered functionality.

5 Discussion and Conclusions

This paper presented our user-centered software engineering process framework, MuiCSer , and showed how it is currently instantiated to redesign a complex user interface into a sustainable user interface. The process makes extensive use of different models, of which the task model is the most prominent during the first stage.

---

[7] http://www.welie.com/patterns/index.php

The user interface management system, although still very much work in progress, is already used with a selection of models to support consistency and correctness during interface design. The fact that models are reused later in the design process improves the maintenance of these models and eases the evolution of the system since (part of) the design choices are still up-to-date for subsequent iterations.

In our experience this simple yet effective approach to combine several artifacts helps to structure the redesign of a user interface for a complex system, and to support collaboration among different members in a multi-disciplinary team. We were able to communicate clearly to the company's development team how the task model is reflected in the user interface, and how changes in task structure are propagated toward the user interface design. Furthermore, designers were able to create designs with their own tools, in this case Microsoft Expression, and check whether the created designs covered all tasks that need to be supported. This provides us with the necessary means to combine creative activities with the more rigid approach that is typical for model-based user interface design.

Acknowledgements. This research was performed in the context of the IWT project Warhol of Punch Graphix in cooperation with usability researchers of IBBT-CUO (KULeuven). The MuiCSer Framework is also based on our experiences in the IWT project AMASS++ (IWT 060051). Part of the research at the Expertise Centre for Digital Media is funded by the ERDF (European Regional Development Fund) and the Flemish Government.

References

1. Haesen, M., Luyten, K., Coninx, K., Van den Bergh, J., Raymaekers, C.: MuiCSer: A Multi-disciplinary User-Centered Software Engineering Process to increase the overal User Experience. In: Proceedings of the 10th International Conference on Enterprise Information Systems, Barcelona, Spain (June 2008)
2. International Standards Organization. ISO 13407. Human Centred Design Process for Interactive Systems. Geneva, Swiss (1999)
3. Mori, G., Paternò, F., Santoro, C.: CTTE: support for developing and analyzing task models for interactive system design. IEEE Transactions on Software Engineering 28(8), 797–813 (2002)
4. Paternò, F., Santoro, C.: One model, many interfaces. In: Kolski, C., Vanderdonckt, J. (eds.) Computer-Aided Design of User Interfaces III, Proceedings of the Fourth International Conference on Computer-Aided Design of User Interfaces, vol. 3, pp. 143–154. Kluwer Academic Publishers, Dordrecht (2002)
5. Pruitt, J., Adlin, T.: The Persona Lifecycle: Keeping People in Mind Throughout Product Design. Morgan Kaufmann, San Francisco (2006)

A Model-Based Approach to Supporting Configuration in Ubiquitous Systems

Tony McBryan and Phil Gray

Department of Computing Science,
University of Glasgow, Lilybank Gardens, Glasgow, G12 8QQ, UK
{mcbryan, pdg}@dcs.gla.ac.uk

Abstract. This paper presents an approach for representing, and providing computer support for, the configuration of interactive systems, particularly ubiquitous systems, that offers a flexible method for combining a wide range of configuration techniques. There are many existing techniques offering dynamic adaptation, ranging from fully automatic through context-sensitive to user-driven. We propose a model that unifies all of these techniques and offers a rich choice of ways of combining them, based on the concept of configuration possibilities, evaluation functions applicable to sets of these possibilities and approaches for parameterising the functions and combining the results. We present a concept demonstrator implementation of the model, designed for home care systems, and describe a set of use cases based on this prototype implementation that illustrate the power and flexibility of the approach.

Keywords: ubiquitous systems, dynamic configuration, model, evaluation.

1 Introduction

Ubiquitous systems typically use large numbers of sensors to detect the state of the environment of use [1] and offer multiple different devices and methods of interacting with users [2]. The multiplicity and volatility of these contexts of use, including the presence or absence of devices and resources, especially when the users or devices are mobile, leads to a demand for systems that are capable of extensive and regular reconfiguration in regards to choice of interactive techniques and components. In addition, as the opportunities for reconfiguration grow, so does the likelihood that users will attempt to appropriate their systems to exploit this flexibility to provide new application functionality in new ways.

This situation has led to the development of software architectures and technologies that enable this dynamic reconfiguration to take place and also to the development of a variety of techniques for carrying out this configuration. The latter range from conventional preference settings through interactive configuration interfaces to autonomic context-sensitive systems that adjust the form of interaction to the current state of the user and setting; perhaps based on sophisticated policies or via matching to previous similar patterns of use. Each of these techniques is useful in certain circumstances and, indeed, combinations of the techniques are also possible.

T.C.N. Graham and P. Palanque (Eds.): DSVIS 2008, LNCS 5136, pp. 167–180, 2008.

From both a design and implementation point of view, it would be desirable to treat all of these techniques in a unified way, as variants of a single coherent model of configuration, so that they can be more easily compared, transformed, combined, refined and swopped. This paper presents such a model, based on the notions of configuration possibilities and evaluation functions over such possibilities. We shall argue that this model offers a rich design space for a range of configurations, making it easier to combine techniques and to develop new variants of existing ones.

In Section 0 we briefly review related work on the configuration of user interfaces to identify the techniques we wish to unify.   Section 3 presents our model-based approach to configuration followed by Section 0 that describes a proof of concept based on a set of configuration examples in the home care domain, implemented using a software framework we have built. Section 0 offers our conclusions and an indication of future work.

2 Related Work

Many techniques for choosing an appropriate interaction technique or device have been developed in the context of ubiquitous systems design. In this section we summarise some of the most popular approaches with some exemplar implementations. This section is intended to discuss the use of the system from the perspective of a typical user and does not compare architectural features of particular approaches.

Thevenin and Coutaz [3] present the notion of plasticity that identifies equivalence of usability as the primary criterion for assessing interaction adaptation. Their implementation demonstrates automatic and semi-automatic generation of user interfaces exhibiting plasticity.

Manual configuration is frequently used to allow the user complete control over a configuration. Using a manual approach it is necessary for the user to specifically make a modification to the configuration when circumstances change. This configuration can be stored in a configuration file, possibly expressed in an appropriate specification language [4] but often commonly manipulated by an interactive editor such as Jigsaw [5] which uses a "jigsaw pieces" metaphor to enable a user to see the interconnection of devices and to manipulate them to meet changes in demand. Another similar approach is Speakeasy [6] that allows direct connections, as in Jigsaw, but also employs a task based approach where templates are "filled out" with the appropriate devices by the user.

Context sensitive systems are systems that choose the interaction techniques to use based on data gathered from the user's environment – their context.   Schmidt [7] describes a hierarchical model of context which includes the user model(s), social environment, task model, environmental conditions and physical infrastructure from which adaptations are derived.

Another approach is to define a "utility function" that automatically decides which interaction styles or devices should be used to communicate with the user. These utility functions may then make use of any contextual data gathered as part of the function. This is the approach taken by Sousa and Garlan [8] where a utility function is used to express the combination of the user's preferences, the suppliers preferences and quality of service preferences. The task of making a choice is then an effort to maximise this utility function. This approach is also found in Supple [9] which performs user interface adaptation according to a utility rule based on pre-assigned weights for screen components.

Rule based reasoning can be used to select appropriate interaction techniques automatically based on rules or policies manually set by the user. In the work of Connelly and Khalil [10] this takes the form of policies for devices and interaction spaces being combined to determine the interaction methods that are allowed to be used. This approach is also a clear influence on the current work being undertaken by W3C Ubiquitous Web Applications [11] where content and presentation are selected based on selection rules based on the characteristics of the device(s) currently in use.

Another approach used by the Comet (Context of use Mouldable widgET) architecture [12] is to employ introspective components that publish quality of use guarantees for a set of contexts of use. Adaptations are triggered by policies; at which point the current context of use will be derived and compared against the quality of use guarantees published by available Comets to make a decision on which component should be used. Each component must therefore be able to identify its own quality of use statistics in each of the contexts of use it is possible to appear in.

It is also possible to use "recommender" or collaborative filtering techniques to make the decision. A recommender algorithm may use a collection of preference or usage histories and compare them to similar information, either from the same user or from multiple users. This approach is used in the Domino system [13] to determine which components a user has access to using a history of frequently used components from other users.

A final approach to be considered is employed by the ISATINE framework [14] based on the USIXML mark up language. ISATINE is a multi-agent architecture that decomposes the adaptation of a user interface into steps that can be achieved by the user, the system and by other external stakeholders. The user can take control of the adaptation engine by explicitly selecting which adaptation rule to prefer from an adaptation rule pool in order to express the goal of the adaptation more explicitly but does not provide a mechanism to utilise multiple configuration techniques at run-time.

All of these techniques are useful in certain circumstances, but currently no system provides a unified method of offering them all, both separately and in combination. Our approach, described below, is intended to provide this unification.

3   Unified Model-Based Approach

Our approach to the configuration of interactive systems is to represent each of the techniques discussed in Section 0 within a unified model. This approach allows designers to provide many configuration techniques in parallel or in combination and are potentially modifiable at run-time and capable of being driven by user interaction.

3.1 An Application Context

Our work has been carried out as part of MATCH[1], a multi-university research project devoted to investigating infrastructure support for dynamically configurable, multimodal

---

[1] http://www.match-project.org.uk

ubiquitous home care systems. For that reason, we illustrate our approach by the use of a running example taken from this domain. In this example Fred and Shirley are an older couple with chronic conditions that could be ameliorated by appropriate use of ubiquitous home care technology. In particular, Shirley has worsening arthritis and is no longer able to move around the house easily; she relies on Fred for tasks such as controlling the heating system, closing the curtains and for most household chores. Fred recently had a stroke. He is still physically fit but has become more and more forgetful since the stroke and requires continual reminders for when to take his medication. He is also hard of hearing.

3.2 A Unified Model of Configuration

The model we present here is designed around the concept of *evaluation functions* that are responsible for both identifying opportunities for change as well as reflection on the alternatives available to make a change.

To do this we introduce concept of a *configuration possibility* (hereafter, 'possibility', for short) which is an *encapsulated solution (consisting of interaction components, techniques and devices) that can offer interaction between a system task and a user.* A possibility includes any software components needed to perform data transformations related to the interaction as well as references to the components that will be responsible for rendering the interaction via physical devices.

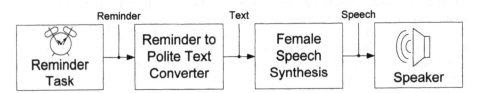

Fig. 1. A typical configuration possibility

Consider a medication reminder for Fred; one of the possibilities, as shown in Figure 1, might be to deliver the reminder via a speech synthesis system. The possibility would include the component representing the physical device (the speaker), the component representing the speech synthesis system (responsible for converting text to speech) and the component that converts a medication reminder into the appropriate textual alert.

To construct a set of possibilities it is possible to use a service discovery system that models relationships between components to construct a directed graph of the available components suitably configured. By identifying interactive components it is possible to traverse the graph with the goal of constructing a set of possibilities that can be used with the application task.

Figure 2 shows a typical, albeit simple, graph that may be constructed from the data in a service discovery system. In this graph we can deduce many different possibilities (such the speaker using polite text and a female voice); we have shown a speaker that requires the choice of two of the intermediate components as well as a GUI that does not require intermediate components. By starting from the reminder task as the root node we can perform as simple breadth first traversal to determine each possibility in the graph.

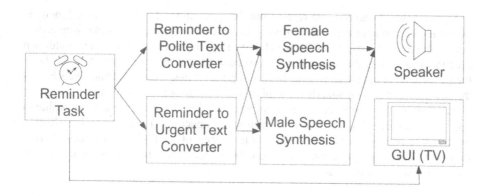

Fig. 2. A typical graph

More complicated graphs including cycles will require a more robust traversal algorithm to determine every possibility. Some unanswered questions currently remain over the likelihood of graph explosion, and what impact this may have on performance, given unrestricted, large numbers of possibilities. This will be a subject of future research and is not addressed here; to date we have not experienced performance problems with graphs of moderate complexity (~70 nodes, ~120 edges).

Once the graph has been built and traversed to create a set of possibilities we can begin to analyse the appropriateness of each possibility. To do this we evaluate each possibility by using one, or many, evaluation functions.

The purpose of an evaluation function is to rank, filter or otherwise analyse these possibilities such that a configuration decision can be made. Evaluation functions can have a many-to-many relationship with task assignments; there may be many evaluation functions used to review the possibilities for the medication reminder task while a single evaluation function may be used simultaneously for many tasks.

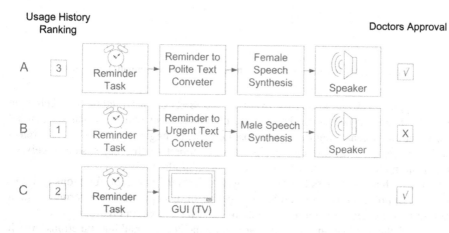

Fig. 3. Example results from the application of a ranking evaluation function and an approval evaluation function

Figure 3 shows one possible result from the application of two evaluation functions (a ranking and an approval function) to some of the possibilities we could have generated in the previous step. The Usage History Ranking is an example of an evaluation function which uses the recommender approach to rank possibilities while the Doctor's Approval function allows or disallows possibilities; here the Male Speech synthesis is disallowed as it sounds too similar to Fred and can confuse Shirley.

To allow multiple evaluation functions to be used with a single task it is possible to use evaluation functions to combine results via function compositions (in effect a *meta-evaluation function*). This allows the results of multiple approaches (implemented as evaluation functions) to be combined together into a single function that can be mapped onto the task.

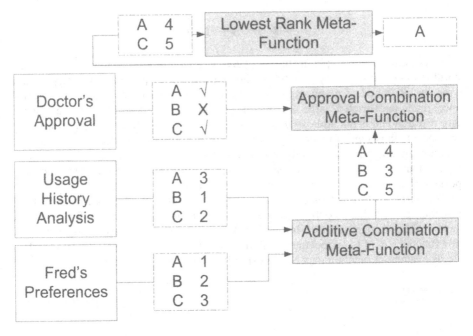

Fig. 4. Example results from the combination of three evaluation functions

This approach would allow, for example, the selection of an interaction technique for the notification task to be based on a combination of context sensitive, manual and/or automatic reasoning. A typical example of this might be that the users' preferences are weighted against the results of a collaborative filtering system receiving input from multiple users, based on the success of similar tasks.

Figure 4 shows one possible method by which three evaluation functions (2 ranking and 1 approval) might be combined together in this approach to determine which possibility to use from the three available possibilities shown in Figure 3.

Two of the evaluation functions are implemented as ranking functions which "score" each of the possibilities. The individually ranked results of both ranking functions are first combined together using an additive meta-function before the results of this are combined with the results of the doctor's approval evaluation function. The result of this is that possibility 'A' was the possibility with the lowest combined rank that had also been approved and was therefore selected.

The meta-functions can be replaced or changed at will to provide different results, for example the choice of meta-function to combine the results of the two ranking functions could have instead been multiplicative in nature which may have had a different result.

A useful result of this is that the system has inbuilt support for multiple, conflicting stakeholders using the system. Each stakeholder in the task can have their own evaluation function(s) modelled after their views or requirements – the results of which can then be combined within the same framework. This allows the natural specification of how conflicts can be solved by changing the meta-evaluation function being used to combine the results.

The result of an evaluation function (or set of evaluation functions) should be the set of possibilities to use for interaction; as shown in Figure 4. In this case, a single technique has been selected, although functions might also enable multiple concurrent techniques to be used.

Evaluation functions are a flexible method of reasoning about the available possibilities and can be applied at different levels of granularity; some evaluation functions may consider an entire possibility while others may only operate over selected portions of a possibility; for example an evaluation function may only consider the choice of physical output device in its reasoning. Evaluation functions may utilise external sources of data such as context or usage history and can be parameterisable such that a single evaluation function may be reused in multiple situations (such as gathering of user preferences from multiple stakeholders) or even called recursively.

3.3 Interactive Evaluation Functions

Evaluation functions can, and often must, be interactive components themselves. Users can (i) provide inputs prior to function creation or use (e.g., preference files read by a function), (ii) interact with an evaluation function directly as part of the evaluation process, (iii) indicate a changed opinion thus triggering a re-evaluation or (iv) interact implicitly, in which some evaluation functions gather usage information or indications of the user's satisfaction over time to determine how to rank or filter possibilities.

Similarly, a meta-evaluation function can be interactive. In the example, in Figure 4, the "lowest rank" meta-evaluation function could be replaced with a function that presents the two remaining choices to the user along with the current rankings and asks them to choose which should be used.

The process of allowing for user interaction as a part of this process means that an evaluation process may need to be deferred until the user has responded. In this case a provisional decision may have to be made in the meantime to provide a service until the user has had sufficient time to complete their interaction.

Since we can combine approaches systematically, we can have a combination of automatic and manually-controlled evaluation function in use at the same time. We may also have policy-based evaluation functions mixed in – we may even have multiple different policy specification languages being used at any one time.

We envisage two primary modes of interaction: (i) one-off or sporadic interaction where the user specifies their needs and wants in advance and rarely changes them, and (ii) continuous interaction where the user frequently interacts with the system, or plans to interact with the system, to assist in the choice of suitable interaction techniques.

In addition, we believe that evaluation functions (and meta-evaluation functions) may be required to provide explanatory information or reviews on the current state of the system or on previous choices they have made so far; similar to the approach in the Crystal application framework [15]. This allows users to have an idea of the reasoning by which an interaction technique was chosen (why is the system behaving as it is?) or to be presented with the currently available choices and the ways in which the system can assess them (how might the system behave if changed?).

In summary this approach allows us to combine together automatic reasoning functions together with interactive functions within a unified model where conflicts between stakeholders can be represented explicitly.

3.4 Interaction Evolution

One of the aims of this approach is to support *interaction evolution*. The concept of evolution we use here is influenced by Dourish [16], MacLean [17] and Fickas [18]. Each of these authors identifies the ability to appropriate, tailor and evolve a system over time as a key feature of ubiquitous systems. We define interaction evolution as *multiple related instances of interaction configuration that have a directed goal to change some aspect of the system with respect to certain attributes of quality.* For example, an elderly user might develop a visual impairment (e.g., cataracts) that requires a reduction in dependency on conventional visual displays. Over time their visual capacity might deteriorate, perhaps resulting in the invalidation of the current configuration choice. Our approach enables us to build evaluation functions that operate over longer periods of time (sequences of choices), thus supporting such evolution by exploiting persistence.

4   Validation of Our Approach

In the remainder of this paper we will discuss an initial validation of our approach through example concept demonstrator applications, based on the scenario presented in Section 3.2 (see section 4.2 for more details).

4.1 The MATCH Software Framework

These demonstrators have been implemented in a software framework developed within the MATCH project. This section describes the architecture briefly; further details of the implementation of this framework are available in [19].

Within the framework architecture (Figure 5) sets of application tasks are controlled by a Task Manager component, responsible for starting, stopping and otherwise controlling tasks and their parameters.

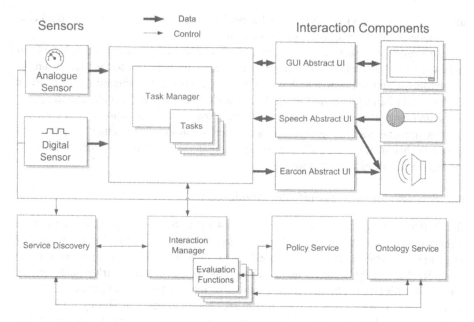

Fig. 5. MATCH Architecture

Components such as sensors and interaction components are provided as logical software "bundles" within the system which can be dynamically added and removed at runtime. Components are not limited to those which are locally accessible; for instance some components may be implemented as web services which are hosted remotely. Interaction components and tasks are registered with a service discovery system, supported by an Ontology Service [20], that can be used to hold high-level descriptions of components and tasks. Evaluation functions benefit from the Ontology service which allows reasoning about classes of related components and their effects on the user based on the information held by the ontology service.

Communication between components and tasks is brokered by a publish/subscribe message handler.

The Interaction Manager subsystem is responsible for the implementation of the approach described in Section 0. When a task is started, it will request from the Interaction Manager any bindings to interaction components it requires. The Interaction Manager has a repository of assigned evaluation functions and will query the appropriate evaluation functions to determine the allocation. Evaluation functions can additionally notify the Interaction Manager that a change has occurred requiring re-evaluation, performed subject to meta-evaluation approval (to allow for deferral of re-evaluations).

Since some evaluation functions may be implemented as rules or policies we have provided a Policy Service [20] component which is capable of reasoning over sets of policies and is a service available to evaluation functions. Other services, such as alternative policy services, recommender services or usage history services could also be made available to evaluation functions to use.

In the rest of this section we present a number of use-case examples that have been built with this framework to demonstrate the basic suitability of our model for unifying automatic and interactive techniques for configuration. The implementations use a SHAKE [21] battery-powered multi-sensor pack equipped with accelerometer, gyroscope and magnetometer to detect movement traces. The interaction devices we use for this implementation are currently simulated versions of the actual devices mentioned in this section (e.g., TV and phone emulators) and the user interfaces to the evaluation functions remain primitive.

4.2 Scenario for the Demonstrator Applications

Recall that Shirley has worsening arthritis restricting her mobility. Fred wants to be informed about Shirley's activity levels so that he does not worry. Fred is interested in seeing this data on his mobile phone both at home and away. He does not need to be notified about the status if he is currently in the room with Shirley since he can observe for himself. The monitoring data is of interest to external agencies such as Shirley's doctor who would like to be kept apprised of changes in Shirley's condition.

To this end Shirley wears a wireless accelerometer that captures her movement in real time and delivers it to the MATCH framework as a sensor stream. A task exists in the framework that interprets the raw sensor data and generates notifications when there has been little movement or unusual movement patterns.

4.3 Example 1 – Utility Function, Multiple Resolutions

We can imagine that Shirley's doctor has prepared an evaluation function which selects a "default" hardcoded configuration. This evaluation function is designed to advise both himself and Fred of Shirley's condition on an ongoing basis. This default evaluation function is a utility function designed to maximise benefit by using preselected interaction components.

Utility functions are the simplest type of evaluation function to implement as they can be completely self-contained and use extremely simple logic to perform their task.

As discussed in Section 0 an evaluation function has as input a set of possibilities available and returns as an output the set of possibilities to select.

In this case the set of available possibilities may include:

- SMS to the doctor's phone (perhaps provided for emergency conditions or for another task)
- HTTP post submission to a shared monitoring screen at the doctors surgery
- A television in the living room
- A loudspeaker which is audible throughout the house
- A monitoring application on Fred's mobile phone

The utility evaluation function is hardcoded to select the HTTP post submission as well as the audible loudspeaker and will simply return both of these possibilities which are both started, discarding all other possibilities.

4.4   Example 2 – Manual Configuration

Since the previous approach was entirely hardcoded it does not specifically address Fred and Shirley's needs for the monitoring application; it does not deliver the required information to Fred's phone and the frequent loudspeaker announcements are annoying to Shirley and difficult to hear for Fred.

To resolve this, Fred and Shirley decide to manually specify the devices to be used. To implement a manual choice in the form of an evaluation it is only necessary to create an approval style evaluation function that knows the user's choice and only approves the appropriate possibility.

In this scenario Shirley has created a connection via the HTTP based surgery monitor and manually adds and removes connections to Fred's phone and to the television in the living room depending on whether or not Fred is home.

4.5   Example 3 – Simple Preferences

Eventually, despite the additional control that manual configuration provides, Shirley tires of manually changing the device between Fred's phone and the television and decides that what is actually required is to use the preferences evaluation function.

Fred selects a set of preferences (Phone > TV > Loudspeaker) and changes the monitoring task to use the preferences evaluation function with his set of preferences.

The evaluation function will take the set of available possibilities and return a single possibility of the highest preference, i.e. if the phone is available then the phone possibility will be used, otherwise the television and finally the loudspeaker.

Since the system only considers available possibilities Fred starts turning his phone off when he's in the house so that it is marked as unavailable and cannot be selected. This causes his second preference, the television, to be used.

4.6   Example 4 – Combining Evaluation Functions

Previously the preferences were configured only for Fred's usage and ignored the needs of the doctor who needed to monitor Shirley's condition over a period of time.

Thus it is necessary to combine the doctor's needs with Fred's preferences. To do this, the simplest approach is to have two evaluation functions – one for the doctor's needs and one for Fred's. One evaluation function selects the doctor's surgery monitoring application, if available, and otherwise the SMS function, the other duplicates the preferences in the previous example.

These can both be implemented as two instances of the same basic preferences evaluation function but with different sets of preferences.

In order to combine these evaluation functions we can use a meta-evaluation function (election system) to the task which operates over a selection of sub-evaluation functions. When the meta-function is queried it simply queries each sub-function in turn and returns as its result the union set of the results from each sub-function. In this case it would return the set of the result of the doctor's preferences (the surgery monitoring application) and Fred's preferences (the phone or television depending on availability).

We could extend this to add an evaluation function for Shirley which may provide an "anti preference", i.e. devices she doesn't ever want used which may have higher precedence than the meta-evaluation function discussed here.

Other tactics of combining evaluation functions could be formed by providing alternate meta-evaluation functions (i.e. the intersection or union of the results of multiple approval functions).

4.7 Example 5 – Context Sensitivity

In the previous two examples; Fred has had to turn his phone off when he enters the house to cause the preference based system to switch to using the television. This situation is not ideal since Fred may receive phone calls while his phone is turned off.

To address this problem, it is decided that Fred's preference evaluation function should be replaced with a context sensitive evaluation function to control the configuration based on Fred's behaviour. Here the appropriate contextually sensitive evaluation function would detect if Fred is at home or not and return the appropriate possibility. Other contextual evaluation functions which might be used by Fred and Shirley are monitoring of light levels to determine which rooms are in use to only use interfaces available in those rooms, or monitoring ambient sound levels to adjust the volume of audio alerts or to determine if they are appropriate at all.

This can be extended further by simply turning the context sensitive function into a switch between two sub-evaluation functions – your preferences in one situation vs. your preferences in another situation. This can be further extended to create logic trees of evaluation functions which control the sub-evaluation functions to be used.

It is also possible that the actual data being monitored could be contextual, such that if Shirley has not moved for an extended period of time then the choice of interaction technique might change (i.e. to send an SMS to the doctors phone) rather than using the passive monitoring provided by the surgery.

5 Conclusions

In this paper we have presented a model-based approach to supporting configuration. This approach allows for the combination of multiple techniques ranging from fully automatic to fully interactive approaches for configuration and including various intermediate combinations.

The approach described here expressed composition and function without using a specific specification or description language but instead supports the combination of multiple disparate languages (for example; Java, ACCENT [22], MATLAB) within a single configuration if so desired. This approach is intended to be realised as a tool-supported configuration system where evaluation functions can be combined together and specified by the stakeholders. However, it may prove useful to express configurations in the model via a custom language.

Our initial examples, described above, only involve the selection and configuration of output components. We are now extending our use cases to support the selection, combination and configuration of components involving both input and output. We are working on more sophisticated interactive meta-evaluation functions, including their user interfaces, intended for typical users of a home care system. We are also working on applying techniques from voting systems to the model by viewing evaluation functions as voters in an election and meta-evaluation functions as the election systems themselves.

In the longer term, we believe that this approach is more broadly applicable than we have described here, including the selection and configuration of application tasks and sensors and involving multiple stakeholders with conflicting requirements. This will be the focus of further research.

Acknowledgements

This research was carried out within the MATCH (Mobilising Advanced Technologies for Care at Home) Project funded by Scottish Funding Council (grant HR04016). We wish to thank our MATCH colleagues for their contribution to the ideas presented here and for their work in developing the MATCH software framework.

References

1. Dey, A.K., Mankoff, J.: Designing mediation for context-aware applications. ACM Transactions on Computer-Human Interaction (TOCHI) 12(1), 53–80 (2005)
2. Oviatt, S.: Ten myths of multimodal interaction. Communications of the ACM 42(11), 74–81 (1999)
3. Thevenin, D., Coutaz, J.: Plasticity of User Interfaces: Framework and Research Agenda. In: Proceedings of Interact, vol. 99, pp. 110–117 (1999)
4. Magee, J., Dulay, N., Eisenbach, S., Kramer, J.: Specifying Distributed Software Architectures. In: Proceedings of the 5th European Software Engineering Conference, pp. 137–153 (1995)
5. Humble, J., Crabtree, A., Hemmings, T., Åkesson, K.P., Koleva, B., Rodden, T., Hansson, P.: Playing with the Bits-User-configuration of Ubiquitous Domestic Environments. In: Dey, A.K., Schmidt, A., McCarthy, J.F. (eds.) UbiComp 2003. LNCS, vol. 2864, pp. 12–15. Springer, Heidelberg (2003)
6. Edwards, W.K., Newman, M.W., Sedivy, J., Smith, T., Izadi, S.: Challenge: Recombinant Computing and the Speakeasy Approach. In: Proc. MOBICOM 2002 - The 8th Annual International Conference on Mobile Computing, pp. 279–286 (2002)
7. Schmidt, A., Beigl, M., Gellersen, H.W.: There is more to context than location. Computers & Graphics 23(6), 893–901 (1999)
8. Sousa, J.P., Garlan, D.: Improving User-Awareness by Factoring it Out of Applications. In: Proc. System Support for Ubiquitous Computing Workshop (UbiSys) (2003)
9. Gajos, K., Christianson, D., Hoffmann, R., Shaked, T., Henning, K., Long, J.J., Weld, D.S.: Fast and robust interface generation for ubiquitous applications. In: Beigl, M., Intille, S.S., Rekimoto, J., Tokuda, H. (eds.) UbiComp 2005. LNCS, vol. 3660. Springer, Heidelberg (2005)
10. Connelly, K., Khalil, A.: Towards Automatic Device Configuration in Smart Environments. In: Proceedings of UbiSys Workshop (2003)
11. W3C Ubiquitous Web Applications, Content Selection for Device Independence (DISelect) 1.0, http://www.w3.org/TR/2007/CR-cselection-20070725/

12. Calvary, G., Coutaz, J., Daassi, O., Balme, L., Demeure, A.: Towards a new generation of widgets for supporting software plasticity: the comet. In: Preproceedings of EHCI/DSV-IS, vol. 4, pp. 41–60 (2004)
13. Bell, M., Hall, M., Chalmers, M., Gray, P., Brown, B.: Domino: Exploring Mobile Collaborative Software Adaptation. LNCS. Springer, Heidelberg (2006)
14. Jaquero, V.L., Vanderdonckt, J., Montero, F., Gonzalez, P.: Towards an Extended Model of User Interface Adaptation: the ISATINE framework. In: Proc. Engineering Interactive Systems 2007 (2007)
15. Myers, B.A., Weitzman, D., Ko, A.J., Chau, D.H.: Answering Why and Why Not Questions in User Interfaces. In: Proc. ACM Conference on Human Factors in Computing Systems, Montreal, Canada, pp. 397–406 (2006)
16. Dourish, P.: Developing a Reflective Model of Collaborative Systems. ACM Transactions on Computer-Human Interaction 2(1), 40–63 (1995)
17. MacLean, A., Carter, K., Lovstrand, L., Moran, T.: User-tailorable systems: pressing the issues with buttons. In: Proceedings of the SIGCHI conference on Human factors in computing systems: Empowering people, pp. 175–182 (1990)
18. Fickas, S.: Clinical Requirements Engineering. In: ICSE 2005, pp. 140–147. ACM, New York (2005)
19. Gray, P., McBryan, T., Martin, C., Gil, N., Wolters, M., Mayo, N., Turner, K., Docherty, L., Wang, F., Kolberg, M.: A Scalable Home Care System Infrastructure Supporting Domiciliary Care. University of Stirling, Technical Report CSM-173 (2007)
20. Wang, F., Docherty, L.S., Turner, K.J., Kolberg, M., Magill, E.H.: Services and Policies for Care at Home. In: Proc. International Conference on Pervasive Computing Technologies for Healthcare, pp. 7.1-7.10 (2006)
21. Williamson, J., Murray-Smith, R., Hughes, S.: Shoogle: excitatory multimodal interaction on mobile devices. In: Proc. SIGCHI conference on Human factors in computing systems (2007)
22. Turner, K.J., Reiff-Marganiec, S., Blair, L., Pang, J., Gray, T., Perry, P., Ireland, J.: Policy Support for Call Control. Computer Standards and Interfaces 28(6), 635–649 (2006)

Exploiting Web Services and Model-Based User Interfaces for Multi-device Access to Home Applications

Giulio Mori, Fabio Paternò, and Lucio Davide Spano

ISTI-CNR, HIIS Laboratory, Via Moruzzi 1,
56124 Pisa, Italy
{Giulio.Mori, Fabio.Paterno, Lucio.Davide.Spano}@isti.cnr.it

Abstract. This paper presents a method, and the corresponding software archi-tecture and prototype implementation to generate multi-device user interfaces in the home domain. The approach is based on Web services and model-based user interface generation. In particular, it focuses on multi-device interfaces ob-tained starting with XML descriptions of home Web services, which are then mapped onto user interface logical descriptions, from which it is possible to then generate user interfaces adapted to the target devices. During use, the gen-erated interfaces are able to communicate with the home Web services and can be dynamically updated to reflect changes in domestic appliances available and the associated state.

Keywords: User Interface Generation, Web Services, Logical Interface De-scriptions, Home Applications.

1 Introduction

Our work takes into account current technological trends and research results and aims to provide integrated solutions able to allow users to flexibly access functional-ity important for their daily life. In particular, the approach is based on three main aspects:

- In recent years, model-based user interface generation has stimulated increas-ing interest because it can support solutions for multi-device environments ex-ploiting XML logical descriptions and associated transformations for the target devices and implementation languages.
- Web services are increasingly used to support remote access to application functionalities, in particular in ubiquitous environments. They are described using WSDL (Web Services Description Language) files, which are XML-based descriptions as well.
- The home is becoming more and more populated by intelligent devices with the ability to communicate information, thus allowing remote access to their state in order to query or modify it.

The goal of our solution is to allow users to access their domestic appliances from anywhere using any available interactive device. This is obtained by supporting

T.C.N. Graham and P. Palanque (Eds.): DSVIS 2008, LNCS 5136, pp. 181 – 193, 2008.

automatic generation of user interfaces for home applications in such a way as to be able to handle dynamic configurations of home appliances. The resulting environment allows users to dynamically access their home applications involving access to domotic devices such as lights, alarm sensors, media players and so on. We aim to provide dynamic access through multiple interactive devices to multiple functionalities available through Web services (see Figure 1). Regarding the home appliances (such as lights, shutters, air conditioning, video recorders), they can communicate using various types of network protocols. We assume the existence of an intermediate middleware supporting interoperability among such home devices (for example, we have considered the open source environment DomoNet [9]), which provides access to the home devices through Web Services independently of the communications protocols. Thus, the devices can use their original protocol to communicate (examples are UPnP, Konnex, BTicino ...) but then such communication goes through a home server, which makes their services accessible to any client through a unifying format. The goal is also to obtain an environment able to support access even when changes in the available home devices occur.

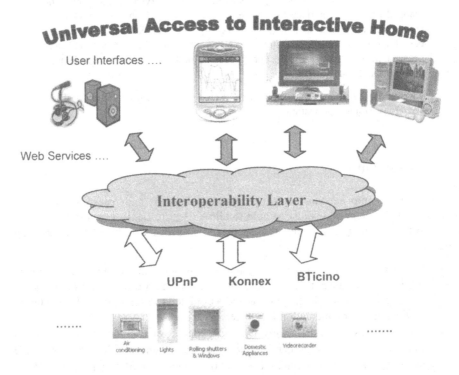

Fig. 1. The Overall Approach

The paper is structured as follows: we first discuss related work, next we provide some background information useful to make the paper self-contained, then we present the overall approach proposed, and show an example application. Lastly, some conclusions are drawn along with indications for future work.

2 Related Work

The increasing availability of interaction device types has raised interest in techniques able to support adaptation of the user interface. In Web applications, the adaptation process can take place in the application server, or in the proxy server or in the client device. Digestor [2] and Power Browser [3] have been solutions that use proxy-based transformations (as in our case) in order to modify the content and structure of Web pages for mobile use. However, they do not use logical descriptions of user interfaces in order to reason about page re-design or apply analysis of the sustainable costs of the target device, as happens in our case. Supple [6] is a tool able to support adaptation by applying intelligent optimization techniques.

One solution that has raised a good deal of interest is the model-based approach in which the logical user interface descriptions are usually represented through XML-based languages (examples are TERESA XML[12], UIML[1], USIXML[7]). In the CAMELEON project [4] a framework describing the various possible abstraction levels was refined based on the experience acquired in this area. A number of tools have been developed aiming to implement such framework (see for example, Multi-modal TERESA [12], ….).

Such logical descriptions have also been exploited in other environments. For example, in Damask [8] they are used along with a sketch editor and the possibility to exploit a number of patterns. PUC [10] is another interesting environment, which uses some logical description but focuses on the automatic generation of consistent user interfaces for domestic appliances (such as printers, copy machines, …). In PUC, logical descriptions of the device to control are downloaded by a mobile device in which the corresponding user interface is automatically generated.

In general, little attention has been paid to the use of user interface model-based approaches for the generation of applications based on Web services. Some work has been dedicated to the generation of user interfaces for Web services [13] [14] but without exploiting model-based approaches to user interfaces. In [15] there is a proposal to extend service descriptions with user interface information. For this purpose the WSDL description is converted to OWL-S format, which is combined with a hierarchical task model and a layout model. We follow a different approach, which aims to support the access to the WSDL without requiring their substantial modifications in order to generate the corresponding user interfaces, still exploiting logical interface descriptions. We aim to address this issue, with particular attention to home applications, which are raising increasing interest given the increasing availability of automatic domestic appliances.

3 Background

In this work we want to investigate solutions for the combined use of Web services and model-based user interfaces. Regarding the description of the logical user interfaces, we have extended TERESA XML [12]. Since this language has already been considered in other papers, herein we just recall the basic concepts in order to make this paper self-contained, highlight the more relevant parts, and indicate its evolution in order to better address the issues raised by this work.

TERESA XML is a set of languages able to describe the various abstraction levels for user interfaces. We consider the levels highlighted by the CAMELEON reference framework [4], which is based on the experiences of the model-based user interface community. There are two platform-independent languages, which means that they are able to describe the relevant concepts for any type of device. They are the language for the task model (which is the ConcurTaskTrees notation [11]) and the language for the abstract user interface description. Then, there is a set of platform-dependent languages, one for the concrete description of each platform considered. We mean for platform a set of devices and associated software environments that share similar interaction capabilities (e.g. form-based graphical desktop, vocal, ...). Such concrete languages are implementation-language independent but depend on the interaction modalities associated with the considered platform (examples are: the desktop direct manipulation graphical platform, the form-based graphical mobile platform, the vocal platform, ...). Each language part of TERESA XML is associated with an XML Schema. We initially used DTDs for this purpose, but their expressiveness is limited.

The abstract description is composed of presentations and connections indicating how to move from one presentation to another. The presentations can include composition operators and interactors. The composition operators are declarative ways to indicate how to put together groups of interactors, in particularly in order to achieve some communication goal, such as highlighting that a group of elements are semantically related to each other (grouping) or that some elements somehow control another group of elements (relation). Associated with groups of elements it is possible to specify the level of importance of the composing elements or whether there is any specific ordering among them. The interactors are declarative descriptions of ways to present information or interaction objects.

All the concrete description languages share the structure defined by the abstract language and refine it by adding elements indicating how the abstract elements can be better defined for the target platform. Thus, the concrete elements are mainly defined by adding attributes to the abstract elements, while still remaining independent of the implementation language. For example the form-based desktop description language can be used to describe user interfaces implemented in XHTML or Windows Forms or Java Swing.

Our work on the home case study has been useful to identify some of the abstractions missing in previous versions of TERESA XML, such as alarms, the possibility to enter numerical values within a range, the possibility to have activators associated with multiple functionality selectable by the user. One important modification has been the introduction of dynamic connections, which means the possibility of moving to a presentation dynamically, in such a way that the actual target presentation depends on some condition tested at run-time.

4   The Proposed Approach

In order to reach our goals, the proposed environment is based on a user interface generator (UIG) server, whose architecture is represented in Figure 2, which receives access requests from the user.

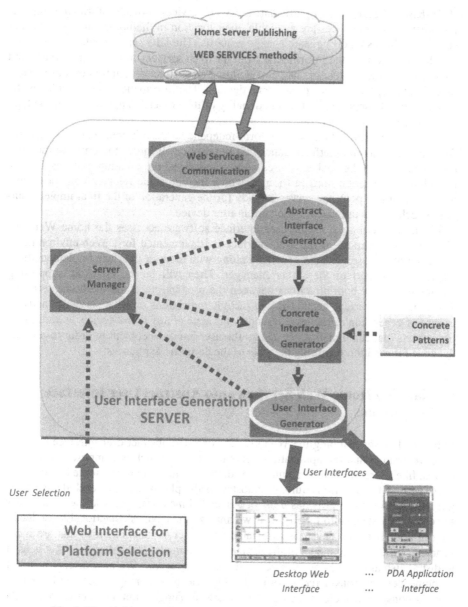

Fig. 2. The Architecture for Platform-dependent User Interface Generation

The first request is the selection of the environment that the user prefers to use in terms of type of device (mobile, desktop, vocal, ...) and implementation language preferred (XHTML, Java, C#, ...).

At the time of the request, the UIG server accesses the home server, which supports access to the home appliances. Such home server is accessible through Web services, which export the list of possible methods and their parameters through an

XML-based WSDL file. In particular, the Web services provide information regarding what home appliances are available, their location in the home, and their current state, as well as supporting state change requests. The UIG server contains a module, which is able to take the information from the Web services of the home server, and then pass it to the module in charge of building an abstract description of a user interface able to support access to the home devices. The information passed includes the list of methods supported by the functionality of the domestic appliances and the type of parameters they can accept.

The abstract description is a platform-independent description, which is then refined into a concrete, platform-dependent description. In order to complete the concrete description, the tool also uses some predefined presentation patterns for the considered application domain (home), which include some relevant content (icons, texts, ...). At this point the server is ready for the generation of the final implementation, which is then uploaded to the current user device.

During the user session, the user interface software accesses the home Web services. For this purpose, if the user interface is implemented for a Web environments then a set of Java servlets are generated along with the user interface implementation, which become part of the server manager. They will be the elements supporting communication in both directions between the user interface and the home services. Thus, the user interface generated will include indications on what servlet to activate in case of generation of requests to modify the state of any home device, as well as on the servlets that can dynamically update the user interface content in order to provide dynamic information regarding the state of the domestic appliances.

5   Mapping Home Web Services onto Abstract User Interface Descriptions

In the module for mapping the Web services onto the abstract user interface description, we assume that the application refers to a home, which is composed of various rooms. In each room there is a number of devices, which belong to some device category (such as DimmerLightBulb, thermostat, media player, ...). For each device category, the Web service provides a list of associated methods, which allow users either to access their state or to modify it. If we analyze the devices' functionality in detail, we can note that each device is associated with a set of functionalities that are independent of the specific model of the device, one parameter is the device id that is used to distinguish among various devices in the same category. We now discuss a subset of home devices considered in order to illustrate how our approach works. Other devices considered include media players able to support remote access to various types of multimedia files.

The *LightBulb* device is associated with the methods:
-       *turnOnLight*: has no return parameters, it is a write-only method with a Boolean as second parameter. Thus, it is used to send two possible values (on and off), each of which can be associated with a specific button.
-       *isLightOn*: has a Boolean return parameter, thus it is a read-only method. The representation of the value can be given by an output-only object

DimmerLightBulb is a device subclass of lightBulb, which adds the possibility to control the brightness value. Its methods are:

- *setDimmerValue*: has no return parameter, it is a write-only method that accepts as input as second parameter a short integer indicating the value that is set for the dimmer. Thus, the corresponding additional interaction element is a numerical_in_range_edit object, whose parameters are the min and max possible values and a Boolean indicating whether the range is continuous.
- *getDimmerValue*: has a return value indicating the state of the dimmer, which can be represented through an output-only object.
- *getDimmerRange*: is useful to know the limits of the possible values, which can be represented through two output-only objects.

The *thermostat* is associated with the methods:

- *setCurrentTemperature*: has no return parameter, thus it is a write-only method, and the second parameter is a short integer, which can be edited through a numerical_edit object.
- *currentTemperature*: has a short integer as return parameter, thus it is a read-only method, which can be associated with an output-only text object.
- *getcurrentTemperatureRange*: is useful to know the range of the possible values independent of the adopted solution for the control.

Sensor represents any type of sensor that can generate an alarm, and it has only one method:

- *getSensorStatus*: has a Boolean as a return parameter, thus it is a read-only method. When the Boolean is set to true then an alarm object is activated.

Alarm represents an alarm device and has the methods:

- *setAlarmState*: has no return parameters, thus it is a write method with the second parameter as integer. Usually three values are used ON/Off and an intermediate value.
- getAlarmState: is a read method, whose return parameter is an integer. The representations of such values can be (Total – Partial - Off) .

In the application of these mappings, we could obtain cases in which an interactive element to set the state of a device is separated from the output element that shows the device state. However, in some cases, for example a mobile user interface in which screen space is limited, it may be useful to have a single interactive element able to cover both aspects (possibility of changing the state and showing actual state). For example, a dimmer can have a slide bar control for both purposes: showing the current value, which can be received from the home device, but also allowing the user to change it sending the new value as result of the interaction. In order to identify such cases, we have developed a heuristic indicating that when in the WSDL we find two methods with complementary structures (such as set xxx value and get xxx value) associated to one device, then they are mapped onto one element able to support both methods instead of two separate interface elements. These mappings are exploited in the building of the abstract user interface.

In this approach, the goal is to obtain an abstract description of a user interface, which when it will be generated it will be able to directly communicate with the Web services. Through this communication, some parts of the user interface will be dynamically filled in (in terms of data values), such as the list of available home devices, eventually filtered by type. Below we show an excerpt of the WSDL considered. At the beginning the types of home devices are defined. All of them are subclass of DomoDevice, which has the common basic attributes (such as room, name, ...).

In the following WSDL excerpt, there is the Light Bulb, which has the methods TurnOnLight and IsLightOn; we can also note that the TurnOnLight has two parameters: the device (LightBulb) and a Boolean:

```
<?xml version="1.0" encoding="UTF-8"?>
<wsdl:definitions ... >
  <wsdl:types>
     ...
     <s:complexType name="LightBulb">
        <s:complexContent mixed="false">
          <s:extension base="tns:Lighting"/>
        </s:complexContent>
     </s:complexType>
     ...
     <s:element name="TurnOnLight">
        <s:complexType>
          <s:sequence>
<s:elementminOccurs="0" maxOccurs="1" name="bulb" type="tns:LightBulb"/>
<s:element minOccurs="1" maxOccurs="1" name="on" type="s:boolean"/>
          </s:sequence>
        </s:complexType>
     </s:element>
     .......
     <s:element name="IsLightOn">
        <s:complexType>
          <s:sequence>
<s:elementminOccurs="0" maxOccurs="1" name="bulb" type="tns:LightBulb"/>
          </s:sequence>
        </s:complexType>
     </s:element>
     ...
  </wsdl:types>
     ...
  </wsdl:portType>
  ...
</wsdl:definitions>
```

6 From the Abstract Description to the Concrete Descriptions and the Implementations

The abstract structure of the resulting user interface is structured as a vertical grouping of three grouping elements (see Figure 3): one dedicated to the header (containing a logo/title), one to the main area, and one to the footer (containing some controls that allow dynamic filtering of the device list, for example according to the type of room or to the type of device). The corresponding user interface is in Figure 4: in the footer grouping there are the buttons associated with the type of rooms available in the home and general controls, such as the Disconnect button. In the main area there are two grouping: one dedicated to the map zone (which provides a graphical representation

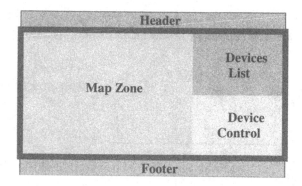

Fig. 3. The structure of the desktop interface

of the rooms available), and one to the device area, which is a vertical grouping of a grouping dedicated to the available devices' list and one to the controls for the currently selected device.

Below there is the excerpt of the abstract description that indicates how this presentation is structured through the composition operators:

```
<?xml version="1.0"?>
<!DOCTYPE interface PUBLIC …  >

<interface>
  <presentation name="Main_Presentation">
    <interactor_composition>
      <operator name="grouping_Application" />
          <interactor_composition>
          <operator name="grouping_Header" />
          …
          </interactor_composition>
          <interactor_composition>
          <operator name="grouping_Central_Zone" />
              <operator name="grouping_Map_ZONE" />
              …
              </interactor_composition>
              <interactor_composition>
              <operator name="grouping_Device_Area" />
              <interactor_composition>
              <operator name="grouping_Devices_List" />
              …
              </interactor_composition>
              <interactor_composition>
              <operator name="grouping_Devices_Control" />
              …
              </interactor_composition>
          </interactor_composition>
        <interactor_composition>
        <operator name="grouping_Footer" />
        …
        </interactor_composition>
</interactor_composition>
  </presentation>
</interface>
```

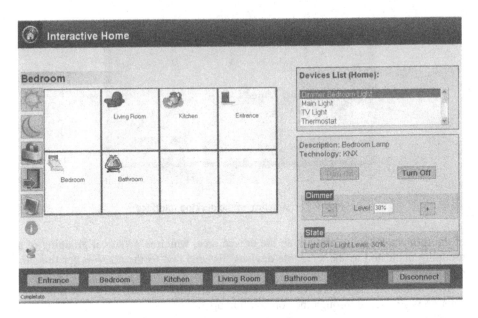

Fig. 4. The desktop interface

More in detail, each area contains specific interactors and composition operators. It is important to note that in the user interface there are some parts, which are dynamic (in particular the Device Control part). This means that, depending on the type of device dynamically selected at run time, different controls will be shown in this part of the user interface in order to operate with them. This has been obtained by extending the TERESA XML language in such a way to include dynamic connections, which means connections in which the target presentation changes depending on a value that is identified at run-time. Thus, through the analysis of the WSDL we are able to identify all the possible target presentations and the associated structure. In addition, we are also able to identify the values (in this case the device type value) which are associated with each of them.

In particular, while in the previous version of TERESA XML a connection was defined through the interactor triggering it and the corresponding target presentation:

interactor ----------- connection ---------------> target presentation

Now, we also associate the interactor with a set of possible values, which are known through an analysis of the WSDL and the connection can have multiple target presentations:

Interactor (values) ----------- connection ---------------> multiple target presentations

the actual value considered is generated at run-time depending on the user interaction with the interactor and determines which target presentation to activate. Thus, in our case at run-time, depending on the actual device selected by the user, different pages with different controls will be shown. This was also obtained through another small extension in the TERESA XML language, for which the activator element can be associated with multiple functionality rather than only with a single one, as it happened in the previous version. This feature is used when the user selects a device from the available device list and depending on the selection a different Web service functionality will be activated. Below we can see the abstract user interface description of the Device Control in the case of a Dimmer Light Bulb type of device:

```
<interactor_composition>
<operator name="grouping_Basic_Device_Control" />
              <interactor id="TurnOn_Button">
                <interaction category="interaction">
                <control type="control">
                <activator object="activator" />
                </control></interaction></interactor>
              <interactor id="TurnOff_Button">
           <interaction category="interaction">
                 <control type="control">
                <activator object="activator" />
                  </control></interaction></interactor>
      </interactor_composition>
      <interactor_composition>
  <operator name="grouping_Advanced_Control" />
        <interactor id="Decrease_Level_Button">
          <interaction category="interaction">
             <control type="control">
             <activator object="activator" />
             </control></interaction></interactor>
             <interactor id="Level_Light">
             <interaction category="interaction">
             <edit type="edit">
             <text_edit object="alphanumeric" />
             </edit></interaction></interactor>
        <interactor id="Increase_Level_Button">
          <interaction category="interaction">
             <control type="control">
             <activator object="activator" />
             </control></interaction></interactor>
        </interactor_composition>
      </interactor_composition>
```

We can note that the grouping_Basic_Device_Control represents the set of basic controls (associated with a Light Bulb), while the grouping_Advanced_Control represents the additional controls (associated with a Dimmer Light Bulb), which provide the additional possibility of choosing the brightness level. Figure 4 shows the resulting user interface for a desktop platform.

The creation of the mobile version is obtained by applying a cost-based semantic redesign transformation in the process of building the concrete description. The starting point is still the same abstract user interfaces. The first version of the concrete description created preserves the same structure but is associated with content for the mobile device in this case. This means smaller icons and, generally, more simplified representations. Then, the concrete description is transformed to better match the currently available resources. Thus, it takes information regarding the screen size of the current device and depending on this it splits the original presentations into presentations more suitable for the current target device. The splitting is based on the logical structure of the user interface. This means that the resulting cost of the composed elements is calculated and if it is too expensive for the device then a new presentation is allocated for this set of elements and the connections to support navigation with it are automatically generated. In our example, simplified versions of the header and footer are generated. Then, the grouping associated with the room list has a cost sufficient to fill in a mobile presentation. The grouping associated with the list of available devices, which is dynamically filled in at run-time is associated with another specific mobile presentation. Also the grouping associated with the device controls has a cost sufficient to fill in a presentation. Lastly, the corresponding user interfaces are generated, Figure 5 shows three presentations for the mobile version.

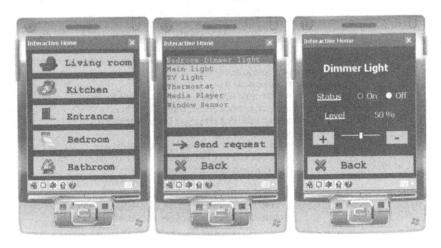

Fig. 5. The interface for the mobile device

7   Conclusions and Future Work

We have reported on a work that aims to bridge the use of Web services and model-based user interface generation for home applications. We have discussed the method developed for this purpose and the corresponding software architecture and prototype implementation. In the paper we have also discussed how TERESA XML has been extended in order to support a more flexible set of interaction techniques and dynamic pages, whose interactive elements depends on information-generated dynamically at run-time in the communication between the user and the home Web services.

Future work will be dedicated to testing the usability of the automatically generated user interfaces for the various interactive devices, considering the use of ontologies for richer semantic descriptions and analysis, and the application to other case studies (such as remote elderly monitoring and assistance).

References

1. Abrams, M., Phanouriou, C., Batongbacal, A., Williams, S., Shuster, J.: UIML: An Appliance-Independent XML User Interface Language. In: Proceedings of the 8th WWW conference (1999)
2. Bickmore, T., Girgensohn, A., Sullivan, J.: Web-page Filtering and Re-Authoring for Mobile Users. The Computer Journal 42(6), 534–546 (1999)
3. Buyukkokten, O., Kaljuvee, O., Garcia-Molina, H., et al.: Efficient Web Browsing on Handheld Devices Using Page and Form Summarization. ATOIS 20(1), 82–115 (2002)
4. Calvary, G., Coutaz, J., Thevenin, D., Bouillon, L., Florins, M., Limbourg, Q., Souchon, N., Vanderdonckt, J., Marucci, L., Paternò, F., Santoro, C.: The CAMELEON Reference Framework, Deliverable D1.1 (2002)
5. Florins, M., Vanderdonckt, J.: Graceful degradation of user interfaces as a design method for multiplatform systems. Intelligent User Interfaces, 140-147 (2004)
6. Gajos, K., Christianson, D., Hoffmann, R., Shaked, T., Henning, K., Long, J.J., Weld, D.S.: Fast and robust interface generation for ubiquitous applications. In: Beigl, M., Intille, S.S., Rekimoto, J., Tokuda, H. (eds.) UbiComp 2005. LNCS, vol. 3660, pp. 37–55. Springer, Heidelberg (2005)
7. Limbourg, Q., Vanderdonckt, J.: UsiXML: A User Interface Description Language Supporting Multiple Levels of Independence. In: Engineering Advanced Web Applications. Rinton Press, Paramus (2004)
8. Lin, J., Landay, J.: Employing Patterns and Layers for Early-Stage Design and Prototyping of Cross-Device User Interfaces. In: Proceedings, C.H.I. (ed.) Proceedings CHI 2008, Floremce (April 2008)
9. Miori, V., Tarrini, L., Manca, M., Tolomei, G.: - An open standard solution for domotic interoperability. IEEE Transactions on Consumer Electronics 52(1), 97–103 (2006)
10. Nichols, J., Myers, B.A., Rothrock, B.: UNIFORM: Automatically Generating Consistent Remote Control User Interfaces. In: CHI 2006, pp. 611–620. ACM Press, New York (2006)
11. Paternò, F.: Model-based Design and Evaluation of Interactive Applications. Springer, Heidelberg (1999)
12. Paternò, F., Santoro, C., Mantyjarvi, J., Mori, G., Sansone, S.: Authoring Pervasive MultiModal User Interfaces. International Journal of Web Engineering and Technology (2) (2008)
13. Song, K., Lee, K.-H.: An automated generation of xforms interfaces for web services. In: Proceedings of the International Conference on Web Services, pp. 856–863 (2007)
14. Spillner, J., Braun, I., Schill, A.: Flexible Human Service Interfaces. In: Proceedings of the 9th International Conference on Enterprise Information Systems, pp. 79–85 (2007)
15. Vermeulen, J., Vandriessche, Y., Clerckx, T., Luyten, K., Coninx, K.: Service-interaction Descriptions: Augmenting Services with User Interface Models. In: Proceedings Engineering Interactive Systems 2007. Springer, Heidelberg (2007)

Resources for Situated Actions

Gavin Doherty[1], Jose Campos[2], and Michael Harrison[3]

[1] Trinity College Dublin, Dublin 2, Ireland
[2] University of Minho, Portugal
[3] Newcastle University, UK
Gavin.Doherty@cs.tcd.ie, Michael.Harrison@ncl.ac.uk,
jose.campos@di.umhinho.pt

Abstract. In recent years, advances in software tools have made it easier to analyze interactive system specifications, and the range of their possible behaviors. However, the effort involved in producing the specifications of the system is still substantial, and a difficulty exists regarding the specification of plausible behaviors on the part of the user. Recent trends in technology towards more mobile and distributed systems further exacerbates the issue, as contextual factors come in to play, and less structured, more opportunistic behavior on the part of the user makes purely task-based analysis difficult. In this paper we consider a resourced action approach to specification and analysis. In pursuing this approach we have two aims - firstly, to facilitate a resource-based analysis of user activity, allowing resources to be distributed across a number of artifacts, and secondly to consider within the analysis a wider range of plausible and opportunistic user behaviors without a heavy specification overhead, or requiring commitment to detailed user models.

1 Introduction

It is typical in human computer interaction when specifying the system to describe the tasks that are the proposed basis for the work to be supported. A process of task analysis elicits the tasks that people carry out with the existing system used as a basis for designing the tasks for which the new design is intended. The problem with this approach is that the way the user actually uses the proposed system in practice may differ from what the designer expects.

In order to reason about the usability of the system we must introduce some notion of plausible user behavior. However, if we introduce overly restrictive or unrealistic assumptions about user behavior, the value and validity of our analysis can be questioned. For example, consider an analysis of whether the user is likely to put the proposed system into an unsafe or undesirable state. We need to introduce assumptions about the behavior of the user because exhaustively checking the system model alone will throw up an unlimited number of spurious problems. Exhaustive analysis corresponds to the assumption that the user will interact with the system (e.g. push buttons) at random. Hence, in looking at the effect of a sequence of user actions on the system, we do not want to consider traces which the user is unlikely to carry out (irrespective of whether they are "good" or "bad" actions).

If we combine the system model with a task model, we assume that the user will follow the pattern of interaction defined by the structure of the task. While this may

T.C.N. Graham and P. Palanque (Eds.): DSVIS 2008, LNCS 5136, pp. 194–207, 2008.
© Springer-Verlag Berlin Heidelberg 2008

still correspond to a large number of possible behaviors, the resulting set can still be criticized as being too prescriptive. This approach can still ignore many highly plausible behaviors and will be unsuitable for many goal directed situations for which the tasks are not well defined. Furthermore, in the real-world, users often behave opportunistically according to the situation they are in, and the resources and actions available to them in that situation.

An alternative approach is to start the other way round. Here the resources that are expected to help the user: to achieve goals; to make choices between actions; to carry out specific activities [10] are considered explicitly. Resources are codified in terms of: status or state; action possibility; action effect information; the plans that are appropriate to achieve goals and goal information. These resources act as constraints on the user and under certain assumptions will create the circumstances in which the goals are achieved. The model makes explicit how these resources are organized and defined in the interface. This can be used in analysis to explore the possible paths that are permitted by the resource organization. In [3] we looked at the resourcing of actions within a task structure; in this paper we develop the analysis a step further, and examine the feasibility of a purely action-based analysis in which we do not commit to a particular task structure, similar to that described in [10] but in this case applied to a formal model. We explore an approach to modeling and analysis based on resource constraints in two ways. We first consider the dyadic relationship between the user and the device. The user has goals and the device supports them in achieving these goals. We explore this relationship and the constraints that are imposed by resources. The device is in practice embedded within a context. This context may additionally constrain the user. Hence the second part of the paper explores the user embedded within a smart environment. We explore a control system where the operator is only able to control aspects of the system when they are within a certain proximity of the system or if they have saved the control for future use. We explore different assumptions about the resources provided to users within this environment, and the potential effects on user strategies and behaviour.

We propose that by looking at the resourcing of individual actions, we can selectively introduce constraints on user behaviors which need not be as restrictive as a task model. We propose that this is also a natural and useful vehicle for analysis of a design, and particularly suited to recent trends towards more mobile, distributed and heterogeneous systems. An added advantage is that we can take advantage of tool support for exploring the consequences of these assumptions.

2   The Resourced Action Approach

Individual user actions are taken as the basic units of analysis. The resourcing of each of these actions is specified independently. The focus of analysis then becomes whether each individual user action is appropriately resourced, or whether appropriate combinations of resourced actions will lead to the achievement of user goals. The starting point is that for an action to be afforded in a particular context, certain information resources must be present in that context. For example, if a mobile phone (the device) has an action to save a draft text message, we could specify that (1) action availability is resourced (the "save" option is currently on the screen), (2) the action is enabled (the message memory is not full), (3) action-effect information is available (is the label "save to drafts" or just "save"?), and (4) required information about the current state is available (have I saved it already?). Regardless of how I ended up editing a text message (did I reply to another message, is it a group text?), or higher level user tasks and goals (which may be varied), the basic resourcing for this action remains much the same.

The specification of the system is thus structured as a set of actions, which affect the state of the system, accompanied by an appropriate model of system state. Various forms of interactive system specification (including interactor models) could provide a means to build this specification, and indeed Modal Action Logic [4] focuses on the actions supported in an interface, but the additional structuring provided by interactor models is not a necessary part of the approach. A difference from other approaches to interactive system analysis is the addition of resourcing requirements to accompany each action. We can consider more sequentially constrained interactions if needed, whether this is through the structure of the system, or due to likely plan-based behavior by the end user. Even if we take the view that actions are situated [9], we can still allow for the possibility by considering plans themselves as resources [10]. It is important to note that this approach is not just a vehicle for automated analysis of behavior, but also leads us to consider, in a methodical fashion, the resourcing of situated user actions. The possibility of tool support however, allows us to more easily and comprehensively identify situations where actions may be inadequately resourced.

The rest of this section considers the steps involved in the analysis. The approach is comparable with a number of other evaluation techniques. For example cognitive walkthrough [8] takes a task or scenario and requires the analyst to ask questions systematically of the interface. The questions have similarities with those that are used in this paper. The main difference between this work and cognitive walkthrough techniques in general is that (i) the information that resources the interaction is considered in more detail in terms of the type of information that it is and (ii) the aim of the activity is to move towards a formal analysis and representation of these resources. Observational techniques on the other hand such as distributed cognition [5] explore the environment in which the work is carried out to characterize how action is resourced. Elements of distributed cognition are also captured in the approach described in the paper. Our basic premise is to specify and examine the resourcing of individual actions. This approach can form a useful vehicle for goal based analysis, as one can ask questions such as whether resourced actions are available which will support achievement of the user's goal. The basic process proposed is as follows:

- specify the actions
- specify the resourcing of actions, and perform initial analysis, possibly redesigning and refining specification
- consider and specify potential user goals
- formulate properties, including those surrounding user goals
- run the properties over the model, and analyze the results, possibly redesigning and refining the specification

Of importance for mobile applications is the fact that actions may only be resourced in particular locations; in this case a location model (however simple) must be included within the analysis. Likewise, certain actions, including those to access particular resources, may only be available in certain locations. We will explore the issue of context and location modeling further in Section 3. We have a choice to make in terms of analysis regarding how much of the user's mental state we wish to include in the analysis; if a current state of knowledge of the user is important to the analysis, then this state of knowledge must be propagated through the steps of the interaction. For the purposes of this paper, we do not pursue this form of user modeling, although it is an attractive proposition for certain types of analysis, for example mode error.

2.1 Specifying Resources

The specification progresses by defining actions. Having specified the actions, we move on to consider the resources which are required for the user to carry out these actions. To do this effectively we must know whether information which is potentially available through the system is visible when the action is to be carried out. Thus some visibility model must be included; this can include what is seen in the environment as well as the device. We have a choice of specifying the exact information to be displayed, or simply indicating the availability of the resource. Existing mechanisms for denoting visible state, such as those in interactor models can be used. Within an automata-based specification language such as Uppaal we can associate resources with states, although use could also be made of integer variables and synchronizations. The system specification defines two things: the resources which are available in a given state, and the actions which can be performed, which affect the set of available resources. Following [10], we consider here what form these may take in terms of typical interfaces.

- *status/visible information* - a resource may simply consist of a piece of information, for example the display indicates that a message is waiting (a resource) in order for the user to perform an action to read the message. This is distinct from the system being in a state where reading a message is possible. The same mechanism can also indicate system status if this is being used in the user's interaction strategy.
- *action possibility* - a resource may consist of information that an action is available. There are two issues here, one is the information that the possibility for carrying out the action exists (e.g. the resource lets the user know they can save an unsent message for resending later, a feature they were unaware of), the second is that the action is enabled (or not) in the current state - perhaps the message memory is full.
- *action effect information* - a resource may let the user know what the likely effect of an action will be. The same piece of information on action availability may also convey information on action effect; "press ok to save" conveys information both on action possibility and on action effect.
- *plan information* - some resources provide plan information, that is, they aid in the sequencing of user actions. For example, interfaces in which an overall task performance sequence is made explicit ("You are in step 3 of 5") are providing a plan resource. We could deal with plan resources in much the same way as for tasks, and either trigger a hardcoded sequence or simply constrain certain aspects of the behavior or sequence - effectively providing a partial model.

- *goal information* - some resources may correspond to user goals, helping the user to formulate and keep track of multiple goals. For example, "there are new messages" could act as a goal resource within the interaction. In complex, real-world situations, there may well be a hierarchy of different goals, and goals may possibly conflict, so denoting resources as goal resources is only a small part of the analysis of goals.
- *internal resources* - some resources may be internal to the user - knowledge in the user's head instead of the world. In terms of modeling, we would be introducing resources and updating them with actions (such as reading the system display).

A question in terms of specification is whether any element of this categorization is contained within the model? Given that a resource may play a number of different roles, this could be problematic, however there is also the issue that a particular presentation of the information may support some uses better than others. While specifying the resourcing for particular actions, it is natural to identify obvious resourcing issues. As the analyst must consider each action and appropriate resources, it may be clear that a particular resource would not be available in the proposed design, and an immediate consideration would be given to the problem. However, many resourcing problems may be more subtle in their evolution, and will not be clear from inspection, particularly if the user has multiple goals, and interleaves actions which contribute to different goals. Other issues could relate to the impact of interruptions on the resourcing of particular actions.

2.2 Using Goals in Analysis

Without assuming a set of predefined tasks we assume the interaction is purposeful in the sense that the user has a goal. The user carries out a set of actions to achieve several goals through simple action or a complicated orchestration of activities. Well designed systems provide relevant information that can be acted upon by the user. This information might remind the user of their goal or the means by which they are to achieve the goal or the possibilities for action or how to invoke the action itself. Our analysis will be carried out with respect to user goals to include:

1. Goal is to obtain information - is it possible to reach a state or resource configuration in which the information resource is available?
2. Goal is to perform a procedure - the actions of the procedure are resourced, and the sequencing of the procedure is possible while providing appropriate resources at each point.
3. Goal is to put the system in a particular state or set of states - fully resourced sequences exist in which state is reached.

By default, this form of analysis will view usability problems in terms of insufficiently resourced actions, and suggest increased resources at key points in the interaction.

2.3 Tool Support for Analysis

If we specify the system state, in terms of resources, and the behavior of the system, in terms of the effects on available resources, we can examine the resource requirements of individual actions. A question which then arises is how tool support can be used to support the analysis. With respect to the three analyses in Section 2.2 above, property (1) is simple reachability - can we reach a state in which the resource is available. This however, does not tell us anything about whether it is plausible that the user would get to this state. Property (2) is the form of analysis introduced in [3] - we have a task structure to be followed, and we need to check that each step in the task is appropriately resourced. With this form of analysis the behaviors considered are plausible, but many plausible behaviors are ignored. The final property (3) tells us that we can reach the goal through an appropriately resourced sequence of actions, but does not constrain this sequence. In terms of the mechanics of the analysis process, we might well split complex goals up into a number of sub-goals, and look at these sub-goals independently and in combination. As stated previously our analyses will generally introduce assumptions about the user behavior - in this case, that the resources we specify for the actions are used by the user in selecting and carrying out those actions. There are a number of distinct modes of analysis based on these:

[Assumptions+Starting situation+Model+Task+Goal -> Boolean] When we combine these assumptions with a model of the system and a model of user behavior (e.g. a task model) and a starting situation we can ask whether the goal state is always reached when we carry out the task.

[Assumptions+Model+Task+Goal -> Starting situations] If we leave the starting situation undefined, we can ask for which starting situations we can/will reach the goal by performing the task.

[Assumptions+Model+Goal+Starting situations -> Behaviours] Alternatively, we can simply give the starting situation and system model, and analyze the range of possible behaviors which result in both positive and negative outcomes. The analysis in this case would focus on the strategies represented by this behavior and if they can be improved or added to by altering the resourcing of user actions.

[Assumptions+Model+Goal -> Starting situations] If we do not specify the starting situations, just as for the task based analysis, we can ask under which conditions we are resourced sufficiently to reach the goal.

Model checking enables exploration of the behavior of a (finite) model of the system. Modeling assumptions and tasks as restrictions on the system's behavior, we can determine whether specific (goal) states can always be reached. This corresponds to the first type of analysis identified above. Regarding the second type of analysis, if the starting situation is left undefined, model checking will attempt to provide counter examples. However these counter-examples identify situations under which the system does not exhibit the desired behavior. The alternative, then, is to generate all possible starting situations (remember that the models must be finite for model checking to work) and reduce the analysis to a series of instances of the first type. The exhaustive generation of these initial situations can, of course, be tool supported. Regarding the third type of analysis, model checking enables, as already noted, the identifications of behaviors that do not result in the achievement of a goal. These behaviors can then be analyzed to understand how the resourcing can be changed to prevent them. In the last type of analysis, and because we are not prescribing a behavior, we can perform an analysis similar to the previous one, but paying attention to the initial states of the behaviors being generated by the tool. The iterative aspect of the process provides an additional advantage over cognitive walkthrough (beyond considering all the behaviors rather than just one).

3 Smart Environment Example

In this section we illustrate the role of resources in specification through a ubiquitous system designed to support a process control system [7]. For the analysis, we make use of a set of Uppaal models [1] which define the state of the system and the mobile device, including its location. There is no space in this paper to describe Uppaal in detail. A detailed explanation of the models is not required to appreciate the approach (see http://homepages.cs.ncl.ac.uk/michael.harrison/papers/pucketmobobsnr2.xml for one version of the model compatible with Uppaal 4.0.6). As stated previously, the analysis is to a large extent independent of the formalism, as long as we can reason about the availability of both actions and information within a particular situation. We can see our model of the setting as comprising a number of components, the plant, incorporating tanks and pumps, the mobile device, and the context.

The details of the process are irrelevant to the current consideration and can be found in [6]. Our concern is how the goal of the process is achieved by an operator, along the lines discussed in section 2.3, as she moves with her mobile device around the plant carrying out appropriate actions. The process that is carried out is depicted in Figure 1. Two goals can be achieved by the process, namely to produce product C or to produce product D. To produce product C a material (A) must be pumped into tank 1 using pump 1 (and the tanks involved must be empty for this process to be carried out successfully). Once tank 1 is full then pump 3 is put into forward mode (pump 3 is directional) to move the material from tank 1 to tank 2 thereby filling tank 2. The pumps then pause while tank 2 cooks the material, changing it from A to C. The flow of pump 3 is then reversed and tank 1, which had previously been emptied, is filled with the product. The final stage involves using pump 5 to remove the product from tank 1. The second goal is achieved in a similar manner. Tank 1 is also used in this process but this time it is fed from pump 2 and the cooking process takes place in tank 3 producing product D.

The questions that our analysis raises are (1) how do we arrive at plausible behaviors for achieving these two different goals? (2) given a specific proposal for the design as represented in a specification, how are these behaviors resourced and should further features of the design be introduced in order to support the actions that the user must carry out?

The model that is illustrated in this paper is designed to demonstrate that a resource based approach will aid the process of design and the exploration of alternatives. The model describes the underlying process (a part of this process is described in the model of Figure 2). Figure 2 describes the bi-directional pumps (3 and 4). This timed automaton captures the actions that are supported by the pumps (*back?*, *forward?*, *off?*, *on?*), the type of material contained in the tanks represented at each side of the pump (*tk1t*, *tk2t*) and volume of material in the two tanks (*t1*, *t2*). It also models the time it takes to pump the material (*t*). This process information therefore reflects an abstraction of the actual state of the pumps and tanks and describes the actions that are available at any given state, regardless of how this information is resourced. This

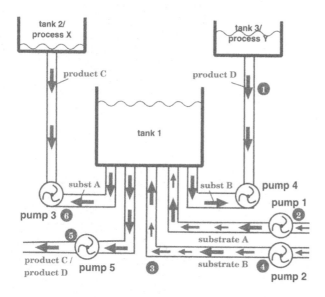

Fig. 1. The process three tanks and five valves

information combined with further aspects of the model, that will be discussed next, represent the system state without any concern for the interface to the operator. The focus has been how to provide a faithful though abstract description of the system.

The important feature of the model from the perspective of the paper is to capture those aspects of the system that combine resource information with the states and available actions. The model of the process as a whole should also include where the operator is in relation to the pumps that are distributed around the physical area of the plant. This information is captured by Figure 5. This model represents where the operator is (LCR represents the control room and LPi the location of each pump i). It represents the physical topology of the space in the sense that for example if the operator is near to pump 5 then it is possible to move to pump 3 or pump 1 without visiting any other locations. Hence in the case of this system the *possibilities* for action will include where the operator is located (it might reasonably be assumed that the operator will know where the values are located in relation to these actions).

The most important part of the model from a resource point of view is the mobile device (see Figure 3, first described in [7]). The model in Figure 4 describes six types of interaction sequence. It simplifies the notion of its location in the sense that there is no notion of being in transit (*move?* moves from one location to another). All "download" (*download?*) actions mapped to the "component selector" therefore act on the location at which the device is and download the controls that are available for the proximal pump (see Figure 3). They appear in the larger display indicated (hence pump 1 is currently available). The switch (*switch?*) feature mapped to the "bucket selector" allows the operator to save controls for future use wherever the device is located. Hence in the example (Figure 3) pump 5 has previously been saved using a switch. It is possible in this case to switch again and make use of pump 5 controls. These features are modeled in Figure 4. The more complicated part of the model

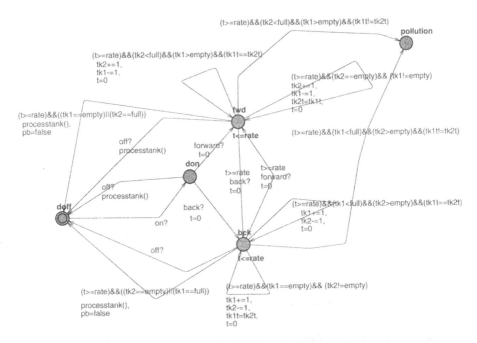

Fig. 2. The bi-directional pump, note the fwd and bck states

describes the actions that are supported by the different types of pump. Depending on the value of "valve" the operator is able to carry out actions that are appropriate to the type of model in the main display. Hence in the present example valve will have the value 1 and if the on button is selected then the model reaches a state (*dp*) where the actions available are all the actions available to the directional pump. These actions themselves control the model described in Figure 2.

The first level of exploration of resourcing involves simply inspecting the models, identifying how the operator's activity is resourced. This involves asking questions about the state of the system, whether the operator should be aware of the state and whether the possible actions appropriate to achieving a goal are clear in that state. In practice it would be feasible to label actions or states to emphasize the role that they play as resources as was discussed in [3]. In this particular case it makes sense to make distinctions between:

Movement actions that change the context of interaction, and the actions available via the mobile device. In this specification we have produced a separate model of location (Figure 5).

Downloading a control affects both the state of the device, and the available information for the end user.

Operating a control affects the state of the plant and also the device.

Reading the display does not affect the system or device models, but could affect the user model if one is included in the analysis. For an analysis based on Uppaal it is potentially convenient to include such actions to facilitate analysis within the tools.

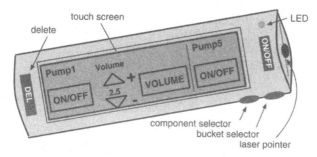

Fig. 3. The hand-held device

The second level of exploration is described in Section 2.3 as the approach: *[Assumptions+Model+Goal+Starting situations -> Behaviors]*. Several assumptions have already been made in the model (for example assumptions about the location of the pumps and the nature of the underlying process). The starting situations are also assumed in the model, that the various tanks are empty for example. The process is iterative. Once behaviors have been considered this leads to the addition of further assumptions about the model to explore more "efficient" behaviors. The goal of producing product C is explored through the LTL property: E<>((tank1==empty)&&(tank1m==C)). This

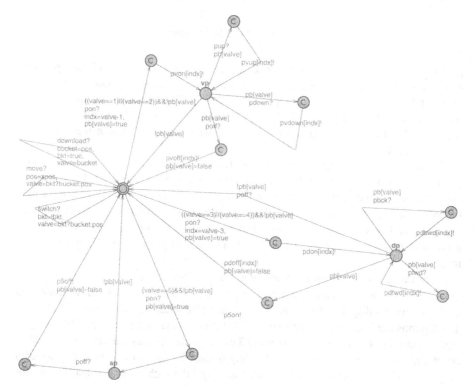

Fig. 4. The model of the hand-held device

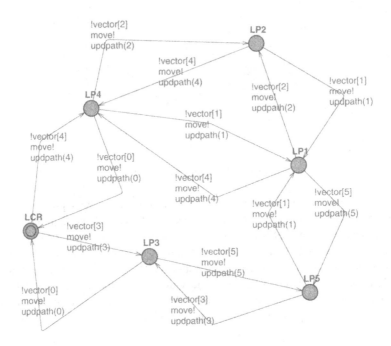

Fig. 5. The model of the space

property is satisfied when pump 5 has been used to evacuate tank 1 and the type of the material is C. The model checker generates a trace in which the operator starts at LCP, visits LP4, then LP1 and uses pump 1 to fill tank 1. The operator then moves to LP5 followed by LP3, using pump 3 first to fill tank 2 from tank1 and then reversing the direction of the pump and filling tank1 from tank 2 with material C, and then going back to LP5 to evacuate tank 1.

The Uppaal system enables the designer to explore the path and at each step to explore each action, asking questions about how each step is resourced. How does the operator know which action to carry out to achieve the goal? Does the operator need to know the status of the process before deciding which pump to progress to? Does the operator know where the relevant pump is? Does the operator know or need to know that the tank is empty? These questions suggest possible modifications to the interface.

Once this trace has been explored, the analyst should observe that this is not the most effective path to achieve the goal. In particular the operator does not make use of the switch facility and therefore it is necessary redundantly to revisit LP5. Further assumptions are therefore added to check that it is always possible to achieve the goal without unnecessarily revisiting pumps. This exploration was carried out by adding constraints to the model, where *updpath(i)* forces the operator to visit any location only once. The goal continues to be achievable and the path generated leads to further exploration of the resources required to encourage the operator to save the pump information at the relevant moment. Further analysis in relation to producing product D, when the locations are not revisited, produces a longer path than necessary. Further constraints enable exploration of shorter paths.

For each path the same questions are asked (corresponding to the list described above). In terms of *movement actions*, how do I know where to go? In terms of *switching a control*, is the save action enabled and visible, is it clear which control will be saved, is it clear what the effect on the device will be of saving the control? In terms of *resourcing for operating a control* is it clear that the action is enabled and visible, is it clear what the effect of the action will be? Appropriate information could be specific values (the operator must know that Tank 2 contains product D), or simply that information is available (the operator can see the level within the tank, regardless of what the value is). The requirement for resourcing of the action of turning a pump on includes the system constraints on it being enabled, plus the mobile device having the pump loaded, plus the display showing the necessary information on the status of the pump.

4 Discussion

The approach presented has opened a number of avenues for further exploration.

Resources and visibility model - We can associate resource availability with particular states (as in Uppaal models), but direct support within the specification language would enable more explicit analysis. While visible state in interactor style models (such as MAL interactors [4]) provides a useful mechanism, support for dynamic visibility within the specification language would make the specifications easier to work with. A more sophisticated approach to the availability of resources would take into account the salience of information, for example visibility of information combined with goal relevance. Information may be potentially available, but the user may have to forage for it; such resource finding activity is much more plausible if cues are provided to the user. For example, in systems in which display space is limited, and multiple actions are available, some interaction may be necessary in order to obtain action-effect information and this itself must be resourced.

Specialized analyses - Although we have concentrated on resource based analysis in the presence of intentional goal based behavior other analyses are advisable. Mode concerns continue to be important and are not revealed directly by the analysis described. Some mode errors will arise from insufficiently (externally) resourced actions, such as lack of mode indicators. Mode errors arising out of user confusions may require some consideration of internal resources, and user mental models. Conflicting activities often provide a setting which is conducive to mode error, and this would be a promising direction for future investigation. For example, where there are two goals to be achieved, opportunistic strategies for achieving both in an interleaved fashion could be explored.

Level of detail - Many analyses can be conducted looking simply at the configuration of information resources, without specifying precisely the content and associated application logic. While this is very attractive from the perspective of reducing the amount of specification and focusing the analysis on the aspects of interest, it is possible that some classes of problem will be missed as a result of this.

Interaction strategies, goals and resources - While we have dealt with the resourcing of actions as dependent only on the situation and the actions themselves, and while such cases are those of most interest to this paper, there are potential dependencies between the interaction strategy taken by the user, the different goals the user might have, and the resourcing of a particular strategy. This issue needs to be addressed in the context of the overall approach to analysis, and in particular the categorization of resources as part of the analysis. In terms of specifying required resources, this should be taken into account, but may also have an explicit role to play in the models (perhaps some requirements should be parameterized with respect to user goals). It would also be worth looking at the analysis in the context of a broader methodology such as DiCoT [2]. The three themes of the DiCoT analysis regarding physical layout, information flow, and use of artefacts all provide potential points of contact with the proposed approach, with tool support allowing us to investigate emergent properties of the space, the dynamic availability of information within an interaction, and the use of (resource-providing) artefacts which exhibit complex behaviour.

5   Conclusions

A conclusion from the example is that the approach appears to be a viable one, and seems to present some particular advantages when considering mobile systems. For situations with less clearly defined tasks or where there are many ways of performing a task, there is the obvious advantage over an analysis where there is no structure to user behavior. However, as can be seen above, even where there is structure to user tasks, the approach still presents advantages, as the focus of the analysis is quite different, and there is no heavy specification overhead. We could also investigate situations where user behaviour arises from a mix of well defined tasks and more opportunistic goal-directed behaviour. The resourced-action based approach is attractive in that it considers opportunistic, situated actions, which are nonetheless purposeful, that is, they are directed towards some goal. Analyst insight obviously comes in to play in the resource analysis, but having an explicit activity can help to make this a more organized and concrete activity. While support for the analysis in tools has been considered, several issues regarding such support require further investigation, particularly support for more sophisticated visibility models, and tool support for more specific analyses (e.g. mode analysis).

Acknowledgments. We acknowledge with thanks EPSRC grant EP/F01404X/1 and FCT/FEDER grant POSC/EIA/56646/2004. Michael Harrison is grateful to colleagues in the ReSIST NoE (www.resit-noe.org).

References

1. Behrmann, G., David, A., Larsen, K.G.: A tutorial on Uppaal. In: Bernardo, M., Corradini, F. (eds.) SFM-RT 2004. LNCS, vol. 3185, pp. 200–236. Springer, Heidelberg (2004)
2. Blandford, A., Furniss, D.: DiCoT: A Methodology for Applying Distributed Cognition to the Design of Teamworking Systems. In: Gilroy, S.W., Harrison, M.D. (eds.) DSV-IS 2005. LNCS, vol. 3941, pp. 26–38. Springer, Heidelberg (2006)
3. Campos, J.C., Doherty, G.: Supporting resource based analysis of task information needs. In: Gilroy, S.W., Harrison, M.D. (eds.) DSV-IS 2005. LNCS, vol. 3941, pp. 188–200. Springer, Heidelberg (2006)
4. Campos, J.C., Harrison, M.D.: Model checking interactor specifications. Automated Software Engineering 8(3-4), 275–310 (2001)
5. Hutchins, E.: Cognition in the Wild. MIT Press, Cambridge (1995)
6. Loer, K., Harrison, M.D.: Analysing user confusion in context aware mobile applications. In: Costabile, M.F., Paternó, F. (eds.) INTERACT 2005. LNCS, vol. 3585, pp. 184–197. Springer, Heidelberg (2005)
7. Nilsson, J., Sokoler, T., Binder, T., Wetcke, N.: Beyond the Control Room: Mobile Devices for Spatially Distributed Interaction on Industrial Process Plants. In: Thomas, P., Gellersen, H.-W. (eds.) HUC 2000. LNCS, vol. 1927, pp. 1–30. Springer, Heidelberg (2000)
8. Polson, P.G., Lewis, C., Rieman, J., Wharton, C.: Cognitive walkthroughs: a method for theory-based evaluation of user interfaces. International Journal of Man-Machine Studies 36(5) (1992)
9. Suchman, L.A.: Plans and Situated Actions: The Problem of Human-Machine Communication. Cambridge University Press, Cambridge (1987)
10. Wright, P.C., Fields, R.E., Harrison, M.D.: Analyzing human-computer interaction as distributed cognition: the resources model. Human Computer Interaction 15(1), 1–42 (2001)

An Architecture and a Formal Description Technique for the Design and Implementation of Reconfigurable User Interfaces

David Navarre, Philippe Palanque, Jean-François Ladry, and Sandra Basnyat

Institute of Research in Informatics of Toulouse (IRIT)
University Paul Sabatier, 118, route de Narbonne, 31062 Toulouse Cedex 9, France
{navarre, palanque, ladry, basnyat}@irit.fr

Abstract. This paper proposes an architecture that provides a means to handle failures of input and output devices. This handling is done by means of previously defined and designed configurations. According to the failure identified at runtime of the interactive system, the most appropriate configuration will be loaded and executed. Such reconfiguration aims at allowing operators to continue interacting with the interactive system even though part of the user interface hardware has failed. These types of problems arise in domains such as command and control systems where the operator is confronted with several display units and can use various combinations of input devices either in a mono-modal or in a multimodal manner.

Keywords: Model-based approaches, ARINC 661 specification, formal description techniques, interactive software engineering, interactive cockpits.

1 Introduction

Command and control systems have to handle large amounts of increasingly complex information. Current research in the field of Human-Computer Interaction (HCI) promotes the development of new interaction and visualization techniques in order to increase the bandwidth between the users and the systems. Such an increase in bandwidth can have a significant impact on efficiency (for instance the number of commands triggered by the users within a given amount of time) and also on error-rate [21] (the number of slips or mistakes made by the users).

Within the HCI discipline, the focus has mainly been on the usability of such interfaces [20, 25] or has addressed this issue in an exploratory mode trying to define, design and compare innovative interaction techniques [22, 17] targeting efficiency. More recent work goes beyond that aspect extending usability concerns to engagement-related aspects such as in the User eXperience trend [13, 9].

Post-WIMP user interfaces [26] provide users with a set of interaction techniques usually based on the direct manipulation paradigm [24]. This includes, for instance, keyboard and mouse as hardware input devices and double click, drag and drop, Ctrl+click, ... as interaction techniques. One of the recurrent characteristics of such interfaces is that the interaction techniques are defined in a static way i.e. remaining the same throughout the use of the application.

T.C.N. Graham and P. Palanque (Eds.): DSVIS 2008, LNCS 5136, pp. 208–224, 2008.

In this paper we address the problem of designing multiple configurations of interaction techniques and making them available to the user according to the operational context. In terms of context we focus here on environmental evolutions related to failures i.e. reconfiguration of interaction techniques related to downgraded and/or degraded modes of an operational system after an input or output device failure has occurred.

Exploiting such possibilities calls for methods, techniques and tools to support various configurations at the specification level (specify in a complete and unambiguous way the configurations i.e. the set of desired interaction techniques and output configurations), at the validation level (ensure that the configurations meet the requirements in terms of usability, reliability, human-error-tolerance, fault-tolerance and possibly security), at the implementation level (support the process of going from the specification to the implementation of the configurations in a given system) and for testing (how to test the efficiency of the configurations and of the re-configured system).

A recent trend in Human-Computer Interaction has addressed the issue of dynamic reconfiguration of interfaces under the concept of plasticity coined by J. Coutaz [10] and extends previous considerations around the notion of adaptive interfaces[1] [6, 15] to the notion of context-aware systems. However, research work on plasticity mainly addresses reconfiguration at the output level i.e. adapting the presentation part of the user interface to the display context (shrinking or expanding presentation objects according to the space available on the display) [7, 8]. In addition, reliability issues and specification aspects of plastic interfaces are not considered. Recent work on website personalisation/configuration [11] and [23] struggles with the same concepts and constraints even though, here again, personalisation remains at a look and feel level and does not deal with how the users interact with the web application. Our work differs significantly as according to the application domain we are considering (interactive cockpits of which fundamental features are defined within the ARINC 661 specification standard) users are pilots who must follow long and intensive training programmes (including on-the-fly training) and thus be trained for authorised reconfigurations while web users passively undergo the reconfigurations.

These issues go beyond current state of the art in the field of interactive systems engineering where usually each interactive system is designed with a predefined set of input and output devices that are to be used according to a static set of interaction techniques which are identified at design time. However, current safety critical systems, for example, the cockpit of the Airbus A380, has 8 display units with 4 offering interaction via keyboard and mouse by means of an integrated input device called KCCU (Keyboard Cursor Control Unit). Applications are allocated to the various display units. If one of the display units fails, (like the importance of the application according to the flight phase) then the applications are migrated to other available display units according to predefined criteria. On the input side, the pilot and the first officer are both equipped with a KCCU and thus multimodal (multiuser) direct manipulation techniques can be envisaged.

This paper proposes the exploitation of a formal description technique (the ICO formalism [19]), architecture and a supporting tool that provide a means to handle both static and dynamic aspects of input and output devices configuration and reconfiguration.

---

[1] In adaptive interfaces the main element of adaptation is based on the notion of user model.

The ICO formalism is a formal description technique dedicated to the specification of interactive systems [18]. It uses concepts borrowed from the object-oriented approach (dynamic instantiation, classification, encapsulation, inheritance, client/server relationship) to describe the structural or static aspects of systems, and uses high-level Petri nets [12] to describe their dynamic or behavioural aspects.

The paper is structured as follows: the next section briefly introduces the ARINC 661 specification while section 3 presents the generic architecture for reconfiguration. Section 4 presents the detailed architecture we propose. Section 0 presents the configuration management and proposes a set of configuration manager models.

2   ARINC 661 Specification

The Airlines Electronic Engineering Committee (AEEC) (an international body of airline representatives leading the development of avionics architectures) formed the ARINC 661 Working Group to define the software interfaces to the Cockpit Display System (CDS) used in all types of aircraft installations. The standard is called ARINC 661 - Cockpit Display System Interfaces to User Systems [2, 3].

In ARINC 661, a user application is defined as a system that has two-way communication with the CDS (Cockpit Display System):

- Transmission of data to the CDS, possibly displayed to the flight deck crew.
- Reception of input from interactive items managed by the CDS.

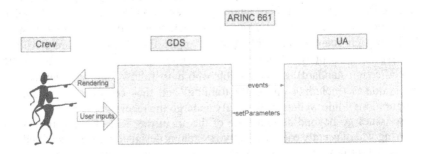

Fig. 1. Abstract architecture and communication protocol between Cockpit Display System and a User Application

According to the classical decomposition of interactive systems into three parts (presentation, dialogue and functional core) defined in [5], the CDS part (in Fig. 1) may be seen as the presentation part of the whole system, provided to the crew members, and the set of UAs may be seen as the merge of both the dialogue and the functional core of this system. ARINC 661 then puts on one side input and output devices (provided by avionics equipment manufacturers) and on the other side the user applications (designed by aircraft manufacturers). Indeed, the consistency between these two parts is maintained through the communication protocol defined by ARINC 661.

3   A Generic Architecture for User Interaction Reconfiguration

In this section we present, a generic extension to the ARCH software architecture [4], to support configuration definitions and reconfiguration management in the field of safety critical application. This architecture aims at describing the various components as well as their interrelations. As stated in the introduction, the architecture targets resilient systems [13] offering a *continuity of interaction service* despite partial failure of an input or output device.

In order to reach this goal, we propose to decompose the interactive system into two parts: the server side[2] (including the window manager, the interaction techniques and the (re)configuration manager) and the application side (including all the graphical components such as widgets ... up to the functional core).

This architecture is generic as it represents the architecture of most interactive systems platforms. However, research work dealing with software architectures for interactive systems typically focus on the application side as they deal with the design and construction of interactive applications. The work presented in this paper covers not only the application side but also the windows manager side that is typically considered has beyond the scope of the architectures.

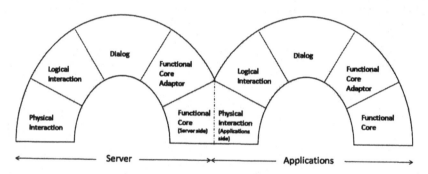

Fig. 2. The server/application dichotomy and their connection point according to the ARCH

Fig. 2 presents the architecture of the two components of the reconfigurable interactive system. The left-hand side shows the architecture of the interaction server (software part of the CDS) while the application architecture is represented on the right-hand side. It is noticeable that both components are compliant with the ARCH model and that their interconnection point is the physical interaction part of the application with the functional core part of the server. More precisely, this "shared" component holds the set of widgets available in the various windows of the application. On the application side they represent the physical interaction (where the crew member can interact with). On the server side these widgets correspond to the data managed by the server.

---

[2] This terminology comes from the ARINC 661 specification standard. While such wording could be questionable in the field of interactive systems engineering we prefer to conform to the standard this work is applied to.

The detail of this architecture (including the structure and behaviour of each component) is detailed in section 4 on a case study in the field of interactive cockpits.

4   An Architecture for Reliable and Reconfigurable Interfaces

One of the aims here is to define an architecture that supports usability aspects of safety critical systems by taking into account potential malfunctions in the input (output respectively) devices that allow the operators to provide (perceive respectively) information or trigger commands (perceive command results respectively) to the system. Indeed, any malfunction related to such input devices might prevent operators to intervene in the systems functioning and thus jeopardize the mission and potentially put human life at stake. In systems offering standard input device combination such as keyboard & mouse, it is possible to handle one input device failure by providing redundancy in the use of the device. For instance a soft keyboard such as the ones defined in [16] can provide an efficient palliative for a keyboard failure[3].

The architecture presented in Fig. 3 proposes a structured view on the findings of a project dealing with formal description techniques for interactive applications compliant with the ARINC 661 specification [5]. Applications are executed in a Cockpit Display System (CDS) that aim to provide flight crew with all the necessary information to try to ensure a safe flight.

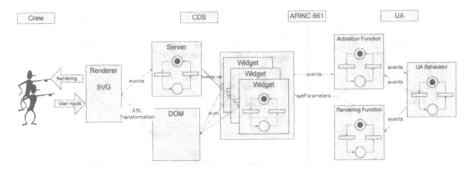

Fig. 3. Detailed architecture compliant with ARINC 661 specification not supporting interaction failures

We are dealing with applications that exclude primary cockpit applications such as PFD (Primary Flight Display) and ND (Navigation Displays) and only deal with secondary applications such as the ones allocated to the MCDU (Multiple Control Display Unit). For previous CDSs (such as the glass cockpit of the A320) these applications were not interactive (they only displayed information to the crew) and inputs were made available through independent physical buttons located next to the display unit. The location in the cockpit, between the pilot and the first officer make it possible for both of them to use such an application.

---

[3] This kind of management of input device failure could and should prevent the typical error message on PCs when booting with a missing keyboard "Keyboard Failure strike F1 key to continue".

A single notation (ICOs) is exploited to model the behaviour of all the components of an interactive application compliant with ARINC 661 specification. This includes each interactive component (called widgets) the user application (UA) per se and the entire window manager (responsible for the handling of input and output devices, and the dispatching of events (both those triggered by the UAs and by the pilots) to the recipients (the widgets or the UAs).

The two main advantages of the architecture presented in Fig. 3 are:

- Every component that has an inner behaviour (server, widgets, UA, and the connection between UA and widgets, e.g. the rendering and activation functions) is fully modelled using the ICO formal description technique thus making it possible to analyse and verify the correct functioning of the entire computer system[4],

- The rendering part is delegated to a dedicated language and tool (such as SVG, Scalable Vector Graphics), thus making the external look of the user interface independent from the rest of the application, providing a framework for easy adaptation of the graphical aspect of cockpit applications.

However, this architecture does not support reconfiguration of input or output devices in the cockpit, neither in case of redesign nor in case of failure while in operation. However, requirements specification for a display unit (DU) like the one of the Airbus A380 explicitly requires the possibility for the co-pilot to read information on the DU of the pilot (in case of failure on his/her side for instance).

The new architecture we propose has been extended to explicitly manage the reconfiguration of applications on the display units. It presents a refinement of the architecture proposed in Fig. 2. In the architecture (presented in Fig. 4), all the elements of which the behaviour is formally defined using the ICO formalism appear in a box featuring a small Petri net inside. Indeed, the input and output devices are formally described using the ICO notation in order to be handled by a configuration manager which is also responsible for reconfiguring devices and interaction technique according to failures. These failures are detected by a software module (called *Device Inspector*) testing on a regular basis the functioning of the input and output devices.

Fig. 4 the dashed-line section highlights the improvements made with respect to the previous architecture:

- The left-hand part of the frame highlights the addition of ICO models dedicated to both input and output devices,

- The right-hand part presents the introduction of a new component named *configuration manager* responsible for managing the configuration of input and output devices

- The *configuration and server rendering* component responsible for representing, on the user interface, the current configuration. In the case study the current configuration is represented to the crew by different mouse cursors. This is why that component is connected both to the *server* (to access

---

[4] Even though we previously worked on broader issues including incidents and accident analysis and modelling, training and user manual design, this paper focuses on the technical aspects of interactive software reconfiguration.

information about the position of the cursor) and to the *configuration manager* to access information about the current configuration.

The upper dark line on top of

Fig. 4 positions the architecture according to the ARINC 661 decomposition while the lower dark line positions the various components according to the generic architecture presented in Fig. 2.

Even though modelling of input devices and interaction techniques has already been presented in the context of multimodal interfaces for military cockpits [5] it was not integrated with the previous architecture developed for interactive applications compliant with ARINC 661 specification. The rest of the paper thus focuses on the configuration manager that is dedicated to the dynamic reconfiguration of user interaction (both input devices and interaction techniques).

5 Configuration Manager Policy and Modelling

This section presents the modelling of different policies to manage both input and output device configuration. We first present two policies and then present a formal modelling of such policies using the ICO formalism.

5.1 Input and Output Management Policies

Configuration management activities may occur at either runtime (while a user interacts with the application) or "pre-runtime" (e.g. just before starting an application or during a switchover of users). To illustrate the different kinds of policy, we present a pre-runtime policy where input devices are involved and a runtime policy for managing output devices.

5.2 Input Device Configuration Manager Policy

A possible use of reconfiguration is to allow customising the interaction technique to make the application easier to manipulate. Even if it is out of the scope of the current version of the ARINC 661 Specification, customisation of interaction techniques may becomes necessary when continuity of interaction service has to be improved allowing users to carry on interacting with the system even though some input and output devices are out of order.

The current case study presents 2 configurations. The standard configuration allows the first officer (FO) and the pilot to interact at the same time on the various widgets of the applications running on the interactive display units of the cockpit. A selection of critical commands requires the pilot and the FO to interact within a short temporal window on the widget. While on the user side, such an interaction technique appears as a simple click for each user, on the system side it is handled as if one user was interacting with two mice and producing MixedClicks i.e. a click with both mice on the same widget. If one KCCU fails then the interaction technique is reconfigured and MixedClicks are replaced by DoubleClicks for triggering critical commands.

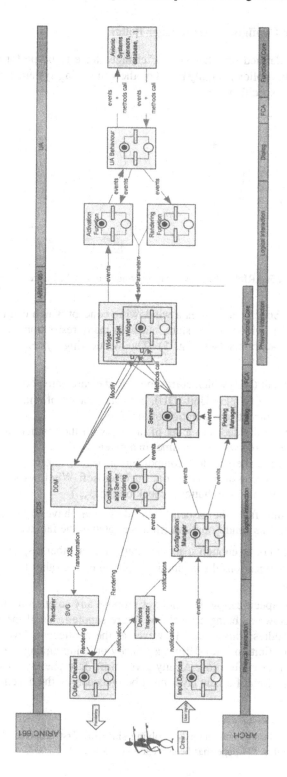

Fig. 4. Overview of the architecture compliant with ARINC 661 specification and supporting interaction failures

5.3 Output Device Configuration Manager Policy

A policy has to be defined on what kind of changes have to be performed when a display unit fails. This policy is highly based on the windowing system adopted by the standard ARINC 661 specification.

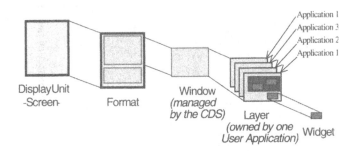

Fig. 5. ARINC 661 Specification windowing architecture

The ARINC 661 Specification uses a windowing concept which can be compared to a desktop computer windowing system, but with many restrictions due to the aircraft environment constraints (see Fig. 5). The windowing system is split into 4 components:

- the display unit (DU) which corresponds to the hardware part,
- the format on a Display Unit (DU), consists of a set of windows and is defined by the current configuration of the CDS,
- the window is divided into a set of layers (with the restriction of only one layer activated and visible at a time) in a given window,
- the widgets are the smallest component on which interaction occurs (they corresponds to classical interactors on Microsoft Windows system such as command buttons, radio buttons, check buttons, ...).

When a display unit fails, the associated windows **may** have to be reallocated to another display unit. This conditional assertion is related to the fact that:

- There might not be enough space remaining on the other display units (DU),
- The other applications displaying information on the other DU might have a higher priority.

The ARINC 661 Specification does not yet propose any solution to this particular problem but it is known as being critical and future supplements of the ARINC 661 specification may address this issue[5]. However at the application level, the UADF (User Application Definition File) defines a priority ordering among the various layers included in the user application. At any given time only one layer can be active. At runtime, the activation of a new layer must be preceded by the deactivation of the current layer.

---

[5] ARINC 661 specification is continuously evolving since the first proposal. The draft 2 of supplement 3 containing 374 pages has been released on August 15th 2007.

The policy that we have defined lays in the definition of a set of compatible windows i.e. windows offering a greater or equal display size. This is related to a strong limitation imposed by ARINC 661 which states that some methods and properties are only accessible at design time i.e. (according to ARINC 661 specification vocabulary) when the application is initialized. Methods and properties related to widget size are not available at runtime and thus any reorganisation of widgets within a window is not possible.

The only policy that can thus be implemented is a policy where first a compatible window has to be found and then the question of priority has to be handled. Since only layers have a priority it is not possible for an application or a window to have a priority. This cannot be done either at design time or runtime and thus the management policy can only take place at the layer level.

5.4 Configuration Manager Behaviour

This section presents possible models for the configuration management according to the policies described above. We first present how input device configurations are managed and then deal with output devices managements.

Input devices Management
The user interface server manages the set of widgets and the hierarchy of widgets used in the User Applications. More precisely, the user interface server is responsible in handling:

- The creation of widgets
- The graphical cursors of both the pilot and his co-pilot
- The edition mode
- The keyboard and mouse events and dispatching it to the corresponding widgets
- The highlight and the focus mechanisms
- ...

As it handles many functionalities, the complete model of the sub-server (dedicated in handling widgets involved in the MPIA User Application) is complex and difficult to manipulate without an appropriate tool, and cannot be illustrated in a diagram.

Events received by the interaction server are in some way high level events as they are not the raw events produced by the input devices drivers. In our architecture, the main role of an input configuration is the role of a transducer [1]; it receives raw events and produces higher level events. The events used by the interaction server, and so produced by an input configuration are (*normalKey, abortKey, validationKey, pickup, unPickup, mouseDoubleClicked, mouseClicked*). These events are produced from the following set of raw events: *mouseMoved, mouseDragged, mousePressed, mouseReleased, mouseClicked* and *mouseDoubleClicked* from the mouse driver, and *pickup* and *unPickup* from the picking manager.

Fig. 6 models the handling of raw events from the KCCU for the production of upper level events such as mouseMove, mousePressed, mouseReleased, etc. The model is common for the two interaction techniques, DoubleClick and MixedClick, each represented within their own model. Switching between these models is performed at the interaction technique level and not at the raw events level. This raw events model first tests the value of a variable "changed" defined in transition *CheckMouseState* (upper transition in Fig. 6) every chosen number of milliseconds (in this model, 100ms) in order to verify if the state of the mouse has changed since the previous check. According to the value of the variable, transition *hasNotChanged* or *has-Changed* will fire.

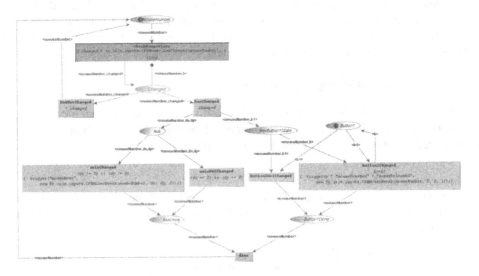

Fig. 6. Model of the raw events handling for both configurations

Following this, there are two further tests, according to the movement of the mouse and the state of the mouse button. The movement test is modelled using transition *axisChanged*, (left hand side of the model) according to x,y coordinates (mouse-Move). Transition *buttonChanged* (right hand side of the model) checks to see if there has been a change in the state of the mouse button which produces mousePressed or mouseReleased events. Only the left mouse button is considered in this example to reduce the complexity of the model. After the *axisChanged* and *buttonChanged* tests, transition *done* is fired placing a token in place *MouseNumber* ready to restart the simulation.

The model in Fig. 7 presents how low level events produced are combined at the interaction technique level to produce higher-level events. Transitions *mouse-Pressed_t1* and *mouseReleased_t1* receives events from transition *buttonChanged* modelled in the "raw events" model shown in Fig. 6. The left part of this model produces a single click from a mousePressed and a mouseReleased from mouse1 (ie. Pilot mouse), while the right hand part of the model performs the same behaviour for mouse2 (ie. First officer mouse). The model states that if a MouseClick is performed (by either person) which starts a timer, and a second event MouseClick (performed with the other mouse) is received before the end of the timer, then the model produces a MixedClick event (transition *triggerMixedClick* at the bottom of the figure).

Fig. 8 represents the DoubleClick interaction technique in the degraded mode i.e. when only one KCCU is available. The model receives events mousePressed, mouseReleased and mouseMoved from the raw events model presented in Fig. 6. They are then processed in order to be able to raise DoubleClick events which occur when the KCCU has been pressed and released twice within a predefined temporal window and without any mouseMove event in-between.

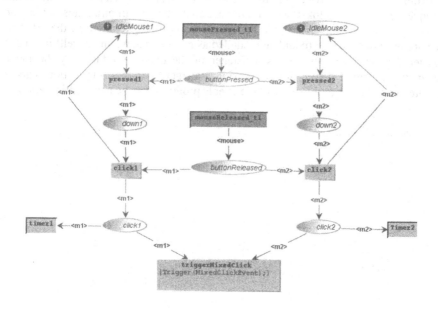

Fig. 7. Model of the mixed (both KCCU) click configuration

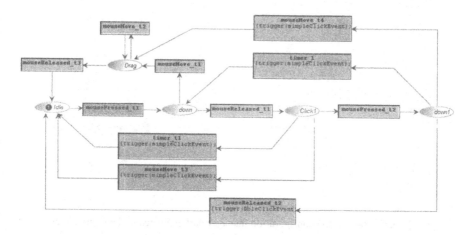

Fig. 8. Model of the DoubleClick configuration

Configurations Management

Fig 9 presents the model responsible for the management of the configurations. The basic principle of the model is that the current configuration has to be removed (unregistered part of the model on the right hand side of the figure) before the new desired configuration is set (register configuration part of the model on the left hand side of the figure).

The four places in the central part of Fig 9 (*MouseDriver, KeyboardDriver, PickingManager* and *InteractionServer*) contain a reference to the set of models corresponding to the input devices and to the interaction server. When a new configuration is requested to be set, a token with a reference to the new configuration is put in place *NewConfiguration*. Following this, the four transitions highlighted on the left hand side are fired in sequence (could be modelled as parallel behaviour as well) in order to register the new configuration as a listener of the events produced by the mouse driver, the keyboard driver and the picking manager. The fourth transition registers the interaction server as a listener of the events produced by the new configuration.

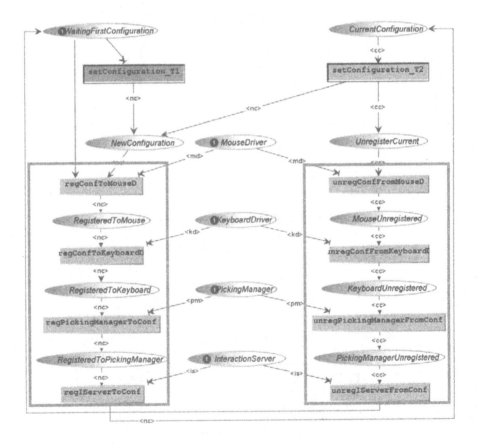

Fig. 9. ICO model of the configuration manager part dedicated to the input devices

If a configuration is already set, when the new configuration is requested, a token is put in place *UnregisterCurrent* in order to fire the four transitions highlighted on the right handside, corresponding to unregister from the different models, in parallel with registering the new configuration.

Output devices Management

In Fig. 10, we present an implementation of the previously defined policy for handling output devices using the ICO formalism. This model is a subpart of the complete configuration manager that can be added to the previous modelling we have done and thus be integrated in the behaviour of our (Cockpit Display System) CDS model [5].

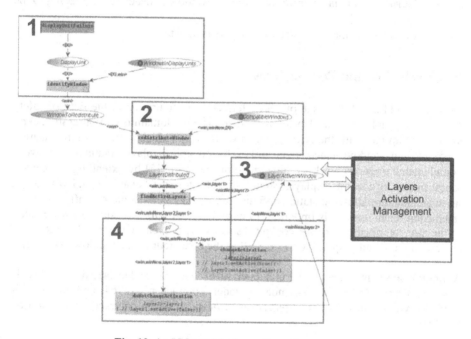

Fig. 10. An ICO model of a configuration manager

The model presented here is based on a very simple case (1 layer per window and 1 window per display unit). This information flow and the operation to be performed remain the same, but it is possible to build models for a much more complex case as ICO proposes a means to handle such complexities:

1. The display unit (DU) notifies its failure (the event may be triggered by a sensor), and then the configuration manager located the window currently displayed in that DU.
2. The configuration manager finds a compatible window for a reallocation of the contained layers (here all compatible windows are listed at creation time) and the layers are transferred to the new window.

3. As in a given window only one layer can be activated, when layers are reallocated, the configuration manager must identify the layer to be activated (among the new set of layers related to the window presented on the non functioning DU).

4. That part of the model determines which layer must be activated according to the layer priority defined at creation time:

   - If the layer from the previous window has a higher priority than the one from the new window, then the layer from the new window is deactivated, sending a notification to the corresponding user application according to the ARINC 661 Specification protocol (the UA may (or may not) request to reactivate the layer depending on its defined behaviour).
   - Otherwise, the layer from the previous window is deactivated (leading to the same effects).
   - In both case, the list of activated layers is updated.

6 Conclusion and Perspectives

This paper addressed the issue of user interface reconfiguration in the field of safety critical command and control systems. The application domain is civil aircraft cockpit systems compliant with the ARINC 661 specification (which defines communication protocols and window management policy for cockpit displays systems). This work complements previous work we have done on this topic [5] by extending the behavioural model of cockpit display system with fault-tolerant behaviour and with a generic architecture allowing static configuration as well as dynamic reconfiguration of interaction techniques. It is important to note that such fault-tolerance is only related to the user interface part of the cockpit display system even though it takes into consideration input and output devices as well as the behaviour of the window manager.

Acknowledgements. This work is supported by the EU funded Network of Excellence ResIST http://www.resist-noe.eu under contract n°026764 and the CNES funded R&T Tortuga project http://ihcs.irit.fr/tortuga/ under contract n° R-S08/BS-0003-029.

References

1. Accot, J., Chatty, S., Maury, S., Palanque, P.: Formal Transducers: Models of Devices and Building Bricks for Highly Interactive Systems (1,1 Mo). In: 4th EUROGRAPHICS workshop on design, Granada, Spain, June 5-7, 1997. Springer, Heidelberg (1997)
2. ARINC 661, Prepared by Airlines Electronic Engineering Committee. Cockpit Display System Interfaces to User Systems. ARINC Specification 661 (2002)
3. ARINC 661-2, Prepared by Airlines Electronic Engineering Committee. Cockpit Display System Interfaces to User Systems. ARINC Specification 661-2 (2005)
4. Bass, L., et al.: A metamodel for the runtime architecture of an interactive system: the UIMS tool developers workshop. In: SIGCHI Bulletin, vol. 24(1), pp. 32–37 (1992)

5. Barboni, E., Conversy, S., Navarre, D., Palanque, P.: Model-Based Engineering of Widgets, User Applications and Servers Compliant with ARINC 661 Specification. In: Doherty, G., Blandford, A. (eds.) DSVIS 2006. LNCS, vol. 4323, pp. 25–38. Springer, Heidelberg (2007)
6. Benyon, D., Murray, D.: Experience with Adaptive Interfaces. The Computer Journal 31(5), 465–473 (1988)
7. Berti, S., Correani, F., Paternò, F., Santoro, C.: The TERESA XML Language for the Description of Interactive Systems at Multiple Abstraction Leveles. In: Proceedings Workshop on Developing User Interfaces with XML UIXML: Advances on User Interface Description Languages, May 2004, pp. 103–110 (2004)
8. Calvary, G., Coutaz, J., Thevenin, D., Limbourg, Q., Bouillon, L., Vanderdonckt, J.: A Unifying Reference Framework for multi-target user interfaces. Interacting with Computers 15(3), 289–308 (2003)
9. Csíkszentmihályi, M.: Flow: The Psychology of Optimal Experience. Harper and Row, New York (1990)
10. Thevenin, D., Coutaz, J.: Plasticity of User Interfaces: Framework and Research Agenda. In: Proceedings of Interact 1999. Edinburgh: IFIP TC 13, vol. 1, pp. 110–117. IOS Press, Amsterdam (1999)
11. Eirinaki, M., Lampos, C., Paulakis, S., Vazirgiannis, M.: Web personalization integrating content semantics and navigational patterns. In: WIDM 2004: Proceedings of the 6th annual ACM international workshop on Web information and data management, pp. 72–79. ACM Press, New York (2004)
12. Genrich, H.J.: Predicate/Transitions Nets. In: Jensen, K., Rozenberg, G. (eds.) High-Levels Petri Nets: Theory and Application, pp. 3–43. Springer, Heidelberg (1991)
13. Hollnagel, E., Woods, D.D., Leveson, N.: Reliability Engineering, Ashgate, p. 397 (2006) ISBN 0754646416
14. Hassenzahl, M.: The Interplay of Beauty, Goodness, and Usability in Interactive Products. Human-Computer Interaction 19(4), 319–349 (2004)
15. Kay, A.: Pragmatic User Modeling for Adaptive Interfaces, and Lies, Damned Lies and Stereotypes: pragmatic approximations of users. In: Proceedings of the User Modeling 94 Conference, pp. 175–184. The Mitre Corporation (1994)
16. MacKenzie, S., Zhang, S.X., Soukoreff, R.W.: Text entry using soft keyboards. Behaviour & Information Technology 18, 235–244 (1999)
17. MacKenzie, S., Oniszczak, A.: A comparison of three selection techniques for touchpads. In: Proceedings of the SIGCHI Conference on Human Factors in Computing Systems, Conference on Human Factors in Computing Systems, Los Angeles, California, United States, April 18 - 23, 1998, pp. 336–343. ACM Press/Addison-Wesley Publishing Co, New York (1998)
18. Navarre, D., Palanque, P., Bastide, R.: A Tool-Supported Design Framework for Safety Critical Interactive Systems in Interacting with computers, vol. 15/3, pp. 309–328. Elsevier, Amsterdam (2003)
19. Navarre, D., Palanque, P., Bastide, R.: A Formal Description Technique for the Behavioural Description of Interactive Applications Compliant with ARINC 661 Specifications. In: HCI-Aero 2004, Toulouse, France, 29 September-1st (October 2004)
20. Nielsen, J.: Usability Engineering. Academic Press, London (1993)
21. Reason, J.: Human Error. Cambridge University Press, Cambridge (1990)
22. Rekimoto, J.: Pick-and-drop: a direct manipulation technique for multiple computer environments. In: Proceedings of the 10th Annual ACM Symposium on User interface Software and Technology. UIST 1997, Banff, Alberta, Canada, October 14 - 17, 1997, pp. 31–39. ACM, New York (1997)

23. Ríos, S.A., Velásquez, J.D., Yasuda, H., Aoki, T.: Web Site Off-Line Structure Reconfiguration: A Web User Browsing Analysis. In: Gabrys, B., Howlett, R.J., Jain, L.C. (eds.) KES 2006. LNCS (LNAI), vol. 4252, pp. 371–378. Springer, Heidelberg (2006)
24. Shneiderman, B.: Direct manipulation: a step beyond programming languages, August 1983. IEEE Computer Society Press, Los Alamitos (1983)
25. Summers, S.: Usability in Battle Management System Human-Machine Interface Design: Assessing Compliance with Design Guide Heuristics. In: Human Factors and Ergonomics Society Annual Meeting Proceedings, Computer Systems, pp. 709-713. Human Factors and Ergonomics Society (2007)
26. van Dam, A.: Post-WIMP user interfaces. Communications of the ACM 40(2), 63–67 (1997)

COMET(s), A Software Architecture Style and an Interactors Toolkit for Plastic User Interfaces

Alexandre Demeure[1], Gaëlle Calvary[2], and Karin Coninx[1]

[1] Hasselt University - tUL - IBBT
Expertise Centre for Digital Media
Wetenschapspark 2, B-3590 Diepenbeek, Belgium
{alexandre.demeure, karin.coninx}@uhasselt.be
[2] Laboratoire LIG, 385, rue de la Bibliothèque - B.P. 53 –
38041 Grenoble Cedex 9, France
Gaelle.Calvary@imag.fr

Abstract. Plasticity of User Interfaces (UIs) refers to the ability of UIs to withstand variations of context of use (<User, Platform, Environment>) while preserving usability. This paper presents COMET, a software architecture style for building task-based plastic interactors. COMET bridges the gap between two main approaches in plasticity: model-driven engineering and interactors toolkits. Interactors that are compliant to the COMET style are called COMETs. These COMETs are multi-rendering multi-technological interactors (WIMP and post-WIMP, Web and non Web as well as vocal). COMETs are extensible and controllable by the user (up until now the designer, in the future the end-user). The COMET architecture and the use of COMETs are illustrated on an executable prototype: a slide viewer called CamNote++.

Keywords: Adaptation, context of use, plasticity, design alternatives, exploration, style sheets, tailored UIs, interactors.

1 Introduction

In the vision of ubiquitous computing users live in dynamic environments that change over time. Interactional, computational as well as communicational resources may arrive and disappear opportunistically. As these changes cannot always be foreseen at design time, there is a need for User Interfaces (UIs) to dynamically adapt to the actual context of use (<User, Platform, Environment>) while preserving usability. We use the term *Plasticity* [17] to denote this UI property. In this paper, we provide the designer (in the future the end-user) with tools for building plastic UIs and for exploring alternative renderings at design time as well as at runtime. The corner stone is a software architecture style called COMET (COntext Mouldable widgET) [3]. COMET compliant interactors are called COMETs.

COMETs are task-based interactors. They group together presentations that support a particular user's task. For instance, a set of radio buttons, a combo-box, a list and a pie menu (Fig. 1-A-1) support the user to *select one option among N*. As a result, they are gathered in one and the same COMET which purpose is to select one

T.C.N. Graham and P. Palanque (Eds.): DSVIS 2008, LNCS 5136, pp. 225–237, 2008.

option among N. In the same way, COMETs based on task operators are defined. For instance, the interleaving COMET groups together several presentations for rendering interleaving. This can be done by putting the interleaved subtasks side by side in a certain window (Fig. 1-A-1), by using multiple windows (Fig. 1-A-2) or a navigation interactor such as a menu (Fig. 1-B). These two kinds of COMETs rely on the same architectural style: COMET.

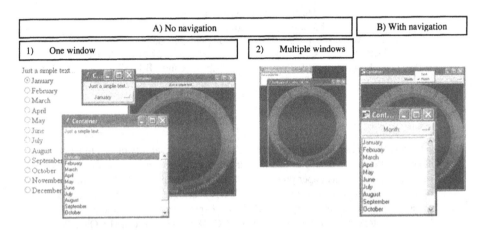

Fig. 1. Functionally equivalent interactors that vary from different points of view: navigation (A versus B), number of windows (A1 and B versus A2) and interactors presentations

COMET, the proposed architectural style, is fashioned for supporting polymorphism (i.e. multiple presentations) where presentations can belong to different rendering technological spaces (e.g. HTML, OpenGL, vocal). The goal of COMET(s) is to sustain the following four requirements:

- Sustaining UI adaptation at any level of abstraction: tasks and concepts, abstract, concrete and final UI as elicited in model-based approaches [2].
- The ability of UIs to be simultaneously rendered in several technologies including web and non web, WIMP and non WIMP, and also textual input and voice output.
- The ability of UIs to be dynamically transformed including enrichments with external and tailored UIs.
- The ability for the user (designer and/or end-user) to explore design alternatives by substituting presentations of COMETs at design time as well as at runtime.

Fig. 2 provides an overview of the global approach. The principles are threefold: (1) a UI is fully defined as a graph of COMETs, (2) the graph can be tuned through transformations, (3) transformations can take benefit from a semantic network [8] to retrieve components (COMETs as well as presentations of COMETs) and update the graph of COMETs accordingly.

This paper focuses on the graph of COMETs. The transformations are not described because of space. The semantic network is described in [8]. Section 2 presents the related work. Section 3 describes an executable demonstrator implemented with COMETs. Section 4 is devoted to the COMET architectural style. Finally, section 5 is about development using COMETs.

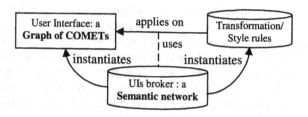

Fig. 2. An overview of the COMET-based approach

2 Related Work

In plasticity, the state of the art can be roughly categorized into three main approaches: Model Driven Engineering (MDE), window managers and widget toolkits.

MDE is probably the area [2,7,9] that recently received the most attention. Separation of concerns is the core principle. A UI is described from different perspectives (task, concepts, abstract UI (AUI), concrete UI (CUI), final UI (FUI)), each of them giving rise to a specific model. In the same way, the functional core and the context of use can be described along a set of models. Models are linked together through mappings. Mappings convey the widgets rationale (the tasks they support) as well as the UI deployment among the set of available platforms [4]. So far, MDE has been widely explored for the forward generation of standardized UIs.

Façade [16] investigates another approach: the adaptation is performed at the windows manager level. Adaptation is fully driven by the end-user who can dynamically copy/paste/replace parts of the UI. Façade is limited to graphical UIs. It relies on the widgets toolkit for the introspection mechanisms and the set of available widgets. As in practice none of these toolkits reaches the task level, adaptation can not be performed at a high level of abstraction (task or dialog).

Table 1. Analysis of the state of the art with regard to our four requirements

	Levels of abstraction	Technological coverage	Extensibility	Controllability
MDE [2,7,9]	All	Multiple	Hard	Depends on the underlying infrastructure
Windows manager [16]	CUI/FUI	Graphics	Irrelevant	End-user
ACE [11]	~Task	C++ toolkit	Easy	Designer
WAHID [10]	CUI	MFC	Hard	System
XFORMS	~Task/AUI	Web	Impossible	System with the help of the designer
FRUIT [12]	~Task	Depend on shells	Impossible	System
Multimodal Widgets [6]	~Task	Java/SWING	?	System with the help of the designer
Ubiquitous interactor [14]	~Task	Depends on interpreters	Impossible	System and designer

Widget toolkits have already extensively been explored. They tackle specific plasticity issues such as multimodality [6,12], polymorphism [10,11,14], or post-WIMP UIs [13]. None of these covers the tasks operators: sequence, interleaving, or operator, and so on [15]. As a result, all the transformations changing the way the navigation is rendered are lost (Fig.1) (e.g., switching from a menu to hyperlinks, tabbed panes, blanks or separators). In addition, only some approaches [11] support extensibility easily. Presentations are mostly mono-technological, and adaptation is neither foreseeable nor controllable.

Table 1 summarizes the state of the art with regard to the four abovementioned requirements. It shows that mixing MDE and widget toolkits may be promising for meeting all the requirements. This is the core principle of COMET(s).

3 CamNote++, A Running Demonstrator of COMET(s)

CamNote++ is a presentation software (like PowerPoint) that can be used by two kinds of users: speakers and spectators. CamNote++ is capable of adapting to the screen size and takes into account hardware capabilities such as graphical hardware acceleration. Therefore, CamNote++ can be considered plastic with regard to the platform dimension of the context of use. CamNote++ is built with COMETs implemented in TCL. It can be rendered using several technologies according to the user's platform. For instance, if the user accesses CamNote++ via a web browser then AJAX/HTML is used. Both WIMP (e.g. form-based UIs) and/or post-WIMP UIs (e.g. multiple interaction points and speech UIs) can be used to render the application and interact with it. WIMP UIs rely on standard widgets available on the platform whereas post-WIMP UIs make use of toolkits such as OpenGL or Microsoft SAPI when available. WIMP and post-WIMP renderings can be used simultaneously.

From the end-user's perspective, CamNote++ first requires the user to log in (*Identify* task). The following tasks depend on the user's role: either speaker or spectator. In both cases, the current slide is rendered to the user. Two modes are available: presentation mode and question mode. The question mode corresponds to the case where the speaker is interrupted by someone for asking a question. In the presentation mode, only the speaker can control the viewer. In the question mode, spectators can also browse the slides using a dedicated controller. This is useful for supporting questions such as *"In slide N, what do you mean by ...?"*.

Fig. 3-1 shows CamNote++ in action for a speaker using a PC. The rendering is post-WIMP. At the beginning (A), CamNote++ is not operating in full screen mode: two windows are displayed to show both the current slide and the slides controller. When the speaker activates the full screen mode, the slide controller smoothly merges with the current slide (B) until being completely embedded in the slide (C). A picture of a keyboard is faded in and out (C) to make the user aware that he/she can now control the slide viewer using the physical keyboard (D). The keyboard controller is retrieved in the semantic network (a description of this approach is beyond the purpose of this paper).

Fig. 3-2 shows the web version of CamNote++ for a remote watcher. The current slide is updated using AJAX. In A, no style sheet is applied: the slide controller (in the upper part of the window) is composed of buttons and a dropdown menu for setting the current slide number. The current slide is displayed just beneath. An input field is placed at the bottom of the window to support taking notes. In B, a style sheet (specified by the designer) is applied for both improving the grouping (black boxes are added to better delimit workspaces) and for expanding the text area. In C, a tailored presentation is preferred for the slide controller: its container is a moveable translucent window. In D, the user's tasks (controlling the slides, perceiving the current slide and taking notes) are not directly observable in this case: they are browsable through tabbed panes. Style sheets (i.e., transformations) are not described in detail in this paper.

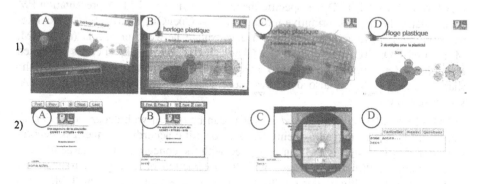

Fig. 3. 1) The OpenGL-based post-WIMP version of CamNote++ for the speaker. 2) The AJAX/HTML versions of CamNote++ for a spectator.

The next section describes the cornerstone of the toolkit: the COMET architectural style.

4 The COMET Style

COMET is driven by three principles: (1) Separation of concerns, (2) Reuse of existing toolkits (e.g., AJAX/HTML, TK, vocal, OpenGL), and (3) Recursivity so that a COMET can recursively be composed of COMETs.

This section describes the architectural style: first, the structure, then the event propagation. Finally we show how engineering interactive systems takes place when using COMET.

4.1 Structure

A COMET is composed of three facets. Each of them is responsible of one specific concern (Separation of concerns principle):

• A Logical Consistency (LC) represents the user's task (e.g., control the slides) or the task operator (e.g., interleaving) that the COMET supports. It denotes the semantics of the service that the COMET provides. The semantics gives rise to a specific API, called *semantic API* (e.g., next slide, previous slide...). The LC is associated to one or many Logical Models (LM). If many, LC is in charge of maintaining consistency between these LMs.

• A Logical Model (LM) is in charge of a specific concern related to the realization of the semantics. Usually, a distinction is made between the presentation and the abstraction (i.e., functional core). Whatever the concern is, each LM has to implement the semantic API of the corresponding LC (e.g., next slide...): this semantic API is the language that LC and LM share. The API can be extended to take into account specific concerns (e.g., blurring the slide). In turn, a LM is associated to one or many Physical Models (PM). If many, LM is in charge of maintaining consistency between these PMs. It also provides PM factories for instantiating PMs on the fly.

• A Physical Model (PM) is a specific means for realizing a LM. A presentation PM encapsulates the code of primitive toolkits such as OpenGL, HTML, SAPI, etc. (Reuse principle). A functional PM would encapsulate network protocols (e.g., AIM, MSN, YAHOO, IRC, etc.) in case of a Chat COMET. Encapsulated codes are called *technological primitives*. A PM has to implement its LM semantic API: this API is the shared language. A PM also describes the context of use it requires (e.g. JAVA, screen size, etc.).

LC, LM and PM are called *nodes*. Nodes can be tagged with decorations. For instance, a LC can be tagged as being frequent or critic according to the task decorations in the task model. A LM can be tagged with the concern it is in charge of (e.g., presentation). A PM can be tagged with the interaction path length it requires for achieving the task. Fig. 4 depicts the COMET architecture style as an UML class diagram (A) and in a dedicated graphical representation (B).

Constraints ensure that a node can only be plugged with compatible ones: LCs with LCs, LMs with LMs, PMs with technological compatible PMs (e.g. HTML presentations).

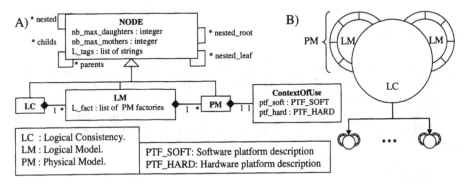

Fig. 4. The COMET architectural style: A) A UML class diagram. B) A dedicated graphical representation.

In the following we take the CamNote++ *"Remote Controller"* COMET as an example. Several presentations can be envisioned (Fig. 5-A) using different technologies: vocal, web, post WIMP, etc. Each presentation gives rise to a specific presentation PM. From a functional point of view, the controller can convey commands using different network protocols (Fig. 5-B).

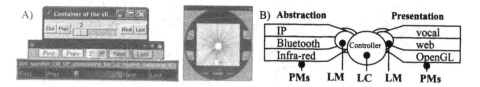

Fig. 5. A) Few presentations for the Remote Controller COMET. B) A graphical representation of the Remote Controller COMET.

Consistency among the different facets is ensured by a communication mechanism based on event propagation.

4.2 Events Propagation Inside a COMET

Events may be fired by two sources: either by a program that calls a COMET's function (e.g. set the current slide number) via its LC (Fig. 6-A) or by the user interacting with a PM (e.g. via the OpenGL presentation of the CamNote++ slides controller) thus triggering an event (Fig. 6-B). Each time an event is triggered, it is propagated along the COMET to the other facets in order to ensure consistency (Fig. 6). Ensuring consistency among presentation PMs can be seen as a multimodality issue if presentation PMs are seen as interaction modalities and multimodality as a combination of modalities.

The CARE properties [5] provide a framework for reasoning about the combination of modalities. Only Redundancy and Equivalence are addressed yet in COMET. Assignment is out of scope of our work presented in this paper. Complementarity as defined in the "put that there" paradigm [1] goes far beyond our work. Only basic forms of complementarity are covered up until now: (1) Input complementarity of modalities is used to achieve an elementary task. For instance, the task "Specify text" is achieved by alternatively using a keyboard-based and a voice-based PM. COMET supports this by design. (2) Input complementarity of modalities to achieve composed tasks (e.g. typing text and changing its colour). It is possible to use different modalities for the different sub-tasks. Again, COMET supports this by design. (3) Finally, output complementarity is achieved by using several PMs for a presentation LM.

To support Redundancy (R) and Equivalence (E), we have defined a domain specific language: COMET/RE (R for Redundancy and E for Equivalence). The idea is to associate a COMET/RE sentence to each function of the semantic API of a presentation LM. These sentences specify the way events must be processed. For instance, "R(E(gfx), E(vocal))" associated to the function F (e.g. switch to diaporama mode) means that the call of F has to be propagated to the LC if and only if one graphical PM (gfx) and one vocal PM (vocal) at least (E) are used in a redundant way (R). In case of redundancy, the propagation to the LC is conditioned by the activation of the corresponding PMs. In case of equivalence, the propagation to the LC is done as soon as an equivalent PM is activated. Fig. 6-B illustrates the COMET/RE sentence "E(*)": it means that all PMs (*) are equivalent (E) for F.

The next subsection elaborates on interactive systems as graphs of COMETs.

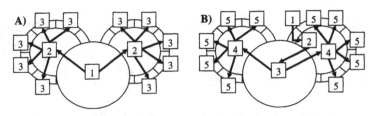

Fig. 6. Propagation of events (arrows) inside a COMET. Numbers represent the calls ordering. A) Propagation starting from the LC. B) Propagation starting from a PM. The propagation from 2 to 3 depends on the evaluation of the associated COMET/RE sentence.

4.3 Graphs of COMETs

Using COMETs, an interactive system is a graph of COMETs. More precisely, there are three types of interconnected graphs: a graph of LCs, a graph of presentation LMs and a set of graphs of presentation PMs, one per PM rendering technology (TK, OpenGL, etc.) as for instance a TK PM can only be rendered inside another TK PM. In all the graphs, the "parent-child" relation has the same meaning: the child expresses itself with regard to its parent (e.g. a PM child is rendered in the PM parent).

Consider CamNote++ for example. Fig. 7-A depicts the graph of COMETs for the spectator's UI: a text specifyer (to take notes), a slide controller and a slide viewer are interleaved. All the LCs are linked together in a graph. All the presentation LMs are linked together in another graph. All the presentation PMs are linked together in mono-technological graphs (one for TK, one for vocal, etc.). COMET ensures the interconnection between these graphs. For readability, only the graph of LCs is depicted in Fig. 7-A. Fig. 7-B shows the rendering of the AJAX/HTML-based graph of PMs.

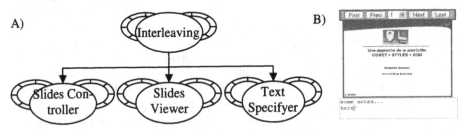

Fig. 7. A) Graph of COMETs for a spectator. B) A corresponding AJAX/HTML UI

Each node that contains a graph of COMETs (Recursivity principle) is said to be composite by opposition with atomic nodes (which do not contain a graph). Fig. 8 illustrates how recursivity is used in the CamNote++ COMET. The LC part of the COMET is composed of COMETs that correspond to the different roles (speaker or spectator) of CamNote++ users. All the COMETs (speaker or spectator) share a same COMET slides viewer, thus ensuring the slides synchronisation among users. Besides the recursivity in the LC, there is a recursivity of presentation PMs. Each PM of

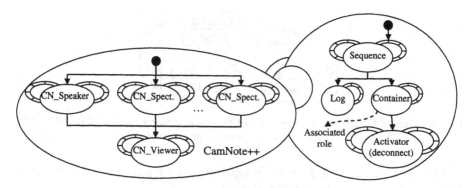

Fig. 8. The CamNote++ COMET. The composite PM is in charge of log in the user to the right role (speaker or spectator). The composite LC manages the different roles (modeled with dedicated COMETs). All the roles share a same COMET slides viewer.

CamNote++ is in charge of identifying the user and setting his/her role. In practice, each time a user accesses CamNote++ by mean of a new UI (e.g. when opening a web browser), he/she is asked to identify his/herself so that CamNote++ can display the right UI (speaker or spectator).

There is no straightforward rule to know when and how to use composite nodes. It is up to the designer to decide about using this feature. However, we can say that task decomposition is likely to be translated into a composite LC; workspaces organisation is likely to be translated into a composite presentation LM, and widgets decomposition is likely to be translated into a composite presentation PM. As shown in Fig. 8, a composite PM can also be used to manage access to a COMET for different users.

In practice, designers only have to specify the graph of LCs. The presentation LM graph (respectively PM graph) is automatically generated according to the LC graph (respectively LM graph). The graph of PMs is built with respect to the context of use: an AJAX/HTML PM is plugged into AJAX/HTML compatible PMs. Note that graphs of presentation LMs and PMs are automatically generated. Indeed, COMETs always contain presentation facets. This is not the case for other facets such as abstraction.

5 Developing with COMETs

This section puts the COMET style in action. Three kinds of requirements are considered to show how COMET can be used for tuning CamNote++ and target additional contexts of use.

5.1 Distributing the Slides Controller on a PDA

Imagine the designer decides to distribute CamNote++ (for the speaker role) on a PC and a PDA: the Slides Viewer on the PC using OpenGL; the Slides Controller on the PDA using HTML. To do this, the designer only needs to plug an OpenGL and an

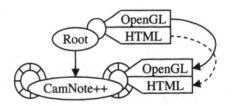

Fig. 9. Graph of COMETs corresponding to CamNote++ rendered in OpenGL and HTML. Links (arrows) between presentation PMs are automatically generated based on the LC links.

HTML PM to the COMET Root which expresses that the graph of COMETs will be rendered using these two technologies (Fig. 9).

Once the graph (Fig. 9) is built, the designer configures the presentations to be rendered. For instance, he/she specifies that the HTML Slides Controller has to fit the web page. This can be done using a style/transformation rule that, if necessary, calls the semantic network for retrieving presentations. Fig.10 provides an example without any detail about the syntax. The example (A) asks for replacing the HTML slides controller with a skinable version (B) to be retrieved in the semantic network.

A)   B)

```
#CN_Speaker->PMs[soft_type == HTML](SlideController) {
    type            :            SlideController_CUI_skinnable;
}
```

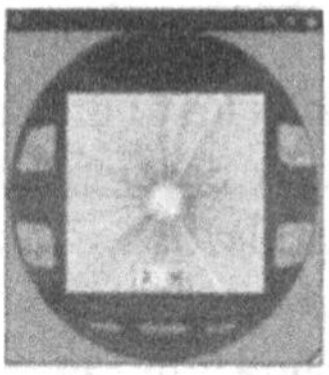

Fig. 10. A) A transformation rule for substituting the HTML presentation of the Speaker's Slides Controller by the one shown in B

5.2 Requiring Redundancy for Switching the Presentation Mode

Imagine switching between full screen and window-based modes appears to be a critical task. Requiring redundancy for changing the mode may be an option to prevent the user from making errors,. In that case, the speaker has to ask for a switch using both the HTML and OpenGL UIs. Such a modification can simply be done using a single transformation rule (Fig. 11). This rule specifies that the mode activator COMET can only be activated if both the OpenGL and HTML presentations are activated in the same temporal window of 2000 milliseconds.

```
#CN_Speaker(Activator.DIAPORAMA->_LM_LP) {
    COMET_RE_expr : activate  R(2000,E(HTML),E(OpenGL)) ;
}
```

Fig. 11. A transformation rule for requiring redundancy between OpenGL and HTML presentations when switching between full screen and window-based modes

5.3 Integrating the Pixels Mirror Feature into the OpenGL Slides Viewer

Imagine the designer decides to include a pixels mirror when possible (i.e., in case a camera is connected to the PC). Using COMET, this is achieved either at design time or at runtime by (1) encapsulating the OpenGL "Slides Viewer" presentation PM into a composite PM, adding a Video COMET in charge of displaying the camera images, and adding an integer Choice COMET to set the translucence level of the video (first rule in Fig. 12-A, *"Eval : U_encapsulator_PM $obj "Container(, \$core, Video(), ChoiceN(set_range \"0 100\"))";").* Then (2) the COMET choice is linked to the video OpenGL presentation PM so that every time a new value is set, the translucence level is updated accordingly (second rule of Fig. 12-A, an Event Condition Action is defined by *"ECA : set_current, true,   set video [CSS++ "#CN_Speaker->PMs[type==OpenGL] CN_Viewer(Video)"] --- $video set_translucidity [expr $value / 100.0];").* Finally, the last two rules express how the presentations are laid out. Fig. 12-B graphically describes the COMET Slide Viewer before and after applying the rules.

A)
```
#CN_Speaker->PMs[type==OpenGL] CN_Viewer {
   Eval : U_encapsulator_PM  $obj "Container(, \$core, Video(), ChoiceN(set_range \"0 100\")";
}
#CN_Speaker->PMs[type==OpenGL] CN_Viewer(ChoiceN) {
   ECA : set_current, true
       , set video [CSS++ "#CN_Speaker->PMs[type==OpenGL] CN_Viewer(Video)"] ---
         $video set_translucidity [expr $value / 100.0];
}
#CN_Speaker->PMs[type==OpenGL] CN_Viewer(Container, Video) {
   Layout : Fit_parent;
}
#CN_Speaker->PMs[type==OpenGL] CN_Viewer(ChoiceN) {
   Type : Slider;
   Layout : Bottom;
}
```

B)

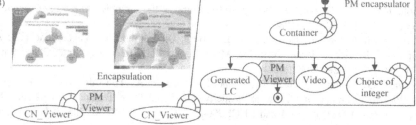

Fig. 12. Four transformation rules, a dozen of lines of code to integrate the pixels mirror feature in CamNote++

6 Conclusion and Future Work

In this paper, we present COMET, a new software architecture style specially crafted for plasticity. COMET bridges the gap between two main research areas in plasticity:

MDE and interactors toolkits. COMET meets four main requirements that had never been simultaneously satisfied so far. The four levels of abstraction and the multi rendering feature are ensured by design concepts: tasks-concepts, AUI, CUI and FUI are respectively embodied in LCs, presentation LMs, PMs and technological primitives. Technological primitives target different languages and toolkits in a non exclusive way. Extensibility and controllability are satisfied with two additional tools (not described in this paper): style sheets for specifying transformations, and a semantic network for retrieving existing UI elements.

The COMET style has been implemented in TCL giving rise to a COMETs toolkit that contains classical interactors (e.g., select one option among N) as well as more innovative ones in charge of task operators (e.g., interleaving, sequence). Each interactor can be polymorphic including exotic custom-made presentations. In turn, the COMETs toolkit has been used for implementing CamNote++, an executable plastic presentation software that illustrates the architecture and concepts proposed in this paper. We show the powerful COMET capabilities for extending and tuning UIs, and for exploring design alternatives. This can be done both at design time and at run time.

In the future, we aim at exploring UIs for visualizing and transforming COMETs at runtime. We keep in mind the difficult issue of evaluating the architecture model and the toolkit. Using the proposed approach in teaching situations could provide an initial evaluation.

Videos are available at **http://iihm.imag.fr/demeure/**.

Acknowledgments. Part of the research has been funded by the SIMILAR European network and ERDF (European Regional Development Fund), the Flemish Government and the Flemish Interdisciplinary institute for BroadBand Technology (IBBT).

References

1. Bolt, R.A.: "Put-That-There": Voice and Gesture at the Graphics Interface. Computer Graphics 14(3), 262–270 (1980)
2. Calvary, G., Coutaz, J., Thevenin, D., Limbourg, Q., Bouillon, L., Vanderdonckt, J.: A Unifying Reference Framework for Multi-Target User Interfaces. Interacting With Computers 15/3, 289–308 (2003)
3. Calvary, G., Coutaz, J., Dâassi, O., Balme, L., Demeure, A.: Towards a New Generation of Widgets for Supporting Software Plasticity: The "Comet". In: Bastide, R., Palanque, P., Roth, J. (eds.) DSV-IS 2004 and EHCI 2004. LNCS, vol. 3425, pp. 306–324. Springer, Heidelberg (2005)
4. Clerckx, T., Luyten, K., Coninx, K.: The mapping problem back and forth: customizing dynamic models while preserving consistency. In: Proceedings of the 3rd Annual Conference on Task Models and Diagrams, TAMODIA 2004, November 15 - 16, 2004, vol. 86, pp. 33–42. ACM Press, New York (2004)
5. Coutaz, J., Nigay, L., Salber, D., Blandford, A., May, J., Young, R.: Four Easy Pieces for Assessing the Usability of Multimodal Interaction: The CARE properties. In: Arnesen, S.A., Gilmore, D. (eds.) Proceedings of the INTERACT 1995 conference, June 1995, pp. 115–120. Chapman&Hall Publ., Lillehammer (1995)

6. Crease, M., Brewster, S.A., Gray, P.: Caring, sharing widgets: a toolkit of sensitive widgets. In: 14th Annual Conference of the British HCI Group, Sunderland, England, September 5-8, 2000. British Computer Society conference series, pp. 257–270 (2000)

7. da Silva, P.: User Interface Declarative Models and Development Environments: A Survey. In: Palanque, P., Paternó, F. (eds.) DSV-IS 2000. LNCS, vol. 1946, pp. 207–226. Springer, Heidelberg (2001)

8. Demeure, A., Calvary, G., Coutaz, J., Vanderdonckt, J.: The COMETs Inspector: Towards Run Time Plasticity Control Based on a Semantic Network. In: Coninx, K., Luyten, K., Schneider, K.A. (eds.) TAMODIA 2006. LNCS, vol. 4385. Springer, Heidelberg (2007)

9. Gajos, K., Weld, D.: Preference elicitation for interface optimization. In: UIST 2005: Proceedings of the 18th annual ACM symposium on User interface software and technology, Seattle, WA, USA, pp. 173–182 (2005)

10. Jabarin, B., Graham, N.: Architectures for Widget-Based Plasticity. In: Jorge, J.A., Jardim Nunes, N., Falcão e Cunha, J. (eds.) DSV-IS 2003. LNCS, vol. 2844, pp. 124–138. Springer, Heidelberg (2003)

11. Johnson, J.: Selectors: going beyond user-interface widgets. In: CHI 1992: Proceedings of the SIGCHI conference on Human factors in computing systems, pp. 273–279 (1992)

12. Kawai, S., Aida, H., Saito, T.: Designing interface toolkit with dynamic selectable modality. In: Proceedings of the Second Annual ACM Conference on Assistive Technologies Assets 1996, April 11 - 12, 1996, pp. 72–79. ACM Press, New York (1996)

13. Lecolinet, E.: A molecular architecture for creating advanced GUIs. In: Proceedings of the 16th Annual ACM Symposium on User interface Software and Technology UIST 2003, November 02 - 05, 2003, pp. 135–144. ACM Press, New York (2003)

14. Nylander, S., Bylund, M., Waern, A.: The Ubiquitous Interactor – Device Independent Access to Mobile Services. In: Proc. of 5th Int. Conf. of Computer-Aided Design of User Interfaces CADUI 2004, January 13-16, 2004, pp. 269–280. Kluwer Academics, Dordrecht (2005)

15. Paterno', F., Mancini, C., Meniconi, S.,, C.: A Diagrammatic Notation for Specifying Task Models. In: Proceedings Interact 1997, Sydney, pp. 362–369. Chapman & Hall, Boca Raton (1997)

16. Stuerzlinger, W., Chapuis, O., Phillips, D., Roussel., N.: User Interface Façades: Towards Fully Adaptable User Interfaces. In: Proceedings of UIST 2006, October 2006, pp. 309–318. ACM Press, New York (2006)

17. Thevenin, D., Coutaz, J.: Plasticity of User Interfaces: Framework and Research Agenda. In: Edinburgh, A.S., Johnson, C. (eds.) Proc. Interact 1999, pp. 110–117. IFIP IOS Press Publ., Amsterdam (1999)

Executable Models for Human-Computer Interaction

Marco Blumendorf, Grzegorz Lehmann, Sebastian Feuerstack, and Sahin Albayrak

DAI-Labor, TU-Berlin
Ernst-Reuter-Platz 7, D-10587 Berlin
firstname.lastname@DAI-Labor.de

Abstract. Model-based user interface development is grounded on the idea to utilize models at design time to derive user interfaces from the modeled information. There is however an increasing demand for user interfaces that adapt to the context of use at runtime. The shift from design time to runtime means, that different design decisions are postponed until runtime. Utilizing user interface models at runtime provides a possibility to utilize the same basis of information for these postponed decisions. The approach we are following goes even one step further. Instead of only postponing several design decisions, we aim at the utilization of stateful and executable models at runtime to completely express the user interaction and the user interface logic in a model-based way.

Keywords: human-computer interaction, model-based user interfaces, runtime interpretation.

1 Introduction

Model-based software development is becoming more and more popular these days and has been identified as suitable to deal with the increasing complexity of software systems developers have to cope with. While UML made the idea of modeling popular by providing a common language to exchange concepts between developers, the Meta-Object Facility (MOF) and the Model-Driven Architecture (MDA) of the Object Management Group (OMG) provide the key concepts for the widespread utilization of model-based software engineering. However, with the advent of technologies like UML Actions or the Business Process Modeling Language (BPML) the focus of the modeling approaches shifts from static systems to dynamic systems and executable models. While the original static models were mainly able to present snapshot views of the systems under study and could thus only provide answers to "what is" kinds of questions, dynamic models give access to information that changes over time and are thus also able to answer "what has been" or "what if" kinds of questions (see also [4]). Executable models support this approach by providing the logic that defines the dynamic behavior as part of the model. Their structure will be explained in more detail in the remainder of this paper.

The ability to model complex software systems has recently also regained more attention as a technology capable of handling the increasing complexity of user interfaces (UIs). Rising demands for dynamic UIs that adapt to the context-of-use and thus user preferences, multiple devices, the surrounding environment or even multiple

T.C.N. Graham and P. Palanque (Eds.): DSVIS 2008, LNCS 5136, pp. 238–251, 2008.

modalities, induce the need for new ways to express such characteristics. Model-based approaches as described in [14, 11] address these challenges by utilizing models to support the user interface development process and provide the means to derive multiple consistent user interfaces from a (sometimes multi-level) UI model. Additionally approaches that utilize UI models at runtime [7, 10] addressed specific development issues. There is however still the lack of a well accepted common User Interface Description Language (UIDL) as different approaches focus on different aspects. UsiXML currently seems to be the most feasible candidate for such a language.

In this paper we present an approach that facilitates the development of User Interface Management Systems that address:

- supporting different UIDLs and models by introducing a common meta-layer
- the consideration of the predictive as well as the effective context of use [5]
- the specification of syntax and semantics as part of a model
- support for the easy extension of systems based on the coupling of multiple models
- the unification of design models and the runtime data structures of interactive systems

The model-based approach we describe in the following therefore facilitates the utilization of "executable" user interface models at runtime. Although we propose a set of models, the general system allows the utilization of various UIDLs on different levels of abstraction. The approach therefore addresses the definition of a meta-meta-model providing building blocks for meta-models that also contain the model semantics. Furthermore the system allows the developer to monitor, maintain, manipulate and extend interactive applications at runtime and thus manage the continuously changing requirements of user interface development.

After introducing the current state of the art in the next section, we give an introduction to the idea of executable models, providing the possibility to combine syntax and semantic with state information to support direct model execution. Next we present a meta-meta-model, distinguishing definition-, situation- and execution parts our executable models are comprised of. Following that section, we give an overview of the meta-models and the mapping meta-model we utilize for the UI development and the underlying concepts. We then introduce the architecture of our runtime system and elaborate on the possible applications of the approach. We describe how the development process can be supported by the ability to directly modify the models at runtime using Eclipse and EMF, which also allows runtime inspection, modification and debugging of the models.

2 State of the Art

The recent shift towards model-based software development aims at solutions to cope with the increasing complexity of current and future systems. While UML made the idea of modeling popular by providing a common language to exchange concepts between developers, MOF and MDA provide the key concepts for the utilization of model-based software engineering. Technologies like Executable UML, UML Actions or BPML focus on the shift from static- to dynamic systems and executable models. These developments also influence user interface research. The current state of the art in model-based user interface development shows the need for a common language [11] and a tendency towards a common understanding of the new challenges and approaches [2, 1]. However, there are also approaches to build architectures, tools and methodologies to support the designer during the development as well as the creation of adaptive user interfaces and their adaptation at runtime. [10] for example deals with the execution of CTT-based user interface models and [7] presents a runtime system that targets the creation of context-aware user interfaces.

Sottet et al. [19] propose keeping the models alive at runtime to make the design rationale available. This means, that the final UI code should not be generated at design-time, but at runtime, taking the context adaptations into account. Demeure et al. [8] presented the Comets, which are prototypical user interface components capable of adaptations due to the application of models at runtime. Preserving the models at runtime opened the possibility for the implementation of plasticity-enabling features like their Meta-UI. Yet, the black-box nature of the Comets seems problematic at runtime, as the system has no indications about a Comet's inner state. Clerckx et al. [6] extend the DynaMo-AID design process by context data evaluated at runtime, supporting UI migration and distribution. Their approach allows the designer to define context-dependent information in the models. However, although the models are then interpreted dynamically, their adaptation at runtime is not possible. To support the linking of multiple models, Sottet et al. [20] propose to model transformations which should also be available at runtime. However, none of the solutions we are aware of enables to identify the common components of multiple models and links between the models, which could pave the road to interoperability between different UIDLs. In our approach, we utilize executable models to derive user interfaces at runtime. We define a meta-meta-model and conceptually introduce a mapping meta-model. This allows us to connect different models and concepts to build advanced user interfaces.

3   Executable Models

Recent developments in the model-based user interface development community show the increasing importance of models as a basis for development support and also as basis at runtime. Currently there is still a focus on the usage of static models, providing (only) a snapshot of the system under study at a given point in time. Research in model-driven engineering of user interfaces has brought up various approaches to use models for the derivation of user interfaces for different purposes. However, future interactive systems are required to adapt to different contexts at runtime and thus deriving multiple UIs at design time does not seem to be feasible anymore. Keeping the model(s) at runtime allows postponing design decisions to runtime and thus performing adaptations to the runtime circumstances rather than predicting all possible context situations at design time. We think that the executable models approach introduced in this section can support a more extensive usage of models at runtime. In contrast to common static models, executable models provide the logic that defines the dynamic behavior as part of the model, which makes them complete in the sense that they have "everything required to produce a desired functionality of a single problem domain" [12]. They provide the capabilities to express static elements as well as behavior and evolution of the system in one single model. Executable models run and have similar properties as program code. In contrast to code however, executable models provide a domain-specific level of abstraction which greatly simplifies the communication with the user or customer. Combining the idea of executable models with dynamic elements as part of the model gives the model an observable and manipulable state. Besides the initial state of a system and the processing logic, dynamic executable models also make the model elements that change over time explicit and support the investigation of the state of the execution at any point in time. We can thus describe dynamic executable models as *models that provide a complete view of the system under study over time*.

3.1 A Meta-Meta-Model

Combining the initial state of the system, the dynamic model elements that change over time and the processing logic in one model, leads to the need to clearly distinguish between the different elements. We thus distinguish between definition-, situation- and execution elements in the following. A similar classification has also been identified by Breton and Bézivin [4].

Definition Elements define the static structure of the model and thus denote the constant elements that do not change over time. Definition elements are defined by the designer and represent the constants of the model, invariant over time.

Situation Elements define the current state of the model and thus identify those elements that do change over time. Situation elements are changed by the processing logic of the application when making a transition from one state to another one. Any change to a situation element can trigger an execution element.

Execution Elements define the interpretation process of the model, in other words the transitions from one state to another. In this sense execution elements are procedures or actions altering the situation elements of a model. Execution elements also provide the entry points for data exchange with entities outside of the model. Defining execution elements as part of the model allows the incorporation of semantic information and the interpretation process as part of the model itself and thus ensures consistency and an unambiguous interpretation. This approach makes an executable model complete and self-contained.

Distinguishing these elements leads to the meta-meta-model of dynamic executable models depicted in Fig. 1. The meta-meta-model provides a more formal view of executable models and summarizes the common concepts the models are based on. It is positioned at M3 layer in the MOF Metadata Architecture [15] (see also Fig. 4). The clear separation of the elements provides clear boundaries for the designer, only working with the definition elements and the system architect, providing the meta-models. A definition element as the basic element finally aggregates situation- and execution elements that describe and change situations for a given definition element. Using such models in a prescriptive way (constructive rather than descriptive modeling) allows defining

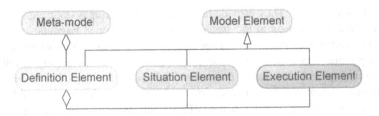

Fig. 1. Meta-Meta-Model of Dynamic Executable Models

systems that evolve over time, reason about the past and predict future behavior. Dynamic models are often used to build self-adaptive applications, as for example Rohr et al. [17] describe. In this context, the role of the models is often that of monitoring the system. In the following we illustrate the implications of the meta-meta-model by introducing the realization of a CTT-based task-meta-model as executable meta-model using the Eclipse Modeling Framework.

3.2 Modeling with EMF

For our current implementation we have utilized the Eclipse Modeling Framework (EMF), which is a modeling and code generation framework integrated into the Eclipse IDE. EMF provides means to define meta-models, create models and appropriate editors. Beyond that, for each meta-model EMF is capable of generating Java class structures representing it. These can then be enriched by a programmer just as usual Java code can. This way it is possible to add execution logic into the meta-model in form of Java code fragments.

ECore is the meta-model of EMF and thus the meta-meta-model of all models defined in EMF. It resides on the same layer as the meta-meta-model of the executable models. Choosing EMF as the implementation technology makes it necessary to map definition-, situation- and execution elements - the entities of our meta-meta-model - to entities in the ECore meta-meta-model. In our approach, the definition elements are represented by EClasses in ECore. The situation elements find their representation in the ECore's EStructuralFeatures although not all EStructuralFeatures are situation elements as some attributes of an element (EAttribute) may describe runtime state data. The differentiation is therefore done by the adoption of an extra EAnnotation. Finally, the execution elements are in ECore expressed as EOperations, which allows adding execution logic into a meta-model in form of Java code fragments. In Java the execution logic is defined within methods and these are represented by EOperations within ECore.

3.3 Executable Task Models

In the following we use the task model as an example to illustrate the executable models, the usage of the meta-meta-model and the realization with EMF. The task model we use is based on the CTT notation which is well known in model-based UI development. Task models are also known to be executable [10] and define the tasks the user has to accomplish and their temporal relations. They thus provide an over-view of the workflow of the application. To be able to utilize the CTT-based task model for our purposes we extended the static part of the CTT meta-model with the state information needed to reflect the state of the execution in the model. We intro-duce attributes for each task, identifying the state of the task and thus the situation elements of the model.

Fig. 2. The Task-Meta-Model in EMF

Fig. 2 shows the EMF meta-model structure for task models. As one can see in the graphic, every task model is comprised of a root task with a set of children tasks. Each task is a definition element which also comprises situation elements. While name, type, description, relation (temporal relation to neighbor task) and the iterative flag are defined by the designer, state and suspended state (the last state before sus-pension) are annotated as situation elements as they change over time. During execu-tion at runtime - starting with the root task - the setNewState operation is used to change the state of the task as well as all related child-tasks (according to their tempo-ral relations). This allows to explicitly store the execution state of the model as part of the model. During execution the Enabled Task Set (ETS) is derived and then each task in this set is set to state "enabled". Once the task is completed it is set to "done". Using this interpretation we distinguish InteractionIn (user input) and InteractionOut (system output) and application tasks (backend call without user intervention) to model the workflow of the application.

This example illustrates how the task model and its execution logic can be embed-ded into a single executable model while keeping design time and runtime informa-tion separate, but also making the runtime state of the model explicit.

3.4 Summary

The executable models introduced in this section support the creation of models that define systems and their behavior over time, while also exposing all state information for manipulation and inspection. The meta-meta-model of executable models de-scribes the building blocks of such models. We exemplified this principle using ex-ecutable task models.

Looking at current model-based approaches [2, 11] there is a clear trend to provide multiple models for the different aspects (e.g. levels of abstractions) rather than a single model. We introduce an approach, combining multiple models to create user interfaces at runtime, in more detail in section 5. Such relations between models are not reflected by the meta-meta-model, as executable models are first of all self-contained to ensure executability. The next section thus introduces a mapping meta-model, that allows to express the relations between multiple models. The model itself is executable as well, and provides the required event hooks in the execution logic to interconnect multiple models. The mapping meta-model is positioned on layer M2 of the MOF architecture [15] (see also Fig. 4).

4 Mapping-Meta-Model

The mapping model connects multiple executable models and allows to define relations between their elements based on the structures given by the meta-meta-model. The mappings defined in this model are the glue between the models of our multi-model architecture. The mapping meta-model as well as the other related meta-models is thereby located at M2 layer of the MOF architecture. Providing an extra meta-model solely for mappings also enables to benefit from tool support and removes the problem of mappings hard-coded into the architecture, as has been already advised by Puerta and Eisenstein [16]. The mapping meta-model allows the definition of the common nature of the mappings and helps ensuring extensibility and flexibility. A mapping relates models by relating elements of the models whereas the models are not aware of their relation. An example of a mapping meta-model, consisting of a fixed set of predefined mapping types only, can also be found in UsiXML described by Limbourg [11]. Sottet et al. [18] have defined a mapping meta-model, which can also be used to describe transformations between model elements at runtime. However, in contrast to their approach we put a stronger focus on the specific situation at runtime and the information exchange between dynamic models. Especially interesting at runtime is the fact, that the relations can be utilized to keep models synchronized and to transport information between two or more models. The information provided by the mappings can be used to synchronize elements if the state of the source elements changes. Mellor et al. [13] also see the main features of mappings as construction (when the target model is created from the source model) and synchronization (when data from the source model is propagated into the existing target model). Our mapping model contains mappings of the latter kind. Focusing on runtime aspects, we see a mapping as a possibility to alter an existing target model, based on changes that happen to the related source model. In contrast to the most common understanding of mappings the mappings we utilize do not transform a model into another one. Instead, they synchronize runtime data between coexisting models. Mappings connect definition elements of different models with each other. They are always triggered by situation elements and activate execution elements.

The conceptual mapping meta-model is provided in Fig. 3 and combines mapping types and mappings. Mapping types are the main elements of the mapping meta-model, as they provide predefined types of mappings that can be used to define the actual mappings between elements on M1 layer. A mapping type thereby consists of two definition elements as well as of well-defined links between the two. The definition elements are the source and the target of the mapping and the mapping synchronizes the runtime data between these two elements. The links consist of a situation

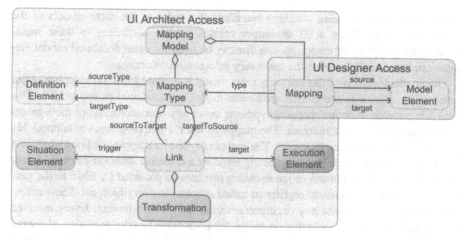

Fig. 3. Mapping Meta-Model

element, an execution element and a transformation. The situation element is the trigger of a link. Whenever a situation element in a model changes, the link is triggered and the referenced execution logic is executed to synchronize the two definition elements of the mapping. The execution logic is thus the logical target of the link. The optional transformation associated with the link describes how the situation data, which activated the trigger, is transformed into (input) data needed by the target execution element in the other model. This transformation might be required, especially when models with distinct data types and structures are linked by mappings. To simplify the usage of the model, the meta-model supports multiple links in one mapping type, as multiple situation elements (e.g. related to the same definition element) might be relevant to trigger the execution. Supporting more than one link also allows a back linking, as some mapping types might also demand two-way links.

From the designer's point of view, the initial mapping model now provides a set of available mapping types with predefined logic, defined on the meta-model level. Thus to relate two models, the user interface designer extends this initial model by creating new mappings that reference one of the available mapping types. To create such a mapping, the designer has to provide the specific source and target model elements to the mapping and define its type. This leads to a relation between the two elements and their synchronization according to the given execution logic.

Using our meta-meta-model we were able to define the mapping meta-model independent from the concrete meta-models that mappings can be created between. Only the mapping models contain mapping types, which are not of generic nature, but specifically designed for the given meta-models.

4.1 Modeling Mappings with EMF

The EMF implementation of the mappings basically reflects the meta-model illustrated in Fig. 3 and also conforms to the described meta-meta-model of the executable models. The main principle behind the realization of the mapping model with EMF is the ability of EMF to include and reference a model within another model. This feature allows us to create standard mappings that refer to the meta-models of the system to design. Once a UI developer creates models according to these meta-models, the pre-defined mappings can directly be used to relate dedicated model elements and thus easily provide the necessary information exchange.

Our implementation of the mapping meta-model is derived from the mapping of our meta-meta-model with the ECore meta-meta-model as introduced in section 3.2. This way it is possible to define mapping types on top of any executable ECore meta-model (M2) used within our architecture. The mappings use the mapping types to connect M1 entities and thus reference EObjects. The mapping type of a mapping defines what links it contains, whereas each link may be triggered by a different situation element. In our implementation we made use of the eventing mechanism provided by EMF in the generated Java code. It enables to register so called adapters to every EObject. These adapters become notified about any occurrence within the model element. Every received notification contains the information about the EStructuralFeature (situation element), which has undergone a change, its new and previous values. In our prototyping phase we have developed a simple transformation language which we then used to define the transformation elements. Currently we are working on the integration of the ATLAS Transformation Language (ATL)[1] into the mapping meta-model. After a link has been triggered and the transformation produced new data for the target model the Java method denoted by the EOperation of the execution element is invoked. For this purpose we utilize the reflection mechanisms of the Java language.

5   The Multi-access Service Platform (v2)

Based on the concepts of executable models and the mappings, we rebuild our previously developed Multi-Access Service Platform (MASP). The MASP is a UIMS that allows the creation of multimodal user interfaces by interpreting models at runtime. We are currently using the system to build adaptive multimodal interfaces for smart home environments as part of the Service Centric Home project[2]. Utilizing executable models as the underlying concepts for the approach lead to a complete redesign of the system. Based on the meta-meta-models and the mapping (meta-) model we selected a set of models to represent the workflow and the interaction with the application as well as context and backend services (Fig. 5). The selection and design of the models was also influenced by UsiXML models and the Cameleon reference framework, although we decided to go with a slightly adapted syntax in the first step. Fig. 4 shows the components of the MASP in relation to the MOF Meta Pyramid. M1 thereby comprises the loosely coupled models while M2 provides the underlying meta-models. On M2 we also introduced the MASP Core meta-model which provides the means to initially load applications (sets of models) and trigger the execution. The Model contains sessions for the user and application management. Additionally it provides a basic API to access the models, making it easy to build software and management tools for the platform. Besides the models and their execution logic, the

---

[1] http://www.eclipse.org/m2m/atl/
[2] www.sercho.de

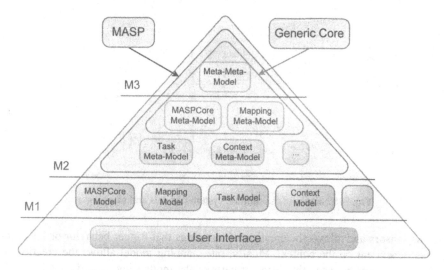

Fig. 4. The MASP in Relation to the MOF Meta-Pyramid

MASP comprises a channel-based delivery mechanism for the delivery of the created final user interfaces to the interaction devices [3] and integrates several sensors (e.g. an Ubisense ultra wide band localization system) for context recognition.

Fig. 5 shows the models we are currently using to develop applications for our approach. The task model defines the temporal relations between the multiple tasks of the application and can thus serve as outline for the interaction. A domain model completes the task model by providing content to the tasks. The model itself on the one hand defines the data structures we are dealing with, but also holds instances of these structures, objects, that become accessible at runtime. The life-time of these objects is determined by the task model again, which also references the objects in the designated tasks [9]. Altering the content of the domain model happens in two ways. On the one hand there are backend services that provide information. These services are on the highest level referenced by the task model in terms of application tasks [9]. A specific description of the service call itself and the referenced objects is provided by a service model. Thus application tasks are mapped to service calls in the service model via the appropriate mappings. The other possibility for new or modified content is the user entering or changing information while interacting with the system. This is realized by the interaction model, related to interaction tasks. Here we distinguish input and output tasks which each identify the interaction on the highest level of abstraction. A reification of the interaction in terms of details is then provided by the interaction model that comprises an abstract interaction description, which is modality independent, and a concrete interaction description, which adds the modality dependent information. Finally, during our work we identified the context model as an important part as soon as the environment, available devices and thus the context of the interaction comes into play. We thus also created a context model, allowing to provide context information. The model is at runtime filled with information delivered by

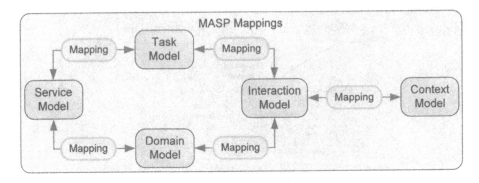

Fig. 5. Structure of the runtime system (models and mappings)

various sensors and allows the creation of mappings that trigger behavior or UI adaptations dependent on the context. Finally, our mapping model allows the creation of various mappings between the different parts of the models and thus links all models together. By linking the task model to service and interaction model, the execution of the task model and thus changing task states to "enabled" triggers the activation of service calls and interaction elements. While service calls activate backend functions, active interaction elements are displayed on the screen and allow user interaction. They also incorporate domain model elements in their presentation and allow their manipulation through user input as defined by the mappings. The context model finally also influences the presentation of the interaction elements that are related to context information. Thus, the execution of the task model triggers a chain reaction, leading to the creation of a user interface from the defined user interface model. The structure underlying this approach also opens the possibility to add additional models or change existing models in the future. Although our current approach follows the well accepted Cameleon Reference Framework and thus provides a similar set of models, it provides a meta-layer, allowing to unite multiple modeling languages and approaches.

6 Applications

Utilizing executable models as described in this paper offers various opportunities for future user interface development. We build a couple of prototypes and smaller trials, which showed great potential for issues like context adaptation at runtime, personalization, debugging and hot deployment as well as extensibility of running systems. In the following we report on our results concerning two multimodal applications (a cooking assistant and an energy manager) we (re-)built based on the MASP as well as several smaller proof-of-concept prototypes.

Both applications, the cooking assistant (CA) and the energy manager, target smart home environments and support multimodal interaction. While the CA, we will focus on in the following, runs in the kitchen and supports the user while preparing a meal, the energy manager provides an overview of the energy usage of the home devices and allows to switch devices on and off. The CA is based on three interaction steps.

First the user selects a recipe, from recommendations or the results of a search. Afterwards the required ingredients are listed and based on the availability in the home a shopping list is displayed. Finally the cooking process is guided with step by step instructions. The central model of the CA is the task model, defining the underlying workflow. Based on the task model, related objects have been modeled as domain model and service calls to the backend (e.g. to retrieve the list of recipes or to control kitchen devices) have been defined as service model. Mappings on the one hand relate application tasks to service calls. Thus as soon as an application task becomes active the related service call is executed. On the other hand the domain objects serving as input and output for the service calls are related to these. In a similar way, interaction tasks are related to interaction objects via mappings. Interaction objects thus become activated as soon as an interaction task becomes enabled. This triggers the delivery of the representation of the interaction objects on the interaction device. The interaction devices are thereby identified as part of the usage context and thus the mappings between interaction model and context model provide the foundation for the delivery of the user interface.

In addition to this complete application we also evaluated some additional features in smaller trials. Based on the developed CA, we explored the runtime inspection of the state information of the underlying models as well as extension mechanisms and further capabilities to adapt the UI to the context of use.

Runtime Development – One feature of the Eclipse Modeling Framework underlying our implementation is the possibility to directly connect the models to Java code. We make use of this facility to build an editor that connects to the models of the running system. Thus any changes we make to the model via the editor are directly propagated into the runtime system, as they also trigger the related events. This approach allows to directly inspect and change the running system. As the situation-elements monitor the state of the execution in various details, there is an enormous potential to access and manipulate the complete state of the system. All modeled information is available. This feature simplifies development and debugging a lot, however, in combination with our strictly model-based approach it also allows the customization of the application by the end user if appropriate tools are provided either as additional software or even as part of the application. The loose coupling of the models and the encapsulation of the execution logic as part of the meta-model also allow easily extending or changing the application, even at runtime, which is an important aspect to manage the continuous changes requested from software developers.

Enhancing a Running System – We evaluated the possibilities to enhance (running) systems in another case study, where we replaced one model with another one (conforming to a new meta-model) at runtime. With current task-based approaches we noted that it is rather difficult to model back and forth navigation e.g. between different screens of an application, as dialog modeling is not the responsibility of the task model. Therefore we will transform the task model into a state machine model and enrich it with additional transitions representing the desired dialog navigation. This case study showed that it is possible to replace models of the system without changing the existing models, simply by providing the model and a set of mappings. In the same way the system can also be extended with additional models, which emphasizes the language-spanning aspects of the approach.

7 Summary and Outlook

We presented an approach to utilize dynamic executable models to build user interfaces. Combining definition-, situation- and execution elements provides the means to make all relevant information explicitly accessible and also helps separating the parts of the models relevant for the UI designer. In combination with the mapping model, this approach allows an easy integration of multiple models at runtime to build complex systems. The loose coupling of models also provides a very flexible structure that can easily be extended and adapted to different needs. This also addresses the problem that there are currently no standard or widely accepted UI models. Combined with development and debugging tools this approach allows to inspect and analyze the behavior of the interactive system on a very low level of details. To evaluate the feasibility of the approach to cope with challenges and requirements for the next generation of user interfaces we developed a model-based runtime system for smart home user interfaces. We use task, domain, service and interaction models and mappings between these models at runtime to interpret the modeled information and derive a user interface. As next steps we want to further evaluate the performance of our EMF- and Java-based implementation to optimize the implementation. However, its current implementation shows that the systems perform very well. We also aim at further refining the models we are using. While the combination of different models seems suitable, especially our current interaction model gives room for extensions and enhancements. The possibility to build self-aware systems using executable models is also a fascinating feature that needs further evaluation. Utilizing the models at runtime however, does not solve all problems of model-based user interface development, but it gives possibilities to overcome the technical challenges in addressing these problems.

Acknowledgements

We thank the German Federal Ministry of Economics and Technology for supporting our work as part of the Service Centric Home project in the "Next Generation Media" program.

References

1. Calvary, G., Coutaz, J., Ganneau, V., Vanderdonckt, J., Demeure, A., Sottet, J.-S.: The 4c reference model for distributed user interfaces. In: Proc. of 4th IARIA International Conference on Autonomic and Autonomous Systems (2008)
2. Balme, L., Demeure, A., Barralon, N., Coutaz, J., Calvary, G.: Cameleon-rt: A software architecture reference model for distributed, migratable, and plastic user interfaces. In: EUSAI (2004)
3. Blumendorf, M., Feuerstack, S., Albayrak, S.: Multimodal user interaction in smart environments: Delivering distributed user interfaces. In: European Conference on Ambient Intelligence: Workshop on Model Driven Software Engineering for Ambient Intelligence Applications (2007)

4. Breton, E., Bézivin, J.: Towards an understanding of model executability. In: FOIS 2001: Proc. of the international conference on Formal Ontology in Information Systems (2001)
5. Calvary, G., Coutaz, J., Thevenin, D., Limbourg, Q., Bouillon, L., Vanderdonckt, J.: A unifying reference framework for multi-target user interfaces. Interacting with Computers 15(3) (2003)
6. Clerckx, T., Vandervelpen, C., Coninx, K.: Task-based design and runtime support for multimodal user interface distribution. In: Proc. of Engineering Interactive Systems (2007)
7. Coninx, K., Luyten, K., Vandervelpen, C., Van den Bergh, J., Creemers, B.: Dygimes: Dynamically generating interfaces for mobile computing devices and embedded systems. In: Chittaro, L. (ed.) Mobile HCI 2003. LNCS, vol. 2795. Springer, Heidelberg (2003)
8. Demeure, A., Calvary, G., Coutaz, J., Vanderdonckt, J.: The comets inspector: Towards run time plasticity control based on a sematic network. In: Coninx, K., Luyten, K., Schneider, K.A. (eds.) TAMODIA 2006. LNCS, vol. 4385. Springer, Heidelberg (2007)
9. Feuerstack, S., Blumendorf, B., Albayrak, S.: Prototyping of multimodal interactions for smart environments based on task models. In: European Conference on Ambient Intelligence: Workshop on Model Driven Software Engineering for Ambient Intelligence Applications (2007)
10. Klug, T., Kangasharju, J.: Executable task models. In: Proc. of TAMODIA 2005 (2005)
11. Limbourg, Q., Vanderdonckt, J., Michotte, B., Bouillon, L., López-Jaquero, V.: Usixml: A language supporting multi-path development of user interfaces. In: Bastide, R., Palanque, P., Roth, J. (eds.) DSV-IS 2004 and EHCI 2004. sixml: A language supporting multi-path development of user interfaces, vol. 3425. Springer, Heidelberg (2005)
12. Mellor, S.: Agile MDA (2004)
13. Mellor, S., Scott, K., Uhl, A., Weise, D.: MDA Distilled: Principles of Model-Driven Architecture (2004)
14. Mori, G., Paternò, F., Santoro, C.: Design and Development of Multidevice User Interfaces through Multiple Logical Descriptions. IEEE Trans. Softw. Eng. 30(8) (2004)
15. Object Management Group. Meta Object Facility (MOF) Specification — Version 1.4 (April 2002)
16. Puerta, A.R., Eisenstein, J.: Towards a general computational framework for model-based interface development systems. In: Intelligent User Interfaces (1999)
17. Rohr, M., Boskovic, M., Giesecke, S., Hasselbring, W.: Model-driven development of self-managing software systems. In: "Models@run.time" at the 9th International Conference on Model Driven Engineering Languages and Systems (MoDELS/UML 2006) (2006)
18. Sottet, J.-S., Calvary, G., Favre, J.-M.: Mapping model: A first step to ensure usability for sustaining user interface plasticity. In: Model Driven Development of Advanced User Interfaces (MDDAUI 2006) (2006)
19. Sottet, J.-S., Calvary, G., Favre, J.-M.: Models at runtime for sustaining user interface plasticity. In: "Models@run.time" at the 9th International Conference on Model Driven Engineering Languages and Systems (MoDELS/UML 2006) (2006)
20. Sottet, J.-S., Ganneau, V., Calvary, G., Coutaz, J., Demeure, A., Favre, J.-M., Demumieux, R.: Model-driven adaptation for plastic user interfaces. In: INTERACT, (1) (2007)

A Middleware for Seamless Use of Multiple Displays

Satoshi Sakurai[1], Yuichi Itoh[1], Yoshifumi Kitamura[1], Miguel A. Nacenta[2],
Tokuo Yamaguchi[1], Sriram Subramanian[3], and Fumio Kishino[1]

[1] Graduate School of Information Science and Technology, Osaka University
2-1 Yamada-oka, Suita, Osaka, 565-0871 Japan
{sakurai.satoshi, itoh, yamaguchi.tokuo, kitamura,
kishino}@ist.osaka-u.ac.jp
[2] Department of Computer Science, University of Saskatchewan
110 Science Place, Saskatoon, Saskatchewan, S7N 5C9, Canada
nacenta@cs.usask.ca
[3] Department of Computer Science, University of Bristol
Merchant Venturers Building, Woodland Road, Bristol, BS8 1UB, United Kingdom
sriram@cs.bris.ac.uk

Abstract. Current multi-display environments (MDEs) can be composed of displays with different characteristics (e.g. resolution, size) located in any position and at different angles. These heterogeneous arrangements present specific interface problems: it is difficult to provide meaningful transitions of cursors between displays; it is difficult for users to visualize information that is presented on oblique surfaces; and it is difficult to spread visual information over multiple displays. In this paper we present a middleware architecture designed to support a new kind of perspective-aware GUI that solves the aforementioned problems. Our interaction architecture combines distributed input and position tracking data to generate perspective-corrected output in each of the displays, allowing groups of users to manipulate existing applications from current operating systems across a large number of displays. To test our design we implemented a complex MDE prototype and measured different aspects of its performance.

Keywords: 3D interactions, graphical user interface, server-client, VNC.

1 Introduction

A variety of new display combinations are currently being incorporated to offices and meeting rooms. Examples of such displays are projection screens, wall-sized PDPs or LCDs, personal monitors, notebook PCs, tablet PCs and digital tables. Users expect to work effectively by using multiple displays in such environments; however, there are important issues that prevent them from effectively taking advantage of all the available displays. MDEs include displays that can be at different locations from and different angles to the user; as a result, it can become very difficult to manage windows, read text, and manipulate objects. If a display is oblique to a user the visibility of information is severely reduced. Moreover, information that is spread over multiple displays appears fragmented making it more difficult to interpret. Another issue is how to provide users with convenient control of the whole environment. If cursors are controlled through indirect input devices such as mice or trackballs, the transitions from one display to

T.C.N. Graham and P. Palanque (Eds.): DSVIS 2008, LNCS 5136, pp. 252–266, 2008.
© Springer-Verlag Berlin Heidelberg 2008

another have to be made easy to interpret; in other words, users must be able to easily understand which movements of the mouse will move the cursor from the original to the intended display.

We have previously proposed solutions to these problems in the form of interaction [10] and visualization techniques [11] that are perspective-aware. Our general approach is based on the idea that we can create more efficient visualization and manipulation techniques if the system can calculate the user's perspective of the environment (i.e. how the displays of the MDE are seen from the point of view of the user).

However, the implementation of this interaction paradigm presents serious challenges because multiple sources of input originating from different machines (mice events, text input, 3D tracking data) have to be processed to generate perspective-corrected output in a distributed set of graphical displays. In this paper, we investigate and describe the implementation details of a previously proposed perspective-aware system. While the interactive principles of the system have been studied in [10] and [11] the architectural and implementation issues have not been investigated before. The focus here is exclusively on the architectural and implementation issues that will help inform the design of future perspective-aware interactive systems.

To validate the proposed mechanisms and architecture we implemented a prototype system and obtained several measures that expose the strengths and weaknesses of our design; we discuss these in the conclusion.

Our work shows how the challenges of providing highly interactive perspective-aware MDEs can be met; we hope that our exploration can serve as a first step towards real implementations of more flexible, easier to use office environments.

2   Seamless Use of Multiple Displays

Ordinary GUI environments are designed with the assumption that the user sits in front of a display which is fixed and perpendicular to her; windows and data are rendered according to this assumption. Unfortunately, the perpendicularity assumption does not always hold in multi-display environments, i.e., the display plane is not always perpendicular to the viewer, especially when the display is flat and covers a large viewing angle or when the user moves around. When a display is too oblique to a user or the graphic elements extend to multiple displays, using it becomes difficult [19].

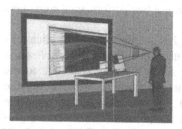

(a) principle of seamless use of displays (b) seamless representation   (c) seamless interaction

Fig. 1. Seamless use of multiple displays

To solve this problem, we proposed a multi-display environment that combines several displays as if they were part of one large virtual GUI environment. The proposed environment defines a virtual plane which is perpendicular to the user as a virtual display. GUI objects (e.g. windows and cursors) on the virtual plane are projected onto the real displays as shown in Figure 1(a). As a result, wherever the user's viewpoint is, the user observes GUI objects (cursors and windows) without perspective distortion; just as if they were perpendicular to the user (see Figure 1(b)). Even if a GUI object extends to several displays, the user observes it continuously beyond the boundaries of the displays.

When the user's viewpoint or some of the displays move, the environment detects these movements with 3D motion sensors and updates the display immediately to maintain the relationship shown in Figure 1(a).

In the environment, the user controls the cursor on a virtual sphere around the user, so that the cursor can move seamlessly between displays as shown in Figure 1(c). This technique is known as Perspective Cursor [10]. Also, the user can interact with the multiple displays not only from a certain specific computer, but also from all computers in the environment.

3 An Architecture Using Server-Client Topology

3.1 General Middleware Architecture

One of the requirements of our design was that displays run by different types of computers should be easy to integrate within the general system. To facilitate the integration of heterogeneous computers into the system we opted for an architecture with multiple servers that take care of the specialized tasks, leaving simpler operations to the clients.

A *3D server* (a dedicated 3D server machine with specific 3D server software) keeps track and processes three-dimensional information of positions and orientations of the users' viewpoints and mobile displays measured through 3D motion sensors. The positions and orientations of user viewpoints and displays are measured by 3D motion sensors that are processed in the 3D server software to calculate the positions and orientations of the GUI objects on the virtual plane. This information is subsequently sent to the *client software* that runs in each of the *client machines*. The client software only renders the display; this way users can use low performance computers like notebook PCs as client machines.

In order to perform ordinary tasks, the system has to run existing applications like text editors, web browsers, etc. Our system uses an independent *application server machine* that runs actual applications and sends the graphical data to the client machines. The software that carries out the functions of broadcasting the graphical data and receiving input from the client software instances is called the *application server software*. Because this function is equivalent to the service provided by a VNC [13] server, we implemented it using RealVNC [24] (an open source VNC server implementation).

In addition to presenting the graphical output of applications the system needs to be able to feed user input to these same applications. Users manipulate regular mice

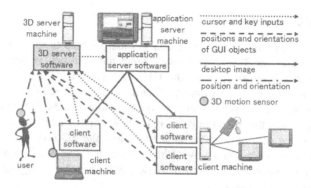

Fig. 2. General architecture of the middleware

and keyboards that are connected to the client machines in order to interact with the applications shown in any display. The client software sends all inputs to the 3D server software, and then the 3D server software relays the inputs to the corresponding windows according to the positions and orientations of the GUI objects in the environment. When the cursor is on top of a window, the 3D server software transfers the cursor inputs to the application server software. For the consistency of the input/output flow, the keyboard inputs on the client machines are sent to the application server software through the 3D server software. In this way, the inputs on all client machines are appropriately processed through the network. Figure 2 summarizes the architecture. We describe the overview of each type of software below.

Client software: Each instance of the client software corresponds to one display. Therefore, the number of instances of the client software running on a particular client machine corresponds to the number of displays connected to that particular machine. The client software receives the 3D positions and orientations of all GUI objects from the 3D server software and the application images from the application server software. Then the windows are filled with the application image which is clipped from the desktop image of the application server machine. The client software also collects all inputs and sends them to the 3D server software.

3D server software: The 3D server software runs on a dedicated machine. It processes and stores positions and orientations of users' viewpoints and all displays; with this information, it calculates the positions and orientations of the GUI objects on the virtual plane. When it receives cursor input from the client software or detects movement of the 3D motion sensors, the 3D server software recalculates the positions and orientations of the GUI objects and resends. In addition, it processes the inputs from the client software and relays them to the application server software.

Application server software: The application server software and any application available to the users run on a single application server machine. The application server software receives the inputs and relays them to the applications. Then, if there is any change of the application images, it sends the altered graphical information back to the client software.

3.2 Network Communication

The client software sends the cursor and keyboard inputs to the 3D server software. On the other hand, the 3D server software sends the positions, orientations, conditions and disappearance notification of the GUI objects to the client software instances which need to render the GUI objects. The messages related to the positions and orientations are sent whenever the user moves the mouse or the 3D server software detects movements of the 3D motion sensors. These communications are robust because even if pieces of data are lost in communication, the 3D server software sends updated data continuously and a newer block of data will eventually replace the missing data. An unreliable network protocol (UDP) is used because high-throughput is required and old data has no value.

Unlike geometric information, other kinds of communication such as conditions and disappearance notifications require guaranteed ordered delivery because the loss of a single packet could set the system in an inconsistent state. These data are therefore transmitted using reliable protocols such as TCP.

There exist two other important flows of information: the desktop image data from the application server software to the client software and the cursor and the keyboard inputs from the 3D server to the application server software; both flows are compressed and sent through the VNC connection.

4 Management of GUI Objects in 3D Space

This section describes the transformations that the three-dimensional data undergoes and how the processed data is subsequently used to render the seamless GUI elements.

In order to provide seamless use of GUI objects across multiple displays, the locations and orientations of these objects are represented with respect to several coordinate systems in the environment. Figure 3(a) shows two three-dimensional coordinate systems; the coordinate system G of the real world and the display's local coordinate systems $D_n(n = 1, 2, ...)$ in which the origin is at the top-left corner of each display. Figure 3(b) shows the two-dimensional coordinate system A which corresponds to the pixel coordinate system of the application server machine.

4.1 Seamless Representation of Information on Multiple Displays

4.1.1 3D Server Software Functionality
The 3D server software receives positions and orientations of users' viewpoints and mobile displays from the 3D motion sensors. These data are expressed in terms of an arbitrary coordinate system G defined by the 3D tracking device that is also used to represent the positions and orientations of the virtual GUI elements (cursors and windows). Positions, orientations and sizes of the fixed displays are configured at initialization time, and are also expressed in terms of the G coordinate system. The resolution of displays is sent from the client software when the client software connects to the 3D server software. All these data represents all the relevant geometrical information of the physical system, allowing the 3D server to perform perspective operations on the virtual GUI elements.

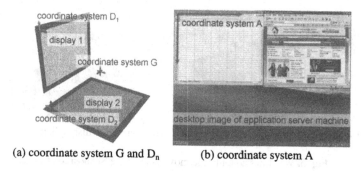

(a) coordinate system G and D_n (b) coordinate system A

Fig. 3. Coordinate systems in proposed middleware

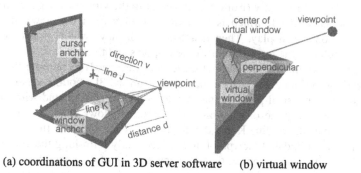

(a) coordinations of GUI in 3D server software   (b) virtual window

Fig. 4. Positions and postures of window and cursor in 3D server software

In order to make a window perpendicular to the user, the 3D server software calculates the position (top-left corner) and orientation of the virtual window which is perpendicular to the user's viewpoint in the coordinate system G. Figure 4(a) shows the data of the virtual window and cursor held in the 3D server software. Using the viewpoint's position and the initial position of the virtual window, the 3D server calculates the distance from the viewpoint to the virtual window (d in Figure 4(a)), the line which passes through the viewpoint and the virtual window (K in Figure 4(a)) and the anchor of the virtual window (the intersection between the line K and the display). If the line K intersects several displays, the anchor is set on the nearest intersection from the viewpoint. Meanwhile, the direction from the top-left corner to the top-right corner (the right direction) of the virtual window is parallel to the horizontal plane in the coordinate system G, and the direction from the top-left corner to the bottom-left corner (the down direction) is perpendicular to both the line K and the right direction. From these data and the size of the virtual window, the 3D server calculates the positions of each corner of the virtual window (see Figure 4(b)). Then, the 3D server software detects all displays which should render the window by calculating the intersections between the displays and the extended lines from the viewpoint to each corner of the virtual window.

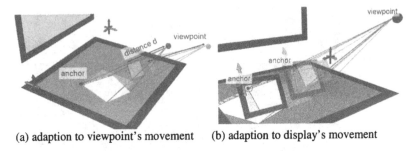

(a) adaption to viewpoint's movement   (b) adaption to display's movement

Fig. 5. Windows adapt to the movement of the 3D position tracker

In addition to the window, the 3D server software holds the information of the virtual cursor. Using direction v (from the viewpoint to the virtual cursor), the 3D server software calculates line J, which is the extension of v from the viewpoint into the cursor anchor on the display. Then it detects all displays which should render the cursor by calculating the intersections of the displays and the line J.

When the viewpoint moves, the 3D server software needs to relocate the GUI objects according to the new positions measured from the 3D motion sensors. The anchor is fixed to a physical pixel so that windows do not float around with the movement of the user; only the orientation of anchored windows changes. This effect is achieved by recalculating line K and the positions of each corner of the window using the anchor and the updated viewpoint and subsequently refreshing the corresponding displays. The distance d is kept so that the apparent size of the window stays constant. Figure 5(a) shows how the virtual window adapts to the movement of the viewpoint. The virtual cursor adapts to the movement of the viewpoint in a similar fashion: the server recalculates v and J, and then sends repaint signals to the appropriate displays.

When a mobile display moves, the 3D server software still maintains windows and cursors anchored to a particular pixel on the display. Figure 5(b) shows a window moving with the display.

4.1.2 Rendering to Display

To simplify rendering in the clients, the 3D server software converts the positions of the viewpoint and each corner of the virtual window into the display's local coordinate system D_n before sending them. When a client instance receives the data it assigns regions to the icon bar, the frame, and the client area of the virtual window (see Figure 6(a)). Then, the client area of the window is filled with the corresponding patch of the desktop image received from the application server. Correspondences between the window client areas and the desktop image patches are maintained and updated by the 3D server software, and expressed in terms of coordinate system A. The result of the rendering process is illustrated in Figure 6(b).

If several windows overlap, the client software renders the windows according to their priority; the highest-priority window always stays on top. A window priority stack is managed independently of the three-dimensional positions in the 3D server. Many priority policies are possible, but our implementation keeps windows on top that have received input recently.

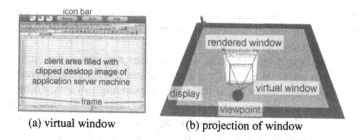

Fig. 6. Client software drawing window

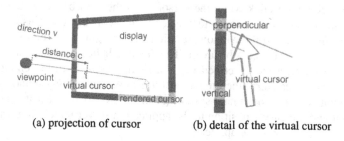

Fig. 7. Rendering of the cursor

To render the cursor to the display, the 3D server software converts the direction v, the vertical vector, and the viewpoint position in the coordinate system G to the coordinate system D_n. Then the 3D server software sends these data to the appropriate instance of the client software. When the client receives these data, it creates a virtual cursor on a virtual plane which is perpendicular to the direction v at the distance c from the viewpoint. The size and distance from the user of the virtual cursor (c in Figure 7(a)) are constant; the orientation of the cursor is calculated using the vertical vector so that the cursor always looks up and points away from the user. Finally, the client renders the virtual cursor to the display surface. Figure 7 shows the rendering of the cursor.

The windows and cursors are re-rendered whenever the 3D or the application servers notify position and orientation movements or when the graphical application data changes.

4.2 Seamless Interaction on Multiple Displays

When the user generates input through a client (e.g., by moving the mouse) the client first sends it to the 3D server software. The data sent includes the type of input (e.g., "click", "move", etc.) and the corresponding magnitude (when appropriate). When the 3D server receives movement input events, it transforms the planar movement data into a rotation of the direction v around the user; the horizontal movement makes v rotate following the parallels of a virtual sphere centered on the user's head. The vertical movement rotates v along the meridians of the same sphere. Then, the 3D server software recalculates the line J and the anchor's position using the updated direction v, and sends back the direction v and the viewpoint's position to the client for rendering.

Figure 8 shows the movement of the cursor in the 3D server software. Note that the spherical nature of the cursor movement mapping makes it possible to point to areas where there is no display.

If the pointing device that controls a cursor does not move, the cursor stays anchored to the same physical pixel of the screen where it is being displayed, regardless of the user's movement; however, if the cursor is pointing towards a direction where there is no display, the anchor is temporally erased, and the direction v is fixed instead. At this time, the direction v is stable against the movement of the viewpoint. The anchor is recreated when the cursor comes back on any display.

The 3D server software also keeps positions and locations of the icon bar, frame, and client area in order to detect clicks on each region of the window. If the 3D server software receives a click while the cursor is on the icon bar, the 3D server software adapts appropriately according to the icon; the icon bar contains icons that allow changing the owner of the window, resizing and dragging the window as well as altering its privacy and resizing behavior. The detailed behaviors of the window including the multi-user case are described in [11]. If the cursor is in the client area, the 3D server software converts the cursor position into a two-dimensional position in the application server's coordinate system (A in Figure 3(b)). Then it sends the type of the input and the cursor position to the application server which, in turn, redirects the event to the corresponding application.

As we mentioned before, the cursor can be located in positions where there is no display. In this case, the cursor cannot be displayed directly but we make use of Halo [2], an off-screen visualization technique to indicate to the user the actual position of the cursor.

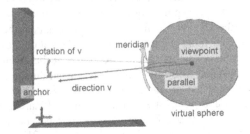

Fig. 8. Movement of cursor

5 Prototype

In this section, we describe the implementation of a prototype system with the features described in section 3 and 4. We also describe the results of measurements of the input/output response time as an aspect of the performance.

5.1 Implementation

We implemented the client software and the 3D server software with Microsoft Visual C++ 2005 on Microsoft Windows XP SP2. The client software uses the OpenGL

Fig. 9. A snapshot of two users using the prototype system

graphic library for the rendering. The communication between the servers and the clients is implemented using DirectPlay [21]. For the application server software, we used one of the several available open-source VNC implementations, Real VNC [24]. The application server receives the inputs from the 3D server software, posts the inputs to the applications, compresses the desktop image, and sends the image to the client software. Because there are Real VNC implementations for Windows, Mac OS and various Linux distributions, users are free to use any of these operating systems on the application server machine (see Figure 10).

For 3D position tracking (users' viewpoints and display position and orientations) we used Intersense's IS-600 Mark 2 ultrasonic tracker.

Figure 9 shows a scenario where two users place and use an editor, a web browser, a multimedia player, and a geographic application on the system. Figure 10 shows some desktop images of the client machine while the application server is running on several operating systems. For illustration purposes, the widow in the figure shows the whole desktop image of the application server machine.

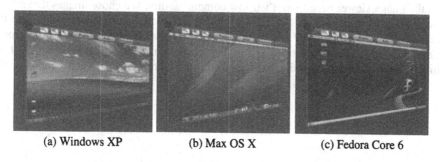

(a) Windows XP   (b) Max OS X   (c) Fedora Core 6

Fig. 10. Display images of client machines with various operating systems

5.2 Measurement of Response Time

In the architecture of the proposed middleware, all inputs/outputs get delayed when they pass through the network. This latency might affect tasks on the system adversely. Thus, it is important to measure at least two types of response time: 1) response time to control the cursor with a mouse, and 2) response time for updating an application image.

5.2.1 Environment for Measurement

The 3D server software and the application server software ran on desktop PCs (CPU: Xeon 2.8 GHz, Mem: 2.0 GB, OS: Windows XP SP2). We also used several desktop PCs (CPU: Xeon 2.2 GHz, Mem: 2.0 GB, OS: Windows 2000 SP4, Graphics: Quadro FX 4000) and a notebook PC (CPU: Core Duo 1.6 GHz, Mem: 1.0 GB, OS: Windows XP SP2, Graphics: Mobile Intel(R) 945 Express Chipset Family) for the client software. Each desktop PC and the notebook PC ran one or two instances of the client software according to the condition of the measurements. All desktop PCs were connected with wired connections (1000BASE-T) and the notebook PC was connected with a wireless connection (IEEE 802.11g).

5.2.2 Response Time for Cursor Control

We measured the time elapsed between a registered movement of the mouse on a client machine and the reception of the updated cursor position by the client machine. Figure 11(a) shows the mean time and the standard deviations of 100 trials in each condition. In conditions G1 to G4, one to four instances of the client software ran on the desktop PCs without the notebook PC. In condition W2 and W5, one instance of the client software ran on the notebook PC with one and four instances on the desktop PCs. The response time measured on the W2 and W5 conditions corresponds to measures taken through the notebook PC.

5.2.3 Response Time for Updating the Application Image

For the application update measurements, we used an image viewer on the application server machine and measured the elapsed time between an update image signal in the client and the complete change of the image in the windows displayed by the client. Because the accurate time when the client machine finishes the update cannot be detected manually, we recorded the display with a video camera (30 fps), and then calculated the time by counting the frames. We chose full colour landscape photos to display on the image viewer because of their low compressibility. We chose images that ranged from 16 × 16 pixels to 1024 × 1024 pixels in size, which correspond roughly to the typical size of a single letter to a medium-sized window. Figure 11(b) shows the mean times and the standard deviations of 5 trials in each connection type and each size of the image. The conditions are the same as those in Figure 11(a). In each condition, the

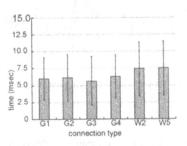
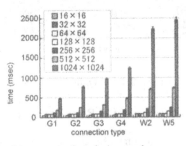

(a) response time for cursor movement   (b) response for window update

Fig. 11. Result of measurement of response time

frame rate of the client software was 60 Hz (16ms per frame). Thus, latency due to communication is about 8 ms less than the values displayed in Figure 11.

6 Discussion

6.1 Effect of Latency

Figure 11(a) showed that the latencies of the cursor controls are shorter than 10 ms in all conditions. Generally, response time should be less than 50-150 ms for simple tasks like cursor control, keyboard typing, and so on [15]. Thus the response time for the cursor controls on the proposed middleware is adequately short and does not impede regular cursor use. We should also consider the latency for the updates of the positions of the GUI objects when the users or the displays move. It can be calculated by adding the latency of the 3D motion sensors (which is approximately 50 ms) and the latency of the communications from the 3D server software to the client software (less than 10 ms). The total latency is about 60 ms. In the field of the virtual reality it has been shown that a latency of 80 ms affects a target tracing task negatively when the user is wearing a half transparent HMD [16]. Although there is no report about the effect of latencies below 80 ms, we consider that these effects are trivial in our system because the movements of the users' viewpoints are usually small when performing a task. We will investigate effects of these latencies more precisely in the future.

The latencies to update the image of 16 × 16 pixels are less than 100 ms in each condition as described in section 5.2.3. Thus, these are adequately short for key typing. On the other hand, the latencies to update the larger images like 1024 × 1024 pixels amount to up to 1000 ms on the wired connections and up to 2500 ms on the wireless connections. These results indicate that the proposed middleware is not suited to deal with applications like movie players which update whole window more frequently than once per second. So users should choose the applications according to the types of connections when users work on the system. Alternatively, it might be a solution to implement special application server software which is optimized to send the application images to multiple instances of the client software, although we would have to implement it on each operating system.

When users use applications which need network communications, these might further increase the response time of the system. But we can separate the communications of the application from those of the middleware by adding another network card to the application server machine. In this way, the communications of the applications will not affect to the response time of the middleware.

6.2 Extensions of the Middleware

In the proposed middleware, the 3D server software can deal with multiple cursors by distinguishing the input messages from different client machines and processing them appropriately. However, existing operating systems on the application server do not support multiple cursors. In order to provide truly collaborative interaction, we need to develop applications which support multiple cursors in the case of multiple users. This problem can also be solved by designing an architecture with multiple application servers where each window corresponds to the desktop image of a different machine. However, the system will need many computers and we will still not be able interact with one window with multiple cursors at same time. The demands towards multiple cursor operating systems in the field of CSCW are, however, increasing and there start to appear experimental systems in which multiple users can interact simultaneously with objects such as Microsoft Surface [22] and Entertaible [9]. We believe that operating systems will support multiple cursors in a few years and that the application server software on such operating systems will overcome the current problems.

In the proposed middleware, the client machines have to render the corresponding display image based on the 3D positions and orientations and the desktop image. According to our measurements, all client software instances rendered at a frame rate of at least 60 Hz. This means that general notebook PCs without specialized graphic hardware has adequate power for the client software. For slower machines, it might be better to adopt a different technique such as server rendering, that is, the 3D server software renders and sends the images for the client software. Another alternative is to use fast 3D graphics libraries for mobile devices like OpenGL ES [23]. We plan to investigate implementations with small devices in the near future.

7 Related Work

In this section, we describe existing research and systems that use multiple displays.

In some systems, the user can interact with multiple displays from one computer. PointRight [8] and mighty mouse [4] redirect the cursor inputs to other computers through a network. Thus, the user can control multiple computers at same time. However, what the systems do are just transmissions of the inputs. The user can not relocate applications beyond the displays because each computer works independently.

On the other hand, some systems support the relocations and the collaborations of the applications beyond the displays. For example, a computer with a graphic board which has multiple outputs treat aligned displays as a large desktop. Mouse Ether [1] can also correct the difference of the resolutions and the sizes between displays for cursor control. Distributed Multihead X [20] sends commands for drawing to multiple computers through a network and creates a huge desktop with many aligned displays. These systems, however, generally assume that all displays are fixed.

Wincuts [17] can transmit copy images of the window on the personal small displays to public large displays but it can only show information to other users. ARIS [3], i-Room [18], EasyLiving [6], and Gaia [14] allow the user to use multiple displays collaboratively which are placed in various positions. In these environments, the user can relocate and interact with the applications beyond displays; however, the GUI spaces are not connected seamlessly but logically. That is, when a cursor goes out of a display, it jumps to another display.

There has been some research on techniques that allow the user to interact with multiple displays seamlessly including mobile displays like notebook PCs or PDAs [12]. Steerable camera-projectors can also be used to create dynamic interactive displays on any plane of the environment (e.g. walls, tabletops and handheld white boards in an environment) [5]. However, in these systems the relationship between the user viewpoint and the display is not considered.

In the field of ubiquitous computing, many architectures and frameworks have been proposed for using multiple devices [7]. Although this work can be used to inform the design of general data-exchange architectures for multi-display systems such as ours, the particular requirements of a perspective-aware environment required a specific study of the interaction architecture.

8 Conclusion

In this paper, we investigated the implementation issues of a multi-display system which allows users to use all displays seamlessly and effectively in common cooperative scenarios. We proposed a double server-client architecture and detailed the data processes necessary to make the system perspective-aware. We also implemented a working prototype and measured its performance in terms of interactive throughput. In the future, we intend to further evaluate the usability of the system and to improve the interaction architecture in order to achieve higher responsiveness and flexibility of use.

Acknowledgement

This research was supported in part by "Global COE (Centers of Excellence) Program" of the Ministry of Education, Culture, Sports, Science and Technology, Japan.

References

1. Baudisch, P., Cutrell, E., Hinckley, K., Gruen, R.: Mouse ether: accelerating the acquisition of targets across multi-monitor displays. In: Conference on Human Factors in Computing Systems, pp. 1379–1382 (2004)
2. Baudisch, P., Rosenholtz, R.: Halo: a technique for visualizing off-screen objects. In: Conference on Human Factors in Computing Systems, pp. 481–488 (2003)
3. Biehl, J.T., Bailey, B.P.: ARIS: an interface for application relocation in an interactive space. In: Graphics Interface, pp. 107–116 (2004)
4. Booth, K.S., Fisher, B.D., Lin, C.J.R., Argue, R.: The "mighty mouse" multi-screen collaboration tool. In: 15th annual Symposium on User Interface Software and Technology, pp. 209–212 (2002)
5. Borkowski, S., Letessier, J., Crowley, J.L.: Spatial control of interactive surfaces in an augmented environment. In: 9th IFIP Working Conference on Engineering for Human-Computer Interaction, pp. 228–244 (2004)
6. Brumitt, B., Meyers, B., Krumm, J., Kern, A., Shafer, S.A.: EasyLiving: technologies for intelligent environments. In: 2nd international symposium on Handheld and Ubiquitous Computing, pp. 12–29 (2000)
7. Endres, C., Butz, A., MacWilliams, A.: A survey of software infrastructures and frameworks for ubiquitous computing. Mobile Information Systems Journal, 41–80 (2005)
8. Johanson, B., Hutchins, G., Winograd, T., Stone, M.: PointRight: experience with flexible input redirection in interactive workspaces. In: 15th annual Symposium on User Interface Software and Technology, pp. 227–234 (2002)

9. Loenen, E., Bergman, T., Buil, V., Gelder, K., Groten, M., Hollemans, G., Hoonhout, J., Lashina, T., Wijdeven, S.: Entertaible: a solution for social gaming experiences. In: Workshop on Tangible Play: Research and Design for Tangible and Tabletop Games (in International Conference on Intelligent User Interfaces), pp. 16–19 (2007)

10. Nacenta, M.A., Sallam, S., Champoux, B., Subramanian, S., Gutwin, C.: Perspective cursor: perspective-based interaction for multi-display environments. In: Conference on Human Factors in Computing Systems, pp. 289–298 (2006)

11. Nacenta, M.A., Sakurai, S., Yamaguchi, T., Miki, Y., Itoh, Y., Kitamura, Y., Subramanian, S., Gutwin, C.: E-conic: a perspective-aware interface for multi-display environments. In: 20th annual Symposium on User Interface Software and Technology, pp. 279–288 (2007)

12. Rekimoto, J., Saitoh, M.: Augmented surfaces: a spatially continuous work space for hybrid computing environments. In: Conference on Human Factors in Computing Systems, pp. 378–385 (1998)

13. Richardson, T., Stafford-Fraser, Q., Wood, K.R., Hopper, A.: Virtual network computing. IEEE Internet Computing 2(1), 33–38 (1998)

14. Román, M., Hess, C., Cerqueira, R., Ranganathan, A., Campbell, R.H., Nahrstedt, K.: A middleware infrastructure for active spaces. IEEE Pervasive Computing 1(4), 74–83 (2002)

15. Schneiderman, B.: Designing the user interface, 3rd edn. Addison-Wesley, Reading (1998)

16. So, R.H.Y., Griffin, M.J.: Effects of lags on human-operator transfer functions with head-coupled systems. Aviation, Space, and Environmental Medicine 66(6), 550–556 (1995)

17. Tan, D.S., Meyers, B., Czerwinski, M.: WinCuts: manipulating arbitrary window regions for more effective use of screen space. In: Conference on Human Factors in Computing Systems, pp. 1525–1528 (2004)

18. Tandler, P.: Software infrastructure for ubiquitous computing environments: supporting synchronous collaboration with heterogeneous devices. In: Ubiquitous Computing, pp. 96–115 (2001)

19. Wigdor, D., Shen, C., Forlines, C., Balakrishnan, R.: Perception of elementary graphical elements in tabletop and multi-surface environments. In: Conference on Human Factors in Computing Systems, pp. 473–482 (2007)

20. Distributed Multihead X Project. http://dmx.sourceforge.net/

21. Microsoft DirectX Developer Center, http://www.microsoft.com/japan/msdn/directx/

22. Microsoft Surface, http://www.microsoft.com/surface/

23. OpenGL ES, http://www.khronos.org/opengles/

24. RealVNC, http://www.realvnc.com/

Graphic Rendering Considered as a
Compilation Chain

Benjamin Tissoires[1,2,3] and Stéphane Conversy[2,3]

[1] DGAC / DSNA / DTI / R&D.
7 avenue Ed. Belin, 31055 Toulouse, France
Benjamin.Tissoires@aviation-civile.gouv.fr
[2] ENAC, Laboratoire d'Informatique Interactive.
7 avenue Ed. Belin, 31055 Toulouse, France
stephane.conversy@enac.fr
[3] IRIT - IHCS, Université Paul Sabatier.
118 route de Narbonne, 31062 Toulouse Cedex 4, France

Abstract. Graphical rendering must be fast enough so as to avoid hindering the user perception/action loop. Traditionally, programmers interleave descriptions and optimizations to achieve such performances, thus compromising modularity. In this paper, we consider graphic rendering as a compilation chain: we designed a static and dynamic graphical compiler that enables a designer to clearly separate the description of an interactive scene from its implementation and optimization. In order to express dependencies during run-time, the compiler builds a dataflow that can handle user input and data. We successfully used this approach on both a WIMP application and on a demanding one in terms of computing power: description is completely separated from implementation and optimizations while performances are comparable to manually optimized applications.

Keywords: interactive software, computer graphics, compiler, dataflow, modularity.

1 Introduction

Interactive systems have to be efficient. In particular, graphical rendering must be fast enough so as to avoid hindering the user perception/action loop. In addition, as any other software, interactive systems have to be modular, in order to maximize maintainability and reliability. The need for modularity is even more important with interactive systems. Making software modular minimizes the cost of modification. As designing good interactive systems requires designers to implement, test, and tweak a large set of alternative solutions iteratively, modular software maximizes the quality. Traditionally, programmers implement graphic rendering in interactive software using an imperative paradigm. They use graphical libraries, and often introduce optimization during the first stages of development so as to maximize performances. This leads to code in which description and optimization are interleaved, which hinders designers' ability to rapidly test new designs. It can even harm safety, as manual

T.C.N. Graham and P. Palanque (Eds.): DSVIS 2008, LNCS 5136, pp. 267–280, 2008.

optimization may change the graphical semantics and introduce bugs that are noticeable only with precise situations.

Computer science literature contains solutions for these kinds of problem. Researchers have designed compilers, i.e. systems that transform a high-level language to a low-level one. They enable programmers to focus on description, while leaving low-level optimization to the compiler. In order to address the problems encountered by interactive systems programmers, we introduce in this paper a new approach to graphical rendering implementation. We consider the transformation from input devices and data to graphics as a compilation chain. We design a static and dynamic graphical compiler: it enables a designer to clearly separate the description of an interactive scene from its implementation and optimization.

We first describe three scenarios illustrating how today's designers implement graphical rendering and cope with description, efficiency and modularity. Based on these examples, we explain why graphical rendering implementation can be considered as a compilation chain. We describe the principles of the graphical compiler, and report on the results we obtained with two examples.

2   User Interface Development Scenarios

In this section, we present three scenarios concerning the development of user interfaces. These scenarios are the basis of our reflexion.

Using Graphic Toolkits

Since the rise of the WIMP (Window Icon Menu Pointer) paradigm, most programmers use User Interface toolkits, such as Motif or Qt. UI Toolkits allow programmers to rapidly construct an interface by juxtaposing widgets, i.e. independent units of graphics and behaviour, on the interface. However, the widget model is not suitable for the implementation of post-WIMP interactions. WIMP interfaces implicitly use a model where widgets are juxtaposed, and they can not be used in scene where graphics lay on top of each other. For example, programmers can not use widgets to implement a radar image that contains flight elements on top of sectors. In addition, programmers do not have access to the inner mechanisms of the toolkit. Hiding implementation details eases use and prevents misuse, but it also prevents some of the optimizations that may speed up the rendering process [15] [10]. There exists a few post-WIMP toolkits [3], but they are internally optimized for a specific part of the rendering process (e.g. culling small or out-of-screen ZUI items).

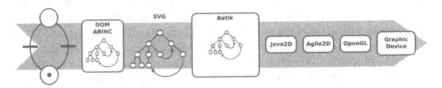

Fig. 1. The chain used in the model of ARINC 661 by [2]

Model-Based Approach

Conversy et al. in [8] present a model-based approach to separate behaviour from rendering. The idea is to describe the behaviour of the application with Petri Nets together with a conceptual model of the interactive elements, and the rendering with an SVG scene (Scalable Vector Graphics [22]). When user input occurs, the Petri Net modifies the conceptual model, which in turn is transformed into a new SVG scene through an XSLT stylesheet (Extensible Stylesheet Language Family Transformations [23]). The SVG scene is then redrawn on the screen (Fig. 1). This model-based approach allows the designer to clearly separate descriptions of appearance and behaviour (look and feel), to use models based on formalism, and to use SVG, which is an exchange format between coders and graphic designers ([7]). However, the execution process of this chain is costly in terms of performance: each time a change occurs; the whole transformation chain is triggered, and slows down the system. Moreover, the system is based on completely separated stages: each intermediate data structure is completely rebuilt, and does not benefit from invariant behaviour of the front stages. Since there can be seven stages between the Petri Nets and the final pixels, performances are extremely low. Thus, the system is completely modular, but not reactive enough to be used in real-time.

Working With the Graphic Device to Optimize Performance

One solution to render fast interactive applications is to work at a low level of programming, with the help of libraries close to the hardware, such as OpenGL (Open Graphic Library[1]). At this level, programmers can use optimizations that mainly consist in caching a maximum amount of data or commands on the graphic device. For instance, the programmer can use display lists - a record of a list of OpenGL commands that can be called at once - or memoization of a computed image into a texture.

However, working at such a low level forces the programmer to interleave description of the graphical scene and optimizations. Moreover such optimizations need to be known by the programmer and programmed by hand, and influence his way of writing the application at the cost of readability. These optimizations speed up the whole application but as they are too tightly linked with the rest of the code, it is hard to change either the description or the optimization.

Discussion

These three scenarios show that with the available tools and methods, a programmer has to do the job of a compiler to build non-standard modular and efficient user interfaces. He has to allocate registers (OpenGL texture or display list), to manage caches of data (render into textures), and to reorganize his optimizations in order to have the fastest code possible. He can even implement parts of a Just In Time compiler (JIT), by designing optimizations triggered at the run-time (such as display lists).

---

[1] OpenGL, The Industry's Foundation for High Performance Graphics: http://www.opengl.org

3   Graphical Rendering = Compilation Chain

In this section, we explain why the graphical rendering process can be considered as a compilation chain. Then we define the notion of a graphical compiler (GC^2) and of intermediate graphical languages.

Fig. 2. The "classical" rendering process

Why it Is a Compiler Problem

Writing an interactive scene needs several steps to produce the final application. Fig. 2 shows what most programmers do: before trying to display something, some data are needed; then, these data are transformed into a high-level description; if the rendering process needs it, this high-level language is usually displayed and a loop analyzes this language in order to apply changes that occur between two frames (this is the case of scenario number 2). When high performances are needed, the programmer converts by hand the high-level description into a lower-level one, which in turn is rendered to the screen (scenario number 3). This requires the programmer to implement a scheme in which the programmer has to take care of the synchronization between a high-level API and a lower level one. This figure also shows the different refresh loops that are used in graphic rendering. The solid loop to the right symbolizes the video controller that scans the video memory at each refresh of the screen. The two dotted loops symbolize the fact that the loop can be either on the high level, or on the low level. Thus, in scenario number 2 (the model-based one), the loop is placed on the high-level description, and in the scenario number 3 (the OpenGL one) the loop stands on the low-level description.

Hence, writing an interactive interface consists in a chain of transformations, which can be handled by a compiler:

> A compiler is a computer program, or set of programs, that translates text written in a computer language - the *source* language - into another computer language - the *target* language. [1]

In the problem of rendering graphical scene, the data can be considered as an input language and the drawing commands as the target language (Fig. 2). In order to explain the structure of the GC (Fig. 4), we will compare it to the structure of the Java programming environment (Fig. 3). The graphical compiler chain consists in the

---

² In Computer Science, GC traditionally stands for Garbage Collector, but in the rest of the article, we will abbreviate graphical compiler by GC.

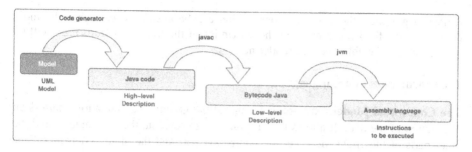

Fig. 3. The compilation chain used in Java when starting from UML...

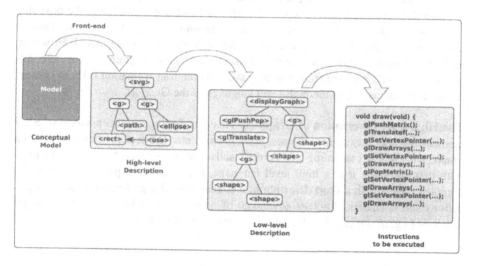

Fig. 4. ...and its equivalent when rendering applications

different transformations between languages. The high-level description of the graphical scene - through an SVG-like syntax - is equivalent to Java code written by the programmer. The low-level description which is strongly linked with the hardware we used at the end (abstracted with OpenGL) is the equivalent of the bytecode produced by the Javac compiler. At the end of the chain, a backend either interprets (JVM) or generates (a native Javac compiler) the instructions that are executed on the hardware.

In addition, the GC includes another front-end, the conceptual model and the rules needed to transform it into SVG. This stage is equivalent to recent environments that generates Java code from UML description. We will see that it allows the GC to handle in a uniform way all the transformations, so that optimizations are applied in the whole program.

By considering the process of rendering graphical scene as a compiler chain, we expect the following benefits: this architecture makes it possible to separate the description of the graphics and the optimizations; concepts such as optimizations that have been well-studied in the compiler problem can be transposed to the problem of rendering graphics; the high-level description can be abstracted enough to be independent of the final renderer used; the semantics of the transformations used will be clear enough to be able to check rendering.

Transformations and Languages

The Conceptual Model. The first language of the graphical compilation chain is an abstraction of the data. It allows the programmer to separate the presentation and the other parts of the application, i.e. the interaction part and the dialog controller. This part contains elements such as the value used to describe a model of a slider in a WIMP application, or the string of characters of a text field [8].

Once the conceptual model of the elements to be drawn is available, the next step is to transform it in terms of graphical shapes. As said before, we extend the standard model of a compiler by adding a stage on the front: the conceptual model. However, as the GC does not know this specific language used by the programmer, the latter has to give to the GC both the front-end language and the transformation rules to convert his specific language into the high-level language of the GC.

The High-level Description of Graphics. This description contains a subset of SVG elements such as *rectangles, ellipses, path, groups,* etc. The scene is described with a graph, with nodes containing geometrical and style transforms. SVG was designed with two purposes: it is a high level language, i.e. it makes it possible to describe complex scenes with a short description; it is also an exchange format between applications and designers. Another advantage of using a SVG-like language is that its structure (a graph) is highly adapted to an implementation in OpenGL.

Fig. 5. A shape with a fill and a stroke can be divided into two elementary shapes

Before the low-level description, the GC inserts another stage which consists in converting every shape into a path and the direct cyclic graph into a tree. Thus, a shape made up of a fill and a stroke is divided into two elementary shapes with the same semantic as a group of shapes (Fig. 5). This reduces the language to a kernel, i.e. the minimum set of primitives needed to express the semantics of SVG. It thus minimizes the complexity of the subsequent transformations. Such stages are also included in most standard compilers: they convert the input source into an intermediate representation. This step also allows the compiler to produce an optimized code.

The Low-level Description. The GC converts high-level primitives into primitives suitable for the hardware: the low-level description. The previous language is thus converted into a tree containing the instructions needed to render the scene: the display graph. As the current renderer used is OpenGL, this part contains the instructions such as *glPushMatrix*, *glTranslate* or the instructions needed to tessellate and render a path.

4 Expressing Dependencies with a Dataflow

The static compiler produces the equivalent of a "binary" program written in the low-level description. Executing the program consists in interpreting the display graph at "run-time". However, the dynamic compiler executed at run-time needs to know the dependencies of the different variables. We chose to express the dependencies with a dataflow. The GC statically compiles this dataflow. The dynamic graphical compiler does not need to recompile the scene when a change occurs between two frames. For example, if the change consists in the modification of the position of an element, the produced code is the same, except the part concerning the changed variables (Fig. 6).

The programmer needs to specify which variables are input so as to help the compiler to know which parts will change during run-time, and to optimize the produced code. The GC caches all the static data during the static compilation.

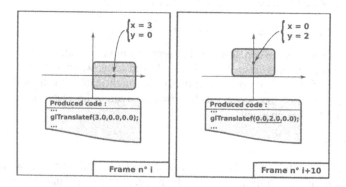

Fig. 6. Changes in the produced code when moving one object

Implementation

Language. The language used for the dataflow is a mathematical one. The designer specifies it by expressing formulas. Our compiler overloads operators in Python[3] to build the parser. For instance, we can write:

```
x0 = var('x0',5)
y0 = var('y0',10)
x1 = var('x1',x0+200)
y1 = var('y1',y0+250)
```

---

[3] Python Programming Language - Official Website: http://www.python.org

This code builds two inputs x0 and y0 and two dependent variables x1 and y1. Building and naming variables allow further references in the description of the scene. For instance, x0 and y0 may be the anchor of a shape and x1 and y1 the anchor of another shape that has to be moved (200,250) relative to the first one:

```
rect0 = rect(-5, -5, w=10, h=10, fill=(1.0,0.0,0.0),
transform=transform(x0,y0))

rect1 = rect(-5, -5, w=10, h=100, fill=(1.0,0.0,0.0),
transform=transform(x1,y1))
```

Execution. Dataflow can have two modes of execution. The first one is interpretation and the second one is compilation. Interpretation is very useful when one wants to debug and test one's design. It allows new variables and formulas to be created at run-time. The counterpart of this flexibility is that it is very costly when it comes to execution, as it requires a tree traversal and the interpretation of each node each time a value has to be computed.

The second possibility, when formulas do not change often at run-time, is to use compilation. The GC implement dataflow compilation by attaching to each variable the function that contains the formula. The execution speeds up but this scheme forces the programmer to do a static compilation of the application.

In the previous example, the GC transforms the declarative description into a list of OpenGL commands. The list of commands contains the two following lines:

```
glTranslate3f(5.0f, 10.0f, 0.0f);
(...)
glTranslate3f(205.0f, 260.0f, 0.0f);
```

The GC remembers the dependences between the input variable ('x0' for example) and the produced memory case ('5.0f' here). At run-time, when a change occurs, the executive part of the GC propagates directly the modification towards the memory that is used to render the scene. Such principle avoids the tests needed to know whether a variable has changed.

Optimizations

As dataflow is a mathematical language and also a functional one, we can apply two types of optimizations. Optimizations can be relevant to the semantic of the functions themselves. For example, writing 'x+x+x+x+x+x' can be transformed into '6*x', thus reducing the number of operations from five to one (if there is no cache implemented, the access to a variable is costly and the overall cost is then reduced). The GC can also find optimizations more relevant to the implementation, as in all languages, so as to accelerate the time spend inside the propagation of the data.

5   Implementation and Optimizations of the Graphical Compiler

Implementation

We wrote the compiler in the Python language as it allows quick development. Nevertheless, in order to achieve good performances with OpenGL, we wrote the run-time of the graphics in a C module of Python.

The production of the low-level description of the scene follows standard transformation rules. For each element in the graph, the GC produces the corresponding elements. Optimizations are made during the productions by testing whether we should add decorators or not, as seen before.

After the production of the low-level description, the renderer can be executed asynchronously. We designed our toolkit to be asynchronous so as not to penalize all the parts of the process if one is slow. The toolkit uses threads and buffers to implement this mechanism. The list of calls from Python to the run-time uses a strategy similar to the OpenGL double-buffering mechanism. There are two lists available: the first is the one which is executed, and is protected from any changes except local changes coming from the dataflow. The second one allows the compiler to allocate and free the memory needed and is allowed to be modified by other processes.

Optimizations

The low-level description is what we call a display graph, an abstract tree that represents the graphical code that will be executed eventually.

Static Optimizations. We have written our low-level language with the help of design patterns. The help of the design pattern decorator allows the GC to construct the tree so as to avoid tests while walking through it. For example, if the element does not contain any *scale* transformations, the compiler simply does not include the decorator *scale* over the element. The produced tree contains the minimum elements needed to render the scene.

The second possibility offered by this approach is that the compiler can factorize elements by detecting common subexpressions. For instance, if the same transformations occur between two groups, it can factorize them into a bigger group containing the common transformation.

Dynamic Optimizations. Working with a tree allows the GC to make optimizations during run-time, to implement a Just In Time compiler (JIT). Nevertheless, walking through the tree has a significant cost in term of instructions to be executed. The time spent to evaluate the display graph, plus the time needed to transform it into graphic call, plus the time of execution has to be inferior to a minimum refresh-time rate (maximum 0.04 seconds per frame to achieve 25 frames per second). To achieve such performance, the run-time transforms this tree into a list of OpenGL calls. This transformation allows caching of operations that have to be executed. It also puts in cache all the tests that need to be done. For instance, the programmer can activate or deactivate a part of the tree through a variable. The produced code is empty if the condition is set to false. By transforming the tree into a list of really executed code, the run-time of the GC avoids a re-evaluation of this test. If the condition changes the run-time re-parses the tree in order to execute the right code. This optimization is known as *dead-code elimination*.

When a change in the inputs that occurs does not imply a rebuilding of the list of OpenGL calls, the dataflow propagates the change by modifying the previously produced code.

Other Optimizations. As we have seen, a graphical compiler can make optimizations over the display graph. The GC can produce both local optimizations and cross-procedural optimizations as it knows the entire display graph. Because of the lack of room, we list other techniques that are available in the GC to speed up the rendering in the light of compiling techniques:

- *Common subexpressions*: the optimizer can detect such graphical common subexpressions and factorize them.
- *Propagation of the constants* corresponds in the graphic field to the operation of caching a maximum amount of data, most of the time on the graphic device.
- *Programmer's hints*: the programmer can specify that a non-trivial or non-detectable optimization concerning his own problem (this optimization corresponds to *aliasing* or the keyword *register* in the C language).
- *Other JIT optimizations*: a Just In Time compiler (JIT) can handle other optimizations that the static compiler can not discover.

6   Results

We assessed the approach by writing two different applications with the GC. The first consists in a demonstration of the use of standard widgets to build a WIMP interface (Fig. 7). This application illustrates scenario number 2. The programmer specifies the conceptual model by specifying the abstraction of the different elements, and then gives to the system the transformations needed to compile the elements to SVG. The GC statically compiles the dependencies and produces the final application. The resulting program contains no interpretation of SVG constructs, as much as a binary does not contain C constructs. As such, it is closed to the minimum program needed to implement this sysytem in the C language with OpenGL.

The second one, a radar view displaying planes (Fig. 8), is demanding in terms of computing power. This application has to display up to 500 planes, each of them made up of 10 elementary shapes. In fact, this proof of concept can display more than 10000 triangles and handle user events with a very low system load: the framerate is up to 500 frames per second. A previous version with a run-time in the Python language with a JIT enabled only reached 140 frames per seconds. The same code without the dynamic compiler and the programmer hints achieved around 4 frames per seconds.

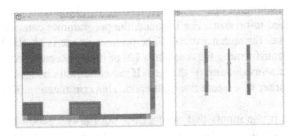

Fig. 7. Example of a WIMP application rendered with the help of our GC

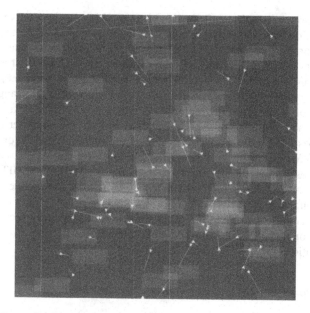

Fig. 8. Example of a radar display application rendered with the help of our GC

The GC weighs in 4000 lines of code in Python and the run-time in C is 4000 lines. Applications using the GC are small: the radar view application is made up of only 500 lines and consists only in the description, as expected. Though more feature complete, a previous radar application written in C++ and OpenGL weighs in 85 000 lines.

7   Related Work

The use of transformations starting from a high-level description has been studied in the Indigo Project [4]. Contrary to the X11 server, both rendering and interaction are in charge of the *Servir*, the server of the Indigo architecture. This idea of transformations was then extended with the implementation of the set of widgets ARINC 661 [2] and later by the MDPC model [8].

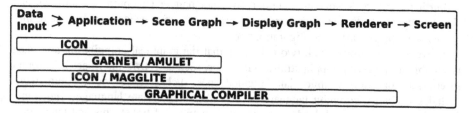

Fig. 9. Dataflow span in different toolkits

Many researchers used dataflow language to describe interactive applications (Fig. 9). Some of these dataflows handle data from the inputs to the application (InputConfigurator [11] or Magglite [14]) while others express graphical constraints (Garnet/Amulet [18], [20]). In the GC, the dataflow can manage the transformations from the data and the inputs down to the screen. In [19], the researchers present a way to reduce the storage of the dataflow, which can be a problem in large applications.

The notion of compilation in graphics was introduced by Nitrous, a compiler generator for interactive graphics [12]. However, as in [17], the compiler is only pixel-based, and does not handle the inputs coming from physical devices or from the application. LLVM [16], with its OpenGL stack developed by Apple, can efficiently abstract the description of the interface from the hardware. The JIT included in LLVM can optimize the different shaders available in order to have the most efficient implementation.

Finally, dynamic compilation has been studied with languages such as Smalltalk [9], Self [13], or Java. LLVM can also be executed with a JIT and can do interprocedural optimizations [5].

8 Conclusion

In this paper, we have proposed a new approach to graphical rendering, in order to make it both modular and efficient. We show that an interactive application is a list of transformations of intermediate graphical languages, which can be considered as a compilation process. We described how a graphical compiler can help designers and programmers to implement efficient rendering code. The programmer writes a front-end of a language describing the objects to be interacted on, and a transformation function to a high-level graphical API. The graphical compiler can then generate low-level code that implements the application. During the different transformations, the GC detects and applies optimizations in order to generate efficient code. Thanks to the dataflow which is produced at compile time, the dynamic compiler avoids unnecessary recompilation at run-time. The latter can take time to optimize the produced code on the fly.

The architecture we have presented has some limitations. It can not handle dynamic changes of the structure of the conceptual model. With the radar view, flights are filtered out when they are not visible, and the conceptual model elements are recycled for new flights. However, implementing a vector graphic editor is not possible with such description, because it is not possible to know in advance the number of shapes.

Furthermore, the graphical compiler does not handle UI control. Dataflows can simulate control with tests, but a more general approach is needed, such as state machines switching dataflow configurations [6].

However, we showed with two examples that the graphical compilation approach is suitable for a range of applications: static ones, such as WIMP interfaces now found in cockpits, or semi-dynamic, data-bounded ones, such as radar view. Future work includes finding a common language to describe intermediate languages and transformations. This approach leads to verifiable semantics of transforms and languages. We plan to enhance the compiler so as to produce verified code, and make critical systems safer.

References

1. Aho, V., R., S., Ullman, J.D., Ullman, J.: Compilers: Principles, Techniques, and Tools. Morgan Addison-Wesley, Boston (1986)
2. Barboni, E., Conversy, S., Navarre, D., Palanque, P.: Model-based engineering of widgets, user applications and servers compliant with arinc 661 specification. In: Doherty, G., Blandford, A. (eds.) DSVIS 2006. LNCS, vol. 4323, pp. 25–38. Springer, Heidelberg (2007)
3. Bederson, B.B., Grosjean, J., Meyer, J.: Toolkit Design for Interactive Structured Graphics. IEEE Transactions on Software Engineering 30(8), 535–546 (2004)
4. Blanch, R., Beaudouin-Lafon, M., Conversy, S., Jestin, Y., Baudel, T., Zhao, Y.P.: Indigo : une architecture pour la conception d'applications graphiques interactives distribuées. In: 17th conference on Conférence Francophone sur l'Interaction Homme-Machine, pp. 139–146. ACM Press, New York (2005)
5. Burke, M., Torczon, L.: Interprocedural optimization: eliminating unnecessary recompilation. ACM Trans. Program. Lang. Syst. 15, 367–399 (1993)
6. Chatty, S.: Defining the behaviour of animated interfaces. In: IFIP TC2/WG2, pp. 95–111. North-Holland Publishing Co, Amsterdam (1992)
7. Chatty, S., Sire, S., Vinot, J.-L., Lecoanet, P., Lemort, A., Mertz, C.: Revisiting visual interface programming: creating GUI tools for designers and programmers. In: 17th annual ACM symposium on User interface software and technology, pp. 267–276. ACM Press, New York (2004)
8. Conversy, S., Barboni, E., Navarre, D., Palanque, P.: Improving modularity of interactive software with the MDPC architecture. In: EIS (Engineering Interactive Systems) conference 2007, joint HCSE 2007, EHCI 2007 and DSVIS 2007 conferences. LNCS. Springer, Heidelberg (2008)
9. Deutsch, L.P., Schiffman, A.M.: Efficient implementation of the smalltalk-80 system. In: 11th ACM SIGACT-SIGPLAN symposium on Principles of programming languages, pp. 297–302. ACM Press, New York (1984)
10. Dourish, P.: Using Metalevel Techniques in a Flexible Toolkit for CSCW Applications. ACM Trans. Comput.-Hum. Interact. 5, 109–155 (1998)
11. Dragicevic, P., Fekete, J.-D.: The input configurator toolkit: towards high input adaptability in interactive applications. In: AVI 2004: working conference on Advanced visual interfaces, pp. 244–247. ACM Press, New York (2004)
12. Draves, S.: Compiler Generation for Interactive Graphics using Intermediate Code. In: Danvy, O., Thiemann, P., Glück, R. (eds.) Dagstuhl Seminar 1996. LNCS, vol. 1110, pp. 95–114. Springer, Heidelberg (1996)
13. Hölzle, U., Ungar, D.: A third-generation self implementation: reconciling responsiveness with performance. In: 9th annual conference on Object-oriented programming systems, language, and applications, pp. 229–243. ACM Press, New York (1994)
14. Huot, S., Dumas, C., Dragicevic, P., Fekete, J.-D., Hégron, G.: The magglite post-wimp toolkit: draw it, connect it and run it. In: 17th annual ACM symposium on User interface software and technology, pp. 257–266. ACM Press, New York (2004)
15. Kiczales, G., Lamping, J., Lopes, C.V., Maeda, C., Mendhekar, A., Murphy, G.: Open implementation design guidelines. In: 19th international Conference on Software Engineering, pp. 481–490. ACM Press, New York (1997)
16. Lattner, C., Adve, V.: LLVM: a compilation framework for lifelong program analysis & transformation. In: IEEE international symposium on Code generation and optimization, pp. 75–86. IEEE Press, New York (2004)

17. Peercy, M.S., Olano, M., Airey, J., Ungar, P.J.: Interactive multi-pass programmable shading. In: 27th Annual Conference on Computer Graphics and interactive Techniques International Conference on Computer Graphics and Interactive Techniques, pp. 425–432. ACM Press, New York (2000)
18. Zanden, B.T.V., Halterman, R., Myers, B.A., McDaniel, R., Miller, R., Szekely, P., Giuse, D.A., Kosbie, D.: Lessons learned about one-way, dataflow constraints in the garnet and amulet graphical toolkits. ACM Trans. Program. Lang. Syst. 23, 776–796 (1994)
19. Zanden, B.T.V., Myers, B.A., Giuse, D.A., Szekely, P.: Integrating pointer variables into one-way constraint models. ACM Trans. Comput.-Hum. Interact. 1, 161–213 (1994)
20. Zanden, B.T.V., Halterman, R.: Using model dataflow graphs to reduce the storage requirements of constraints. ACM Trans. Comput.-Hum. Interact. 8, 223–265 (2001)
21. ARINC Specification 661-3 Cockpit Display System Interfaces to User Systems, Aeronautical Radio Inc. (2007)
22. Scalable Vector Graphics (SVG) 1.1 Specification. W3C Recommendation (2003), http://www.w3.org/TR/SVG/
23. XSL Transformations (XSLT) Version 1.0. W3C Recommendation (1999), http://www.w3.org/TR/xslt

Towards Specifying Multimodal Collaborative User Interfaces: A Comparison of Collaboration Notations

Frédéric Jourde[1], Yann Laurillau[1], Alberto Moran[2], and Laurence Nigay[1]

[1] Grenoble Informatics Laboratory (LIG)
38042, Grenoble, France
{fjourde,laurilla,nigay}@imag.fr
[2] Facultad de Ciencias, UABC,
Ensenada, Mexico
alberto_moran@uabc.mx

Abstract. Interactive systems including multiple interaction devices and surfaces for supporting the collaboration of a group of co-located users are increasingly common in various domains. Nevertheless few collaborative and multimodal interface specification notations are proposed. As a first step towards a notation for specifying a design solution prior to its software design and development, we adopt an empirical approach. We applied and compared four existing notations for collaborative systems by considering a case study, namely, a system for supporting informal co-located collaboration in hospital work. This paper reports the conclusions from this empirical comparison.

Keywords: CSCW, multimodality, multi-devices, specification notation.

1 Introduction

The multimodal domain, including multi-surface and multi-device areas, has expanded rapidly. Significant achievements have been made in terms of both modalities and multimodal applications especially for Computer-Supported Cooperative Work such as co-located collaboration in a smart room. Real collaborative multimodal systems are now built in various domains [12] including the medical one [10]. Moving away from research prototypes, we now observe the need for specifying such interactive systems especially in the context of industrial projects. In this article, we address this problem of specification of multimodal collaborative User Interfaces (UI).

Specifying user interfaces is a well-established discipline and various notations have been proposed for specifying the tasks, the dialog elements, the sequences of interaction, concrete UI elements, dynamics of group behavior and so on. Such a variety of notations both in terms of their descriptive qualities, their syntactic structures and the amount of support that they offer according to the development phases has already been highlighted ten years ago in [5]. In [9], the review of notations for interaction design underlines that the most common interaction representational needs are covered by four models: task, domain, abstract and concrete UI. Many of these notations are dedicated to single user WIMP interfaces and we are interested in studying the proposed extensions of these notations and more recent notations dedicated to

T.C.N. Graham and P. Palanque (Eds.): DSVIS 2008, LNCS 5136, pp. 281–286, 2008.
© Springer-Verlag Berlin Heidelberg 2008

collaborative and multimodal UI. To do so, our approach for studying existing notations for specifying multimodal collaborative UI is in the first instance empirical: we start from existing collaboration notations and we apply them for specifying a case study: a system for supporting informal co-located collaboration in hospital work.

2 Empirical Comparison of Collaboration Notations

The relationships between collaborative and multimodal interaction open a vast world of possibilities that has not been systemically explored in terms of specification notations. We aim at going further than considering multimodal aspects such as the CARE properties [2] for the concrete UI and collaborative aspects for the abstract UI. In our empirical comparison, we first focus on existing notations for specifying collaborative UI. Since we are interested in also modeling multimodal interaction, while studying collaborative UI specification notations, we also examine the power of expression of the notations for specifying concrete UI. A complementary approach to ours would be to start from multimodal UI specification notations.

2.1 Scope of the Comparative Study

In [1], three dimensions for evaluating an interaction model are described: descriptive power (i.e., ability to describe a UI), evaluative power (i.e., ability to help assess multiple design alternatives) and generative power (i.e., ability to help designers create new designs). As a starting point for our comparative study, we are focusing on the descriptive power of UI specification notations. Their impact on the design including their evaluative and generative powers will be studied afterwards. Moreover, our study does not aim at evaluating the selected notations that can be studied in light of the criteria identified in [5] and of the notational dimensions of the framework "cognitive dimensions of notations" [4]. Since the selected notations differ in their descriptive qualities, some focusing on collaborative tasks while others on the users' roles and on collaborative situations, our goal is to assess their complementary aspects and their projected ability to specify a multimodal collaborative user interface.

2.2 Rational for the Selected Notations

Our review of existing collaboration notations highlights the fact that the notations such as CTT [11], CUA [4], GTA [15] and MABTA [8], mainly focus on both individual and collaborative tasks. Such notations aim at accommodating several aspects of collaborative work situations into a task specification and thus extend task specification with contextual information. Some notations also focus on other aspects than individual and collaborative tasks such as TKS [7] which focuses on users' knowledge involved in task behavior and UML-G [14] on modeling shared data.

Amongst the existing notations, a first way for selecting the ones to be applied to our case study would be based on the syntactic structure of the notations (i.e., graphical, tabular, textual approaches) as in [6]. This solution was not satisfying since most of the notations imply several types of representations. Moreover since our study focuses on the specification of a collaborative user interface, we did not consider the notations that are not dedicated to interaction tasks and system behaviors, although they may be complementary to the other notations. We therefore exclude TKS. Moreover although CUA is focusing on individual and collaborative tasks in the context of scenarios, its main focus is on modeling the tasks for the needs of groupware evaluation. As a conclusion, we selected four notations, CTT, GTA, MABTA and UML-G that involve different background disciplines. UML-G is an extension of a standard in Software Engineering. CTT is a well established notation for task analysis in Human-Computer Interaction, while GTA and MABTA aims at extending task analysis with elements from Social Sciences (social psychology, sociology) in order to capture key elements of the nature of groupworking.

3   Specifications Based on the Selected Notations

We apply the four selected notations to specify a collaborative multi-surface [10] that provides a support for informal co-located collaboration by allowing multiple users to study medical documents. As highlighted by the field study described in [10], hospital medical workers including physicians and medical interns are very mobile and need to opportunistically and informally establish co-located collaboration while focusing on a particular patient. Using the system, two physicians can share extracts from a patient medical displayed both on the large screen (i.e., Public Screen) and on the PDA screen (i.e., Private Screen): (i) on the public screen, physicians can only annotate the medical information using a virtual pen ; (ii) on the PDA, a physician can initiate a shared session, select documents to share, edit documents and stop a session. For illustrative purpose, we partly present the CTT specification of our case study while the complete specifications along the four notations are available at [16]. Applying CTT, collaborative activities are described at a high-level of abstraction through a collaborative task tree; individual task trees (one per role) describe concrete tasks. A collaborative task tree contains collaborative tasks and high-level individual tasks, related to one of the multiple individual task trees. Figure 1 shows the collaborative task tree for our case study and one individual task tree associated with the public screen user's role. The

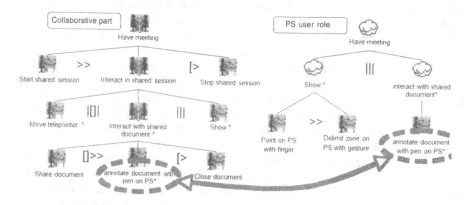

Fig. 1. CTT collaborative and public display (PS user's role) individual task trees

CTT notation includes five types of tasks: system, mental, abstract, individual (user) and collaborative tasks. A collaborative task is an abstract task that must be composed of individual tasks. Relation operators between tasks are inherited from LOTOS. In particular, Figure 1 highlights the coupling between the PDA and PS (|[]| operator) and the document sharing between users ([]>> operator).

Difficulties or limitations identified by applying CTT include the fact that the links between the tasks of different trees are not explicit (i.e., no role is specified for a task) and are only deduced from the task identifiers. Moreover to specify the modalities of a concrete task, the only means is to use the task identifier (e.g., *Annotate document with pen on PS*). In addition, the notation does not provide any means of representing shared objects and of specifying a policy for the sharing. For example, we are able to specify that the telepointer is controlled by the PDA but we are not able to specify that the telepointer can be observed by both roles.

4   Conclusions from the Comparative Study and Future Work

About role specification, the four notations explicitly support user's roles specification in working group. While GTA and MABTA advocate a dedicated representation to roles and relationships between users, we describe roles using UML-G with a class diagram and the involved objects for each role. As opposed to UML-G that focuses on the manipulated objects per role, CTT describes the tasks per role in individual task trees (Figure 1).

About group and individual work specification at abstract level, on the one hand, CTT and MABTA advocate a dedicated representation that combines collaborative tasks, and individual tasks that take part directly in the group work coordination, such as *start shared session* in Figure 1. However, CTT operators refine the MABTA "influence" relation for the case of temporal interdependencies only. As pointed out in [3], in addition to temporal interdependencies related to the activity level, interdependencies are related to the object level and describe the multiple participants' access to the same set of objects. In [13], they define a set of generic mechanics of collaboration as elementary abstract tasks for such coordination issues surrounding how objects are assessed. Such elementary abstract tasks are generic since they are common to a variety of social and organizational work groups. For example one abstract task "Obtain resource" could be part of the CTT and MABTA group work representations.

On the other hand, GTA and UML-G represent together group and individual work. Using GTA, it is possible to annotate each task with the roles and the manipulated objects. As for GTA, with UML-G, group work is implicitly described within the class diagram by different roles manipulating the same object. Collaborative activities are further described in the UML-G activity diagram that highlights the relationships between the individual tasks over time.

Individual tasks are described hierarchically in CTT, MABTA and GTA for each role. MABTA refines the work group tasks into sub-tasks while maintaining the columns for describing the roles and adding new individual tasks that are not related to the group work. GTA advocates only one representation for both group and individual works. Links between tasks of different roles can be specified by triggered task and hence corresponds to the "influence" relation of MABTA. As opposed to MABTA and GTA, CTT does not explicitly describe the links between the tasks of different roles. This link is deduced from the group work representations that share tasks with the individual task trees (Figure 1). In contrast to the hierarchical refinement approach of CTT, MABTA and GTA, the activity diagram in UML-G shows individual work and interdependencies with respect to time and roles. Moreover only GTA and UML-G enables us to represent task flows respectively in terms of activity diagram and sequence diagram.

Finally, about group and individual work specification at concrete level, CTT and MABTA advocate the same representation for abstract and concrete tasks. The GTA elementary abstract tasks are described using NUAN which enables a precise description of both users' actions, system feedback and dialogue states. For UML-G, concrete tasks can be described by sequence diagrams along with state-transition diagrams. For each object, the users' actions on it as well as its reactions are described. Nevertheless such a specification would be extremely tedious for a complete user interface.

To conclude, by applying four existing notations for specifying a simple groupware where two users are working on a medical image using a PDA and a public display enables us to identify some complementary aspects in the induced representations as well as some missing aspects. We underline three key issues from this empirical study. Firstly, the distinction between group work and individual work (per role) is useful in a specification for describing at different level of detail (i.e., abstract and concrete) a collaborative user interface from its two facets, the group and the users. However a unified representation of group and individual work enables us to depict interdependencies between users with respect to time and roles. Classical hierarchical representations such as CTT are suitable for individual tasks, while group work representations need to include specific aspects of collaboration such as in MABTA where tasks are decorated with concepts from coordination theory. Secondly, temporal relationships between tasks for describing group work are not sufficient: Temporal interdependencies are at the activity level and interdependencies related to the object level are required for describing the multiple users' access to the same set of objects. UML-G focusing on shared objects can be used for describing such interdependencies. Thirdly, the specification of concrete multimodal interaction as concrete tasks involves extending the selected notations dedicated to WIMP user interfaces. For example, it was not possible to explicitly specify the redundancy (one of the CARE properties of multimodality [2]) of the display (PDA and public display) of our case study. Further studies must be done on the description of tightly coupled multimodal interaction (a concrete multimodal group task corresponding to an abstract group task) and on loosely coupled multimodal interaction (concrete multimodal individual tasks corresponding to abstract individual tasks that define a composed abstract group task).

As further work, we plan to experiment on the complementary usage of the studied notations on another case study, namely a collaborative and multimodal military command post. The focus will be on studying the links between the activity (task) and shared resource (object) aspects and on extending the notations in order to depict multimodal interaction. For multimodal interaction, distinguishing abstract/concrete tasks as well as group/individual tasks allows us to identify: (1) tasks that require tightly coupled multimodal interaction when two users are continuously engaged with the accomplishment of physical actions for realizing a concrete group task. (2) Tasks that require loosely coupled multimodal interaction when two users are performing actions along different modalities for realizing two concrete individual tasks that define an abstract group task. For specifying these two types of multimodal group tasks, one of our research avenues is to study extensions of the ICARE notation [2].

References

1. Beaudouin-Lafon, M.: Designing Interaction, not Interfaces. In: AVI 2000, pp. 15–22. ACM Press, New York (2000)
2. Bouchet, J., Nigay, L., Ganille, T.: ICARE Software Component for Rapidly Developing Multimodal Interfaces. In: ICMI, pp. 251–258. ACM Press, New York (2004)
3. Ellis, C.A., Wainer, J.,, J.: A Conceptual Model of Groupware. In: CSCW 1994, pp. 79–80. ACM Press, New York (1994)
4. Green, T.: Instructions and descriptions: some cognitive aspects of programming and similar activities. In: AVI 2000, pp. 21–28. ACM Press, New York (2000)
5. Johnson, C.W.: The Namur Principles: Criteria for the Evaluation of User Interface Notations. In: DSVIS 1996. Springer, Heidelberg (1996)
6. Johnson, C.W.: The Evaluation of User Interface Design Notations. In: DSVIS 1996, pp. 188–206. Springer, Heidelberg (1996)
7. Johnson, H., Hyde, J.: Towards Modeling Individual and Collaborative Construction of Jigsaws Using Task Knowledge Structures. In: TOCHI, vol. 10(4), pp. 339–387. ACM Press, New York (2003)
8. Lim, Y.K.: Task models for groupware and multitasking: Multiple aspect based task analysis (MABTA) for user requirements gathering in highly-contextualized interactive system design. In: TAMODIA 2004, pp. 7–15. ACM Press, New York (2004)
9. Markopoulos, P., Marijnissen, P.: UML as a representation for Interaction Design. In: OZCHI 2000, pp. 240–249 (2000)
10. Mejia, D.A., Morán, A.L., Favela, J.: Supporting Informal Co-located Collaboration in Hospital Work. In: Haake, J.M., Ochoa, S.F., Cechich, A. (eds.) CRIWG 2007. LNCS, vol. 4715, pp. 255–270. Springer, Heidelberg (2007)
11. Mori, G., Paterno, F., Santoro, C.: CTTE : Support for Developing and Analyzing Task Models for Interactive System Design. In: TOSE, vol. 28(8), pp. 797–813. IEEE Computer Society Press, Los Alamitos (2002)
12. Oviatt, S., et al.: Designing the user interface for multimodal speech and gesture applications. In: HCI 2000, vol. 15(4), pp. 263–322. Taylor & Francis, Abington (2000)
13. Pinelle, D., Gutwin, C., Greenberd, S.: Task Analysis for Groupware Usability Evaluation. In: TOCHI, vol. 10(4), pp. 281–311. ACM Press, New York (2003)
14. Rubart, J., Dawabi, P.: Shared data modeling with UML-G. In: IJCAT. Inderscience, vol. 19 (3/4), pp. 231–243 (2004)
15. Veer, G., Welie, M.: Task Based Groupware Design: Putting Theory into Practice. In: DIS 2000, pp. 326–337. ACM Press, New York (2000)
16. http://iihm.imag.fr/laurillau/four-notations-comparison.pdf

Towards Characterizing Visualizations

Christophe Hurter[1,3] and Stéphane Conversy[2, 3]

[1] DGAC DSNA DTI R&D 7, Avenue Edouard Belin 31055, Toulouse, France
christophe.hurter@aviation-civile.gouv.fr
[2] ENAC LII 7, Avenue Edouard Belin 31055, Toulouse, France
stephane.conversy@enac.fr
[3] IHCS – IRIT, Université Paul Sabatier,
118 route de Narbonne, 31062 Toulouse Cedex 4, France

Abstract. The ability to characterize visualizations would bring several benefits to the design process. It would help designers to assess their designs, reuse existing designs in new contexts, communicate with other designers and write compact and unambiguous specifications. The research described in this paper is an initial effort to develop a theory-driven approach to the characterization of visualizations. We examine the Card and Mackinlay characterization tool and we show its limitations when it comes to performing a complete characterization.

Keywords: Information Visualization, Evaluation Tools, Design, Graphical Coding.

Topics: Development Processes, Verification and Validation, Specification of Interactive Systems.

1 Introduction

Research in HCI has led to the design of methods and tools to evaluate the effectiveness of interfaces. *A posteriori* methods rely on user tests to check if an interface is usable. They involve developing parts of the interfaces, which are costly. *A priori* (or *heuristic*) methods use models of the system and the user to predict effectiveness before the development of the interface. *A priori* methods are less expensive, and they enable designers to design and compare a large set of solutions and help them produce better interfaces. *A priori* methods include the keystroke-level model, to help compute the time needed to perform an interaction [5], or the CIS [1] model, which extends keystroke by taking into account the context in which the interaction takes place. Both keystroke and CIS are *predictive* models, i.e. they can help compute a measurement of expected effectiveness, and enable quantitative comparison between interaction techniques. These tools have proved to be accurate and efficient when designing new interfaces. *Descriptive* models only help describe phenomena. They are less powerful than predictive models, but are nonetheless very valuable, since they help designers organize their thinking along relevant dimensions. Even if not supported with quantitative data, designers are able to make better design decisions since they use relevant dimensions of analysis. For example, the cognitive dimension framework [6] is an analysis tool that helps designers to recognize patterns of important interaction dimensions, discuss them with other designers using the same vocabulary, and help them find the right solutions during the design process.

T.C.N. Graham and P. Palanque (Eds.): DSVIS 2008, LNCS 5136, pp. 287–293, 2008.

Although methods do exist for *a priori* evaluation of interaction effectiveness, very few exist for *a priori* evaluation of visualizations. The lack of efficient models to describe visualization hinders the design process. For example, designers sometimes inappropriately transpose the existing features of a particular visualization to another one, because they have no means of analyzing visualizations in detail, so as to really understand them, and they have no way of comparing visualizations. In addition, the lack of description tools makes specification writing tasks very difficult. Many specifications use prose to describe a visualization, which is cumbersome to read, subjective and error-prone: we observed during our engineering projects that there were a lot of differences between an expected system that we designed and a delivered system coded by a third party.

This paper describes the first steps towards building a method to describe visualization systematically. In particular, we try to characterize visualizations, i.e. to find a precise and compact description that unveils similarities and differences, and allows for comparison. We seek to answer the following questions: what information is displayed on the screen? How many information are displayed? How is information displayed? At first sight, it seems that the answer is trivial: the information on the screen is exactly what the designer wanted to put there when he designed the visualization. However, we will see that the answer is more complex, as it does not take into account information built up from our perception system. We want to insist on the fact that we do not try to assess the effectiveness of different representation. We only identify what is displayed and not how well a user perceives it.

To bridge the characterization gap, we use the Card and Mackinlay model from the Information Visualization field (InfoVis). We apply this tool to particular visualization, and show the usefulness of the result. Finally, we show why this tool is not satisfactory, especially when characterizing emerging information.

2 Characterization Model: Card and Mackinlay

Card and Mackinlay [4] (C&M) attempted to establish comparison criteria of visualizations. They proposed a table for each transformation function (Table 1). The C&M table is completed with the notations in Table 2.

Table 1. C&M representation model

Name	D	F	D'	automatic perception					-	[]	Controled perception
				X	Y	Z	T	R		CP	

Table 2. C&M Model notations

S	Size	Lon, Lat	Longitude, Latitude
Sh	Shape	P	Point
f	Function	O	Orientation
N, O, Q	Nominal , Ordered, Quantitative		

The horizontal rows correspond to the input data. The column D and D' indicate the type of data (Nominal, Ordered or Quantitative). F is a function or a filter which transforms or creates a subset of D. Columns X, Y, Z, T, R, -, [] are derived from the visual variables of Bertin [3]. The image has four dimensions: X, Y, Z and time, T. R corresponds to the retinal perception which describes the method employed to represent information visually (color, form, size,etc.). The bonds between the graphic entities are noted with '-', and the concept of encapsulation is symbolized by '[]'. Finally, a distinction is made if the representation of the data is treated by our perceptive system in an automatic or controlled way. Card and Mackinlay depicted some well-known InfoVis visualizations. However, they did not explicitly demonstrate how to use their model, nor its usefulness. We applied this model to visualization from Air Traffic Control (ATC), which we describe in the next section.

3 Rich and Dynamic Visualizations from ATC

Air traffic controllers aim to maintain a safe distance between flights. In current ATC environments, air traffic controllers use several visualization systems: radar view, timelines, electronic strips, meteorological views, supervision, etc. Each visualization is rich and dynamic: it displays numerous visual entities that evolve over time. These visualizations are complex and each visual detail is important. The following section details the design of two Radar visualizations.

3.1 ODS: The French Radar Screen

ODS is the main French radar view for air traffic controllers. It is a top view of the current flying aircrafts. Its main goal is to display aircraft positions and to help controllers to space aircraft beyond the safety minima.

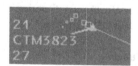

Fig. 1. The ODS comet of an evolving aircraft, the image exhibits direction and acceleration changes

The radar track presents aircraft positions, speed (speed vector), name, altitude and speed as text (Fig. 1). The design of the comet is built with squares, whose size varies with the recentness of the aircraft's position: the biggest square displays the last position of the aircraft, whereas the smallest square displays the least recent aircraft position. The Speed Vector (SV) is a line which starts from the current aircraft position and ends at its future position (3 minutes later). The X axis of the screen codes the latitude of each aircraft; the Y axis of the screen codes the longitude of each aircraft. We applied the C&M characterization of the comet in Table 4 and of the speed vector in Table 3.

3.2 ASTER: A Vertical Visualization

ASTER [2] is a vertical view of the current position of an aircraft. The X axis of the screen codes the current aircraft distance from a reference point (IAF) and the Y axis of the screen codes the Flight Level (FL or altitude) of each aircraft.

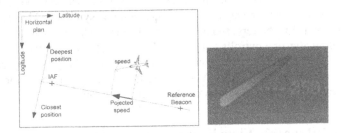

Fig. 2. Aster projection plan (left) and comet (right)

The head of the comet shows the position of the aircraft in the vertical view. Its orientation codes the aircraft vertical speed (or its incidence) and its length codes the projected aircraft speed (Fig. 2). We applied the C&M characterization of the ASTER comet in Table 4.

4 Applying C&M Model

This section deals with the use of the C&M model. First, we show how the C&M characterization enables to compare the ASTER comet and the Speed Vector. Second, we explain why this model is a partial characterization, especially because it lacks characterization of emerging data. Third, we define the notion of 'emerging data'. Finally, we explain why the transformation function alone is not sufficient to fully perform a characterization of static visualization.

4.1 Unveiling Similarities: Success

The characterization of the radar speed vector (Table 3.) shows that its size or length changes with the aircraft's speed.

As we can see by comparing Table 4 and Table 3. , the same information is coded by the length of the ASTER comet and by the speed vector of the radar's comet. The ASTER comet is thus equivalent to the radar's speed vector, modulo a translation.

Designers and users use the term comet to describe the aircraft position in ASTER visualization, but the ASTER comet has not the same semantic as the ODS comet.

Table 3. C&M Speed vector characterisation

Name	D	F	D'	X	Y	Z	T	R	-	[]	CP
speed	Q	f	Q					S			
direction	Q	f	Q					O			

Table 4. C&M ASTER Comet characterization

Name	D	F	D'	X	Y	Z	T	R	-	[]	CP
Plot	Lat Lon (QxQ)	f	Q	P				Shape			
Afl	Q	f	Q		P						
Vert. speed	Q	f	Q					O			
speed	Q	f	Q					S			

Table 5. C&M Radar Comet characterization

Name	D	F	D'	X	Y	Z	T	R	-	[]	CP
X	QLon	f	Q Lon	P				Emerging Shape			
Y	QLat	f	Q Lat		P						
T	Q	f(Tcur)	Q								

This mistake can lead to false information being perceived: for instance, the tail of the ASTER comet is not a previous aircraft position. As a first result, we show the usefulness of characterizing visualizations: it is the characterization and the comparison which allows us to link two visualizations, and thus to give elements of analysis to the designer. This result highlights the importance of carefully analyzing what is displayed in order to make perceivable the right information when building and justifying a design.

4.2 Unveiling Differences: Failure

In the ODS comet, the last positions of the aircraft merge by Gestalt continuity effect (alignment and progressive size increase of squares). A line does appear with its particular characteristics (curve, regularity of size increasing of the past positions, etc). In this case, it is not possible to characterize the radar comet as a single graphic entity using the C&M transformation model. But we can characterize the shapes that build the comet. With this intention, we introduce the concept of current time (Tcur: the time when the image is displayed). The size of the square is linearly proportional to current time with respect to its aging. The grey row and column are two additional items from the original C&M model (Table 5).

However, the characterization cannot take into account the controllers' analysis of the evolution of aircraft latest positions (speed, evolution of speed and direction). For instance, in Fig. 1, the shape of the comet indicates that the plane has turned 90° to the right and that it has accelerated (dots spacing variation). These data are important to the air traffic controller. The comet curvature and the aircraft acceleration can not be characterized with the C&M model because they constitute emerging information (there is no raw data called 'curvature' to design a curving comet). A precise definition of 'emerging' will be given in the next section.

4.3 Emerging Data

In Fig. 3, raw data are transformed with many Transformation Functions to the view. They are displayed and then perceived by the user as visual entities. In an efficient design, the perceived data and the raw data are the same. If there are more Raw Data (RD) than Perceivable Data (PD), the non-perceived data are useless. As we said earlier, the emerging data are perceived data which are not transformed from raw data, which means that there are more perceived data than raw data. The ODS comet curvature is an example of emerging data; there is no item of raw data named 'curvature' that needs to be transformed to the view, even if we can perceive the aircraft rotation tendency. Pd-Rd is a characterizing dimension (we call it the level of integration) which helps us to characterize a design (Fig. 3).

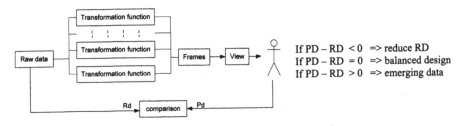

Fig. 3. Emerging Data

4.4 Characterizing with Emerging Data

If we consider the amount of coded information as a design efficiency dimension, the C&M model rates the ASTER comet higher than the ODS comet (Table 6). Therefore, we may think that the ASTER comet codes more information than the ODS comet. However, we have already explained that emerging data are not listed with the C&M model. Even with emerging data, this characterization is still incomplete, as the dynamic of the image codes additional information. When the visualization is updated, the ASTER comet evolves. The information about change is visually coded; the user can perceive the movement and thus perceive the aircraft's tendency. Hence, ODS and ASTER comet code the same amount of information (Table 7).

Table 6. ASTER and ODS coded information with C&M model

ASTER coded information	ODS coded information
Aircraft position	Aircraft position
Flight Level	Time of each position
Vertical speed	
Horizontal speed	

Table 7. ASTER and ODS information with C&M model and emerging data

ASTER coded information	ODS coded information
Aircraft position	Aircraft position
Flight Level	Time of each position
Vertical speed	*Aircraft speed*
Horizontal speed	*Aircraft tendency (left, right)*
Tendency (animation)	*Aircraft acceleration*

5 Conclusion

Whereas Card and Mackinley depicted some InfoVis visualizations without explicitly demonstrating how to use their model, we have shown the practical effectiveness of the C&M model when performing the ASTER comet and the ODS speed vector comparison. Although the C&M tables make visualizations amenable to analysis as well as to comparison, this model does not allow essential information to be highlighted for designers, and does not allow any exhaustive comparison of different designs. In this article, we managed to apply the C&M model. We extended this model with the characterization of emerging data. The ODS comet is richer than the Aster comet (when comparing the amount of coded information), although the characterization of C&M seems to indicate the opposite. The wealth of information transmitted by each representation is thus not directly interpretable in the characterizations.

Designers need to be able to evaluate and reuse their work, as well as to communicate effectively. This work is an initial attempt to meet these needs by giving them the supporting tools to measure their design. A tool that is descriptive, predictive and prescriptive would be a valuable aid to designers. As a descriptive tool, visualization characterization and issues related to it form the core of the present paper. Predictive tools may forecast the visual coded information with a given visualization, while prescriptive tools have the ability to find a solution to a specific problem. There are currently no such tools in existence, and our goal is to converge on such a solution.

References

[1] Appert, C., Beaudoiun-Lafon, M., Mackay, W.: Context matters: Evaluating interaction techniques with CIS model. In: HCI 2004 (2004)
[2] Benhacene, R.: A Vertical Image as a means to improve air traffic control in E-TMA. USA, DASC California (2002)
[3] Bertin, J.: Graphics and Graphic Information Processing. deGruyter Press, Berlin (1977)
[4] Card, S.K., Mackinlay, J.D.: The Structure of the Information Visualization Design Space. In: Proc. Information Visualization Symposium 1997 (1997)
[5] Card, S.K., Moran, W.P., Newell, A.: The keystroke-level model of user performance time with interactive systems. Communication of the ACM 23 (1980)
[6] Green, T.R.G.: Instructions and Descriptions: some cognitive aspects of programming and similar activities. In: AVI 2000 (2000)

Towards Usability Evaluation
for Smart Appliance Ensembles

Gregor Buchholz and Stefan Propp[*]

University of Rostock, Institute of Computer Science, Albert Einstein Str. 21,
18059 Rostock, Germany
{gregor.buchholz, stefan.propp}@uni-rostock.de

Abstract. Smart environments comprise users and devices to form ad-hoc an ensemble and assist the users to fulfill their tasks more efficiently and more conveniently. This introduces new challenges for usability evaluations. To cope with theses issues, we propose the application of task models. Following this approach the behavior of the users can be interpreted as a trace through the corresponding task model. We discuss our method of capturing, visualizing and analyzing traces through task models within smart environments. The paper provides the first results of a prototypical implementation.

Keywords: Smart Appliance Ensembles, Task Models, Usability.

1 Specifics of Usability Evaluation in Smart Environments

According to [12] we define a smart environment (SE) as being capable of gathering and applying knowledge about the environment and its occupants so as to provide automated assistance in reaching goals. Automation in this context can be described as a repeated cycle of "perceiving the state of the environment, reasoning about the state together with task goals and outcomes of possible actions, and acting upon the environment to change the state" [1]. A main characteristic of smart (or pervasive) environments as ensembles of smart (or intelligent) devices operating as a coherent unit is their effective invisibility to the user [1]. Furthermore, we strongly emphasize the cooperative aspect of the use of smart environments. Out of this, the challenge of developing, applying and evaluating adequate usability test methods emerges. Evaluation methods for measuring the usability of single devices are widely spread and, of course, necessary to be applied on every single device in the ensemble. Beyond this, the combination of several devices, linked by an intelligent authority that coordinates the devices' funtionalities affords a lot of aspects to be evaluated. Usability "just means making sure that something works well" [5]. When dealing with the usability of smart environments it has to be ensured that the automatically initiated actions are based upon an appropriate and correct collection of knowledge about the environ-

---

[*] Supported by a grant of the German National Research Foundation (DFG), Graduate School 1424, Multimodal Smart Appliance Ensembles for Mobile Applications (MuSAMA).

T.C.N. Graham and P. Palanque (Eds.): DSVIS 2008, LNCS 5136, pp. 294–299, 2008.
© Springer-Verlag Berlin Heidelberg 2008

ment's state and its actors, a reliable and learning component to interpret the users' intentions, and proper interaction modalities to initiate or (in the worst case) revert actions caused by misinterpretation of sensor data or faulty knowledge affecting the intention recognition in an unfavorable way.

A lot of work has been done in the field of employing task models in usability tests of interactive systems [3]. Among others, Paternò describes the use of task models within the evaluation of mobile applications [8], providing methods and tools for conducting evaluations and analyzing the results by presenting the collected data in several visualizations. As we attach importance to the idea of basing both the developers' and the usability experts' work not only on the same concepts but on the same artifacts as well, an integrated tool support is presented for developing and testing task models and evaluating systems that are built onto them.

2 Model-Based Design of Smart Environments

Within the domain of HCI task modeling is an established technique. Originally, task models were only used to capture the structure of tasks a user has to fulfill. Subsequent research efforts developed methods to also use task models as an initial model for model-based development of interactive systems, particularly UI development [9]. Some recently developed approaches also apply task modeling for the model-based design of smart environments.

Trapp et al. [11] describe the capabilities of each device with a task model chunk (device functionality model, DFM). When a new device connects to the room infrastructure this DFM fragment is added to the current task model (room task model, RTM). The combination of available DFMs provides some new combined functionalies, e.g. a scanner and a printer offer a combined copying functionality. Sinnig et al. [10] suggest the "Task-Constraint Language" (TCL). Every user in the room is described by a task model and additional constraints specify the dependencies of collaboration, e.g. that person "A" finishes his presentation, to give person "B" the floor. Feuerstack et al. [2] enhance the task model notation CTT to serve as a runtime model. For instance domain concepts are annotated and an object flow is modeled. Different users' task models are synchronized with domain objects.

Our objective is to provide usability evaluation methods independent of a specific modeling technique. Therefore we define an evaluation scenario as a set of users and devices, each charatarized by properties and specific task models. Every user owns one or more roles and every role is described by a certain task model. Every device is associated with one or more types described by a set of properties and a usage model in a CTT like notation, which defines a set of task sequences a user can perform with the specific device type. To evaluate a smart environment based on a specific modeling technique, the model artefacts stored in the devices are firstly gathered. Subsequently the task model chunks, which describe user behavior and device usage, are mapped to a CTT like notation as used in the evaluation tool and additional information is annotated. The aim is to track the interaction between user and environment and validate the interaction according to the model in an analysis stage.

3 Model-Based Usability Evaluation

Due to the intended relative independence from a specific modeling technique and the early development stage of our environment a test setup is suggested wherein at least two experimenters act as mediators between the smart environment room and the task model interpreter. Such Wizard-of-Oz experiments are a common technique for early stage tests of window based software systems and have been conducted to evaluate speech-based ubiquitous computing systems with natural language interaction [4, 6], among others. As described in the following, experimenters in our evaluation approach have to bear a little more responsibility than just to mediate between the observed environment and the task model interpreter.

The goals of the evaluation can be devided into two subgoals: One aim is to validate the devices' and roles' task models and the other one is to identify weak points in the environment's sensors and the interpretation of the users' behavior. We will outline the procedure of a usability evaluation and point out, which kinds of problems are addressed.

The evaluation preparation includes the definition of a scenario that is to be carried out by one or more users in the smart environment room. Therefore, the task models of all devices and roles participating in the proposed scenario are gathered and a model describing the scenario has to be developed. This task model is composed of subtrees of the devices' and roles' models and augmented with new inner nodes to structure the task model chunks according to the scenario's intention and define hierarchical and temporal relations between them.

The users taking part in the evaluation are now instructed to fulfill the tasks defined in the scenario. They do not know the complete task models in detail but only the goal and a list of subgoals so as to avoid them to behave more unnatural than inevitable.

During the evaluation the experimenters are provided with all user movement information that is produced by the sensors in the smart environment room, video streams from cameras placed in the SE and an audio stream to keep track of the users' activities. Furthermore, the current states and properties of the devices are displayed. All these data flows are recorded to be used in subsequent analysis, too. We developed an Eclipse plug-in to simulate multiple task trees describing a role's action or a device's capabilities and functions. An experimenter can define a set of task trees for an evaluation and activate the simulations simultaneously. Each time the experimenter observes an action he journalizes it using the task model simulation (see figure 1).

We distinguish three situations that can occur during the test session:

1. In one case, the action executed by a user with or without the help of a device is valid regarding the current state of the according task model simulation(s). The experimenter then only has to click in the appropiate task model tree(s) and select "Run Task" (executing a sequence of "Start" and "Stop" immediately), "Start Task", "Stop Task" or "Crash Task" respectively in the popup menu of the according task node(s) to execute a simulation step.

2. The experimenter may notice the starting or stopping of a task that can not be started or stopped at that time due to the modelled temporal relations in the task model. For example, the user may start a task that is disabled in the simulation because another task is modelled to be finished before. If so, the popup menu

provides "Forced Start" and "Forced Stop" items to produce an entry in a protocol that lists behavior not covered by the modelled task trees. An input field for entering a comment is offered. In figure 1 these items are disabled because the clicked task "Show next slide" can be started, actually.

3. The third case is the occurrence of tasks not modelled at all but observed in the test session. For these situations a panel is provided for entering time stamped actions, saved in a protocol as well.

Another experimenter is responsible for initiating the effects on devices in the SE. Tasks that are marked as system tasks in the devices' models are started and stopped in the simulation and delivered as commands to the appropriate devices. Thus, the information flow out of and into the smart environment room is complete: Observed actions are recorded using the model simulation and an additional protocol for tasks not modelled so far, and the environment's reactions are simulated by an operator sending the commands to the devices in the SE room. The users performing activities in the smart environment room interact with the room's devices as if the task model engine was triggering them according to the task models. The subsequent analysis of the recorded events reveals several shortcomings of the SE system developed so far.

- Actions initiated through the use of the "Forced Start/Stop" items indicate restrictions in the chronical ordering of tasks expressed by the temporal relations in the models that do not comply with the very behavior of the users or the actual operation mode of devices. It has to be decided whether to loosen the ordering restrictions or not. If the achievement of subgoals does not suffer from the loosening the choice in most cases will be to allow the diverging task order by changing temporal operators or restructuring parts of the model tree.

- Tasks protocolled outside the already modelled task trees uncover possible activities in the SE room that may benefit from task model based assistance. While the capabilities of the SE are evolving, the task models should cover as many processes as possible. The more detailed the behavior of users is trackable the more precise become the automatically suggested or executed assistance activities like preparing a device for a specific usage. If single subtrees of a role's task tree turn out to be useless in terms of possible assistance they can be removed or reduced later.

- By comparing the data provided by the movement sensors their accuracy and reliability can be checked. Therefore, the display of executed tasks in the users' task trees is reduced to show movement-related tasks only. This list of activities is compared to the protocol of the movement sensors in the SE room to discover divergencies. A floor plan can be utilized to visualize the users' motions as tracked by the sensors and together with the technicians, which are concerned with the functionality of the sensors their improvement is forwarded.

The evaluation process presented so far primarily targets functional facets of the SE as a first step to establish usability tests within the SE's development and, of course, the future evaluation process has to cover more usability aspects.

4 Visualization and Analysis for the Usability Expert

While the task traces of the interactions between users and the system are captured, the usability expert is provided with a number of visualizations. Figure 1 depicts our usability evaluation environment which is implemented as Eclipse plug-in to ensure a seamless integration into the design tools which are used for the task model-based development of interactive systems.

Figure 1 is devided into three parts. The left-hand part shows a model of the planned usability evaluation and includes a description of the relevant elements of our smart environment. The behavior of all user roles is described by a task model, while the functionality of all device types is described by a usage model in task model notation. Such a defined test series can be carried out several times in order to conduct several evaluation sessions in the same scenario setup with improved model descriptions. The middle part of figure 1 depicts one individual test scenario with certain concrete users, based on the defined model at the left. It allows both (1) the simulation of a scenario for validation of the models in early development phases of the smart environment and (2) the evaluation of scenarios within an already established environment. As described in the previous chapter, one usability expert is required to track the interaction in a real environment by observing the user behavior and activating the modeled tasks accordingly. If the interactions differ from the models the expert annotates the differences for later analysis. Hence the annotations are instantly available within the development environment, at the specific location, where they are needed for further improvement.

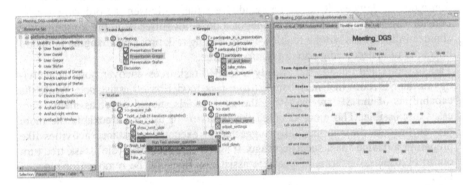

Fig. 1. Usability Evaluation Environment (Usability Model, Simulation, Visualization)

The right-hand part visualizes the captured task traces of a completed subtree ("presentation Stefan") of the "Team Agenda" task model and the involvements of two users. A gantt chart depicts the progress of a meeting according to a timeline, based on aggregation and filtering of tasks. The fulfilled tasks are visualized as blue lines and the tasks are grouped by task models depicted as green lines. In this example a person gives a presentation while other persons are listening and welcomed to interactively ask questions to the presenter.

Depending on the information interest of the expert, different visualization techniques are available, e.g. a timeline to compare several scenarios as suggested by Maly et al. [7] for classical applications.

5 Conclusion

In this paper we presented a model-based usability evaluation method for smart environments. Since model-based techniques for the design of smart environments evolve, usability evaluation methods are needed to exploit the arising oppurtunities. Therefore we describe the behavior of persons in the environment in terms of task models and interpret the interactions as trace through these models. The advantages are twofold: on one hand the usage of the same models within system design and evaluation simplifies the discovery of the cause for a detected usability issue within the design model. On the other hand an abstract description of the usage of different devices with task models allows comparing interactions with these different devices directly and further enables the user to begin a task on one device and finish it on another device. Compared to other task-based usability evaluation approaches, we not only integrate design and evaluation at conceptual level, but also at the same artefacts.

Future research avenues comprise further work on the link between real smart environments and the usability evaluation engine to natively capture the system changes and further sensor data.

References

1. Cook, D.J., Das, S.K.: How smart are our environments? An updated look at the state of the art. Journal of Pervasive and Mobile Computing 3(2) (March 2007)
2. Feuerstack, S., Blumendorf, M., Albayrak, S.: Prototyping of Multimodal Interactions for Smart Environments based on Task Models. In: AMI 2007 Workshop on Model-Driven Software Engineering, Darmstadt, Germany (2007)
3. Ivory, M.Y., Hearst, M.A.: The state of the art in automating usability evaluation of user interfaces. ACM Comput. Surv. 33(4), 470–516 (2001)
4. Johnsen, M., Svendsen, T., Amble, T., Holter, T., Harborg, E.: TABOR – A Norwegian Spoken Dialogue System for Bus Travel Information. In: Proceedings of 6th International Conference of Spoken Language Processing (ICSLP 2000), Beijing, China (2000)
5. Krug, S.: Don't make me think, New Riders, p. 5 (2000) ISBN 978-0789723109
6. Mäkelä, K., Salonen, E.-P., Turunen, M., Hakulinen, J., Raisamo, R.: Conducting a Wizard of Oz Experiment on a Ubiquitous Computing System Doorman. In: Proceedings of the IPNMD Workshop, Verona, December 14-15, 2001, pp. 115–119 (2001)
7. Malý, I., Slavík, P.: Towards Visual Analysis of Usability Test Logs, Hasselt, Belgium, pp. 25–32 (2006)
8. Paternò, F., Russino, A., Santoro, C.: Remote evaluation of Mobile Applications. In: Winckler, M., Johnson, H., Palanque, P. (eds.) TAMODIA 2007. LNCS, vol. 4849, pp. 155–168. Springer, Heidelberg (2007)
9. Reichart, D., Forbrig, P., Dittmar, A.: Task models as basis for requirements engineering and software execution. In: TAMODIA 2004, Czech Republic, Prague (2004)
10. Sinnig, D., Wurdel, M., Forbrig, P., Chalin, P., Khendek, F.: Practical Extensions for Task Models. In: Winckler, M., Johnson, H., Palanque, P. (eds.) TAMODIA 2007. LNCS, vol. 4849, pp. 42–55. Springer, Heidelberg (2007)
11. Trapp, M., Schmettow, M.: Consistency in use through Model based User Interface Development. In: Workshop at CHI 2006, Montreal, Canada (2006)
12. Youngblood, G.M., Heierman, E.O., Holder, L.B., Cook, D.J.: Automation Intelligence for the Smart Environment. In: Proceedings of the Nineteenth International Joint Conference on Artificial Intelligence 2005, Edinburgh, Scotland, pp. 1513–1516 (2005)

Task Model Refinement with Meta Operators

Maik Wurdel[1], Daniel Sinnig[2], and Peter Forbrig[1]

[1] Department of Computer Science,
University of Rostock, Germany
{maik.wurdel, peter.forbrig}@uni-rostock.de
[2] Faculty of Engineering and Computer Science,
Concordia University, Montreal, Quebec, Canada
d_sinnig@encs.concordia.ca

Abstract. In model-based user interface (UI) development task models are successively refined into more detailed task specifications. To ensure that analysis information is correctly translated into requirements and design artifacts it is important to verify that for each transformation step the derived task model is a valid refinement of its base specification. In this paper we present a versatile refinement relation between task models based on the principle of *mandatory scenario equivalence*. Which scenarios are mandatory is determined by meta-operators. These operators are assigned to tasks by the requirements engineer depending on the role of the task model in the development lifecycle.

Keywords: Task models, requirements engineering, refinement, scenarios.

1 Introduction

In modern software engineering, the development lifecycle is divided into a series of iterations. With each iteration a set of disciplines and associated activities are performed while the resulting artifacts are incrementally perfected and refined. Task modeling is no exception to this rule. An analysis level task model may be further refined into requirements- and/or design level task models. In order to ensure that elicited analysis and requirement information is correctly transferred to the design stage it is important to verify that the involved refinement steps are valid.

In the field of model-based UI development task models play a central role. While analysis task models serve as a starting point for development, design level task models are used as specifications for the envisioned UI. Different notations for tasks models have been introduced. A comprehensive overview of existing approaches can be found in [1]. ConcurTaskTrees (CTT), the most common notation, promotes hierarchical task trees and distinguishes between several task types. In addition to the tree structure CTT offers a set of temporal operators which restrict the potential execution order of tasks. A detailed description of CTT can be found in [2].

Refinement between two specifications has been investigated for decades and definitions have been proposed for various models [3-6]. But to our knowledge a generically applicable notion of refinement has never been defined for task models. Various refinement and equivalence criteria have been defined for labeled transition systems. Among the most popular ones are trace-, testing- and bisimulation equivalence [7]. In this paper we use a notion similar to trace equivalence, called *mandatory scenario equivalence* to

T.C.N. Graham and P. Palanque (Eds.): DSVIS 2008, LNCS 5136, pp. 300–305, 2008.
© Springer-Verlag Berlin Heidelberg 2008

verify that one task specification is a valid refinement of another task model. A scenario is defined as a sequence of tasks which represents a single complete run through the task model. Which scenario is mandatory depends on the usage of meta-operators, which will be introduced in the next section. In Section 3 we provide a set of heuristics and guidelines for creating meaningful task model refinements. Finally we conclude and provide an outlook to future avenues.

2 Instruments of Refinement

Refinement between task models is possible in two different ways: *structural refinement* and *behavioral refinement*.

Structural Refinement: The refined task model may contain more detailed information than its base model. This can be achieved by further refining the atomic units (i.e. the leaf tasks) of the superordinate model. It is, however, important to retain type consistency. That is, the task type of the refined task may need to be revised such that it corresponds to the task types of its newly defined subtasks (e.g. as per CTT semantics [2] an *application* task can only have subtasks which are also of type *application*). An exception to this rule are tasks that have been marked with the *deep binding* meta-operator (will be explained in the context of behavioral refinement). These tasks cannot change their task type and the respective subtasks need to be chosen such that type consistency is ensured.

Behavioral Refinement: Whether a behavioral refinement is valid or not depends on the usage of meta-operators in the respective task models. Unlike temporal operators, meta-operators do not determine the execution order of tasks, but define which tasks must be retained or may be omitted in the refining task model. As depicted in Table 1, we distinguish between three different meta-operators: *shallow binding*, *deep binding*, and *exempted binding*. All three operators denote tasks which need to be preserved in all subsequent refining task models. While *shallow binding* only applies to its direct operand task, *deep binding* applies to the entire subtask tree.

We can now define behavioral refinement as follows: Let TM_1 be a task model and TM_2 be a refining task model. Furthermore, let $TM_{1_{red}}$ be the task model obtained from TM_1 by removing all subtasks of shallow bindings and $TM_{2_{red}}$ be the task model

Table 1. Meta-Operators in Support of Behavioral Refinement

Meta-Operator	Interpretation
Shallow Binding ($\odot$)	Denotes a mandatory task which needs to be preserved in subsequent refining models. Subtasks may be omitted or modified and the task type may be changed.
Deep Binding ($\otimes$)	Denotes a mandatory task which, *including* all its subtasks and their types, needs to be preserved in subsequent refining models.
Exempted Binding ($\ominus$)	Denotes a newly introduced mandatory task, which is not present in the base task model, but which (including all its subtasks) should be preserved in all subsequent refining task models.

obtained from TM_2 by removing all structural refinements (relative to TM_1). Moreover, let $\mathfrak{S}_{TM_{1_{red}}}$ be the set of all scenarios which only contain mandatory tasks (i.e. tasks marked with any of the meta-operators) of TM_1 and let $\mathfrak{S}_{TM_{2_{red}}}$ be the set of retained scenarios which only contain mandatory *non-exempted* tasks (i.e. tasks marked with *shallow* and *deep binding*) of TM_2. Then TM_2 is a valid behavioral refinement of TM_1 if, and only if $\mathfrak{S}_{TM_{1_{red}}} = \mathfrak{S}_{TM_{2_{red}}}$.

Table 2. Behavioral Refinement Example

In order to illustrate behavioral refinement, let us consider the example task models given in Table 2. TM_1 is the original task model and TM_2 is the refining task model. In order to compare TM_1 and TM_2 the reduced task models $TM_{1_{red}}$ and $TM_{2_{red}}$ are derived first. As depicted, $TM_{1_{red}}$ is obtained from TM_1 by removing $A1$ and $A2$, which are direct subtasks of A. Task A, is marked with the *shallow binding* operator and should be retained in all refining task models. Its subtasks as well as its type, however, may be changed in subsequent refining models. $TM_{2_{red}}$ is obtained from TM_2 by removing the subtasks $A3$ and $A4$. Both are structural refinements of A relative to TM_1, or, more precisely $TM_{1_{red}}$.

In order to verify that TM_1 is correctly refined by TM_2 we need to obtain the sets of mandatory and retained scenarios of $TM_{1_{red}}$ and $TM_{2_{red}}$, respectively. Clearly, the set of mandatory scenarios of $TM_{1_{red}}$ is the singleton set $\{\langle A, C1, C2\rangle\}$. Equally the set of retained scenarios of $TM_{2_{red}}$ is also $\{\langle A, C1, C2\rangle\}$. Due to equality of both sets we can now state that TM_2 is a valid refinement of TM_1. Please note that in the case of TM_2 task E has been *exempted* from the refinement comparison with the base model TM_1. It will, however, be taken into account for all subsequent refinement checks of T_2.

Behavioral refinement is heavily depending on the usage of meta-operators. The decision of which task should be marked with which meta-operator can only be made by the requirements engineering and domain expert. In the next section we provide a set of heuristics for the assignment of meta-operators to tasks depending on the role of the target task models in the development lifecycle.

3 Applied Task Model Refinement: From Analysis to Design

Based on our experiences while working with task models we found the following general guidelines useful:

(1) Tasks marked as binding should remain binding in all subsequent refining task models. Bindings can only be modified to more rigid ones (e.g. shallow to deep).
(2) Exempted binding is only to be used for newly introduced tasks which must be preserved in subsequent refining models.
(3) Throughout development, structural refinement can be used to gradual refine the superordinate model as long as type consistency is preserved.

In addition to the general guidelines we also discovered a set of heuristics which, depending on the role of the task model in the software engineering lifecycle, help the developer with the assignment of meta-operators to tasks. In what follows, we consider three phases of development where task models play a major role: analysis, requirement and design.

Analysis Task Models. The purpose of analysis is to understand users' behavior such that the requirements/design artifacts for the envisioned software can be defined as closely to "natural" human activity as possible. The analysis task model captures the current work situation and highlights elementary domain processes as well as exposes bottlenecks and weaknesses of the problem domain. It is important, that refinements of analysis models retain all crucial processes of the domain. Therefore, as a rule of thumb, tasks that correspond to elementary business process should be either marked with the *shallow binding* operator, or, if the process is crucial and fixed in its tasks, with the *deep binding* operator.

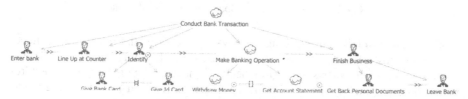

Fig. 1. Analysis Task Model for an ATM Machine

Fig. 1 shows the analysis task model for the development of an ATM machine. As typical in analysis the current situation (without taking into account the envisioned ATM machine) is depicted. While banking operations are performed manually, the tasks "Identify", "Withdraw Money" and "Get Account Statement" are marked as *shallow binding* tasks denoting elementary business processes of the domain. As a consequence, any refining model needs to retain these tasks.

Finally we note that an excessive usage of the binding operators is not advisable. When moving to the requirements stage, the changes to the model are usually substantial due to the introduction of the envisioned system. An overkill of meta-operators (especially *deep binding*) unnecessarily restricts the specification of the requirements, which is often undesirable and counterproductive.

Requirement Task Models. In Fig. 2 a valid refinement of the analysis task model is given. Clearly the structural refinements are type consistent and the set of retained scenarios equals the set of mandatory scenarios of the analysis task model. Generally, requirement task models specify the envisioned way tasks are performed using the system under development. The artifacts gathered during requirements specification are part of the contract between stakeholders about the future application. Therefore, we recommend to mark most tasks with the *deep binding* operator to ensure that all refining models truly implement the requirements. In Fig. 2, the tasks "Withdraw Money", "Get Account Statement" and "Finish Transaction" are marked as *deep binding*, requiring all subsequent refining models to implement the tasks in the same manner. Only the task "Identify" is marked as *shallow binding*. In our example, the requirements merely state that identification is needed to perform a bank operation. *How* identification is performed is not yet specified and will be determined by the UI designer in the next phase. Additionally the *exempt* task "Check Card Lock" was introduced. It constitutes a technology specific requirement and as such was not part of the analysis task model.

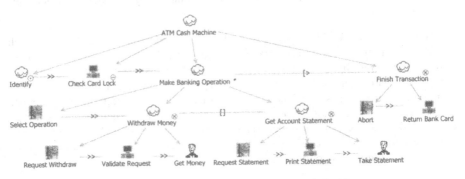

Fig. 2. Requirement Task Model for an ATM Machine

Design Task Models. During design, the various tasks of the requirements model need to be "instantiated" to a particular user interface. It is important to ensure that the design truly implements the requirements. Typically, when moving from requirements to design, mainly structural refinements are used, which further detail a previously atomic task into a set of design specific subtasks. Fig. 3 depicts a valid design task model (relative to the requirements task model of Fig. 2) for our ATM example. It structurally refines many tasks of the requirements model. Note that due to space constraints only the refinement of the task "Identify" is shown. Structural refinements of "Request Withdraw", "Request Statement", and "Finish Transaction" are abbreviated using the symbol ⊞. In addition to structural refinement, new, design specific, tasks may also be introduced. If these tasks need to be carried on to subsequent design phases they have to be integrated using the *exempt binding* operator.

Fig. 3. Design Task Model for an ATM Machine

4 Conclusion and Future Work

In this paper we proposed a refinement relation for task models, in which an artifact may be either structurally and/or behaviorally refined. While the former is generically applicable, the latter can be "guided" by the requirements engineer by assigning meta-operators to tasks. More precisely meta-operators define whether a task is deemed mandatory and should be preserved in refining models, or not. We believe that the usage of meta-operators makes our refinement relation more flexible and versatile, than traditional refinement relations which are often based on plain trace inclusion.

Currently, the verification of refinement is done manually. However, as the specifications become more complex, efficient refinement verification requires supporting tools. We are currently investigating how our approach can be translated into the specification languages of existing model checkers and theorem provers. Another future avenue deals with the definition of additional meta-operators such that bindings cannot only be assigned to single tasks (including their subtasks) but also to a set of temporally related tasks and temporal operators. After doing so our ultimate goal includes the computer aided placement of meta operators since manual assignment can be very tedious in particular for large specifications.

References

1. van Welie, M., van der Veer, G., Eliëns, A.: An Ontology for Task World Models. In: DSV-IS 1998. Springer, Abingdon (1998)
2. Paterno, F.: Model-Based Design and Evaluation of Interactive Applications. Springer, London (1999)
3. Khendek, F., Bourduas, S., Vincent, D.: Stepwise Design with Message Sequence Charts. In: Proceedings of the IFIP TC6/WG6.1. Kluwer, B.V. (2001)
4. Brinksma, E., Scollo, G., Steenbergen, C.: Lotos specifications, their implementations and their tests. In: Conformance testing methodologies and architectures for OSI protocols, pp. 468–479. IEEE Computer Society Press, Los Alamitos (1995)
5. Sinnig, D., Chalin, P., Khendek, F.: Consistency between Task Models and Use Cases. In: Proceedings of Design, Specification and Verification of Interactive Systems 2007. Salamanca, Spain (2007)
6. Sinnig, D., Wurdel, M., Forbrig, P., Chalin, P., Khendek, F.: Practical Extensions for Task Models. In: Winckler, M., Johnson, H., Palanque, P. (eds.) TAMODIA 2007. LNCS, vol. 4849, pp. 42–55. Springer, Heidelberg (2007)
7. Bergstra, J.A.: Handbook of Process Algebra. Elsevier Science Inc., Amsterdam (2001)

Utilizing Dynamic Executable Models for User Interface Development

Grzegorz Lehmann, Marco Blumendorf, Sebastian Feuerstack, and Sahin Albayrak

DAI-Labor, TU-Berlin
Ernst-Reuter-Platz 7, D-10587 Berlin
firstname.lastname@DAI-Labor.de

Abstract. In this demonstration we present the Multi Access Service Platform (MASP), a model-based runtime architecture for user interface development based on the idea of dynamic executable models. Such models are self-contained and complete as they contain the static structure, the dynamic state information as well as the execution logic. Utilizing dynamic executable models allows us to implement a rapid prototyping approach and provide mechanisms for the extension of the UI modeling language of the MASP.

Keywords: human-computer interaction, model-based user interfaces, runtime interpretation.

1 Introduction

Ambient environments comprising numerous networked interaction devices challenge interface developers to provide approaches that exploit these new capabilities. Multimodality, runtime context adaptation, personalization or even end-user development are examples for related challenges. We see two major features that can significantly empower user interface development. First is the possibility to modify the UI models at runtime. This feature allows to build self-adaptive user interfaces, which react to the current context of use. Furthermore it enables to close the gap between the design time and the runtime as the UI designer can alter the models of a running UI and see the results of his work immediately. The second feature is the possibility of extending the modeling language by extending its meta-models. This way the designer is no longer limited to one modeling language and is flexible enough to deal with challenges that will appear in the future. Moreover the architecture can then be customized for specific applications.

In this paper we present an approach based on executable models comprising static and dynamic information as well as the execution logic to form a foundation for the utilization of user interface models at runtime. In the next sections we present our realization of the Multi-Access Service Platform (MASP) using the Eclipse Modeling Framework (EMF). The demonstrated architecture allows the designer to work on models of a running application via model editors as well as the easy extension of the system (even at runtime) according to continuously changing requirements or end-user needs and preferences.

T.C.N. Graham and P. Palanque (Eds.): DSVIS 2008, LNCS 5136, pp. 306–309, 2008.

2 Multi Access Service Platform (MASP)

The MASP is a model-based runtime architecture which creates user interfaces from a set of models conforming to different meta-models. The user interface results from the execution of a model network comprising the task, domain, service, interaction and context models connected with customizable mappings [6]. The peculiarity of our approach lies within the executable nature of MASP's models and meta-models. In contrast to common static models, our executable models have a clearly defined execution logic and behavior specified in their meta-models. This makes them complete in the sense that they have "everything required to produce a desired functionality of a single problem domain" [5]. The executable meta-models provide the capabilities to express static elements as well as behavior and runtime evolution of the system in one single model. Additionally, the notion of the execution state as part of the model itself leads to models with an observable and manipulable state. Combining the initial state of a system, the processing logic, and the state information as part of dynamic executable models allows us to describe them as *models that provide a complete view of the system under study over time*. Thus, executable models run and have similar properties as program code. Other than code however, executable models provide a domain-specific level of abstraction which greatly simplifies the communication with the user or customer.

For our current implementation we have utilized the Eclipse Modeling Framework (EMF), which is a modeling and code generation framework integrated into the Eclipse IDE. EMF provides means to define meta-models, create models and appropriate editors. EMF is also capable of generating Java class structures for each meta-model and allows to express execution-defining meta-model elements in form of operations for which it then generates Java methods. These can afterwards be supplemented with Java code fragments which allowed us to define the execution logic inside our executable meta-models. One main feature of the Eclipse Modeling Framework supporting our runtime approach is the possibility to create model editors for the defined meta-models. We made use of this facility to build editors (Figure 1) that connect to the models of running MASP applications. This allows us to manipulate running applications and observe the effects of any changes immediately as they are instantly taken into account by the execution logic of the models.

3 Rapid Prototyping with Executable Models

We demonstrate the feasibility of our approach by showing the development process of an interactive recipe finder, allowing to search recipes, that match selected predefined criteria. When the search is completed the results are presented in form of a recipe list. The user may then either restart the search or select a recipe and proceed to its detailed description.

After defining basic model like the task model, providing the application workflow, and the domain model, providing access to application data, the application can already be executed because of the nature of the executable models. However, none of the models does provide a detailed description of the anticipated user interface or the interaction yet. We therefore proceed with the specification of the interaction model

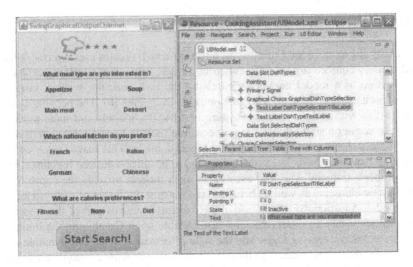

Fig. 1. Modifying an executable model of a running MASP application

containing abstract and concrete user interface elements as proposed by the Cameleon reference framework [4]. While the application is already executed, we create elements allowing the user to provide the search criteria and start the search. The UI elements represent interactions for specific tasks and are therefore connected with tasks inside the task model by the means of mappings. While the models are connected with each other the UI starts to emerge on the display because the mappings synchronize the state of the UI elements with the current ETS of the task model. This way we can see the results of our work immediately. The UI elements representing the recipe search criteria are also connected to appropriate objects in the domain model, so that they appear on the screen immediately. Figure 1 shows the resulting (running) recipe finder UI on the left and the editor connected to the interaction model on the right.

In contrast to an earlier approach we presented in [1] the manipulations the UI designer performs happen directly to the model data structures, which are the same at runtime as well as at design time. Therefore the border between both becomes blurred. Being able to manipulate the models at runtime also paves the road for end-user development and self-adapting systems.

4 Extending the Modeling Language

In the second part of our demonstration we show the extensibility of the MASP by replacing one model with another one (conforming to a new meta-model) at runtime. We complete the definition of the interaction model with the creation of UI elements responsible for the navigation inside the Recipe Finder application. It should be possible for the user to navigate back and forth through the application, for example from the recipe details view either to the recipe list or to the initial search criteria configuration. As dialog modeling is not the responsibility of the task model a new model should be introduced. Therefore we will transform the task model into a state machine model and enrich it with additional transitions representing the desired dialog navigation. To achieve this we remove the mappings between the tasks and the UI elements and map the latter with states and transitions in the state machine model.

In order to achieve the described extensibility we have defined a meta-meta-model for the MASP. It distinguishes between definition-, situation- and execution elements of its executable models. A similar classification has also been identified by Breton and Bézivin [3]. The resulting structure of the meta-meta-model allows to generalize executable meta-models and relates them with each other by the means of mappings. As each executable model is an encapsulated entity on its own, to orchestrate multiple, independent models into one application we have also developed a special mapping meta-model. It enables the definition of custom mappings between elements conforming to different meta-models based on the structures given by the meta-meta-model. Providing an extra meta-model solely for mappings also allows to benefit from tool support and removes the problem of mappings hard-coded into the architecture, as has been already advised by Puerta and Eisenstein [6].

5 Summary and Outlook

In this paper we briefly described our approach of applying executable models to user interface development in order to enable the investigation of stateful models at runtime. The approach allows the inspection and manipulation of the application at runtime and provides easy extensibility of the utilized modeling language. The prototypical recipe finder application demonstrates the feasibility of our approach. In the near future, we want to further evaluate our approach, by implementing multiple models from different approaches like e.g. UsiXML[1] and we want to further investigate the implications of our approach to user interface development by creating enhanced UIs that facilitating context adaptation, self-awareness and self-adaptation.

References

1. Blumendorf, M., Feuerstack, S., Albayrak, S.: Multimodal User Interfaces for Smart Environments: The Multi-Access Service Platform. In: Advanced Visual Interfaces 2008 (2008)
2. Blumendorf, M., Feuerstack, S., Lehmann, G., Albayrak, S.: Executable Models for Human-Computer Interaction. In: DSV-IS 2008 (submitted, 2008)
3. Breton, E., Bézivin, J.: Towards an Understanding of Model Executability. In: FOIS 2001 (2001)
4. Calvary, G., Coutaz, J., Thevenin, D., Limbourg, Q., Souchon, N., Bouillon, L., Florins, M., Vanderdonckt, J.: Plasticity of User Interfaces: A Revised Reference Framework. In: TAMODIA 2002 (2002)
5. Mellor, S.J.: Agile MDA (June 2004)
6. Puerta, A.R., Eisenstein, J.: Towards a General Computational Framework for Model-Based Interface Development Systems. In: Intelligent User Interfaces 1999 (1999)

---

[1] www.usixml.org

Author Index

Lecture Notes in Computer Science

Sublibrary 2: Programming and Software Engineering

For information about Vols. 1– 4498
please contact your bookseller or Springer

Vol. 4824: A. Paschke, Y. Biletskiy (Eds.), Advances in Rule Interchange and Applications. XIII, 243 pages. 2007.

Vol. 4821: J. Bennedsen, M.E. Caspersen, M. Kölling (Eds.), Reflections on the Teaching of Programming. X, 261 pages. 2008.

Vol. 4807: Z. Shao (Ed.), Programming Languages and Systems. XI, 431 pages. 2007.

Vol. 4799: A. Holzinger (Ed.), HCI and Usability for Medicine and Health Care. XVI, 458 pages. 2007.

Vol. 4789: M. Butler, M.G. Hinchey, M.M. Larrondo-Petrie (Eds.), Formal Methods and Software Engineering. VIII, 387 pages. 2007.

Vol. 4767: F. Arbab, M. Sirjani (Eds.), International Symposium on Fundamentals of Software Engineering. XIII, 450 pages. 2007.

Vol. 4765: A. Moreira, J. Grundy (Eds.), Early Aspects: Current Challenges and Future Directions. X, 199 pages. 2007.

Vol. 4764: P. Abrahamsson, N. Baddoo, T. Margaria, R. Messnarz (Eds.), Software Process Improvement. XI, 225 pages. 2007.

Vol. 4762: K.S. Namjoshi, T. Yoneda, T. Higashino, Y. Okamura (Eds.), Automated Technology for Verification and Analysis. XIV, 566 pages. 2007.

Vol. 4758: F. Oquendo (Ed.), Software Architecture. XVI, 340 pages. 2007.

Vol. 4757: F. Cappello, T. Herault, J. Dongarra (Eds.), Recent Advances in Parallel Virtual Machine and Message Passing Interface. XVI, 396 pages. 2007.

Vol. 4753: E. Duval, R. Klamma, M. Wolpers (Eds.), Creating New Learning Experiences on a Global Scale. XII, 518 pages. 2007.

Vol. 4749: B.J. Krämer, K.-J. Lin, P. Narasimhan (Eds.), Service-Oriented Computing – ICSOC 2007. XIX, 629 pages. 2007.

Vol. 4748: K. Wolter (Ed.), Formal Methods and Stochastic Models for Performance Evaluation. X, 301 pages. 2007.

Vol. 4741: C. Bessière (Ed.), Principles and Practice of Constraint Programming – CP 2007. XV, 890 pages. 2007.

Vol. 4735: G. Engels, B. Opdyke, D.C. Schmidt, F. Weil (Eds.), Model Driven Engineering Languages and Systems. XV, 698 pages. 2007.

Vol. 4716: B. Meyer, M. Joseph (Eds.), Software Engineering Approaches for Offshore and Outsourced Development. X, 201 pages. 2007.

Vol. 4709: F.S. de Boer, M.M. Bonsangue, S. Graf, W.-P. de Roever (Eds.), Formal Methods for Components and Objects. VIII, 297 pages. 2007.

Vol. 4680: F. Saglietti, N. Oster (Eds.), Computer Safety, Reliability, and Security. XV, 548 pages. 2007.

Vol. 4670: V. Dahl, I. Niemelä (Eds.), Logic Programming. XII, 470 pages. 2007.

Vol. 4652: D. Georgakopoulos, N. Ritter, B. Benatallah, C. Zirpins, G. Feuerlicht, M. Schoenherr, H.R. Motahari-Nezhad (Eds.), Service-Oriented Computing ICSOC 2006. XVI, 201 pages. 2007.

Vol. 4640: A. Rashid, M. Aksit (Eds.), Transactions on Aspect-Oriented Software Development IV. IX, 191 pages. 2007.

Vol. 4634: H. Riis Nielson, G. Filé (Eds.), Static Analysis. XI, 469 pages. 2007.

Vol. 4620: A. Rashid, M. Aksit (Eds.), Transactions on Aspect-Oriented Software Development III. IX, 201 pages. 2007.

Vol. 4615: R. de Lemos, C. Gacek, A. Romanovsky (Eds.), Architecting Dependable Systems IV. XIV, 435 pages. 2007.

Vol. 4610: B. Xiao, L.T. Yang, J. Ma, C. Muller-Schloer, Y. Hua (Eds.), Autonomic and Trusted Computing. XVIII, 571 pages. 2007.

Vol. 4609: E. Ernst (Ed.), ECOOP 2007 – Object-Oriented Programming. XIII, 625 pages. 2007.

Vol. 4608: H.W. Schmidt, I. Crnković, G.T. Heineman, J.A. Stafford (Eds.), Component-Based Software Engineering. XII, 283 pages. 2007.

Vol. 4591: J. Davies, J. Gibbons (Eds.), Integrated Formal Methods. IX, 660 pages. 2007.

Vol. 4589: J. Münch, P. Abrahamsson (Eds.), Product-Focused Software Process Improvement. XII, 414 pages. 2007.

Vol. 4574: J. Derrick, J. Vain (Eds.), Formal Techniques for Networked and Distributed Systems – FORTE 2007. XI, 375 pages. 2007.

Vol. 4556: C. Stephanidis (Ed.), Universal Access in Human-Computer Interaction, Part III. XXII, 1020 pages. 2007.

Vol. 4555: C. Stephanidis (Ed.), Universal Access in Human-Computer Interaction, Part II. XXII, 1066 pages. 2007.

Vol. 4554: C. Stephanidis (Ed.), Universal Acess in Human Computer Interaction, Part I. XXII, 1054 pages. 2007.

Vol. 4553: J.A. Jacko (Ed.), Human-Computer Interaction, Part IV. XXIV, 1225 pages. 2007.

Vol. 4552: J.A. Jacko (Ed.), Human-Computer Interaction, Part III. XXI, 1038 pages. 2007.

Vol. 4551: J.A. Jacko (Ed.), Human-Computer Interaction, Part II. XXIII, 1253 pages. 2007.

Vol. 4550: J.A. Jacko (Ed.), Human-Computer Interaction, Part I. XXIII, 1240 pages. 2007.

Vol. 4542: P. Sawyer, B. Paech, P. Heymans (Eds.), Requirements Engineering: Foundation for Software Quality. IX, 384 pages. 2007.

Vol. 4536: G. Concas, E. Damiani, M. Scotto, G. Succi (Eds.), Agile Processes in Software Engineering and Extreme Programming. XV, 276 pages. 2007.

Vol. 4530: D.H. Akehurst, R. Vogel, R.F. Paige (Eds.), Model Driven Architecture - Foundations and Applications. X, 219 pages. 2007.

Vol. 4523: Y.-H. Lee, H.-N. Kim, J. Kim, Y.W. Park, L.T. Yang, S.W. Kim (Eds.), Embedded Software and Systems. XIX, 829 pages. 2007.